FLASHING SABER

Three Years in Vietnam

Matthew Brennan

Revised Edition

ISBN: 1503102947
ISBN 13: 9781503102941
Library of Congress Control Number: 2015903691
CreateSpace Independent Publishing Platform
North Charleston, South Carolina

"If all men were just,

there would be no need for valor."

Agesilus

444-400 B.C.

"Happiness and sadness

I will remember forever.

North Vietnamese soldier's diary

Soui Ca Mountains

February, 1967

CONTENTS

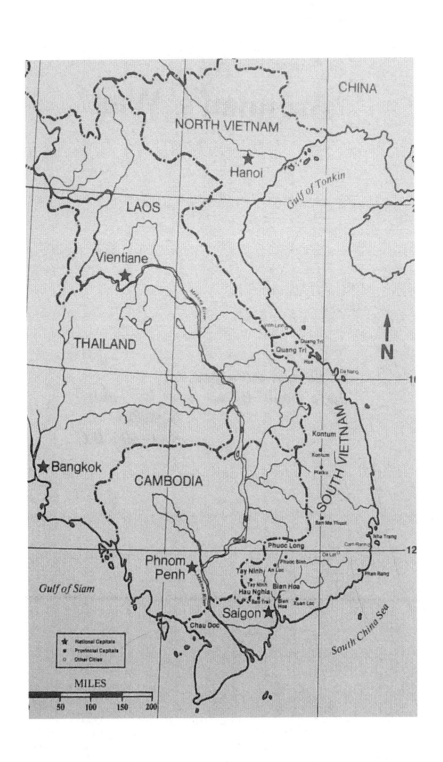

PROLOGUE

The First Air Cavalry Division was the Vietnam War's premier fire brigade, never staying long in one place. About one-half of the enemy dead claimed by the division were caused by the elite reconnaissance squadron, the 1/9th Cavalry, which also started a majority of its battles, large and small. There were many, almost daily, firsts, including an engagement described herein where a regimental command post was overrun and the largest number of high-ranking enemy officers (division and regimental staff) of any air-ground action of the war became casualties. I was there.

Most of this book is about life with the 9th Cavalry's small infantry [Blue] platoons. Our missions varied from capturing prisoners, to starting battles, to landings in the wake of B-52 strikes, to long, silent patrols, or rescue and recovery of downed choppers and their crews. The Blues jumped from moving helicopters, hung from the skids and dropped, and sometimes rappelled, all of this under the shield of brave scout helicopter and gunship crews. A division commander once called the Blues "the division's expendables," meaning that if they couldn't get us out of a situation, only our perpetually understrength platoon would be lost.

I was a patriot and a military history buff in high school and planned to make the Army my career. My favorite books were personal war memoirs; I dreamed of someday experiencing combat and writing about it. I wasn't going to be another Erich Maria Remarque, but perhaps I could contribute something to human and military literature. That motive was my deepest secret. By sheer chance, I stumbled into a unit that was legendary throughout Vietnam, although personally knowing nothing about all of that.

Over the past thirty years, I have been able to research Vietnam War history, clarify some descriptions and add others, eliminate inaccuracies, and correct some time sequences in an original memoir, **Brennan's War.** I have also used the real names I could recall, with the exception of a few men who can't, or shouldn't, be named. Readers will find this book quite different from the original.

I do not aim to glorify war or its consequences, but all of us should remember the real heroes, those volunteers and draftees who didn't know that they were part of something unique. Many of them, privates and pilots alike, left us too soon to ever know what they had helped accomplish. In the Ia Drang Valley, in 1965, Ninth Cavalrymen fought daily air and ground battles, relentlessly attacking the North Vietnamese for seventeen days prior to the famous 7th Cavalry landing at LZ X-Ray. Some of these pre-X-Ray actions by the 9th Cavalry and other units resulted in hundreds of enemy casualties. The reconnaissance squadron's daily battles continued for years, ceasing only when its last elements departed Vietnam in 1972. Here is a small part of an extraordinary story.

Chapter 1

DECISIONS

(1965)

In early 1965 I was serving alongside 300,000 other Americans as a teen-age private in West Germany. News about a war in Asia was found mostly in latrines and beer halls in those days, and the Army's rumor mill was going full tilt. The Marines were at Da Nang. The paratroopers of the 173rd Airborne Brigade were in War Zone D. Men with certain special skills were suddenly transferred back to the United States for redeployment to Vietnam. We listened to an ex-helicopter gunner from another unit, a skinny fellow with jet black hair and piercing blue eyes, repeat the same stories about "hunting dinks" time and again.

Something big had to be brewing. About twenty members of my artillery battery volunteered for Vietnam service and were just as quickly turned down. Our captain called a meeting of the Vietnam volunteers, during which he thanked us for our patriotism, but explained that units in Europe were understrength. We could not be spared.

I returned to America in September 1965 to attend the United States Military Academy Prep School at Fort Belvoir, Virginia. There I first read about the bloody battles being fought by the 1st Air Cavalry Division in the Ia Drang Valley. I was sure that the war would end while I was wasting away in boring classrooms, so I let my grades slip until a third request for resignation was accepted by the class commander.

My tactical NCO, a man who proudly displayed a captured Viet Cong flag on his office wall and wore two rows of decorations, told me not to be so eager. The war, he said, would be there when I graduated from West Point in 1970. I couldn't imagine a war lasting for five more years.

A volunteer could pick his unit. I chose the 1st Air Cavalry Division.

Soon I arrived at a replacement depot in Oakland, California to await a flight across the Pacific. That vast warehouse of humanity was a beehive of activity. Units in the United States were being cannibalized to supply fresh blood for the battalions already in Vietnam. Always there were endless lists of men called for shipment to the war zone. Always new faces arrived in a steady stream of cabs and military buses.

Many of the replacements were from the 82nd Airborne Division, the All-American division of World War II fame, recently returned from a police action in the Dominican Republic. Those loud, swaggering para-troopers sat on the crowded bunks until the early morning hours, sharpening assorted trench knives, boot knives, and bayonets, cleaning and oiling "unauthorized" pistols, some of which had accompanied fathers, brothers and uncles to wars in other places, and bragging about how they would finish off the dinks in nothing flat.

"DR," the only conflict the younger men had experienced, had gone easy on most of them. They believed that was what war was all about. I would encounter some of those same men months later – thinner now, dirtier, with expressionless faces and hollow eyes, their bravado only a memory.

Most of us didn't understand what was happening in Vietnam. We believed that the war had reached its final stages and that we might arrive after the last big battles were won. Replacements at Oakland felt and acted like part of a conquering army. All of us were proud of America's strength and her ability to end guerrilla wars quickly. Some soldiers bribed replacement depot staff to be moved up on flight manifests and go over a day or two sooner. We were too naïve to be afraid.

My group left for Vietnam on a commercial jet in mid-December 1965. The flight was uneventful except for one (or two) events. A pretty, blond stewardess began a hushed conversation with an equally blond, barrel-chested airborne sergeant who was seated in the aisle seat across from mine. He had a plea, being a poor paratrooper on his way to possible death. Could she? The stewardess eventually led him back to the curtained kitchen area and performed her patriotic duty. A few hours later, she was persuaded to help out the sergeant's taller, darker, sidekick in the window seat. As the jet winged its way over the Pacific Ocean those two noisily discussed their fun.

Twenty-two hours after the flight began, the plane taxied up to a wooden terminal building at Tan Son Nhut Air Base outside of Saigon. We walked onto a steaming and unhurried airfield that could have been a large civilian airport, except for the uniforms most people wore. Soldiers scrambled for shade in a futile effort to stem the sweat already staining our uniforms. We had expected battle lines to be drawn right on the edge of the airfield, but instead of being issued combat gear and hustled off to waiting units, a short, wiry Transportation Corps lieutenant, wearing a freshly starched summer dress uniform and a single row of ribbons, herded us into the rear of several large cargo trucks. The trucks roared to life and gave us a bumpy ride the short distance to a tent city called Camp Alpha.

At Camp Alpha, the Vietnam Army's replacement depot, we were ushered through the tedium of processing once again – paperwork, long lines, and more immunization shots. Recruits stayed in big brown army squad tents and slept on cots, or on the ground between cots. I spent the first night alternating between napping on the damp ground and walking guard between rows of dark tents. In future years, Alpha would be outfitted with spring bunk beds, mattresses, pillows and blankets, wooden buildings, an excellent mess hall, game rooms, shops, paved roads, and an extensive public address system. In 1965, it was a field of mud and canvas tents.

Before we left Alpha, the Army treated us to the standard briefing for new arrivals. A grim lieutenant warned us that U.S. military personnel were guests in that country. Vietnamese were to be treated with the utmost respect. This was an ironic touch because, up to this point, we had seen Vietnamese only from a distance. The officer followed with a verbal horror show about the various types of poisonous snakes, scorpions, centipedes, and spiders in the country, and the equally numerous varieties of venereal disease. The dangers not mentioned were our VC [Viet Cong] and PAVN [Peoples' Army of Vietnam] enemies. From that lecture I learned two things – always shake out you boots before putting them on and always wear a rubber.

A four-engine Air Force C-130 took the replacements for the 1st Air Cavalry Division hundreds of miles north and west to Pleiku, a provincial capital and military headquarters in the Central Highlands. We were stored aboard, alongside Vietnamese families carrying bundles of clothes and household goods, and wicker cages with chickens and young pigs.

We bounced along in that roaring plane as moisture condensed on the ceiling and fell on our backs and necks. I wasn't near a window, but managed to lean over a couple of chicken cages and an elderly woman to catch a view of Vietnam. I had imagined that we flew above rice paddies and irrigation canals. Instead I saw a confusion of high mountains and seemingly endless ridges reflecting a kaleidoscope of green, purple, and brown hues.

A twin-engine Army Caribou transport [Army pilots still flew some fixed wing aircraft at the time] was waiting for us at the Pleiku airfield. Our group was off the C-130 and filing aboard the banana-shaped Caribou within minutes of landing. We were flown eastward toward the 1st Air Cavalry Division base at An Khe, a place soon to be named Camp Radcliff in honor of the executive officer of the 9th Cavalry reconnaissance squadron - the division's first fatality in Vietnam. The story of Major Donald Radcliff's death is a tale worth telling.

Radcliff had been in Vietnam only a few days as part of a site selection team for a possible base camp when he learned that the Marines were about to launch their largest operation of the war to date: Operation Starlight. Major Radcliff and his crew volunteered to fly one hundred miles north to participate. Their gunship escorted the first lift of Marines into a firestorm at a place called LZ [Landing Zone] Blue, which happened to be surrounded by a Viet Cong battalion. Major Radcliff died at LZ Blue as his gun bird attacked positions pinning down our Marines.

I spent the ride watching row after row of truly rugged mountain peaks glide beneath us. The tangled trees and mat of green jungle canopy looked like a scene from an alien planet.

The Caribou landed at An Khe airstrip in late afternoon, and we waited, resting in the shade of a half-dozen skinny trees and a single tent. Behind the tent, a black soldier lounged in a stripped-down, sandbagged jeep, and spoke with someone on a backpack field radio. Almost at dark, two battered Army dump trucks, each with a heavily sandbagged bed, arrived for us. The drivers laughed when they told us that the sandbags were for protection against mines. Our trailing dump truck moved more slowly through the sleepy town of An Khe than the first.

An Khe was little more than a string of shanty houses and shops along both sides of French Colonial Route 19. Some of the shop owners were apparently confused about our nationality. They had dusted off old inventory and were doing a brisk business in French badges, patches, and decorations. A silver emblem the size and shape of a French parachute badge featured spread legs, instead of spread wings. These were called "Boom-Boom" wings. Boom-Boom wings probably had more significance for French paras than they did for us.

Our driver stopped for a hitchhiker, a muscular black soldier with white chest bandages showing under the green of his jungle shirt. He flashed a wide grin, probably at the thought of riding with a bunch of "fresh meat" just in from the United States. I managed to catch his eye, hoping he would say something. He did.

"Replacements, huh?"

"Yeah. We've just been here a couple of days. What happened to your chest?"

"Got hit by a mortar in the Ia Drang. Bad shit. Gave me a chance to get out of the field for a while."

That man had my instant respect. His carefree attitude caught the attention of every replacement in the truck. "That must have been some fight. Could you tell me what the division is like?"

He grinned again before answering. "Wait and see, man."

"Has there been much fighting lately, or was the Ia Drang the last of it?" (Translation: Did I miss the war?)

He was getting bored. Obviously new dudes weren't worth spending time on. "Man, you sure do ask questions. Listen, my buddies been beating the bush around Pleiku for weeks and ain't seen nuttin'. I think it's 'bout over. We might all be home in a couple of months." He turned away and stared towards the green mountains in the distance.

We were too late after all, I thought, and I had blown the chance to go to West Point. The dump trucks passed under an arch woven from branches with the division's horse head symbol and its motto, "The First Team." The wounded soldier wanted off, so we shouted for the driver to slow down. A quick thumbs-up signal and the truck left him in a cloud of red dust.

The trucks ground to a halt at a processing center located at the foot of a large jungle hill crowned by a wooden sentry tower. Its name on the maps was Hon Con, but everyone called it Hong Kong Mountain. There were no tents for replacements. A gruff supply sergeant gave each of us a thin, Army-issue wool blanket and pointed to a field of saw grass. We made nests in the grass and began fighting losing battles with the insects we had disturbed. I had never seen such a variety of insect life. My nest became a highway for at least three types of ants and several long, black cockroaches. Mosquitos and tiny biting flies were drawn to our sweating bodies in swarms. Bats made erratic, skittering flights through the insect clouds.

The tropical night arrived with its usual suddenness, along with a Donald Duck cartoon being shown on a white bed sheet somewhere inside the camp. Eleven thousand miles from home, a world away, and here was Donald Duck in full, living color. Then it started raining and didn't quit until morning. Of all the miserable nights I would spend in Indochina that was probably the worst. I was wet and alone and wondering what I had done, and what in the hell I was doing in that field.

At dawn a sleepy cook served a meal of stale bread and powdered eggs that had already turned green. There would be times when green eggs were a welcome substitute for C-rations, but that morning, I only ate the bread. Clerks gathered our papers and directed us to a large tent for a briefing. We waited in the heat of the tent for an hour, watching a GI taunt a rhinoceros beetle with a stick. The huge black beetle would rear up on its back legs, hiss, and grab the stick between two enormous pinchers. The soldier would lift him off the ground, shake him loose, and start over again. It never occurred to the aggressive beetle to retreat from the stick.

A tough-looking sergeant-major stepped into the tent. Games and laughter ceased. The rhinoceros beetle disappeared beneath its torment-er's boot heel with a final hiss and a loud Pop!

"Teng Hut!" bellowed the sergeant-major.

We jumped to our feet like puppets and stood at more or less rigid attention. A man behind the sergeant-major walked in, a real one-star general. He glanced briefly around the tent and began his presentation.

"At ease, men. Please be seated. Could some of you roll up the tent flaps and get some air in here? Gentlemen, I'm General Wright, the assistant division commander. The division commander couldn't make the briefing today, so I'm filling in.

"On behalf of the officers and men of the First Cav, I welcome you to the best damned division in Vietnam. Many of you have already read about some of the things we've accomplished since arriving here. We cut this base out of bush and built the biggest helipad in the world, mainly with axes, saws, and machetes. This is a hard-working bunch of men with a tremendous spirit, and we expect the same from you.

"A couple of months ago, everyone was working at clearing bush when a couple of black pajama boys stepped out on a rock ledge up on Hon Con and took a few pot shots at the camp. The whole division must have grabbed rifles and opened up on them. It must have scared them half to death because we haven't had any trouble from up there since. That's the kind of spirit we have.

"We've met and defeated the enemy every time they've shown themselves. Our biggest problem is finding enough of them to fight. We can go anywhere at any time. The division has over four hundred helicopters and is completely airmobile. Contrary to what you may have heard, our small arms are proving themselves to be superb. In the Ia Drang Valley, the M-16s had such a flat trajectory that the enemy simply couldn't crawl in under them.

"We all have a hard job to do, and all we ask is that when you get to your units, you do your part. Thank you."

The sergeant-major stepped forward, bellowed another "Teng Hut!" and it was over. They left, and then we left to stand in the intense heat and wait for assignments.

I had an artillery specialty called FDC, or fire direction control. The common title was FDC computer. This training allowed a soldier to compute the trajectories of rockets and cannon using slide rules and thick volumes of tables, or be a member of an FO [Forward Observer] team. I wanted to be an artillery forward observer with an infantry company, but when my name was called, I was assigned to Division Artillery Headquarters. I didn't know what the job entailed, but knew I wouldn't like it.

A jeep delivered me to a new home in another sweltering squad tent. Across a dirt road was the giant helipad with its rows of olive drab helicopters. The helipad had been a stretch of jungle three months before; now it had been cleared so well that it was called the "Golf Course." The Golf Course was enormous enough to hold the cavalry division's entire arsenal of 435 helicopters.

I was sitting on an empty cot when the headquarters company first sergeant pulled up in a jeep and poked his head through the doorway of the tent.

"You the new FDC man they sent us?"

"Yes, Sergeant."

"Good. I'm First Sergeant Barley. Glad to have you aboard." He gave me an unexpectedly warm handshake. I had never been close enough, or allowed, to shake a first sergeant's hand. "Unpack your duffel bag and then go over to the supply tent and draw field gear. Get some sleep and report to the orderly room tent tomorrow at seven sharp. We have a lot of sandbags that want filling."

So my new duty was to fill sandbags. This seemed like a good time to bring up the subject of a transfer. "Sergeant, I may not be here long. I'd like to request a transfer to an artillery battalion."

He stepped away as if stung by a bee. "Any particular reason?"

"Yeah. I want to be a forward observer."

He shook his head. "That would be a, 'Yes, Sergeant.' Boy, that's crazy talk. Anybody who wants to be an F.O. must be dumber than the headlight on my jeep. It's not so bad here. You'll be doing a lot more than filling sandbags. It's just to keep you out of trouble until the forward CP returns to pick you up."

"Sergeant, I'd like to try anyway."

He adapted the patient, impatient attitude of a teacher trying to reason with a wayward student. "Look, boy. The life expectancy of a forward observer can be measured in days, sometimes minutes. They live in the bush like animals, and they're begging for a safe job like you'll have."

"Maybe we could arrange a swap, Sergeant."

He looked me square in the eye, a stop-this-bullshit sort of look. "If you apply for a transfer, it'll be refused. We're short of men the way it is, and the replacement center has been waiting for someone with your scores for weeks now. Report to the orderly room tent tomorrow at seven." He disappeared through the doorway of the tent.

I sat on the cot and cursed the air. First Sergeant Barley was trying to help me, but I was too angry to care. I finally fell asleep to the booming of cannon, the perpetual thunder of Vietnam.

Chapter 2

FORWARD COMMAND POST

(January-December, 1966)

For a few days I piled sandbags around a house-sized bunker that held Division Artillery Headquarters. Over the next months, whenever the forward command post was at Camp Radcliff, if only for a few hours, the enlisted men were ordered to repair and expand the bunker. Before 1966 was through, it had a lawn, beds of flowers to please the colonel, neat white gravel sidewalks bordered by crimson-painted artillery shell casings, and God knows how many sandbags. It became an object of our hate and scorn.

I have a vision of that bunker as it was in March, 1969. The cavalry division was gone by then, far to the south among the lowland jungles northwest of Saigon. Camp Radcliff was now protected by 173rd Airborne Brigade troopers, some of whom were rejects from the combat units who sported beards, lopped off uniform shirt sleeves, bead necklaces, shoulder-length hair and earrings. I was returning from the hospital in Japan and had made a special trip to see the hated bunker.

The flowers had died; the grass was two feet high all around; the red shell casings were dented, chipped, and scattered. Rain was rotting the timber supports as sandbags slowly poured their contents into the damp interior. A large rat and I crawled around on top of the decaying heap until the rat thought better of it and scurried away through a hole in the roof. I was alone with my thoughts. The bunker of many sandbags was going the same way as the war, I thought, a lot of sweat and suffering had gone into building an illusion, and now everything was crumbling.

I joined the forward CP [Command Post], also called the Jump CP, when it returned from a short operation in the mountainous Soui Ca Valley to the northeast. My main job would be communications – developing targets for the artillery batteries, verifying that no "friendlies" would be shelled by mistake, planning harassment fires, etc. I would work with a small group of operations officers and NCOs that supported cavalry operations from small forward bases, following the action from one campaign to the next. The forward CP was really airmobile in those days. Everything and everybody could be loaded in two jeeps and several three-quarter-ton trucks with trailers. In 1966 we could dismantle the equipment and move in a matter of minutes, and we did.

On New Year's Eve, 1965 a fellow soldier suggested a walk through a grove of skinny trees behind the big bunker. "Tell me what you hear," he said.

An animal's warning call was answered by the same call from the other side of the grove. I wasn't sure how to describe the calls until he explained that we had just been serenaded by two fuck-you lizards. The lizards' nocturnal cries did sound vaguely like "fuck you/fuck you!" [the call of the beautiful Tokay Gecko Lizard]. Thereafter I thought of that place as "fuck you forest."

That midnight we watched from the grove as tracers from rifles and machine guns, and flares of various colors, lit up the sky in a 360-degree circle. I would watch similar fireworks displays at Bong Son, Chu Lai and Quan Loi on New Year's Eve of 1966, 1967, and 1968, respectively.

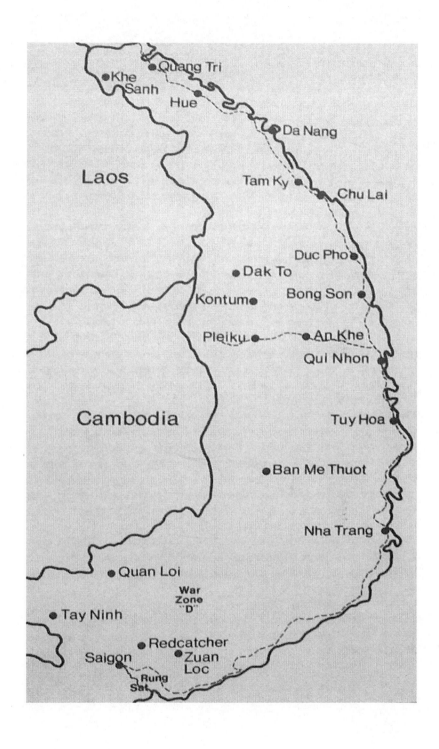

My first ground's-eye view of Vietnam came when the CP traveled west to Pleiku down Colonial Route 19. Our jeeps and trucks, each with a layer or two of sandbags on the floor, rolled through the Mang Yang Pass. The sheer wildness of the terrain was unlike anything I had ever experienced or imagined. In some places, fields of elephant grass stretched from the road to the first ridgeline; in other places were hairpin curves or steep drop-offs; in still others, a tangled wall of trees grew to within a few feet of the crumbling pavement. The convoy inched around demolished bridges and passed a cluster of fire-gutted APCs [Armored Personnel Carriers, also called "tracks"].

I realized for the first time how nervous everyone was, especially the officers. Every officer rode with a pistol or automatic rifle across his lap. They frequently signaled for vehicles to stay a good distance apart. Soldiers in each vehicle were constantly sweeping the countryside with their eyes and weapons. Single troop-carrying helicopters [called slicks or lift birds], with the yellow crossed sabers of the 9th Cavalry painted on their noses, roared over at regular intervals to set down their "Blue" infantry squads in the tall grass beside the road. Saber-painted gunships prowled the jungle and surrounding ridges at tree-top level.

I asked the machine gunner on our truck what was going on. "What's all the fuss about? Are all convoys like this?"

He relaxed his grip in the trigger, but his eyes never left the trees we were passing. "They're supposed to be, but here it's for real. The One-Oh-First Airborne got their asses kicked up through here right before the Cav arrived. Everybody's afraid of ambush going through Mang Yang. The major back there" –he pointed to an officer in the passenger seat of the jeep behind us- "looks like he's going to have a baby." The major was staring into the distance with bloodshot eyes and jerking his head back and forth like a mechanical doll.

When the 101st Airborne Brigade secured the area around An Khe prior to the cavalry division's arrival, one of its companies had taken a severe beating in the pass. The 101st Airborne was like us, a fire brigade that never stayed long in one place. The fact that those tough paratroopers had been bloodied at Mang Yang Pass gave the place a special aura of evil.

Our convoy continued down the road to Pleiku, passing a six-foot-tall stone marker almost swallowed by weeds. The machine gunner said that a French convoy had been wiped out here and the stone was their memorial. I don't recall seeing this as we passed, but a plaque on the marker was inscribed with the words in Vietnamese and French:

Here, on June 24, 1954 Soldiers of France and Vietnam Died for Their Countries.

On the way to another operation in April, the convoy stopped at just the right place, and I had time to walk among the gravestones of a weed-choked French cemetery. I felt that I walked with the ghosts of heroes.

Shortly after the French surrender at Dien Bien Phu 600 miles to the north, *Groupement Mobile 100*, a regiment on wheels, was ordered to abandon An Khe and withdraw westward through Mang Yang Pass toward Pleiku. It was ambushed by a Viet Minh regiment. These were the French graves. Then I understood why the officers had been so nervous that day in the pass. Perhaps the major was a student of military history.

The CP set up at a place called Monument Hill which was crowned by a large statue of the Virgin Mary. She gazed down Colonial Route 19, across a grassy plateau toward the mountains along the Cambodian border. Evidence of the French war was there as well. When mortars rounds explode with evil thunder, they leave their stabilizing tail fins embedded in the ground. As I climbed the hill to the statue, I stumbled over many badly rusted 60mm and 81mm mortar tail fins. That they were lying so thickly on the surface of the hill indicated someone had once taken a serious pounding. More tail fins turned up every time we erected a tent or dug up the ground.

A French unit had been surrounded and overrun on Monument Hill shortly after *Groupement Mobile 100* was destroyed in the Mang Yang Pass.

The days at Monument Hill were uneventful: long shifts inside a busy operations tent, and long hours filling sandbags or digging in the rocky red soil. Once we were troubled by a sniper who consistently missed, and that was about it.

The operation we supported was taking place miles to the west along the Cambodian border. It was largely a failure in military terms. The biggest day was when an artillery observation helicopter happened upon about one hundred men carrying huge sacks of rice with sewn-on shoulder straps through a region of elephant grass. All guns within range hit the target. The porters were taken by surprise, and many of them just stumbled around through the shell bursts. Others ran to their spider holes in Cambodia but couldn't get into them with those big sacks of rice on their backs. Many of the shells were airbursts and the result was a slaughter. As the pilot described the carnage, I tried to understand how men could be so frightened that they would forget to throw off their baggage.

On a moonless night, one of our captains begged a helicopter ride along the Cambodian border. An infrared mission by a Mohawk reconnaissance plane had detected the heat of cooking fires on a mountainside. The captain wanted a look-see. When the helicopter reached the dark mass of the mountain, the crew observed a campfire, suddenly extinguished, so the gunner decided to fire his machine gun in that general direction. The entire mountainside lit up with the red muzzle flashes of return fire. The helicopter pulled away as our captain began calling for something, anything, to hit the mountain.

He asked for "Armed Falcon" [ARA or Aerial Rocket Artillery. These were pairs of Huey gunships armed with forty-eight rockets each, also called "heavy hogs"]

None available.

Puff the Magic Dragon [a C-47 equipped with flares and miniguns].

No dragon ships within range.

Artillery?

No artillery can reach the mountain.

Air strikes?

No.

The frustrated captain took no more nighttime tours.

The enemy's designation changed during the operation. The U.S. military had been calling the North Vietnamese what they called themselves: PAVN [People's Army of Vietnam]. Someone decided that using PAVN would sanction the communist cause and give them recognition as the people's army. They would henceforth be known as NVA [North Vietnamese Army]. I never understood what difference the change could possibly have made..

After three weeks at Monument Hill, the CP returned through the Mang Yang Pass with the usual heavy gunship and infantry protection. We spent a night at Camp Radcliff and left at dawn to descend toward the sea, through the Deo Mang Pass on the opposite side of the An Khe Plateau. Here the countryside was even more rugged than at Mang Yang, but mining incidents and ambushes were rare. The reason was obvious.

The hills commanding the long pass were occupied by South Korean platoons and companies. The Vietnamese had great respect for the fighting ability and ruthlessness of their fellow Orientals. Stories about Korean ferocity and cruelty in battle were told throughout the Central Highlands. They did not make a habit of taking prisoners.

We passed the last and largest of the lonely hilltop outposts as morning mists drifted across the southern wall of the pass, and watched as the Koreans practiced Tae-Kwon-Do in white boxer shorts and T-shirts. The North Vietnamese *Sang Vao* [Yellow Star] Division, that had controlled Deo Mang before the Koreans arrived, had withdawn northward into base areas in the An Lao Valley and the Soui Ca Mountains. The Koreans were left to their martial arts exercises.

I believe that it was on that first convoy through the Deo Mang that we saw something unusual. A half-mile or so beyond the last Korean outpost, an entire Air Force "Bird Dog" spotter plane balanced in the tree tops of the steep southern slope. We assumed that the little aircraft had been shot down, and indeed it had been – miles away from where it now rested. The Viet Cong had taken it apart and reassembled the plane. Of course it was booby-trapped.

In the foothills of the Deo Mang, the convoy came to a full stop for a mechanical breakdown up ahead. Suddenly, jarringly, about twenty bearded soldiers stood up in foxholes on the high north bank beside us and climbed out to watch. Those fellows looked worn out – totally exhausted. Beards were rust-red from the iron oxide in the tropical soil; heavy cotton trousers and shirts had become tattered, rotting, rust-colored rags; black leather boots were scraped white, ripped, and decaying under layers of dull mud. Everything about them was some shade of tropical red.

About eight of them carried foreign weapons – AK-47s and two RPD squad machine guns. Some of them wore belts of machine gun bullets crisscrossed over their chests, looking for all the world like Cuban guer-rillas or Mexican banditos. Curious as usual, I asked one of the soldiers why he was using a communist weapon.

"My M-16 jammed in the Ia Drang." He explained that the missing U.S.-issue rifles were broken up and buried, or rusting in pieces at the bottom of village wells. "Gook weapons," he said, "don't jam." That was a lesson for the future.

That chance encounter was so unusual that, from our all-seeing headquarters perch, I followed that infantry company's patrols and bat-tles, little victories, and loses to mortars, farmer-snipers, and booby-traps, for months thereafter.

The convoy reached the sandy coastal plains and headed north along Colonial Route One until we arrived at the small town of Bong Son. As we drove over a concrete bridge into the village, we passed a long bamboo platform about fifty meters downstream that jutted from a high bank about forty feet above the river. I didn't understand its purpose until a woman in black pajamas walked to the end of it, dropped her drawers, squatted, and released a black bomb that seemed to take an eternity to plop into the water. The platform got heavy use. Sometimes we would drive to the bridge and park, just to watch the queue of people walking, one at a time, down that wobbly platform to bomb the river. I called it "walking the plank."

Foreign soldiers were still a rarity in Bong Son, so citizens filed out of their shops and homes to silently watch our jeeps and trucks rumble down the muddy main street. Some of them gave us looks of pure hatred. Only the children, being children, displayed any positive emotion.

The coastal province of Binh Dinh (and Quang Ngai Province to its north) had been under Viet Minh domination since 1945. In a bizarre reversal of the situation in America's war, the French loosely held the mountains and the communists ruled the rich coastal plains. Any open opposition to that rule had been long since eradicated by Viet Minh murder committees, and "re-education" camps in the mountains from which few returned.

The area around Bong Son is among the most beautiful regions any-where. Mountains stand in the distance, gradually giving way to a slop-ing countryside covered in coconut palms, these yielding in turn to the white sands and deep blue water of the South China Sea coast. In later days, when the slicks took the 9th Cavalry Blue platoons above the palms on the way to assault landings, even the hardest men could appreciate the view: purple mountains, green fronds, brown thatched roofs, white sand, blue ocean, and the occasional multi-hued checkerboards of paddy fields. The Bong Son Plains is a place for communing with nature, provided there isn't a war going on.

The CP set up outside the wire of a little Special Forces camp. The camp had a trench inside the barbed wire obstacles for the SF strikers [merce-naries] and another trench outside the wire where lived Army of Vietnam soldiers and their families – read cannon fodder or human tripwire. A stony dirt track leading to a small airstrip ran in front of that trench. About one hundred meters down the track, near its end and smack dab in the middle, was a lone pup tent (my home).

While digging a shallow, coffin-sized sleeping hole for protection against incoming bullets and fragments, my entrenching shovel kept striking jagged pieces of metal embedded in the upper foot or so of earth. I uncovered the unexploded half of an old artillery shell that started steaming when I knocked the mud away. A young Special Forces staff sergeant saw the smoking chunk of metal and strolled over.

"That's Willy Peter. This place is littered with old pieces of junk like that. This was commie country back in the French war and they shelled it a lot from offshore."

"Oh. What's Willy Peter?"

The SF man gave me an "I'm-the-veteran-campaigner-here" sort of look. "You must be new, partner. You know, white phosphorous."

The forward CP erected its single squad tent beside the airstrip and very quickly began business as usual. Reports poured in about infantry and helicopter battles in all directions. Project Delta Special Forces teams had been landed in the An Lao Valley, within sight to our west. We knew something was going on, but were given few details. The SF teams made immediate contact and suffered heavy casualties. Ninth Cavalry gunships helped rescue two survivors of one of those teams. A couple of weeks later, the reconnaissance squadron's Blue infantrymen would begin their own landings in the An Lao Valley with the same result. Immediate contact almost every place they set foot.

Meanwhile, in the opposite direction along the coastal plain, companies and battalions were pinned down and taking heavy losses. American casualties in one place, "the graveyard," were 140 dead and 220 wounded.

Targets were everywhere. Ninth Cavalry gunships destroyed an enemy roadblock about two miles north of us. Tax collectors and their enforcers had been standing beside strips of PSP [Perforated Steel Plate] used for instant runways, ready to bridge a trench dug across the pavement once a toll was paid.

Aerial rocket artillery heavy hogs soon killed forty-four enemy soldiers in a coconut grove northwest of the roadblock. At first the body count was not believed, but it was repeatedly verified by high-ranking sightseers. Everyone of rank was clamoring for a flyby. Operation Masher had begun.

Scout pilot David Bray and gunship door gunner Mike Kelley give vivid accounts of the early days of Operation Masher in the book, **Hunter-Killer Squadron**.

Early on the afternoon of February first, Major Rankin joined me in the shade of the palm tree where I usually ate a C-ration meal. He was the artillery liaison officer with the 9th Cavalry, and although he had often smiled and nodded, we had never talked. His rank made me nervous, and I was sure he had come to talk about some mistake I must have made in the operations tent.

"Is something wrong over at the CP, Sir?"

He answered with a troubled look, "No. Not at the CP. We lost our first F.O. today. Strickland. A boy of about your age. He was humping a radio with one of the Blue platoons of the Ninth Cav. I just can't seem to get him out of my mind. I've known him since the States."

"How'd it happen, Sir?"

"They were in the Crow's Foot walking some ridges and he was on point, radio and all. I told him not to walk point, and I thought we had an understanding about that. He came over the crest of a hill and they shot him. The rest of the platoon high-tailed it down the trail. Just left him there. When they got their nerve back, he was dead. The VC took everything – his radio, his rifle, even his belt and boots."

I didn't know what to say, mumbling that what had happened was a shame and that I was sorry. The major sat there for a while longer, looking dejected and tired, and then left for the CP. I seldom saw him smile after that day. Whatever the bond had been between Strickland and him, it had been deeply felt.

LTC (Ret.) Teddy H. Sanford, Jr., leader of the thirteen-man patrol that included Hiram Strickland, provides a detailed eyewitness account of that engagement in his online family genealogy, ***Out of the Mist of Times Past.***

PFC Hiram D. Strickland's last, unmailed letter home, a moving and wonderful letter in which he expresses his pride in America, was published in a book called ***Letters from Vietnam.*** It begins,

"You've probably already received word that I'm dead and that the government wishes to express its deepest regret. Believe me, I didn't want to die, but I know it was part of my job ..."

For a short time I made the acquaintance of a captured NVA battalion commander. His small tent was pitched in the middle of a thirty-foot square of grass enclosed by a tall farm fence. The compound was guarded by a single MP who sometimes tried to shoo me way. The NVA commander was slightly-built and clothed in black pajamas –friendly, with a warm smile and sparkling eyes– not at all what I expected an enemy to be like. We shared some C-ration meals, sitting a couple of feet apart, nodding and smiling, and passing ration cans back and forth through the fence.

On February fourth, 1966 South Vietnamese Premier Ky, a pilot, accompanied by his pretty wife, landed a small plane at the Bong Son airstrip. They wore sunglasses and matching black flight suits. Hers was form-fitting and accented by a yellow scarf. I stood to the side in a small crowd as the couple walked down the stony path and stopped at my pup tent. Premier Ky stared at the tent for a few seconds (his wife wasn't interested). They turned around and headed back to the airstrip, trailing a pod of local military dignitaries. Ky and his beauty didn't stay around for long. That was my first experience with a photo opportunity.

They took my prisoner friend away soon after Premier Ky's visit.

All the dying was still secondhand to me, so I spent free time swinging in a blue canvas North Vietnamese hammock stretched between two palm trees and bathing in the light of an enormous tropical moon. That little pleasure made up for the monotonous work and C-ration meals, and made the days seem worth living.

I could neither dream of, nor imagine, my world of a few months later, a world inhabited by hardwood forests, razor-sharp grass, spiked vines, elephants, tigers, monkeys, tiny deer, feral water buffalo on mountaintops, noisy herds of wild boar, parrots, peacocks, giant tortoises, green bamboo vipers, gecko lizards in rainbow colors, fat black scorpions, freshwater crabs, huge insects, three varieties of leeches, dangling hornet and fire ant nests, eight-inch, shiny, yellow-and-black banana spiders, and one very large Day-Glo orange centipede.

The war did touch us indirectly at times. Once the CP orchestrated a division TOT [Time on Target]. This is an artillery method in which all available pieces are aimed at a certain target, and firing is timed so that the first shells land simultaneously in an avalanche of steel. The target was a factory camp, dug into a hillside and camouflaged. Guns of all sizes, high explosive and white phosphorous shells, instant, delayed [for ground penetration] and airburst fuses were used. The barrage continued for half an hour, and the Air Force observer watching the fireworks was thrilled.

"That's beautiful, just beautiful! The whole place is going up! Keep it coming! Keep it coming!"

We crowded outside the tent to see the flashes of light and better hear the muffled detonations. Something must have been hit because explosions shook the hill for hours afterward.

One night a string of eighteen 82mm mortar shells thundered past our operations tent. The explosions had two immediate effects. They put an Air Force spotter plane out of action for a few days, and put the fear of God in me for a few hours. The spotter plane had been busily engaged in dropping propaganda leaflets over the An Lao Valley. It was the only aircraft permanently stationed at the airstrip, and the pilot routinely parked it beside our operations tent at night. Those mortars walked a line right between us and the plane.

The funniest part of that attack was when an officer heard the first mortar hit and let out a yelp. He ran to the nearest tent wall and frantically clawed it, like a cat scratching on a screen door, then tried to run through the wall and was trampoline-knocked on his ass. He flipped over and slithered away beneath the tent's side flap. Most of us were so enthralled by the man's antics that we didn't take cover or pay much attention to the debris thumping on canvas overhead. We found fragmentation holes in the canvas roof of the operations tent the next morning.

A captain looked up, saw sunlight filtering through a splattering of rips and tiny pinholes, and asked, "Were those there before?"

A graves registration [GR] tent was set up down a slope and across a narrow dirt road from the CP. A helipad on a hill behind the tent received chopper-loads of the cavalry division's dead heroes. Ironically, the helipad was built over a bulldozed graveyard. The graves registration team would transport the bodies on bouncing "mules" [little four-wheel-drive cargo vehicles that looked like platforms on wheels] back to the processing tent. Bodies usually arrived neatly stored in body bags, but if things were really rough somewhere, the GR helipad could be a horror. I never believed anything like that could happen to me, but did go out of my way not to look in the direction of the GR helipad or walk down the road below it.

I was insensitive enough to ask two GR men if their work bothered them. The first answered, "No. I don't mind my job much." The other nodded in agreement and replied, "Somebody has to do it." Their eyes told a different story. Perhaps that's why they were perpetually drunk.

In a pattern that seldom varied over the next year, the CP convoyed over crumbling French colonial highways in support of operations across the breadth of central Vietnam. Later in March, we were back in Pleiku, coordinating artillery fires for an Operation, called Lincoln, in the dangerous region along the Cambodian border where numerous battles (including the LZ X-Ray landing) had been fought the previous November. The same enemy units were still there, replenished now by a steady stream of replacements down the Ho Chi Minh Trail.

The major engagement during Lincoln began on March 29th, 1966 when a single slick carrying a squad of Blues from Alpha Troop [about five or six men] conducted a "snatch mission." Snatch missions were a favored 9th Cavalry tactic - swoop down, grab a prisoner, and get the hell out. The target area that day was riddled with spider holes, bunkers, and trenches close by the Chu Pong Massif. Two North Vietnamese prisoners were snatched.

The next morning, the troop commander decided to put his entire Blue platoon of about twenty men back into the same complex with orders to take another prisoner. Lift pilot Joe Salamone in the book **Hunter-Killer Squadron** describes the scene immediately after the Blues jumped from the slicks:

"I lifted off, and as I was clearing the trees in front of me, I saw countless VC within the tree line, moving in and out like the fangs of a dark, ferocious beast. The sight was unbelievable. "We should be dead," I thought. "Why didn't they shoot while we were on the ground? As vulnerable as we are, why aren't they shooting now?"

Meanwhile, the infantry platoon engaged North Vietnamese in spider holes and took a few prisoners, one of whom stated that there were a thousand more soldiers in the area. The Blues reported that they were not encountering strong resistance, but the troop commander now realized what they were facing and ordered an immediate withdrawal to the original drop-off point. The Blues ran one hundred meters through a gauntlet of enemy fire and arrived as the clearing was hit by mortars, RPGs, and machine guns.

Of the four slicks that tried to pull them out, two were shot down in the clearing; another was flown a short distance away and then crash-landed. The last helicopter made it back to Alpha Troop's staging area at the Plei Me Special Forces Camp. It was piloted by a crew chief who removed the dead pilot from his seat and, working with the seriously wounded co-pilot, managed to fly it back with shot-out hydraulics.

During that horrific rescue attempt, gunship and scout crews ran out of ammunition and reverted to pistols and M-16 rifles until those were empty as well. One gunship crew continued attacking the swarming NVA by throwing C-ration cans at them. Bob Emery, a Blue infantryman, was wounded three separate times during the battle, including being clubbed on the head with a rifle butt. He also survived his helicopter being shot out of the sky by an RPG. Emery played dead and lived through the night. The Blue infantry and Blue Lift platoons were effectively destroyed.

A crack paratrooper company was air assaulted in, suffered heavy casualties in a battle that would stretch throughout the night, and couldn't reach the original drop-off point until the next morning. The engagement was outside of tube artillery range, so fire support was provided by teams of aerial rocket artillery heavy hogs that fired almost thirteen hundred rockets.

———◆———

In early April, we left Pleiku and journeyed north on Colonial Route 14 to the mountain city of Kontum, a place heavy with the brown stucco architecture of the French era. Kontum was famous for an open-air market where various nations of hill tribesmen sold beautiful brass work, multicolored fabrics, and woven baskets. We slung hammocks in an old French barracks. For the first time in Vietnam, I had a real roof over my head, even if it did leak like a sieve. A straight, narrow dirt road, used by Montagnards [hill tribesmen] as a trade route between the city and their mountain homes, ran beside the barracks. We never tired of watching a steady trickle of loin-clothed men and bare-breasted women.

That road holds my best and worst memories of Kontum. One evening at dusk, a jeep driver from a neighboring command unit was decapitated by a wire stretched across the road at neck level. We had often raced down that road with jeep windshields folded down, which was the only way to get cooled off in the stifling heat. Jeeps whizzing past the French barracks, trailing clouds of red dust, had become a common sight. Our behavior had evidently not been lost on a local communist cell. Now one of us was dead. An official order was issued to drive all jeeps with windshields raised. No one had to tell us.

One fine market day morning, three of us drove down the road toward the mountains until we saw a male ocelot in a dead tree. The cat's front paws dangled over a barren limb, probably its daily perch, as it swiveled it head to watch the mountain people come and go. As we stared upward, a sinewy hill tribesman, his face a well-used map of lines and wrinkles, padded down the trail. He offered to sell the bamboo cage he carried and catch the ocelot for a grand total of two dollars. He shimmied up the tree, barefoot and bar-handed, and threw a brown cape over the spotted cat before it could react.

The soldier who paid the old Montagnard was going home soon and planned to take the ocelot with him and sell it for big bucks in America. I tried to buy the cat with all the money I had to set it free. No deal. For two days, the cat never made a sound as it relentlessly paced back and forth inside its cage, refusing water or even the tiniest morsel of food. That beautiful animal was dead in its cage on the third morning. I will forever admire its decision to live free or die.

On a pleasant April evening, I hitched a ride to the American advisors' compound in Kontum, rumored to have a spacious beer hall and a real wooden bar, just like those found back home. The place was filled with a dirty, chattering crowd of infantrymen – no open tables, standing room only at the bar. After threading a way between tables to the right corner of the famous wooden bar, I ordered a cold, ten cent beer.

Through the door walked four skinny, sunburned men wearing faded blue bandanas around their necks. They weaved through the tables and ended up milling about my corner.

The low hum of voices suddenly became a roar. About twenty infantrymen stood up from their tables and began migrating toward my corner. I got the hell out of Dodge. The blue bandana boys formed a tiny shoulder-to-shoulder semi-circle in front of the corner and silently faced a growing crowd of men shouting things like "There they are!" and "Get the bastards!"

A big sergeant first class, a bear of a man, intervened. "Let them be!" he roared. "Get yo' asses back to your tables! Leave those men have a beer in peace!" And just like that, the confrontation was over.

I didn't know who those four men represented at the time, but had to ask the question, "What was that all about?"

They told me.

A patrol of 9th Cavalry Blues was climbing a trail into the foothills when the point man killed two enemy soldiers nonchalantly walking toward them with their rifles slung over their shoulders. The patrol continued into a hardwood forest. Abruptly, the North Vietnamese opened fire. Gunships made rocket runs, but the rockets exploded in the tree tops and had little effect. The Blues were pinned down and in trouble, so the troop commander called for reinforcements.

An infantry company soon arrived. Those were the soldiers seated at the tables around us. They saw no casualties (already evacuated) and received no enemy fire. When the Blues came back down the trail to be picked up, some of the grunts booed and jeered, or cursed them. The infantry company walked up the same trail and was ambushed.

I later experienced this hostility firsthand on a narrow trail high in the mountains. Our Blue infantry platoon met a platoon of soldiers who had been part of a reaction force that relieved them during a serious battle. The two patrols squeezed by each other in total silence, but their eyes said it all. For soldiers whose only wish was to make it home alive, relieving a Blue platoon usually spelled trouble.

The four blue bandana boys that evening in Kontum drank one beer apiece and then quietly padded out of the bar like a pack of wary foxes.

———◆———

The CP returned to Camp Radcliff in late April. In line with some new duties, I became a courier on H-13 observation helicopters [they looked like Plexiglas bubbles with erector-set tails] carrying dispatches to artillery positions in the field.

One of the courier missions took me closer to the fighting than I had been before. A battle was raging on a jungle ridge in the Crow's Foot, near an artillery base in a valley below it. Artillery shells were bursting on top of wooded hills – flashes, tree limbs and trunks hurtling into the air before whirly-gigging down into the black smoke. The reason for the shooting was on display at Bird. Outside the artillery command post tent were two Chinese 12.7mm heavy machine guns on wheels with a major standing proudly beside them. He watched me step out of the H-13 with my document pouch and called me over. Beaming like a new father, he pointed to the trophies.

"They're really something, aren't they?"

"Yes, Sir. They sure are."

"You know what happening out there? The Seventh Cav is having a field day. A scout ship flies over and draws fire from those guns and we pound them with our one-oh-fives. All the infantry has to do is go and police them up. There's another one on the way in now. You tell those rear-echelon bastards back at Divarty [Division Artillery Headquarters] what you saw here."

The battle wasn't as simple as the major's version. The first observation helicopter that day had not only found a 12.7mm, it had been shot down. What had begun as a rescue mission had become a gun hunt, tempered by certain infantry casualties the major might not have known about. An enemy anti-aircraft unit had probably moved onto the ridge and been drawn into a fight before its soldiers were dug in and prepared to defend themselves.

An H-13 returning to Radcliff on the same route, fifteen minutes ahead of our return flight, was shot down. I entered the big bunker to find the colonel and his staff staring wide-eyed, looking like they were seeing a ghost. They thought the dead courier was me.

The major's comments were not repeated.

———◆———

Our next operation was in the Vinh Thanh Valley, or Happy Valley, so named because a previous operation had supposedly killed, or driven out, the enemy. Now the place was "Happy." We set up the CP at a narrow artillery base, called Cobra, about halfway down the valley and beside a mud road leading to a Special Forces camp. The cavalry division was maneuvering to protect the camp from an impending enemy assault.

It was May. The air was heavy with humidity from the last monsoon rains, and the surrounding upland jungles choked off any breezes that might have cooled us. We occupied a wrecked building that had been built for the French colonial administrators of the valley. Its roof had been destroyed long before; the walls were pitted with bullet holes and other battle scars. The rubble was cleared away, and the CP tent erected in one of the open rooms. Ponchos were strung between the naked walls of another room to protect supplies and C-rations from the constant rain. Soon it was business as usual: an endless cycle of duty, digging and sleep.

I carried daily intelligence dispatches between Cobra and the Special Forces camp. The trips were a good opportunity to escape the routine of Cobra and rest in the shade of the trees near an underground bunker [team house] in the center of the camp. They also gave me a chance to listen to the Green Berets' war stories. A balding sergeant would shake when he talked about the war, squinting his blue eyes before telling a favorite story.

"We set up a claymore [an antipersonnel mine named after the famous two-handled Scottish sword] ambush beside this little footbridge and were waiting for something to happen. Then this squad of dinks starts crossing the bridge, real slow-like. When the first one reaches the other side, we blow the mines on the ones that hadn't crossed and get the swinging dicks on the bridge with machine guns. It was bee-u-ti-ful! Blood everywhere! I've never seen so much blood at one time! Not one of those little fuckers got away!"

The ambush at the footbridge had taken its toll on more than the Vietnamese.

One evening the colonel walked into the CP tent and said, "I want a fire box." He put four dots on the acetate overlay wall map and connected them into a rectangle with a red grease pencil. "You will saturate this area with all available artillery."

An enemy regiment was assembling in a region of truly rugged mountains. Our job was to destroy them in place or drive them into infantry screens along the edges of the fire box. Where no infantrymen were available, teargas drops were supposed to seal off escape routes. Everything that could be pinpointed by SLAR [Side-Looking Aerial Radar], people sniffers [urine detectors], infrared [heat detectors] observation helicopters, and Air Force spotter planes -every camp, grove of trees in the fold of a mountain, known or discovered stream, trail, or military crest- was hit by artillery, air strikes and even B-52 bombers.

For seventy-two almost sleepless hours, we hit that box with artillery strikes whose broken blue crosses overlapped so heavily on the big wall map that no open space remained. We erased all of them and started over. The CP staff became practiced at planning artillery strikes down to the minute: when, where, and in what sequence which types of shells would strike targets. In one interrogation report, a North Vietnamese soldier spoke about what the artillery pounding and air strikes were doing. Entire squads had been wiped out as they fled shells impacting elsewhere.

The enemy attacked our perimeter one rainy night at a point about forty meters from my pup tent home. A machine gun burst tore little holes in my pup just above ground level. These were discovered the next morning. The southern staff sergeant who stood over me while I dug a below-ground sleeping hole had done me a great favor. Thank you again, sergeant. I apologize for accusing you of lacking a father.

Two enemy dead from the attack were left behind, and two more, probably a body retrieval party, hid in the tall grass in front of a machine gun until they were captured. One of them was the tallest Vietnamese I was ever to see. The guy wore a khaki shirt with far-too-short sleeves, and khaki trousers that reached about three-quarters of the way down his calves. The Latino rifleman who guarded him reached to the boy's shoulder. To make the scene more bizarre, both of them were back-slapping and laughing like long-lost buddies. Of course, only one of them had a rifle. General SLA Marshall says that no enemy prisoners were taken during Operation Crazy Horse. I know of at least two.

Soon thereafter, on another wet, black night, we were targeted by a rapid, crashing mortar barrage from the mountains. Rustling death sailed directly overhead and landed about eighty meters away, in a dry rice field outside Cobra's perimeter. I didn't smoke, but had grown tired of smokers begging for the four cigarettes included with every C-ration meal. I was looking for the proper occasion to light up. Those near misses were it.

By chance, I had stepped onto the veranda of the French building for a breath of fresh air just as the mortars fluttered overhead and detonated. I exclaimed in a teenage macho voice, "Ha! They missed!" This tough guy fished around in his left breast pocket for the little cardboard pack, stuck a cigarette in his mouth, and lit it. A stinging slap and a red spark shower as the cigarette went flying were unexpected.

"Asshole!" I recognized the husky voice of the captain who had begged a helicopter ride along the Cambodian border in January. "All they need is a good aiming point to do it right!" He expanded on the asshole comment and made threats about what would happen "if you try that shit again." I didn't.

The Captain was later one of the Special Forces officers somehow connected to the death of a suspected Viet Cong double agent.

The four artillery pieces at Cobra were newly arrived Italian howitzers that rested on circular bases and could be easily rotated to fire in any direction. About noon on a day in late May, bedlam broke loose. Shirtless artillery crews ran to their pieces, swung them around, and began slamming shells into gun breeches as fast as they could be fired. Amid shouts and orders from the gun commanders, the crews blasted direct fire over open sights onto a hill, LZ Hereford, about two miles away. A small platoon waiting for helicopter pick-up was being overrun there.

Black blossoms erupted in the elephant grass on the crest and marched downhill and across the tops of tangled jungle trees. The howitzers abruptly ceased fire after more shouted commands. The gun crews at Cobra had stopped the enemy attack and helped in the rescue of a few survivors.

This is a tiny part of an amazing tale of bravery. A full accounting of the battle at Hereford can be found in General SLA Marshall's book, **Battles in the Monsoon.**

I was a witness to the Hereford shelling and couldn't have done much else. I had contracted what was probably either Malaria or Dengue Fever [also called Break-Bone Fever]. I remember very little, except for three days of aching pain, chills, fever with hot, sticky sweating, and, toward the end, diarrhea. No one attended me. My buddies brought canteens of water to my bed in a shallow trench with a pup tent overhead as I drifted in and out of consciousness.

A cavalry latrine, a plywood box with a single fanny hole over a sawed-off fifty-five-gallon oil drum, stood about seventy meters away. No provisions were made for privacy at cavalry toilets – just the box. The one trip there and back, on about the third day, was the longest walk of my life. I was so weak that each footstep sapped my strength. I would rest a while, think about taking the next step, and then extend a foot. I have never again experienced such debilitating weakness. On the fourth or fifth day, I ate some C-rations and started getting stronger. End of story, or so I thought.

A day or two later, my right arm felt like someone had taken a base-ball bat and broken the humerus. There was extreme, continuous, mind-numbing pain. I was back to work, but one arm was useless for two or three days.

By the time Operation Crazy Horse was through, I hated everything remotely related to Happy Valley.

———◆———

After Crazy Horse ended, I was reassigned, under protest, to the big bunker beside the fuck-you forest at Camp Radcliff. The part of that job I liked best was the box seat that the daily intelligence reports gave on the war. The cavalry division was conducting simultaneous operations from the Cambodian border to the South China Sea. Its units stretched along two hundred miles of coast, patrolling areas where the French had rarely set foot after 1946. I had a teenager's pride in being part of something so enormous.

My job was coordinating counter-mortar and final defensive fire [*Quick Fire*] through a local base defense radio network [*Base Defense net*], and plotting artillery fire on approaches to the base. We also monitored, gave instructions, and took reports on a parallel and far-flung Division Artillery radio network [*Divarty net*] composed of cavalry division units and artillery bases spread across Central Vietnam

Freak atmospheric conditions sometimes played games with *Divarty net*. One quiet morning, an infantry commander was in heavy combat and begging for artillery support. We didn't recognize the unit call signs, couldn't decipher the locations, and assumed division headquarters had changed codes without notifying us. We were soon staring at a pile of expired, current, and future codes, and nothing matched. The battle was taking place in the Ho Bo Woods, a couple hundred miles to the south.

About a week later, we monitored a similar broadcast from an infantry company in War Zone D, again far to the south. His company had just discovered the vine-encrusted wreckage of an Air Force B-57 bomber. The skeletons of two pilots were still strapped in their seats. The commander kept repeating, *"Has anyone lost a plane?"* Again, call signs and map locations didn't match our information. We were hearing his transmissions, but not the replies to them. Our replies, of course, went unanswered.

On another occasion, we listened on *Divarty net* as a 4th Infantry division base called Oasis was hammered by 400 mortar rounds. As transmissions bounced off clouds and made their way over the high mountains along the Mang Yang Pass, the old hands who had been mortared at Oasis , then called the Tea Plantation, during the Ia Drang Campaign heard the background thump of mortar explosions, exchanged shocked looks, and grew white-faced.

One moonless night in late June or July, I was on duty when the enemy fired a ranging [marking or adjusting] mortar round that overshot the rows of helicopters parked on the huge Golf Course and landed about forty meters from the big bunker. I was able to grab a handset and yell, *"Initiate Quickfire!"* so quickly that the howitzers began booming just as a swarm of mortar rounds exploded among the helicopters. Counter-battery fire was usually an exercise in futility. The enemy would have their mortars reburied and be gone themselves by the time ARA rocketed fires started by artillery shells, and the new counter-mortar radars pinpointed targets that were actually echoes from those same shells.

Fresh eggs almost made me an officer that summer. We had eaten powdered eggs and the deceptively named, canned C-ration entre, "Ham and Eggs Chopped," since I arrived in December, 1965. One fine morning, a shipment of fresh eggs arrived at the mess tent. You probably can't imagine the electrifying effect that the prospect of eating two fresh eggs, cooked any way you want, had on us. Everything remotely connected to eggs had come out of a box or a can; powdered eggs had often turned a lovely shade of green before we could eat them. Now we could feast on two real eggs.

I was on duty in the big bunker when the windfall was announced and the morning trickle of people to the mess tent became a flood. I looked downslope from the back entrance, through the narrow trunks of fuck-you forest trees, toward a line of men queued-up to receive their manna from heaven. Word quickly spread, and diners flooded in from all over the area. The mess sergeant and a headquarters clerk with a clipboard were screening-out men from other units. The cooks had only so many eggs.

The captain on duty began going to the back entrance and returning to pace back and forth and mumble about missing his eggs. I felt the same way. Finally, the captain exclaimed, "Fuck it! I'm going to get my eggs. I won't be gone long," and hurried off down a path through the trees.

The rules required an officer to be present at all times in the bunker; the bunker was, after all, the nerve center of the division's far flung tube artillery and aerial rocket forces. But the morning's radio traffic had been quiet, and neither of us thought much about bending the rules for a few minutes. Within a couple of minutes after the captain left, the division-wide *Divarty net* came to life. A Special Forces patrol was in a heavy firefight in the mountains northeast of the An Khe base. Their strikers had run away, abandoning two Special Forces men and a Vietnamese first sergeant. They were asking for help. Quick map plotting showed no artillery in range to help them.

Now a voice squawked from the *Base Defense net*. The commander of a 105mm artillery battery emplaced three or four kilometers from Camp Radcliff had been monitoring the *Divarty net*. He radioed to say that he could help if he moved his howitzers a few kilometers north to an abandoned artillery position. I made quick calls on a telephone line to the infantry battalion defending Camp Radcliff. Their headquarters did some fast checking and informed me that the road to the old position was not secured or swept for mines, the old firebase had not been swept for mines and booby-traps, and no infantry was available to protect the howitzers during a road march, or guard them when they arrived at the firebase.

I told the folks on both nets to hold for a moment, ran out of the big bunker to the edge of fuck-you forest, and began hollering for the captain. People were still queued-up outside the mess tent, waiting for their precious eggs. A few of them looked in my direction, but no one left his place in line. They probably thought that I was shouting something about those damned eggs. I ran back inside to find the Special Forces men still in trouble and the battery commander telling me to make a decision. I had no safe way to reveal my rank or position over an open radio net. I was on my own.

To make a long story short, I used code words to tell the SF guys that help was on the way, and authorized the captain to move two howitzers and truckloads of ammunition down an unsecured road to the old firebase, using his gun crews for security. My part in the affair lasted less than ten minutes. The SF men were able to escape with the help of the howitzer fire. I went back to quiet radios and ate fresh eggs when I got off-shift at noon.

Two days later, the command sergeant-major approached me on behalf of Colonel Brand, the division artillery commander, and asked if I would accept a direct commission to artillery lieutenant. I turned him down. The reasons were complicated. I was still afraid of officers and didn't think I would make a good one. I also figured that the offer had something to do with the fresh egg caper, and, for me, the real heroes were the battery commander and the Special Forces men.

Refusing that commission was a knuckle-headed decision.

———◆———

The Camp Radcliff vacation ended in early September and I returned to the endless CP operations. The cavalry division was again fighting in Binh Dinh Province, in a coastal region south of Bong Son called the Crescent, where sandy plains, paddy fields, and fishing villages curved around the purple-green mass of the Phu Cat Mountains. We supported a massive head-on clash between the cavalry division and all three regiments of the Yellow Star Division. The campaigns involved were called Irving and Thayer.

The CP convoyed through the rugged Deo Mang Pass and set up shop at a Korean artillery base below the mountains. American bases were becoming well-protected fortresses with multiple rolls of barbed wire, ditches, berms, bunkers, claymore mines, and flares. The small Korean base was laid out in a square and protected by a single roll of barbed wire. The bunkers were flimsy, but spacious and neat, designed for inspections, not defense. The artillerymen didn't man all of those bunkers, so we helped them out. Far from being dug in and protected by multiple layers of sandbags, each Korean howitzer was dug down about one foot into the sand and protected by a neat and tidy, two-foot-high circle of sandbags.

The base had a wooden mess hall that served excellent American meals. The Koreans' main activities seemed to be flag raising and lowering ceremonies, lots of white underwear Tae-Kwan-Do practice, and work parties to keep the place spic-and-span. The Koreans were not being disturbed. The reason was probably an accommodation. Given the Koreans' reputation, the Viet Cong were protecting their relatives in the local villages, with a typical "You don't shoot at me, and I won't shoot at you. You go here, and I'll go there" arrangement.

Had we known the unspoken history of the Korean-occupied region, the reason for the lack of real defenses at the artillery base would have been clearer. There were rumors that the Koreans killed villagers in the vicinity of attacks on their forces, but the truth was far worse. In early 1966, while the cavalry division and the Marines were conducting Operation Masher/White Wing/Eagle Claw farther north, the Koreans were systematically destroying "hostile" hamlets north of the Deo Mang Pass.

The Korean base gave us a front row seat for a heavy fire attack on LZ Hammond, the principal cavalry base in the Crescent. Eight-inch [203mm] howitzers had been slamming 200-pound shells into base areas in the Soui Ca Mountains since the cavalry division's arrival in the Crescent. Our forward CP was plotting the targets. The enemy came down from the mountains to destroy the big howitzers, and so the eight-inch position was blanketed by very accurate mortar and recoilless rifle shells. Every jeep, truck, ammo trailer and howitzer was hit. Throughout that event, the Korean artillery fired not a single shell.

I was sent to Hammond at dawn the next morning to do a damage assessment. When I arrived, the gunners were still dazed and stumbling around like drunks. What impressed me most deeply were a brown paper shopping bag and a pair of boots. They were placed to one side of a field littered with broken glass, pieces of muddy canvas and black mortar craters. The boots were still laced around feet; the bag held part of a rib cage. That was all that remained of the first soldier killed. What I couldn't know at the time was that the three men killed in that attack were an FO team assigned to Charlie Troop of the 9th Cavalry. Their loss would indirectly affect me in the coming months.

When we packed up our equipment for a move to Hammond, I remembered that shopping bag and those boots.

After the move to Hammond, we supported Operation Irving. On the opening day of that campaign, Alpha Troop of the 9th Cavalry started a major battle. It began when the troop commander's gunship crew spotted seven NVA heading toward a (fortified) seaside village. A bitter fight ensued as the troop attacked a battalion of North Vietnamese. Three Blues were killed. Three infantrymen from the relieving paratrooper battalion, the same unit that had relieved Alpha Troop Blues in the long-ago March thirtieth battle near the Chu Pong Massif, also died. Alpha Troop helicopters and Blues had killed 92 enemy soldiers by the time the paratroopers arrived.

Thus began an escalating series of battles and maneuvers that lasted for the next four months and resulted in hundreds of dead American and thousands of North Vietnamese soldiers killed or taken prisoner. Binh Dinh Province, least secure of the forty-nine South Vietnamese provinces throughout the war, was never pacified.

<hr />

Soon the days at Hammond became routine - battles and barrages, targets and results. What made them unusual was the unit stationed nearby. Helicopters with the yellow crossed sabers of the 9th Cavalry took off and returned within easy view of the CP tent. Gunships, slicks, and scout birds would fly over Hammond trailing long streamers of red smoke if a particular mission had resulted in enemy dead. They were using up a lot of red smoke grenades. The Blues, the blue bandana infantry boys I had first encountered in Kontum, walked by our tent wearing captured North Vietnamese star belts and carrying souvenir rifles, and I envied them the "excitement" of their lives. They didn't spend their days talking into a damned radio.

The 9th Cavalry was already becoming a legend in Vietnam, although I didn't know this. What I did know was that the unit's name popped up almost every time a battle began, and that most of our fresh targets for nighttime artillery strikes over the past year had come from their helicopter teams. They were noted for going after the enemy like blood hounds and were called the "Headhunters," although I didn't personally take the name seriously. Every unit seemed to be nicknamed "Hunters," or "Stalkers," or "Tigers," or "Destroyers," or some such thing.

A new artillery liaison officer – compact, energetic and muscular– began coming by the CP tent daily, asking if any radio jockeys wanted to see the war firsthand. I followed him out of the tent one day and asked if he was serious about wanting forward observers. He was serious. He said that he could have me transferred immediately.

I had only a few weeks left in Vietnam, but wasn't proud of my easy tour. The bullets through my pup tent at Cobra and a few mortar attacks were the only times I may have been in real danger. I wasn't sure. Now I could finally be a combat soldier. It was easy to forget the baby-faced major who had so grieved for Strickland, his lost FO, at Bong Son. Nothing like that could happen to me.

Divarty set up its first forward observer training school at An Khe and I was the first graduate. The officers who trained me acted like they were losing a family member, and I felt the same way towards them and all of my friends at the CP. Then I joined Charlie Troop's Blue platoon: the men whose lives I had envied. Their radio call sign was "Brave Fighter Blues." It was a fitting name.

Chapter 3

BIRD

(December, 1966)

Some background. Each of the three air cavalry troops provided intelligence for a brigade of about three thousand men. Because a brigade's assigned area was so vast, most of it was "screened" by an air cavalry troop's ten Huey gunships [Red] and ten H-13 scout helicopters [White]. The infantry [Blue] platoon was carried into battle by four Huey lift ships [Blue Lift]. Lift helicopters were often called "slicks" [no weapons attached to the fuselage] or "lift birds." Charlie Troop's lift pilots were a courageous lot who rode their helicopters as if they were thoroughbred racehorses. They performed amazing aerial acrobatics to keep us alive. Because each Blue squad in a troop was assigned to a specific slick, the pilots and infantrymen worked well together and developed strong bonds.

A Blue platoon varied in strength from eighteen to twenty-two men, including a two-man forward observer team and a medic. The platoon was inserted into LZs [Landing Zones] by slicks with cargo bay doors removed and all seats arranged in a solid bank. Everyone sat facing outward. In-flight firepower was provided by a crew chief on one side and the infantry squad's machine gunner on the other, each manning a machine gun suspended by a bungee cord. As the helicopters approached the LZ, the Blues stepped out on the landing skids and grabbed seat struts with the hands not holding weapons. They tried to jump at the same time from the moving choppers to help the pilots keep the machines in balance.

All-weapons-firing landings and pick-ups were impressive affairs that made the slicks look like they were blazing. Often the accompanying 9th Cavalry gunships, or aerial rocket artillery heavy hogs, attacked the area around the LZ or PZ [Pick-Up Zone] with rockets and other weapons; sometimes there was artillery fire preparation; sometimes the enemy was shooting at us going in or coming out. This was referred to as a hot LZ or a hot PZ, also as red [enemy fire] or green [no enemy fire].

In transit to a landing, the crew chief on one side of the slick, and the infantry squad leader on the other, wore headphones to stay current on events on the ground and keep everyone briefed. Assault landings were called air assaults in the early years and combat assaults beginning about 1968. Many people kept count of their air assaults. My eventual total was about 450.

The Blue platoon was equipped with six infantry radios, one artillery radio, four machine guns, and four grenade launchers. Everyone else carried automatic rifles. Each squad could, and often did, act as an independent recon element.

While some American units avoided trails like the plague, Blue platoons walked straight down them until they found what they were after. This tactic was so unexpected that it usually caught the NVA completely off guard. The last thing the enemy apparently expected was a platoon of Americans prowling down the trail they used every day. We sometimes found guards set out in every direction, except along their "safe" trail.

Our greatest edge came through experience and reflexes. Enemy units spent long periods between battles in mountain "base areas," or in villages inside "liberated zones." Discipline in those areas was not so great. We were in some sort of contact almost daily. By the time an enemy soldier got over the shock of being under attack and remembered what to do, he was dead. Even in face-to-face meetings, the opponent's slight hesitation to pull the trigger almost always made him the loser.

I would soon learn to tie boots so that the laces wouldn't snag and trip you; to silently walk heel to toe; to avoid touching branches and bushes; to avoid disturbing or breaking grass, soil, leaves, and twigs; to glide across the jungle floor and leave almost no trace of my passage; to read trails and perform the hand signals and the occasional whispered word necessary for silent patrolling. Instruction followed on detection of enemy soldiers dressed as farmers by their shorter haircuts, smooth hands [farmers had tough, calloused hands], and pack strap burns.

A special sort of remedial education, in the form of questions and warnings from fellow infantrymen, would come later:

"Have you ever been wounded?" ….. No.

"If you had been (*you fool)*, you wouldn't have stayed. It hurts."

"Have you ever killed someone?" ….. No.

"Can you kill someone?"….. I don't know. I never thought about it.

"Look, man. If you want to live, you have to shoot first. You can't take time to think about it. Forget what they told you at home, in school, in church. This shit is real!"

And it was.

———◆———

Sheets of rain had been coming down for days, until about two hours earlier, on the morning I arrived at Charlie Troop as a forward observer [FO] sergeant. Some helicopters had taken off during the lull and made quick reconnaissance flights toward the mountainous Crow's Foot War Zone. Rain was pouring down again as a pilot and I ate C-rations at a long plank table in the mess tent. Two gunship pilots entered the tent and greeted the pilot at my table.

The seated pilot asked, "Been back to the Crow's Foot?" to which a standing pilot replied, "Yeah. The bodies are still there. It's been three days. You'd think their buddies would've found them with their noses by now. I could smell them in the chopper."

They had killed three North Vietnamese soldiers in a ditch three days before and returned to see if the bodies were moved or buried. To make some sense of this brutal exchange, I mentally converted it into a standard radio report of the type we received at the forward CP.

The rain stopped again and I walked through watery mud to a nearby pup tent camp. Shirtless men with blue bandanas tied around their necks emerged as I arrived, sat on the low sandbag walls around the tents, spread plastic sheets and oil-cloth rags on the ground at their feet, and began cleaning and oiling rifles, machine guns, and grenade launchers. Some of them were sneaking looks at me, sizing up the new FO. I reported to the platoon sergeant, Samuel, who shook my hand warmly and welcomed me to the platoon. Sam was a handsome, athletic, man with a quiet air of authority: a real leader. I liked him instinctively.

Sergeant Sam sat with me on the sandbag wall surrounding his pup tent and explained Charlie Troop's operations. He said that the Blues would see a fraction of the troop's total effort, because gunships and scouts often fought battles in remote places completely inaccessible to helicopter landings. In other cases, the crews landed long enough to collect weapons and documents. When he said that the troop often caused more enemy casualties in a month than the individual infantry battalions, and in some months, more than the entire brigade of three battalions, I didn't believe him.

Sam made a point of reminding me to always secure my grenade pins and never let them dangle loose. Eight months before, a Blue had been killed and four others seriously wounded when a grenade pin caught on a machine gun mount and pulled loose as a soldier jumped from a lift bird.

A story that was probably based on that accident can be found in Steven Phillip Smith's novel, **American Boys**, *which draws upon his experiences with Charlie Troop, 9th Cavalry, in Vietnam. Smith later wrote* **An Officer and a Gentleman.**

After the briefing, Sergeant Sam gave me a quick tour of the barbed wire obstacles and the machine gun bunkers behind them, pointing out fields of fire. He said that everyone, medics, infantrymen, and the artillery team manned the defenses at night. For most of the next twenty-six months I did just that.

Sam showed me to my new home, a makeshift structure thrown together from four tent halves and barely large enough for the team radioman, our equipment and me. The edges were held down by a single row of sandbags; the floor was dug down two feet for more room and protection. As I dragged my field gear into the cramped space, Johnson, the radioman, appeared from somewhere. He stuck his head through the small entranceway, forced a smile, and crawled in beside me.

"Hi. I'm Greg Johnson. I'll be carrying your radio." He started shaking when he said the last sentence.

"Matt Brennan. I hope you know what's happening around here. I'll need a little help getting started."

He nodded and waited a second for effect. "No sweat, but I'll only be here for a couple of days. Just got a radio job over at squadron. Did you just get in from the States?"

This would be a first admission of the greatest sin in Vietnam. "No. I extended my tour."

He gave me a shocked look. "Oh! Well, I'm glad to be leaving." That pale little man meant it. He looked away in embarrassed silence while his body twitched and jerked.

The Blues had recently landed in a quiet place called the 506 Valley, run into unexpected trouble, and spent the night pinned down by two machine guns firing from the edge of a wood. After that experience, Johnson decided the Blue platoon wasn't his line of work. He found excuses not to go on landings, and several times left the platoon without an FO. Sergeant Sam had requested that Johnson be taken off his hands. It gradually dawned on me that the liaison officer who recruited me for this adventure was juggling a forward observer team with no NCO and a vanishing radioman.

I spent the early evening assembling the heavy infantry field gear – fourteen twenty-round magazines, each loaded with eighteen bullets [if the magazines held nineteen or twenty bullets the springs would weaken], four hand grenades, a yellow smoke grenade, two first aid packets, a fighting knife, a thick sock [to muffle sound] holding a couple of C-ration cans stacked and tied tight, an artillery compass, and two canteens of water, all attached to a web belt with a shoulder harness. A bandolier of seven more magazines was worn looped over the shoulder and across the chest. The outfit felt like it weighed a hundred pounds when I tried it on.

I had almost finished cleaning the beat-up rifle that had been my constant companion for a year when a tall medic walked silently over. He sat down beside me on the sandbags, threw a hunting knife into the sand at our feet, and slowly grinned. He was there to check me out for the others.

"Hi, FO. I'm Doc Stone. What do you think of this bunch of clowns?" He indicated the low profiles of tents where those Blues not manning the bunkers were sleeping.

"I don't know them yet, Doc. They seem all right to me."

He nodded his head. "They're a good bunch of men, and they are damned happy to have an F.O. again." He winked like a fellow conspirator. "Gives them a sense of security, you know?"

"Yeah. I guess it does. How do you medics work it on missions?" Landings were called "missions" here.

He hesitated, as if a painful nerve had been pinched. "Well, me and the other Doc [Brad Smith] used to trade off before he got hit on December first. That way we only had to go out every other day. If there's some deep shit, only one gets hit. For a couple of weeks, I've been the only medic, and that gets a bit hairy." He brightened for a moment. "One thing's a fact. You do get a lot of souvenirs around here."

Doc Stone pulled three leather belts from a leg pocket. He dangled the belts so that the stars on the brass buckles would reflect the moonlight. "If you'd like, I'll give you one. They're all the same."

If I told him how much I coveted one of those belts, he would laugh. "Thanks anyway. I'll get one myself sooner or later." One day I would have a collection of eleven different styles of those damned communist belts: officer, NCO, enlisted, dress, web, star, no star, canvas, leather, patent leather, brass, aluminum, etc.

Doc shrugged his shoulders and flashed another grin. "If that's how you want it." He dug his knife out of the sand and disappeared into the night like a silent jungle cat. I hoped that I had been approved.

The whine of chopper engines and shouts of "Saddle Up!" awoke me at dawn. I grabbed the harness, bandolier, and rifle. My leg cargo pockets bulged with acetate-covered maps, code books, and ballpoint pens wrapped in plastic. The palm of my hand would be a writing tablet because paper disintegrates in the rain. Johnson and I ran toward a waiting line of four slicks.

The Blues were already there, standing in a ragged circle and playing their weapons like imaginary guitars. They shouted the lyrics of "Rockin' Robin" above the beat of the chopper blades, swaying and stomping their feet in cadence. *"He rocks in the tree tops all the day long, rockin' and a rolling and a singing this song. Rockin' Robin ... bop, bop, bop."* That gyrating circle of black, and brown, and white men, with mustaches and sideburns, hung all over with belts of ammunition and grenades, was like a scene from a psycho ward. A few minutes later, those same soldiers would be stepping over muddy bodies many miles away.

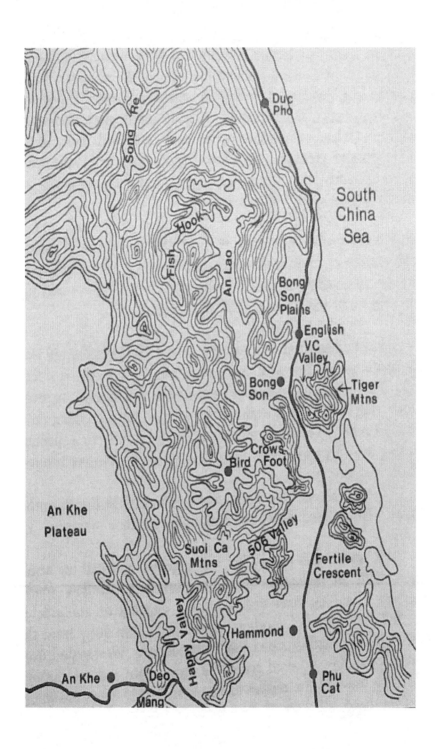

The four slicks lifted off in a swirling cloud of sand and flew us west over rice paddies and peaceful villages bounded by coconut palms along irrigation canals. They began crossing jungle ridges towering above deserted rice valleys with cracked paddies and broken palm trees. Then someone fired at a gunship. The slicks pulled away from the westward route, climbed for altitude, and began circling over a line of green foot-hills. Far below us, gunships rocketed a hill beside an overgrown rice valley. Black explosions sent tree limbs crashing down into the jungle.

Our crew chief listened intently to a message coming over his ear-phones and shouted excitedly over the whomp-whomp-whomp of the chopper blades, "We're going in! Two ships! The gun birds took fire from that valley!" He pointed down and listened to another message. "LZ is hot!"

Yellow smoke marking a landing zone drifted over a clearing on the side of the hill. My ship and another made a tight right turn away from the other choppers and dropped toward the smoke with machine guns firing. We jumped from the slicks as they hovered across the open space and ran through shin-high water to the bushes along its edge. My legs were numb and my head still buzzed from the din of the chopper blades. This was happening too fast. I crouched behind a bush beside Taso, a fat Latin American grenadier. He didn't like it.

Taso jabbed his elbow into my arm and looked me square in the eye. "Look! Would you mind moving off a little? There's plenty of bushes on this hill, man. Hanging together ain't healthy."

He was right. I scrambled to another bush, bothered by his anger, and realized that the rain had already soaked through my uniform. Then I saw it. A few meters in front of me, beside a smoking rocket crater were two mangled bodies. The whole one had fallen forward into the mud with his neck somehow bent double beneath him. The other corpse was just a pair of legs complete with belt and trousers. The torso ended at the edge of the muddy crater – a direct rocket hit. They had been dead only minutes, but already flies buzzed around the remains and a heavy odor hung in the air. My mind screamed, "My God! Those can't be men lying there. They aren't really dead."

A gunship roared over the clearing a couple of feet above the bushes. One of the door gunners tossed a red smoke grenade into some trees forty meters farther up the hillside. The Blues advanced in squads, one moving and one covering, through tangled grass and muddy water, to the place where red smoke floated among the branches.

Two leaning, decaying huts stood under the trees behind the bodies. In a straw lean-to beside the second hut were two khaki packs and a jumble of cracked rice bowls. The bowls were still moist and warm from an early meal. Sam sent one squad under Sergeant Hobson farther up the hill to search for anything of military value. They had barely disappeared up the trail when a rifle stuttered a long burst. We dived into the mud and crawled for cover. Sam remained standing, frowning down on us.

"Let's go, Blue! That was a Sixteen!" Johnson and I were the last to pull ourselves out of the mud.

Sergeant Hobson walked back down the trail, shoving a frightened little man with the muzzle of his rifle. Both prisoner and captor were trembling. Hobson gulped air and reported to Sam. "I just killed a broad back there hiding in the bushes. I didn't know it was a woman. She had her hair rolled up under a VC bush hat. This one" –he flipped a thumb at the prisoner- "didn't move until she bled all over him." Hobson, a thin career NCO from Indiana, had just killed his first human being. He looked confused and sick.

Sam turned away, trying to ignore Hobson's agony by directing questions to our interpreter. "Okay, Minh, ask this one what they were doing here."

The two Vietnamese talked rapidly in their singsong voices. Minh turned to Sam. "He say they farmer."

Sam pointed to the military packs we had found. "How does he explain these?"

"He say they find them."

"Did they have weapons?"

"He say no weapon. Only pack."

The last answer was accompanied by a violent shaking of the prisoner's head. Sam's face lost all expression for a moment. He ran down the trail to the rocket crater, stooped, and pulled an SKS rifle from under the pair of legs. He returned with the rifle and slowly waved the muzzle in front of the prisoner's nose. The man's knees buckled and a Blue pulled him back to his feet.

Sam put the muzzle under the man's jaw and asked one more question. "Now that we know he's a liar, ask him who the woman was."

"He say they farmer and she wife."

"Christ, loyalty unto death. She was more likely a nurse. Get this scum back to the PZ."

We burned the huts and lean-to and threw the packs into the flames, saving only some documents and a few Chinese bullets. Leather belts were striped from the crater bodies by a soldier, but they didn't have stars on their brass buckles and that disappointed him. He wiped off some drying blood on the whole corpse's shirt and on his own trouser leg, carefully folded the belts, and stuffed them into a cargo pocket.

Two Blues ripped cavalry division horse head patches from their shirt sleeves and tossed them on the crater bodies. Another man ran up the trail to the woman's body and placed a patch on her forehead. I had seen the darker fabric on the sleeves of many Blues, where patches had been worn and then torn off, but didn't know where the patches had gone. The platoon was keeping two local seamstresses busy sewing on new patches.

When we pulled back to circle the clearing for security, Sam ordered a weapons test fire. Nine M-16s were on the ground that morning; seven of them fired more than one round. Not a bad score for those damned rifles.

The slicks clattered in, machine guns firing all the way. A mad scramble for seats and then we were away from that desolate place. Even our prisoner seemed happy to be leaving. I had spent a year in Vietnam without getting as wet as I now was. As the choppers climbed through the downpour, I realized the true advantages of a helicopter. The blades keep out the rain and the wind dries your clothes.

That night they gave me a blue bandana.

As a more or less free agent within the platoon, I could attach myself as an extra rifleman on single-ship landings. Extra rifles were always welcome. The next morning, I accompanied Sergeant Haskett's squad on a raid launched from a sandbar near LZ Bird. We chased four Viet Cong up a trail and through their hilltop camp, wounding the tail man. They dived into an overgrown, dead end gulley, abandoning everything – packs, hammocks, cooking utensils, grenades, ammo pouches, and four bolt-action Russian carbines.

We were needed elsewhere, so we burned everything in a hurry, except the explosives, the rifles, and a pack booby-trapped by a primed hand grenade. On a signal from Haskett, all six of us hurled grenades into the gulley and ran like hell down the trail as detonations boomed behind us.

Later that day, a door gunner shot a man who disappeared into a trench concealed by vines trained over a wicker framework. We found blood, but no body. The trench led to an underground cargo bike repair shop concealed under a hut. The shop was blown up.

The next morning we burned an enemy camp in the tall grass behind a peaceful hamlet. The camp was equipped with U.S. Army blankets, ponchos, gas masks, cots and other equipment. Later we followed a trail in the high Soui Ca. The weather had been overcast and raining more or less continuously for days when suddenly the sun broke through the clouds. Minutes later, the distinctive tat-tat-tat-tat of a door gun echoed from high above us, across a deep ravine. Two North Vietnamese soldiers had emerged from a cave, removed their khaki shirts, stretched out on a rock ledge, and began soaking up the sunshine. A door gunner killed them.

At dawn on a mid-December morning, six of us, in a slick escorted by two gunships, were flown over a wasteland of burned huts, abandoned rice fields, broken animal pens, and the bones of a water buffalo beside a smashed two-wheel cart. A Charlie Troop helicopter had crashed and burned on a sandy river bank the evening before, killing both pilots. We jumped in a few feet from the wreck. All that remained of the helicopter were the tips of the main rotor blade, a fire-blackened engine that looked like a giant's discarded toy top, and clumps of melted plastic, metal, and wire.

We were after body parts. Most of us weren't experienced enough to distinguish burned human remains from burnt metal and plastic, so two "old Blues" did the sifting while the rest of us stood guard. All they found fit into about one-half of a sandbag [the size of a pillowcase]. The squad leader, an old-timer named Person, held up the sandbag with a soot-smudged hand and obscenely suggested that he needed to find some gloves.

The next two weeks were mostly spent on clearing operations in the Crow's Foot War Zone. This mountainous region was called the Kim Son, but its interconnected valleys vaguely resembled a bird's foot on maps. The region had once held numerous small farming villages occupied by Roman Catholics who had fled south after the 1954 partition. The Catholics hated godless communism, and this made the Kim Son one of the potentially most loyal areas for any non-communist government, but the valleys were rice rich. The undersupplied communist forces needed that rice and had no qualms about fighting through and around Catholic villages.

The solution to the problem of separating enemy forces from peaceful farmers, while denying the enemy rice, was to declare the Kim Son a war zone. This coming zone of destruction, soon to be the target of artillery, bombers, gunships, and rice-killing chemicals, was not created without considering the people who lived there, that is, if you didn't take into account the misery involved in tearing people from their homes and paddy fields. Spotter planes spent weeks dropping millions of leaflets telling the people to leave within thirty days. The leaflets spread the word to most of the farmers.

Our job was to find the rest and get them out while there was still time. We landed throughout the Kim Son, gathering little families, usually women, children, and very old men, and sending them to resettlement centers on the coast. We were on their side in this war, so there usually was no hostility, just raw emotions. One ancient blind woman had lived for weeks on the rice stored in her hut. She was alone in her dark world; everyone else in the hamlet had left, but she wouldn't, or couldn't, follow. A door gunner spotted her because she was frightened by the noise and scuttled into her hut as the machine roared overhead. There were also the stubborn ones – old men, single women, or occasional families who simply refused to leave their homes. Those people were forcibly dragged to the waiting helicopters.

All of the empty huts and rice storehouses could never be destroyed by bombs and shells, so we had another task. Deserted villages, most with beige stucco churches topped by the one true cross, were searched and burned. Those churches were carbon copies of the Spanish mission churches in America's southwest. Before the French arrived, the first Catholic missionaries in Vietnam had been Spanish. Spain's unique Moorish architecture came with them. It felt strange to be burning Spanish mission churches in lush tropical valleys.

Small rice caches were burned. Larger caches were sacked-up by other units and shipped to the resettlement camps. On some days we would burn so much rice, and so many huts and haystacks, that our route would be marked by dozens of columns of hot white smoke extending back across some silent valley or another. Few of us liked the clearing operations. They only made the world a bit more empty. But they did eventually "work." Those remote valleys became an uninhabited wasteland, abandoned even by the communists.

We patrolled through hamlets where peaceful farmers had lived, and others that looked innocent enough from a distance but were riddled with extensive and well-camouflaged bunker and trench systems. Everything was left in ashes. Earthworks were blown up when we had time to do it. The digging had been going on since the French war, and in some cases, back to Chinese rule. Once, near a hamlet alongside a shallow river in the Crow's Foot, we found two old cannon balls embedded in a field. I have often wondered who fired those and at whom.

Vietnam was a land of contrasts. Beauty and devastation often coexisted in such a peaceful way that the arrangement seemed almost natural. Once we spent the entire afternoon stalking through a destroyed village and its associated hamlets in the Crow's Foot. A great battle had occurred there. Artillery shells had sheared the top from every palm tree and left the few huts still standing without roofs. Nothing stirred. Even the enemy had abandoned it.

Then we found her. At the edge of a hamlet close beside a jungle ridge, sat a pretty young woman on a low stool, nursing her baby. She was in the doorway of what might once have been her home- a bamboo framework with no roof and three missing walls. It was such a strange thing to walk through all that destruction and then to find her. Soldiers begged Sergeant Samuel to halt the patrol for a few minutes. We brave children went into groves bordering the jungle and brought back undamaged bananas and coconuts, laying them at her feet as gifts. The woman smiled, the baby nursed, and the place was transformed. She was our Vietnamese Madonna. In that particular region her husband had to be a Viet Cong fighter, but it just didn't matter at the moment.

Minh asked her one question. "Where is your husband."

She replied with a hand sweep toward a looming jungle ridge. "I don't know."

The patrol continued.

———————◆———————

One night after a long day in the Crow's Foot, I shared a bunker with a big Italian rifleman named Corda. He wanted to warn me.

"FO," he said, "you don't know what you got yourself into. This outfit is a death trap. Man, right now we're rounding up civilians and burning hooches, but it ain't gonna last forever. Why in the livin' hell did you extend?"

That was one question I didn't want to answer. I couldn't very well say I was a career soldier who hoped to write a book someday. "I don't know. I guess it's because it was something I had to experience before I died. I want to experience war, not just read about it in books and have other people tell me about it."

He sadly shook his head. The FO is such a fool. "F.O., before this is over you'll wish you had read about it. I got here three months ago and I'm one of the last ones left. This outfit must have the highest casualty rate in the Army. They're giving us an easy time because we got creamed on December first, lost ten goddamned men, but time's running out, baby. Do you know about December first?"

"Yeah. Johnson said you lost Captain Smith that day. But we've been in contact since I got here and it turned out okay."

"Contact? Chasing a couple of scared gooks is not contact. You don't know what contact is. We're gonna be out in those hills again, and you're gonna be wishin' you'd gone home when you had the chance."

I didn't know what to think. Surely he was trying to frighten me.

*General SLA Marshall describes the December first battle at Phu Huu 2 in his book, **Bird**. A more immediate account of the battle can be found in Medic Brad Smith's book, **A Graveyard called Two Bits.***

———◆———

Fate turned four cards down the next night. In a friendly fire incident, Taso fired a 40mm grenade into the middle of an LP [Listening Post]. Four Blues were seriously wounded, evacuated, and never seen again.

A few days later, we walked a long day on a trail in the foothills of the Soui Ca and were picked up at dusk and flown to a base. We manned dog-eared, falling down bunkers until dawn. It rained all night. Blue boarded the slicks in a steady drizzle at dawn the next morning while a sleepy-eyed three-piece band, sent from somewhere, played George Armstrong Custer's tune, *Garry Owen*. That was a bizarre sendoff.

We were flown to an LZ in the mountains above Happy Valley. Elephant grass grew so thickly there that it was impossible to see the lay of the land. It was like jumping onto a rocky field covered by a seven-foot blanket of impenetrable green fog. We didn't know how, or on what, we might land.

As the four slicks hovered in a line over waving, swirling grass, the soldiers on the right jumped and landed on the edge of a ridge. We hit, felt our feet fly forward as boot soles slipped on wet grass, and slid downhill on our asses. The first B-52 bomb craters were below us, still steaming.

There are two ways to stop a downhill butt-slide in elephant grass. The first is to grab handfuls of the giant blades. The sharp grass accounted for palm cuts and slashed faces. The other method is to slide down behind the fellow in front of you (who is gripping handfuls of grass and holding on for dear life) until your feet plow into his legs or backside.

Those fortunate enough to leap to the left stayed on their feet and tried to carefully walk down the right side's slide paths, steadying themselves by grabbing razor grass. Most of them lost their footing and butt-slid down the slope. They bowled over right-side soldiers who were just struggling to their feet. That caused bruises, sore backs and more cuts. Curses and threats rang out through the thick mist.

The day was spent patrolling a formerly pristine valley. The forest had become a chaos of naked giants [trees without bark], boulders made rubble, streams that had changed course or been dammed by debris, two-and-three-foot wood splinters, and a carpet of blown-down leaves over freshly churned earth.

As we broke through the tangled blast wall of each crater, we saw the woodland casualties – bright green bamboo vipers [tree vipers], a dog-sized deer, and beautifully-plumed birds. Several sizes of centipedes scurried this way and that, searching for new rotten logs from which to hunt. A solitary blue-black scorpion was angry, striking a wood splinter with its stinger, as if the splinter had caused the havoc. Among the leaves, rhinoceros beetles reared up on their hind legs and hissed as we walked by. The beetles knew who did this.

Delicate, powder-blue butterflies, so recently fluttering through the forest in their thousands, were being carried away by convoys of large black ants.

Near dusk, as Sergeant Jefferson's squad on point struggled up another steep elephant grass slope, a joker with an AK-47, a look-out, let loose with a short burst. The point found spent cartridge cases and a downhill path through more of that damned grass. He was allowed to escape.

At the evening briefing, Sergeant Sam said, "Today was a visually-controlled strike by a single bomber." He hesitated a moment before continuing. "You know how much those valleys look alike." When he hesitated again, a bunch of tired, smelly soldiers exchanged puzzled glances. Sam continued, "They bombed the wrong valley."

The fellow with the AK had probably wondered what in the hell we were doing there.

We had recently experienced an Air Force Phantom jet strike in the mountains where four 500-pound bombs landed anyplace but on target. Someone grumbled, "Fuck the Air Force!" and the cursing began.

⎯⎯⎯◆⎯⎯⎯

We had reached the trail at last. I had thought the climb up through the trees would never end. The path was wide, with many sandal prints in the mud heading in the direction we were traveling. Hobson's squad on point had gone less than eighty meters and was already finding black telephone wire hidden in the bushes. At places ahead and behind us were enemy units large enough to have telephone hook-ups. Sergeant Sam was obviously nervous when he radioed the news about the wire to gunships, orbiting out of earshot, a few kilometers to the south. He told Hobson not to cut the wire because the enemy might not know we were on the trail.

Then our point man fired a long burst as he crested a ridge. AK bullets clacked past my head and I dived into the muddy grass beside the trail. Sam crouched, grabbed his ground-to-air radioman's handset and shouted "Contact! Contact! Contact!" Johnson tapped my shoulder and handed me his handset. Lieutenant Sutliff, the airborne artillery observer watching from a gunship circling high above us, said that shells would be landing to our front within five minutes. When I gave Sam the message, he sent squads to the sides of our ridge to form a circular defense.

The AK fire ended with a burst that splintered the bark of a tree beside Sam's head. His radiomen jumped into the bushes, but Sergeant Samuel probably would have been more bothered by a pesky fly: he ducked his head a bit. A radio crackled. The point had taken a prisoner. The captive was a tough-looking North Vietnam soldier of about twenty, dressed in a khaki uniform and bleeding from a bullet wound in his side. His right trouser leg was soaked with blood. The point man shoved him to his knees while Doc Stone pulled off his shirt and wrapped a field dressing around his waist. The man seemed more interested in a black medic than with his wound. Sam questioned him.

"Minh, ask him what he's doing here."

A brief exchange gave a lot of answers. Minh began, "He say he NVA corporal. He in South eight month. He point man for patrol of fourteen who come to check American landing."

"Where is his weapon?"

"He doesn't carry weapon, just that." The man had pulled a few bloody AK bullets from his pocket and was holding them out to Sam. "He say if point man carry weapon and killed, weapon lost." Sergeants Samuel and Haskett exchanged half-smiles and winks. They knew the fellow was lying about his missing rifle.

Sam continued, "Minh, ask him how many of them are along this trail and what they are doing here."

Minh's question produced a long-winded reply from the prisoner. "He say he will not tell you mission. He doesn't know how many, but they many." He interrupted Minh's report with another comment, and the color drained from our interpreter's face. "He say they very many."

Sam grimaced and turned to Sergeant Haskett. "That's just fine! Cut the wire! Cut the damned commo wire!"

Our gunships had strafed the trail ahead with machine guns, rockets, and cannon. Now they pulled away so the artillery could begin. I had to direct the shelling, but only if Johnson would come with me. His eyes jumped out of their sockets as I moved off in a crouch.

"Where you going, Sarge?"

"We've got to get up to the point and bring in some rounds."

"No. Not me. Let's do it from here."

"We can't, man. That would risk hitting our own men."

His eyes were pleading. "Sarge, please. This is my last mission. We can bring it in just as well from here."

I turned back to Johnson, but saw the look on the North Vietnamese corporal's face. He was amused by Johnson's fear. "Come on, Johnson. I need the radio. You're gonna make it."

He followed, then stopped and pointed an accusing finger. "Okay, Sarge. But if I don't make it, it's on your head."

That pointed finger unnerved me for a moment, but as we headed down a prostrate file of Blues toward the contact point, I realized just how alone Johnson must feel among these men. Each soldier gave me a thumbs-up signal or a word of encouragement like "Get some, FO." The same men greeted my radioman with hostile stares and curses.

The first shells had exploded far up the trail. Sutliff carefully walked them back toward us as I tried to estimate how far away they were bursting. When his gunship ran low on fuel, I was on my own. You know how far away shells are hitting in heavy jungle by watching the shrapnel. If it buzzes two or three feet over your head as you lie on your stomach, bring it closer. When fragments start slapping into tree trunks a foot or so above your head, move it out a bit. I was learning these facts for the first time. My two European-style FO training courses had been worthless.

I worked the shells around our hill and across a gulley to our front – each time two explosions and then two more. Whump! Whump! Whump! Whump! Metal whizzed through the air as corrections were called to the gun crews. "Left five zero, drop two zero, repeat platoon two. Rarely is the flash and black smoke of an explosion seen in the jungle.

The artillery was stopped. We moved down the trail past a jumble of broken trees and smashed boulders. The prisoner had said nothing more, only repeating that many of his friends were nearby. Then we began finding the camps. We walked for hours along the trail, discovering so many sturdy bunkers, spider holes, and weapons pits along the military crest of the ridge that we grew indifferent to them. Beside us in the bushes, the line of black communications wire continued.

The camps were spread out, about 100 to 150 meters apart, and each had held a platoon or two. In some camps, uniforms were drying on jungle vines or on black ropes woven from women's hair. The hair was donated by village woman as their personal sacrifice for the liberation. In others were boxes of Vietnamese rations and open American C-rations cans; in still others, a private's belt or a camouflaged bamboo helmet. The enemy was making a determined effort not to be found. He had us outnumbered too many times over to worry much about twenty men, or the two gunships crisscrossing overhead.

The prisoner walked with us the entire way because no helicopter clearings existed. He was smiling, watching our reaction to each new discovery. He knew that at any moment his buddies would stop playing cat and mouse games and rescue him. We expected the same thing. But now a clearing was ahead and we dared to hope that we had been spared.

We passed through one last camp that had an interesting toy. Fastened with a metal ring to a slanted vine cord above the bunkers was an accurately carved wooden model of a Skyraider fighter-bomber. The enemy had been getting lessons on tracking aircraft with rifles.

We broke into a clearing barely large enough for one slick to hover down between tall trees. I leaned my back against a giant, ancient tree perched on the edge of a cliff, and marveled at the emerald beauty of the ridges and valleys below us.

The slicks took us out of there one load at a time by climbing up to tree top level and diving down the mountainside to gather air speed and purchase [lift]. The clearing was a perfect ambush site, and no doubt our progress was being observed by hundreds of men, but our strange enemy let us escape. He was preparing for something bigger: an attack on LZ Bird.

As our slick skimmed the wooded ridges of the Crow's Foot, Johnson hopped up and down on the seat beside me. He shouted above the thumping rotor blades, "We made it, Sarge! We made it! It's a-a-l-l Over! A-a-l-l Over!"

Back at Hammond, he was off the chopper before it touched down. Baggage was soon flying out of the doorway of our tent. Johnson grabbed his few possessions and was gone, not stopping to say goodbye to anyone. I never saw him again.

The day had been important to me as well. No forward observer was ever accepted by the infantry until he proved himself. That was an unspoken rite that I underwent with each group of men with whom I served. I didn't realize how crucial that day had been to my credibility until a succession of tired, dirty Blues stopped by my pup tent home. Each man told me in his own way how good the artillery protection felt, and for the first time, really welcomed me to the platoon.

Johnson's replacement arrived later that evening. I had thought Johnson and I were different sorts, but that was before I met John Martin. He was a tall and incredibly thin Slovak from the mining country of eastern Pennsylvania, with a long face and a shock of thick brown hair that he refused to cut to military regulation length. John was already a college graduate, a rarity among Army enlisted ranks at that time, and one of the finest people I have ever known. He would have a profound effect on my thinking over the next months.

John introduced me to a world of literature and poetry I might never have discovered but for him. He showed me beauty where I had seen terrain, but that was in the future. For now we had only mutual suspicion. I was a sergeant who had committed the unpardonable crime of extending my tour of duty when I could have gone home, which indicated to John that I could not be trusted. He was an outspoken non-conformist and a confirmed private, both of which made me equally wary of him. He would refuse rank and decoration until the day he left Vietnam. I eventually got him a promotion, a Combat Infantry Badge and a meritorious medal, all behind his back. In exchange, he let me know that I was interfering in his life.

Martin had spent time in the stockade in America for a unique offense. He had done so well in a basic communications course that the Army wanted to give him more specialized training. He declined the offer with too much zeal and was jailed. When released, he had to take the training anyway. He was now capable of operating sophisticated electronic equipment, but would be carrying the simplest of all field radios. John was shipped to the 9th Cavalry because he was a thorn in the side of any person in authority. It's an understatement to say that we were mismatched.

Martin tossed his duffle bag through the door of our tent and offered a hand. "Well, Hi, Sarge. I'm John Martin."

"Sergeant Brennan. Why don't you call me Matt."

A grin. "I'll call you Sarge. You probably like that name better. You're a lifer aren't you?"

"I don't know. I never gave it much thought." [a lie]

Another grin. "Aw, come on, Sarge. Did you really extend for this shit?"

It felt like I was branded with the devil's mark. "Yeah. Word travels fast around here."

"Johnson told me. That settles it. You're a lifer."

I mentally cursed whoever had sent this hellcat to Charlie Troop. "We're going to have to work pretty close together. Why not try to get along?"

A derisive stare. "Well, anything you say, Sergeant." End of round one.

The irony of that introduction remains with me. Charlie Blues had just walked through the base camps of at least two North Vietnamese battalions, who had given us an early Christmas present by letting us live, and here we were, arguing over a title.

The next morning we destroyed four huge mounds of salt, tons of salt, stored under bright blue tarpaulins in a hardwood forest on the edge of the An Khe Plateau. The tarps and supporting wooden platforms were burned; gallons of aviation fuel in Jerry cans were poured on what was left. The jungle doesn't provide salt, so each pile represented months of gathering and carrying.

Now we ate C-rations as the slicks orbited above wooded foothills. Below us, an Air Force spotter plane fired a white phosphorous rocket at something on a hillside. Thick white smoke bubbled up through the green canopy. A Phantom jet dived through the clouds, released two bombs and pulled up sharply. Shock waves and black smoke. A second jet followed, releasing two bombs and climbing away. The Phantoms turned high above us, and darted by at what seemed an incredible speed. Four more black explosions and the pilots were on their way back to air conditioning and TV sets.

Gunships rocketed our streambed LZ. I watched tracer streams and the white pinpoints of exploding 40mm cannon shells and hoped the landing would be cold. As the slicks dropped, Martin pointed to the smoking craters and uprooted trees that marked our objective, and folded his hands as if praying that no one would be there.

We ran over dark, slippery rocks in the streambed, stumbling through a swift current at the base of the hill. A gunship roared close overhead, and red smoke blossomed on the hillside above us. We were in too close to see the bomb craters, but the water was littered with fresh leaves, bark, torn branches, and clumps of red earth.

Sergeant Haskett led us in a skirmish line as we jogged upslope. There had once been a long mess hall and a cave. Most of the mess hall was gone, and a bomb had collapsed the roof of the cave. Martin's prayers were answered. The enemy was either buried or gone. Blues made a bonfire of everything burnable.

I was back at the streambed, watching the flames and jiggling a pin on top of one of the big Chinese land mines we had captured, when I had a visitor. Shay, an old Blue from Boston, walked over, pointed to the big brown disk in my hands, and wagged a finger.

"Say, Sarge. You ever handled mines before?"

"Yeah. Lots of times."

He didn't believe me. "Well, watch what you do or you'll get yourself blown up. That pin you're fooling with is the safety."

After Shay had strolled away, Martin looked at me with a cat-eyed squint. "Sarge, you haven't ever handled mines before, have you?"

I looked around to be sure that Shay was out of earshot. "That's right. But he doesn't have to know that."

"I'm curious," continued Martin. "Why did you tell him that you had?"

"Hell. I don't know. Pride I guess."

John Martin lowered his eyes. "Pride. All right. Ah, thanks, Sarge." Score one for Martin.

———◆———

It was 3:00 a.m. and rain was pouring down again. The Christmas truce had been over for three hours as our troop commander walked down the line of four slicks, telling each miserable huddle of Blues that LZ Bird was being overrun. A Blue platoon from another troop would land inside the place to reinforce the defenders. We would land behind the attacking force. It had to be the soldiers who hid from us two days before.

I was shivering in our assigned chopper on its outward facing seat when Sergeant Kaneshiro settled into the next seat. Kaneshiro had been back from leave only a few hours, and he looked exhausted. Here was a man with a reputation. Men in his squad almost whispered his name, rather than speak it aloud, and said that they would follow him anywhere. General Westmoreland had personally handed him a Silver Star for his exploits on December first, and he had been nominated for the Medal of Honor. I wanted to meet him.

"How was your trip home, Sergeant?"

He didn't look surprised that I knew him. He answered in his always gentle voice, "It was very good. I miss my family in Hawaii very much right now. I'm going home for good in six months. They tell me you were a fool and extended, too." So he already knew about me.

"Yeah. I extended. I'm thinking of home myself. Christmas was rough."

He put his hand on my shoulder and smiled. "Welcome to the platoon. I know why you had to stay and I understand." He was the only man who ever understood.

I was thinking of all those men in all those camps on the ridgeline, hoping that Kaneshiro couldn't tell how nervous I was. "What do you think we'll find at Bird?"

"Don't worry," he replied. "It won't be bad. If they wait until dawn to insert us, the VC will be gone. They can't stand up to our choppers in daylight." I hoped he was right. Our slicks took off a few minutes later in total darkness.

Phantom jets had hit a low mountaintop with bombs; a large bomb crater would be our LZ. Artillery and gunships had just finished their fireworks. Dawn arrived as "Guns-a-Go-Go" tore at the mountaintop.

Go-Go was a heavily armored Chinook helicopter with thirty-eight rockets, two miniguns, a 40mm cannon, and several heavy machine guns. It looked and sounded like a prehistoric dragon, spitting fire and death. Two of those monsters tried to flatten the place.

After Go-Go had blasted the jungle with rockets and cannon, the big choppers each made a final run with miniguns blazing. The heavy machine guns in their tails poured down a steady stream of bright red tracers, which disappeared into barely visible trees and bounced back in all directions. The jungle still echoed as Blue and a platoon from Delta Troop, the squadron's "rat patrol" reconnaissance unit, jumped, one shipload at a time, into the muddy crater. The Delta Troop boys used a captured Chinese 61mm mortar with a helmet full of rocks as a base plate to lob shells down the mountainside. I called down howitzer shells around us. The bombardment was all very costly and dramatic, but it was wasted. A wilderness of broken trees was all that greeted us.

As our two platoons moved downhill throughout the morning, I walked howitzer shells ahead of us. Then we began crossing the scattered tree lines and deserted paddy fields of the Crow's Foot War Zone. Here we found the trail of the enemy force retreating from the bloody attack on Bird - a muddy track, made by hundreds of Ho Chi Minh sandals, heading away from us, around the base of that damned mountain. All that remained of the attackers was a row of fresh graves holding bodies that were shrouded in French camouflage parachute silk, buried upright and facing north. The graves or spider holes had been dug before the attack. Some were empty.

The scout helicopters and gunships followed the trail and began killing stragglers. I listened to their dry reports over Martin's radio.

"White One-One. Engaged two NVA with packs and weapons. Two NVA KIA." [KIA = Killed in Action].

"Red Three-Three. Engaged NVA in khaki uniform. One NVA KIA. Area is open. Request permission to collect weapon."

"Red Three-Five. We're receiving AK fire from streambed to your whiskey. Rolling in hot!"

As the patrol continued toward Bird, we searched a few wrecked hamlets and burned everything that had escaped the torch in previous weeks. In late afternoon, we passed an NVA company campsite of the night before, complete with a regulation latrine hole, and took long-distance shots at khaki figures running away in the distance. A brief radio transmission brought two scout helicopters racing after them. Our force passed the smoking wreckage of a gunship and reached the barbed wire defenses of Bird.

Inside the base were rows and piles of enemy corpses killed by point-blank artillery fire as they swarmed toward the howitzers. The gunners had fired the new, Top Secret, "Beehive" flechette rounds that literally stopped the North Vietnamese in mid-stride with a buzzing wall of tiny nail-darts. The survivors of the 22nd NVA Regiment turned and fled. Before their run was through, 266 bodies littered LZ Bird and the trails leading back into the mountains.

We are on a trail in the high hills of a mountain range north of Happy Valley. The target is a hamlet hidden under the trees of a deep ravine. Below us is a small pond with a dead pig lying half in the water. I leave the file to see how it died. I never find out, but glimpse a scene that is both primitive and ageless. A large freshwater crab sits in the shallow water beside the smelly carcass, pulling away chunks of rotting entrails with one of its claws. The crab doesn't mind if I watch.

Here is a Montagnard hamlet of plank houses on stilts. The hill tribesmen have fled so quickly that they spilled some of the gourds of foul-smelling rice wine that they were drinking. We search about twenty huts, finding nothing except fire-blackened hearth stones, baskets of greens, gourds of rice wine, crude three-legged stools, and stacks of curing animal hides.

Perhaps we'll spare this hamlet. But, no. Not this time. Haskett pulls two NVA canvas dress belts and a green star canteen from underneath a pile of reeking hides. Sergeant Samuel decides in an instant.

"Burn it! Three squads back to the LZ for extraction. Hobson's squad, stay here and make sure all the hooches go up. Then get back there on the double."

Soldiers gather handfuls of thatch straw and light the ends. Others pour rice wine on the plank floors and pile cloth and baskets in the corners of huts. As the slicks lift us out, the ravine fills with smoke and the tree tops crackle and blaze.

The slicks flew us north of Hammond in pitch darkness. Beside me was the comforting presence of Sergeant Kaneshiro, looking calm and unconcerned as usual. I cupped my hands and shouted in his ear, "Where are we going at this time of night?"

"All I know, FO, is that we're going to Bong Son for a mission."

The choppers touched down on that familiar airstrip at Bong Son, now dark and empty, where I had once spent innocent nights swinging in a hammock and admiring the moon. I walked down the parked row of scout helicopters, gunships, and slicks and wondered what they had in store for us this time. Kaneshiro rested with his back on a Vietnamese grave mound with an ear pressed to his radio handset. He quietly listened to a transmission and waved me over.

"This could be something. A Lurp [LRRP - Long Range Reconnaissance Patrol] team just got overrun in the An Lao. We are supposed to go in and look for survivors. It's up in the mountains, and the commander is trying to get flares to light up the LZ."

The thought of a night landing in the An Lao mountains chilled me. I remembered the Special Forces and Blue platoon contacts in that valley eleven months before.

"I'll contact the artillery. How do you rate our chances of going in?"

Kaneshiro thought about it for a moment and then shrugged his shoulders. "Very slight. Less than fifty-fifty. Night assaults are tricky business. If they did get overrun, there's not much we could do until morning."

Kaneshiro was right again. A last minute conference decided that the risk of a night assault in those mountains was too great. When an infantry company landed at dawn, it found the place where the long range patrol had been, strewn with empty cartridge cases and a few pieces of equipment. No bodies. Later that day, we patrolled trails around the ambush site and found nothing. That was a double loss. The missing Lurps had been testing one of the new night vision scopes. As far as I know, their fate was never determined.

When I told John Martin about Kaneshiro's ability to guess right, he added a very personal view of the Nisei. "Sarge, Kaneshiro's a killer. His specialty is head shots."

I considered Kaneshiro a brave man and a friend, and defended him. "That just stands to reason. He figures each situation as it comes up. A man's not going to shoot back if he's hit in the head."

Martin threw up his arms in disgust. "That doesn't make it right, Sarge. Besides, I think he likes it." John ended the conversation by walking away.

My pick was still Kaneshiro, any hour, of any day, of any week.

The New Year's truce arrived the next morning. We had hoped for a rest, but truce violations were a habit on both sides. A scout chopper was on a recon mission when the gunner spotted two unarmed North Vietnamese walking down a trail in scrub country near the Soui Ca Mountains. Hobson's squad was launched on a one-ship raid. They landed behind the NVA, away from the mountains. When the Vietnamese tried to run for the safety of the hills, the scout gunner dropped tear gas grenades in front of them.

Seven Americans panted down the trail after them. A couple of flying tackles later and the Vietnamese, still crying from the effects of the tear gas, surrendered at gunpoint. No weapons had been fired, so technically the truce had not been violated. The prisoners were reported as "returnees" to the government cause.

I accompanied Hobson on a one-ship raid to the same area the next morning, a North Vietnamese three-man cell ran farther and faster than we could. They threw personal items into the bushes as they ran, a common tactic designed to entice us to stop and gather souvenirs, giving them more time to escape. I grabbed a beautifully sewn rain jacket with a lining of soft poncho liner fabric and a hood. Unfortunately, the jacket was given away to someone it fit.

Several days after the truce, a visitor from the artillery forward CP asked if I had been along when the Blues picked up "those two gooks who surrendered to a passing helicopter."

I wanted to laugh at his question and tell him why but only said, "No. I missed that one."

A note on unit pride: *When I first went to Charlie Troop in December, 1966 the old-timers still bragged about events that had happened a year before. Eleven days before the famous 7th Cavalry landing at LZ X-Ray, Charlie Blues, led by Captain Chuck Knowlen, sprang an ambush along one hundred meters of trail in the Ia Drang Valley when an enemy battalion padded into their trap. That ambush wiped out a heavy weapons platoon and probably many other soldiers. The Blues retired under fire to a patrol base called Mary [named after reporter Charlie Black's wife] where soldiers from three Blue platoons plus reinforcements fought an all-night battle with the battalion that Knowlen's platoon had just* *ambushed. NVA casualties were estimated at ninety-six, with ten prisoners captured. By the time I arrived, the troop had fought many battles involving large enemy units, but LZ Mary was the first and it was remembered.*

If you are interested, there are at least three excellent accounts of that ambush and fight. The best is by Charlie Black, a reporter with the Columbus (Georgia) Ledger Enquirer *newspaper who was on the ground that night. He published a detailed article in the March, 1966 issue of Argosy* Magazine *entitled, "Trial by Fire." A well-researched account was written by premier reporter and historian Joe Galloway. See also J.D. Coleman's superb book,* Pleiku: The Dawn of Helicopter Warfare in Vietnam.

Chapter 4

MOUNTAINS AND VALLEYS

(January-February, 1967)

The New Year's truce had been over for about fifteen minutes and the sky lightened as our armada of gunships and slicks circled far above a mountain valley in the Soui Ca. A door gunner had killed three enemy soldiers in clearing only minutes before the truce started. The troop commander wanted us to collect weapons and search the bodies. We orbited in a clear sky above a solid blanket of dazzling white clouds. Mountain peaks jutted through, looking like green tropical islands in a rolling white sea.

Beside me, Martin swept the scene with his hand and shouted over the blade noise, "What do you see down there, Sarge?"

"Cloud cover. If it doesn't break, we can't go in."

He hung his head. Not the answer he wanted. "No, Sarge! Isn't it beautiful down there? I hope the clouds stay there forever."

I hadn't expected that comment, but he was right. "Yes. Yes it is beautiful." Those emerald islands remain one of the most beautiful scenes I have ever witnessed.

We remained in the cold morning air for another thirty-five minutes before the choppers returned to Hammond.

It rained in buckets that morning as we waited on a sandbar near LZ Bird. All of us were soaked to the skin. Most of the helicopters had not been able to fly through the downpour, and we hoped that none would be able to leave. Then, as the skies cleared, Sam listened to a pilot's message and threw on his harness.

"Saddle up, Blue! Saddle up!"

Within minutes we were running through a silent hamlet in the Crow's Foot, trying to burn wet haystacks and huts. Only Sam knew our mission, and he was talking excitedly to the gunships roaring overhead. Lots of them. I joined Hobson's squad on point as they passed a hut with a rack of NVA belts, hung with canteens, leather ammo pouches, and several stick grenades. We followed a trail behind the hamlet and almost stumbled over the reason for the landing.

Five North Vietnamese had been running down the trail when a door gunner shot them. They had died in a row, legs pumping even in death. Four were face-down in the mud, but the fifth had turned over to get one last look at his killer. The mud was littered with rifles, mess kits, a loose grenade and AK-47 magazines. The trail was neatly stitched with lines of bullet holes, as if left by a giant sewing machine.

Spider holes lined a bank just above the trail. All were full of water from the heavy rains; one had a green star canteen floating in it. Sharp crashes behind us. Hobson grabbed his radioman's handset.

"Blue Mike [Sam], this is Blue Two-Six. What've you got, over." A long pause. "Oh. Thought you were in contact." Another pause. "Roger that."

I asked Hobson what had happened and he answered slowly, fighting to control his anger. "Well, shit! Some shithead set fire to that hut without getting the grenades first. No one was hurt, but one of Sam's radiomen is shook up pretty bad. You know? We're liable to lose this war without the gooks' help."

Sam ordered Hobson to stop at a clearing at the base of a jungle hill. When we arrived there, I turned back toward Sam's command group. An explosion close ahead sent me scrambling for cover. I looked up. Sprawled on his back on the lip of a spider hole was a dead enemy soldier, fish eyes bulging out of a shocked face. Shay stood over the body, shaking his head in disbelief.

Curious as ever, I asked "Where did he come from?"

"He was hiding in that hole, Sarge. I was walking up the trail and saw this canteen floating in the water. Then I looked again and it was moving like somebody breathing down there. There wasn't any wind coming through the trees. I chucked in a grenade and out he came. Didn't have time to warn you. Just look at that!"

"Look at what?"

"That body, man. Not a mark on it. Concussion must have got him!" The man's canteen had floated free from its pouch as he hid under the water. Shay ripped the Cav patch off his shirt sleeve and slapped it on the corpse's face.

I reached Martin and Sam just as one of Hobson's men walked down the trail behind me with a prisoner. Sam questioned the rifleman.

"Where'd you get this one?"

"We set up at the edge of the clearing like you said, and I went into the grass to take a leak. I looked down and I was almost pissing on this dude here. He started begging for mercy, so I brought him in." The soldier neglected to tell Sam that he had left his rifle back at the trail when he went to pee. Sam wouldn't have understood.

Sam went into high gear at the thought of six dead NVA and one prisoner. "This place must be crawling with Charlies. Get Minh over here." Minh was pulled from the spider hole where he hid and nudged in Sam's direction. As he hurried over, Sam pointed to the muddy prisoner and asked, "What's he doing here, Minh."

A quick dialogue was followed by, "He say his squad harvest rice from paddies. They don't expect helicopters because so much rain."

"What unit is he from?"

"He from Twenty-Seven Company of Eighteen Regiment."

"Where is his company now?"

"He say they on hill where trail goes. They have bunkers and recoil-less rifle." That heavily jungled hill, an extension of some ridge, dominated the trail and commanded a view of the entire countryside.

"In that case, we leave the hill for an air strike." He turned to Haskett. "Get him out to the rice paddy so a chopper can pick him up."

We stayed four more hours in that place while gunships flew criss-cross patterns above us. A teenaged girl died there, firing from inside a plank-sided rice storehouse with an M-16 rifle. She had been very pretty.

Rice was hidden everywhere. We found it under floors, in walls, in huge clay pots that could hold a man, or sometimes just piled to the ceiling of a hut. Control of rice was the essence of the battle for the Crow's Foot. Everything was torched. A soldier was lighting the roof thatch of a tiny hut when Sam received a message from a scout pilot. He ran over and pulled off the burning straw.

"Don't light it yet. Scouts say they shot a man crawling under the hooch. Let's have a look-see."

I found him with a flashlight. He was somehow squeezed into a space a few inches high. It took long minutes and all the strength of three Blues to drag him free. One arm still clutched a battered American carbine. His face was twisted and frozen in absolute terror. The woods reeked of violent death.

As we assembled for pick-up beside the ashes of the hamlet where we had first landed, I saw Sam staring across the open paddies at something I hadn't noticed before. About a kilometer away, in the middle of a lush, green landscape, was a patch of plowed earth – an ugly brown mound where nothing living appeared to grow. Sam had a far-away look, so I asked him why.

"That was December first," he said, pointing at the brown scar, "We lost Captain Smith that day." [December first was the Battle at Phu Huu 2]

On January third, 1967 we jumped into a shallow stream in the An Lao Valley as gunships blasted a ruined hamlet with rockets and cannon. A bullet slapped the water in front of me; another careened off a flat rock behind me. A high, cracking volley echoed down the streambed. The cracks were coming from a high bank in front of the huts and sounded oddly familiar. Sam was the only man still standing.

"We can't stay here! Let's go, Blue! Charge it! Charge it!" The platoon rose from the water in a single mass, shamed by Sergeant Samuel's bravery.

"We're in for it again, Sarge!" It was Martin, gasping as he ran with the weight of the heavy radio.

We stumbled in a yelling mob toward the hamlet as the ones in front sprayed bushes along the high bank. We scrambled, ran, and slid up a bank of mud, through slick grass, and tumbled into the hamlet, panting hard. Behind the bushes was a long trench. Beside it were three riddled, minced-up bodies, the work of a gunship minigun. Even their weapons were chopped to pieces.

Kaneshiro's squad set fire to a hut and tossed the bodies through an open wall. This was supposed to strike fear in the hearts of the enemy. It struck fear in my heart. The burning roof collapsed in a shower of sparks.

One of Kaneshiro's men found a low bunker at the end of the long trench. He looked through the aperture and hollered, "Nobody here, Sergeant!" When he stood up, the man inside fired a burst from his AK-47. Kaneshiro ran over and shoved the soldier away from the opening.

"Back! Get back!" He pulled the pin on a grenade and tossed it into the bunker. Silence. He threw in another and again nothing happened.

He calmly pulled the pin on a third grenade. "Hell! This one has to work!" He lobbed it in underhand. It plopped back at his feet. The poor fellow inside had collected his senses and thrown back the grenade. "Grenade! Hit it!"

The charge went off with a sharp bang, blowing off some roof thatch but injuring no one. Kaneshiro held the fourth grenade for four seconds after pulling the pin and releasing the safety lever. It blew the bunker apart. He crawled into the bunker and returned with the pieces of the dead man's rifle.

Turning to the soldier who had originally informed him that no one was in the bunker, Kaneshiro quietly told him, "You don't clear a bunker by looking inside."

I had bragged to my fellow soldiers that the most recent shipment of hand grenades was manufactured at Crane Ammunition Depot near my home in Indiana. After those two grenades failed to explode, I kept my mouth shut.

We reached the end of the crumbling hamlet without further incident. Jefferson, a squad leader from the inner city of Chicago, searched a large, last hut. He found nothing until he looked up. His shouts rang through the hamlet.

"Hey! Hey! Somebody give me a hand!"

A North Vietnamese was hiding in the rafters, pressed spread-eagle against the roof thatch like a giant spider. Three pointed rifles convinced him to come down and join the party. He dropped from the ceiling, folded his hands, and began bowing to Jefferson. The man was well over six feet tall. An under-sized khaki uniform, a Sad Sack face, and either mange or a spotty haircut, made the man look like a clown.

Sam needed some quick answers. "Okay, Minh. What's he doing here?"

"He say they harvest rice when helicopters come."

"How many are with him?"

"He say about twenty before helicopters come."

"Where is his unit?"

"He say his company in Crow's Foot about twenty kilometer from here."

Sam started to walk away and remembered something. "Where's his weapon?"

The prisoner took a long time explaining something to Minh. The interpreter nodded and turned back to Sam. "He say he have no weapon. This man medic and volunteer to come along in case some soldier get sick. He never carry weapon because his job not to hurt people. There much malaria in his company."

A bag stuffed with East German drugs and Vietnamese bandages had been found in bushes beside the hut, so his story was believed. Our mission was over. The hamlet was burning and we had a prisoner. Clack-Clack! Someone was trying to kill one of Sam's radiomen. The sniper was in a palm grove behind the hamlet. We crawled through the mud once again as helicopter rockets tore apart the palm trees, and then ran in an exhausting half-crouch back through the wood smoke and flames.

I was back at the long trench when a bush that several of us had just walked past moved. A Blue emptied his rifle into it. A perfectly camouflaged, branch-covered body pitched forward into the mud. Sam rolled over the quivering body with the toe of his boot and saw the man's rifle.

"A Sixteen. I thought that was a Sixteen firing at us before. This must be the Charlie who pinned us in the creek. Must have been waiting for another crack at us."

Blue was back at Hammond about thirty minutes later. Maybe the rest of January would be easier than the first two days. Three replacements were waiting for us when we jumped from the moving slicks. I swaggered by them, trying to look like a veteran infantryman.

Martin spoiled my mood in an instant. "You've got something in common with them. Only a year left. Huh, Sarge?"

———◆———

The An Lao is a long rice valley running for miles parallel to the South China Sea, separated from the coastal plains by a chain of mountains running south to north. The inland wall of the valley is composed of mountain ridges rising in emerald steps toward a high plateau stretching toward Kontum. The valley was a place with a different character. The communists had declared it a "liberated zone" after winning a victory there in 1963. In truth, it had been a liberated zone since 1945. The tough, brave inhabitants, in addition to local Viet Cong and a division of North Vietnamese regulars, fought for that valley long after the rice was gone and the village down its center was a ruin.

The cavalry division had raided the valley during Operation Masher in 1966 and would fight there throughout 1967. After we left, the 173rd Airborne Brigade would make the valley "off-limits" – too dangerous. To the soldiers of 1967, An Lao was a sinister place where death always threatened, where the Vietnamese fought on when normal human beings would have quit. There were no routine missions to the valley.

There's a saying we used that goes, "Some days you get the bear, and some days the bear gets you."

On January fourth, Blue waited in the graveyard at Bong Son, a fitting place to be. Sam had briefed the squad leaders and me that we would be returning to the An Lao behind a B-52 strike. I considered B-52 strike zones to be mainly useful as lessons on how to splinter trees and kill birds and snakes with big bombs, but today's strike would be directed at a known base area. There was no doubt that the First Air Cavalry was returning to the An Lao Valley in force, and we would be used as bait to find out what was waiting there.

The slicks dropped toward foothills on the eastern wall of the An Lao. Ahead was a narrow valley, an abandoned paddy field shaped like a horseshoe. Steaming B-52 craters stretched away into the mountains. We jumped into green, scummy water and weeds, triggering long bursts as we ran for cover behind low paddy dikes.

A machine gun chattered and I wondered if Sam would tell the gunner to stop wasting ammunition. I looked around for Sam as a line of bullets kicked up high waterspouts about twenty feet behind me. I dived into the rotten water. The enemy had waited through the bombs, guessing that someone would land here. They had us in horseshoe ambush in a natural horseshoe. At least one machine gun fired from each side of the "U." AKs were at the bend and along both sides. White and green and red tracers flashed overhead.

I was terrified by the screams and noise and prayed like I meant it for the first time in years. "Dear God! Please don't let them kill me!"

Slugs chewed away at the paddy dike corner where Martin and I hid. Shay ran for a corner like ours and was chased by a string of waterspouts. His legs were knocked out from under him as he reached the corner; his head hit the dike with a loud Thud!

Taso was lying behind a tiny dead tree that had once grown from a paddy dike. A machine gun was firing from a bomb crater. Taso fired grenades at it as fast as he could load them. The machine gun crew swung their weapon toward him.

Bullets chopped Taso's little tree into wood splinters as he screamed, "Mama! Mama! Oh! Mama, Mama!"

Sam shouted above the incredible racket, "Somebody help that man! Hold on, Taso!"

Doc Stone jumped across a paddy dike behind Taso and was chased back by bullets. Next came the bravest act I ever saw. Doc leaped back over the dike and crawled through thirty meters of mud, bullets and stinking water. He grabbed Taso's shirt and dragged the fat man back through that hell. Every enemy weapon turned on them. For long seconds, the only targets in that horseshoe valley were a black medic and a wounded Latin American grenadier. The paddy water boiled from bullet hits and churning mud, but they made it. Doc Stone was untouched. I have always hoped that he was given a medal for heroism.

Now they turned their guns on the rest of us. I tried to fight back by shooting at muzzle flashes, or at the crater gun that got Taso, but it seemed useless to be throwing tiny bullets at all those trees. I quickly learned to move very slowly. With any sudden movement a machine gun chopped at the dike beside us, showing me with mud, dirt and rock. That dike saved my life.

As I lay there on my stomach, a large rice paddy leech, in two lovely shades of green, emerged from the water and began crawling toward my face. Rice paddy leeches are thick and muscular, not skinny sticks like their tree leech and freshwater leech cousins. I could barely move and was more afraid than I had ever been, but that leech made me feel truly desperate. I slowly inched my arm above my head and pushed him back. He immediately resumed crawling toward me. I pushed him back again; same result. Next, I took an empty bullet casing and pushed him into the mud all the way to the cartridge's base. That worked for about fifteen seconds, until he squirmed under the cartridge and emerged to continue his crawl. A second cartridge push produced the same result. Then I had a crazy idea. I reached out and turned my green friend around. He crawled away and slid back into the water.

Gunships roared over to rocket the trees around the horseshoe. Artillery shells began falling, but failed to break holes in the jungle canopy. I felt a heavy thump on my back and had the breath knocked out of me by a clump of earth thrown up by a shell, but it didn't matter; the Vietnamese suddenly stopped firing. We were saved. At least some of us were saved.

Shay had been shot through both legs and was unconscious. He would have gone home in two weeks. Taso had taken three bullets in the back.

He had lost a lot of blood and was too weak to call for his mother anymore. Two of last night's replacements were wounded. The third replacement, Joe Keifer, a cheerful fellow who could have become a friend, was dead. We had been talking about home just before the mission.

The commander pulled us out of the horseshoe valley and rewarded us with time off. Sam put it this way. "The major is giving you the rest of the day on stand-down. Be sure to clean your weapons."

An infantry company took our place. They searched the hills and trails around the horseshoe and found three scared local force Viet Cong hiding in a cave. They quickly surrendered; the bombs had unnerved them. Our North Vietnamese attackers had escaped.

The platoon was on patrol in the Soui Ca, hunting for troops of an enemy regiment that had been driven out of the lowlands. The point squad was cutting a path with machetes over rugged hills when it happened upon a gigantic pile of boulders. The place could have been a scenic overlook in any American state park and gave a rare view of the entire lowland plains. We stood on that wooded hilltop, somewhere in central Vietnam, and looked across the flat Crescent, all the way to the South China Sea, a magnificent sight, marred only by the distant specks of brown helicopters searching for prey.

The long patrol had rewarded us with hanging nests of biting red ants and vines with thorns that tore our skin and uniforms. We had frequently stopped to burn leeches off each other after they dropped from trees and painlessly attached themselves to our backs and necks. Our shirts and cuffs were buttoned tight. When men undid their cuffs, blood ran out over their hands and fat leeches tumbled out of shirtsleeves. The leeches had drunk their fill and detached themselves, while the anticoagulant in their saliva kept the blood flowing.

Now the lift birds were on the way to get us out of there. Kaneshiro's squad cut a path downhill toward a clearing until they found a footpath heading back up the hill. Sam sent Sergeant Jefferson's squad to investigate. Corda was on point.

Deep cracks from an M-16, rapid popping sounds from an American carbine, more cracks. Jefferson's men raced down the footpath and threw themselves into the thorn bushes around Sam's command group. Carbine shots popped through the thorns inches over our heads as Corda shouted in a hysterical voice, "Gooks in a cave! Gooks in a cave! Gooks in a cave!"

Sam grabbed Corda's shoulders and shook him back to sanity. "Slow down, boy. Take it easy. Now what have we got up there?"

Corda looked around with wild, bloodshot eyes, as if seeing us for the first time. "There was three VC standing in the cave and just staring at me. I shot one of them, and the other two started shooting. One of them turned to run and I shot him in the back. There's more up there!"

More carbine shots popped through the thorns. Sam grabbed his radio handset and talked excitedly to the gunship pilots covering us.

"Squad leaders, pop smoke! We're in too close for rockets! They're coming in with miniguns! Everybody keep your heads down!"

The beating of chopper blades drew more carbine shots. My ears roared with the harsh buzzing of the minigun. Twigs, bark, and branches fell around us; ricochets from the cave whined through the bushes. More smoke grenades, another minigun run, and the cave was silent.

We ran down the footpath toward the clearing. Kaneshiro's men stopped at rock bunkers along the way, just long enough to gather armloads of enemy equipment. They had left behind everything except their weapons. We reached the clearing and a clattering flock of slicks landed, one at a time, to deliver us. As the lift birds headed back to Hammond in the twilight, the beautiful orange of a FAC's [Forward Air Controller] phosphorus marking rocket blossomed. Two jets dived toward the hill.

And so another day, full of natural beauty, and violence, and a hundred different emotions, came to an end.

Corda was getting more desperate with each passing day. December first, the horseshoe valley, the VC in the cave, and fights in other months had taken their toll. We talked that night at Hammond.

"I told you things would get worse," he began, wagging a finger in my face. "I'm never going to see the City again. They've got my number, Matt."

"That's nonsense. You can make it if you want to. Seven months from now you'll be telling war stories back on the street."

"Eight months. That can be forever in this death-trap unit."

I was beginning to think he had a good point, but his paranoia didn't need more encouragement. "You'll get a job in the rear before that. Just don't give up yet."

Corda shook his head. "No! No jobs with my luck. You don't know how unlucky my life has been. Not with my luck."

"Why don't you try praying or something? That usually helps people."

His eyes went wild again. "Pray? Shit! I don't pray because the world is godless. Think about it. How can men with so much blood on their hands believe in a god?" He wandered off into the night air, pausing once to kick a wooden case of hand grenades.

Most men in the platoon carried side arms and fighting knives as back-up for the inevitable day when their M-16s would jam. I had bought an Army-issue .38 caliber Smith & Wesson revolver from a gunship pilot. Corda would borrow the revolver when he went on outpost duty.

The evening after my talk with Corda, Sergeant Jefferson woke me from a deep sleep. The outpost had VC moving all around them. Those men were from his squad and he needed volunteers for a relief mission.

Jefferson said with a smirk, "You extended for this shit, FO, so I know you'll want to volunteer." I didn't, but I did.

It was raining again. The Blue volunteers threw on their equipment and ran to the barbed wire. From somewhere in the darkness ahead came the sounds of M-16 and carbine fire. Eight of us crawled under the wire and ran toward the shooting. We found Corda behind a tree, groaning and bleeding from an upper leg wound. Jeff and I hoisted him in a fireman's carry and staggered toward the barbed wire. Corda weighed over two hundred pounds and we couldn't carry him the entire distance, so we rested for a moment in the damp sand.

A man in black pajamas walked through a gap in the hedgerow right behind us. He was firing a carbine from the hip, spraying bullets in an arc. We would have been hit if we were standing. I fired a burst and he vanished, stepping backwards through the hedgerow, just like a scene from an old war movie. We picked up Corda again and got the hell out of there. Behind us, 40mm grenades exploded in spark showers along the hedgerow. We had reached the last ditch before the wire when two American machine guns opened up on us.

Corda, the defeated man, lowered his head. "Jesus Christ! We're going to be killed by our own men."

Jeff and I shouted like devils: "Tell those bastards to stop firing!" "Cease fire!" "Stop firing!" "Cut the fire!" "It's Charlie Troop!" "It's Charlie Troop!" and so forth.

Military police on bunker duty had mistaken us for Viet Cong. For fifteen long minutes, we hid in the ditch while tracers crisscrossed and zinged a foot over our heads, and sand from near misses showered down on us. Then it was over. An MP sergeant was waiting at the barbed wire to apologize.

We learned the next day that an Army doctor was getting a Silver Star for our rescue. This brave medic had run all the way down to the barbed wire to wait for Corda. The rest of us weren't even thanked.

What we did was expected. It wasn't until later years, when Blues rarely had the opportunity to fight, that they started receiving numerous medals.

A squadron aid man returned my revolver a few days later. He had a message. "Corda said to give you this. He said to tell you he doesn't need it anymore." I checked the cylinder and found one bullet fired. I have often wondered how Corda was wounded.

A few nights later, a bunker guard from a neighboring unit shot at splashing sounds in a rainstorm and killed an enemy scout armed with a Thompson submachine gun. Blue soon began returning at random times between missions to sweep through the hedgerows, scrub trees, and marshes that surrounded Hammond.

———◆———

On January fourteenth we were on the way to a third landing in five hours. At dawn we had searched a hamlet in Happy Valley that was supposed to be a Viet Cong rest camp. The farmers loaded us with coconuts and bananas; our boots stank from the manure of their American dairy cows. We were in the mountains later, at a breathtaking place where a waterfall flowed over enormous boulders and trees grew at crazy angles from rock ledges. The trails we searched had been made by barefoot mountain tribesmen herding pigs. Now the slicks carried us north of the Special Forces camp in Happy Valley.

We leaped into a field of tall grass. The outlines of old rice fields were visible from the air, but no trace was left at ground level; there were only slight bumps that had long ago been paddy dikes. Red smoke rose beside a narrow, tree-lined stream. Ho Chi Minh sandals drifted in the slow current and five packs were scattered along the muddy bank. Two bodies in black pajamas, a man and a woman, were sprawled face-down in the stream, lodged against black rocks. Their blood mingled with the water flowing past them and made long, pink streaks in the current. They had been carrying rice and hand grenades.

Jefferson's squad was sent to patrol an embankment, probably an incomplete railroad bed, with jungle trees forming a curved canopy above us. I was last in line, and when the patrol had gone far enough, Jefferson walked back to me.

"F.O., you're already there. How about taking the point on the way back?"

I walked along the soft grass of the embankment until I saw a man walking toward me on a footpath. Our eyes met and we nodded to each other. *Viet Cong!* In that long instant, his facial expression told the whole story. It was saying, "I just made a stupid mistake." He reached for something on his belt and jumped soundlessly into the bushes below the berm. I fired by instinct. When the bullets were gone, I dropped the empty magazine at my feet and forgot to reload the rifle. I was shaking with disbelief when Jefferson got to me.

"What were you shooting at, F.O.?"

"I saw a Charlie. He disappeared down there."

Jefferson sprayed the bushes beside the footpath, walked down it for a short distance and quickly returned. He was holding a rusty American pineapple grenade. He slapped me hard on the back. "Dude didn't have the chance to pull the pin. I owe you a beer tonight, F.O. Better reload that rifle." Jefferson was offering me one-half of his two-beer-a-day ration. He was also telling me that I had just killed a human being, and he understood what I was feeling.

I never did look at the body.

We waited for the slicks beside yet another corpse tagged with a Cav Patch. Martin stood to one side with a dark look on his face. I had a terrible, mixed-up feeling of guilt, disgust and euphoria, and needed to talk to someone.

"What's bothering you, John?"

"You know those people didn't have a chance against gunships. They just killed another one. Blew his head off. Sounds like Kaneshiro's work."

"No, John," I said. "It was me." Martin stared away in silence.

———◆———

Next came more landings in the Soui Ca Mountains. This was the base area of the 18th NVA Regiment, a unit that had the great misfortune of being battered by the cavalry division time and again for the past thirteen months. Those brave soldiers had been hunted in the coastal plains and now could find safety nowhere. We often came across them in the mountains – thin, scared men. It was impossible to hate them.

The slicks would fly between mountains with winds buffeting them as if they were toys, knocking them sideways and sometimes dropping them fifteen or twenty feet as they hit air pockets. It felt like flying on a rollercoaster. We would land in the vast open spaces above the hardwood forest and walk down mountains along cool trails under tall trees that never let in direct sunlight or rain. It was a twilight world of deadly beauty.

It was never a monotonous life. Blue would pass wide caves, waterfalls, and clear-running brooks. When we stopped beside those brooks, I would place a small piece of C-ration cake on the bank by the water and would soon be sharing food with a freshwater crab or two.

That landscape was magnificent, and even the deadly things did not seem so dangerous. The elephant grass above the tree lines was filled with thousands of bamboo punji stakes, but they weren't new and they hadn't been made for us. The branches of hundreds of trees had been slit and punji stakes placed in the cuts at every possible angle. But the branches had grown around the stakes and mended themselves and the bamboo was rotting. Here was a glimpse of that other war. The French had access to this region through paratroop drops. These greeting cards were meant for them. The effort used to make, carry, and plant those rotting slivers of bamboo must have been enormous.

We often found crumbling bunker complexes, sides overgrown with moss, and one day we found the granddaddy of them all. Blue walked for hours through a former camp, many years old, on the scale of a city. Some of the bunkers could hold small houses. A regiment had lived there once. I tried to picture the forgotten soldiers, sweating through weeks to carve defenses out of those timeless hills. As the file walked down an ancient trail, someone's boot broke through rotten planks covered with earth. He dug away what remained of the planks, and discovered four British Sten guns wrapped in decaying oilcloth. Who had buried those guns, and why had he never returned to claim them?

Once we landed in the open spaces and followed a forest trail beside a swift-flowing stream. It had been quiet, and our new lieutenant let us rest beside some rotting Montagnard huts on a hillside. The hill tribesmen in that area had been wiped out, ethnic cleansed, by the Vietnamese communists years before. The hatred between the Montagnards and lowlanders had existed for centuries. That made the hill tribesmen natural allies of the French, and also gave the lowlanders another excuse to be rid of them. What little was left of their homes, black, mold-covered bamboo and straw thatch, was soon burning.

I wanted to get away from the heavy smoke and found what had once been a trail. The faint path climbed a steep rise and led to yet another reminder of that other war – an old defensive position in a circle under the trees. It must have once been French because the collapsed foxholes were big like ours, not small and round like spider holes. At one place was a rusting American-type helmet riddled with jagged holes; at another were the ruptured steel canisters of homemade grenades that had exploded unevenly; at yet another, French Army cartridge cases. Excavating one of those foxholes would probably have revealed which side had been left to bury the dead.

As I leaned against a tree whose fragment wounds were so old that they appeared as dark spots in the living bark around them, I wondered if who won that little fight mattered, except to the men who had fought there.

Blue continued following the trail beside the stream. These quiet mountains were a good place to learn the point, so Sam had Patterson, a new man, leading the patrol. Crack! Patterson ran back along our file yelling "Gooks! Gooks! Gooks!" A low branch sent his helmet flying and he stopped, staring at our surprised faces. He had walked into six enemy soldiers munching rice balls in the middle of the trail. His rifle had jammed after one shot. Patterson *threw it at them.*

One of the escaping Viet Cong lost his way. He splashed down the stream below the trail, fighting the strong current with all his strength. He wore soaked black pajamas, a scarf and cape of camouflage French parachute silk, and a leaf-covered French jungle hat. The water boiled around him as a dozen rifles fired at once. He looked up at us with a shocked expression and flipped backwards into the water with a loud splash. His body spun for a moment in the current and wedged between two boulders a little farther downstream.

Gunships chased the other enemy soldiers into the steep hills along both sides of the stream and began making 40mm cannon runs. The sound of the detonations boomed around us like monstrous bomb blasts. We were in natural echo chamber.

Sergeant Haskett almost killed another soldier hiding in boulders in the middle of the stream, but the fellow was too skilled at catching Haskett's grenades and hurling them away. All we saw were flashes of his arm and geysers when the grenades exploded. When Haskett's squad fought through the strong current to the man's boulder pile, he had somehow disappeared.

We collected abandoned rifles and equipment, including one jammed M-16, halfheartedly searched the woods along the stream, and walked the short distance to a clearing. It had been a long day and we wanted to go home. The Viet Cong had been eating lunch almost on the edge of our pick-up zone.

The following day, slicks left us at dawn in the vast open spaces of the high Soui Ca. The point squad cut its way down a mountain through brush, thorns and tangled "wait-a-minute" vines – no trail this time. The platoon finally rested in a place so steep that we had to brace our boots against small trees to keep from sliding farther down the mountainside. I ate canned beans and listened to big shells exploding along a stream below us. Sam was beside me, eating his beans. We always got the worst rations – Sam, because he let everyone else choose first, and me, because I wasn't fast enough. Sergeant Samuel wanted to talk.

"The scouts want us to check out a creek down there. Those are one-seventy-fives hitting it. Out of range of everything else. That's why we broke here. They're afraid of us getting closer in case one of those rounds gets off target.

"I didn't know the pilots cared so much."

He laughed softly. "Neither did I." His eyes grew solemn. "Hey, FO, be careful today. We're a long way into these mountains, and they aren't sure what's going on along that creek."

Sam was going home in a few weeks, but he was still putting the welfare of his platoon ahead of his own. "Thanks, Sam. I'll watch it."

It took another hard hour to reach the stream. We forded it by clinging to a vine rope that the enemy had placed there, and crossed a series of hundred-foot-deep ravines on muddy fallen trees. We shuffled sideways for forty feet or more, using our rifles as balancing sticks. I was very afraid of falling. One false step would have aborted the mission and caused an almost impossible rescue through three hundred feet of hardwood trees and rock walls. That was one of the wildest places we ever visited.

We followed a trail until Sergeant Haskett's point man found an SKS rifle leaning against a pile of rocks. An NVA soldier was sitting inside the rocks, probably as a lookout for something, waiting for the artillery to stop. Maybe he was asleep. Haskett found a small opening in the pile and cupped his hands.

"Lai day! Lai day!" ["Come out! Come out!"]

Silence. He lobbed in a hand grenade, and when it exploded, the man inside scrambled over loose rocks.

"Dammit! *Lai day! Lai day!"*

He tossed in another grenade and the man inside groaned loudly for the few seconds before it went off. I cannot imagine the terror of knowing that you are trapped and living the last seconds of your life. When Haskett looked into the opening, the man saw him and scrambled away for the second time. He turned to the Blue holding his rifle.

"Lousy fuckin' frags. Give me my M-16."

He pointed the rifle through a small opening in the rocks and burned through the entire magazine, then pulled out the body of a man in his late thirties. It was hard to believe a person had been so thin and still lived. Haskett ripped off the man's khaki shirt to look for wounds. Four bullets had entered the smooth skin of his back. The bullet holes were tiny and bloodless, as if someone had been pricked the man several times with a big pin.

The man was left in a jumble beside his rock pile. When the rest of the platoon moved off down the trail, Martin walked back to the body, removed the Cav patch from the corpse's face and covered his head with the khaki shirt. When he had returned to walk behind me, he whispered a bit of spontaneous poetry.

"The Sun suns,
The Moon moons,
The skies sky,
Around punctured prone smoothness,
Left to lie."

A short distance down the trail, Haskett heard female voices. He walked around a large boulder, and came face-to-face with two women in black and a man in khakis. The man smiled and put his hands in the air, then reached for something in his breast pocket. Haskett shot by reflex. By the time Sam's command group arrived, Sergeant Haskett had big tears rolling down his cheeks. The man had been reaching into his pocket to show Haskett the bandages he was carrying there.

"If he had just not moved," he said, "he'd be alive right now."

Sam tried to comfort him. "Don't take it so hard. This is war and people get killed."

"The poor bastard," continued Haskett. "Why did he do it? Why the hell did he do it?" Most of the rest of us were ready to cry along with him.

Sam tried to change the mood. "Okay. What's everyone standing around for? Get these women back to the trail."

Haskett remained by the body. "Why? Why? It was such a stupid thing to do."

Sam was on the other side of the boulder, questioning the women. "Minh, ask them who they are."

"They say they nurses. This hospital area of Eighteen Regiment. They say for us to leave."

"Minh, ask her how many people are there around here."

"They say, yes. There many. Most of them sick."

Patterson had discovered two boulder caves about ten meters behind the medic's corpse. One of the caves was full of straw sleeping pallets, bamboo bunk beds, and boxes of East German medicines. When Patterson looked into the other cave, he jumped away as if stung by a wasp. He saw me watching him and jerked his thumb at the entrance.

"Man, I saw something moving in there. Let's frag it."

Sergeant Hobson didn't like that idea. "Better check with Sam first."

Sam had the women brought to him when he heard about the caves. "Minh, ask them if there is anyone in that cave back there."

"They say, 'What cave?'"

"Minh, explain to them that we don't want to kill unless we have to. Ask them if they had anyone else with them."

The Vietnamese talked for a moment, then one of the women spat toward Sam. She moved about five feet away while the other woman hissed a warning at us, went into a squat, pulled a pajama pants leg up to her crotch, and urinated. Minh was embarrassed. He blushed and said, "Sergeant, they say no more questions."

Sam stared at the women for a long instant, and then looked away. "Frag it, Hobson."

Patterson threw two grenades into the cave and squeezed inside. He returned, dragging the body of a nurse by its long, black hair. One of the grenades had landed squarely on her back, exposing intestines and breaking her spine. As he pulled the body along the ground, it bounced like a jelly manikin. Patterson was shaking with anger.

"They let their friend die! I'll kill those bitches for making me do this."

As he headed for the trail, still dragging the corpse, Hobson grabbed him roughly by the shoulder. "Forget it! There ain't no way Sam's gonna let you do that. Git rid of that gook and git your ass back up there and search those caves."

Patterson let go of the hair and stood there like a cornered animal. "I just hope they try to run!" He stroked his rifle for emphasis.

Our mission was over for today. We climbed uphill to a slanted, rocky one-ship clearing. The slicks that took us home left a platoon from Delta Troop behind in ambush. The enemy was supposed to think all of us had left when there had really been a switch.

Martin had been impressed by the day's events as only he could be. We were becoming friends in the little tent and during those long days on patrol, and we talked more often. He broke a long silence that evening with a thought.

"Matt, those poor little guys. They don't have any place left to hide."

"I know. The one by the rocks got to me. He was so thin."

John nodded. "Listen. I've been thinking. Let's propose a toast to them."

"Name it."

"To the Eighteenth NVA Regiment: may they sleep on firm straw pallets tonight, and may their rice rolls be full." We raised our imaginary glasses.

At dawn the next morning we were back, waiting among the boulders for the Delta Troop platoon. A tired, dirty file of men slid down the trail towards us. They broke into smiles when they saw us. Their night had been hell. Campfires blazed on the mountainsides until our slicks arrived at dawn; groups of North Vietnamese had walked the trail throughout the night, laughing and playing transistor radios. Some of them were listening to rock music on Armed Forces Radio. The Delta Troop platoon's thoughts had turned from ambush to surviving until we returned.

Blue led the way back along yesterday's trail. The thin little man had been rolled on his side, but no attempt had been made to bury him. The bodies of the nurse and the medic were gone. Both platoons then headed in the opposite direction. The patrol continued for another hour as we passed unnaturally quiet caves.

When our force rested in an area crisscrossed by footpaths, the lieutenant sent patrols to investigate. They found the area full of boulder rock caves, walkways floored with woven bamboo mats, bamboo handrails, and bamboo arrows pointing in various directions at intersections. This was certainly the base area of a regiment, and our two platoons continued to exist because of their goodwill or confusion.

Jefferson was curious. He was resting in front of a cave and had to know if people were inside. He borrowed our new lieutenant's .45 automatic and Sam's flashlight and disappeared into a dark hole between two boulders. Seven muffled shots, then Jefferson scrambled out on his hands and knees.

Sam squatted down beside him. "What's in there, hotshot?"

"Two Charlies. They were sitting with their backs against the far wall. Their AKs were right beside them. When I flashed the light, they went for their guns and I shot them. I'm damned sure not going back down there!" Jefferson underhanded the empty pistol to the new lieutenant, who gave him an "I'm not going down there either" look. He had lost Sam's flashlight.

Sam had the same thought. "Sir, if we get a man hurt in one of those caves, we're likely to pay the devil trying to get him out. That's Charlie's homestead down there."

The officer hurriedly agreed. "Right! Nobody goes in a cave." Jefferson breathed a loud sigh of relief.

Hobson's squad led the way down the trail with Gould, a wiry soldier from the rural Midwest, on the point. Gould was a rare combination of survival instinct and bloodlust. Although he was a draftee who hated the Army, he was a natural killer. The first time I saw that small package in action was the day a pretty teenage girl died defending a plank-sided rice storehouse. No one knew that the person firing an M-16 was female. *Sacrificed for the revolution as the Vietnamese would say.* Gould pulled down the front of her black pajama bottoms, leered and asked if anyone wanted some pussy. He then dragged her body back into the storehouse and set the building on fire.

Five minutes after our break, Gould killed a North Vietnamese. He ducked under a branch across the trail and stood up face-to-face with a surprised man in a khaki uniform. The NVA carried an M-16 rifle and a canvas courier pouch with papers. Incredibly, they still seemed to be unaware of our presence.

Minh shuffled through the papers and turned to the lieutenant. "Sir, he messenger for Headquarters Company of Eighteen Regiment. He carry list of rice rations for battalions." The officer's mouth dropped open as he nervously eyed the trees around us.

Eventually the two platoons took another break – strict silence, hand signals only, no smoking. As we sat in the mud of the trail, Gould heard laughter around a bend. Word was passed in whispers that Hobson and Gould would take prisoners, but it didn't reach the Delta Troop platoon behind us quickly enough. They had spotted a khaki-clad man standing high above us on a tree platform, scanning the sky with binoculars, searching for helicopters. When he was shot out of the tree, Hobson and Gould had to act quickly.

Rapid shots from the point, then the message – One enemy dead, one trapped, and two escaped. Hobson had chased an NVA under a rock ledge and shot into the rocks above him as he hollered *"Choi hoi!"* [Surrender!] Now he had a prisoner: a pale teenage boy with jungle rot sores on his face and neck, dressed in a filthy brown uniform. Minh questioned the prisoner as the command group walked up to the little waterfall where the NVA had been joking. A newsman was with us that day. Sam had been told to give him what he wanted, and what he wanted was a human interest story.

The newsman smiled at the prisoner, handed him a cigarette, and turned to Minh. "Where's his home?"

"He say he live in farming village fifty kilometer south of Hanoi."

"Did he join the army or was he drafted?"

"He say they come for him one day when he in rice paddy. He go because he doesn't want to shame parents. He doesn't like army very much. He say he want to go home."

The newsman nodded. "Me, too. This is my kind of guy. How long has he been in the South?"

"He say he here six month."

"What's his job in the army?"

"He say he rice-bearer for Headquarters Company of Eighteen Regiment."

Sam was seething. We weren't standing in small-town America. "Okay, that's enough. Let's see if we can find his buddies."

Jefferson and I sat beside the trail, watching Kaneshiro's squad fan out to search the surrounding jungle and then quickly return past the little waterfall. Jeff couldn't understand how the other two North Vietnamese had escaped so quickly.

"Hey, FO. I wonder where they went. This is pretty solid brush."

I couldn't help him. "The only thing I can figure is they took off as soon as those guys opened up at the one in the tree."

I happened to glance again at the waterfall. An Oriental face peeked out of the bushes and stared in my direction. Our eyes met and locked for a few seconds. He looked like a schoolboy. The next instant he was up in a flash of khaki and jumping over the waterfall.

"There went one."

Jefferson had a suspicious look. The FO is nuts, all right. "Stop kidding, F.O."

"Have it your way, Jeff."

Before we left that day, I had a rare opportunity to talk with Sergeant Haskett, an extraordinarily brave man. I had heard that he fought in the Pacific in World War Two and had to know more.

"Sergeant, Is this like the Pacific?"

"Well, yes and no," he replied. "The weather and the jungle are about the same, but we didn't have to hunt so hard for the Japanese. They would come looking for you."

We landed at the rocky LZ one last time. Soldiers from the 25th Infantry Division would clean out the caves, so we stayed only long enough to protect the place while a convoy of slicks brought in an infantry company. They all carried heavy pouches of explosives. The grunts looked around them at those wild mountains and deep gorges, and stared down the narrow trail that led to the caves. They were already afraid. We left them waiting for another company to arrive.

Their operation continued for days. I would sometimes read about the fight for a hospital and bunker complex southwest of Bong Son and shudder at the thought of the casualties the grunts were suffering. Thanks to my CP work, I could read through military doublespeak and understand what was really being said. The *Stars and Stripes* newspaper called them "moderate casualties," a euphemism for "small units taking heavy losses."

On the Bong Son Plains in late January I experienced what, for me, was a deeply moving event. Large above-ground bunkers, constructed of enormous coconut logs and covered with earth and palm fronds, peppered a village near the mountains. These were more than crude bunkers for family protection, and were being used as cover to fire at our helicopters. Blue moved through that green place, blowing big bunkers apart with lots of plastic explosive.

As the charges were set on yet another bunker, I walked across a courtyard and entered a thatched hut where a withered, ancient woman lay on a wooden table. Family members standing around the table used hand gestures to invite me in and say that she was dying. I walked over to her, bowed with folded hands, said *"Chao"* [Hello], and patted her thin arm.

Big thunder rolled across the courtyard as the bunker blew apart. I bowed farewell and she replied with a blink of her eyes. I had to leave, but would rather have stayed with those people who invited me into their home. I paused in the doorway and looked back to find the old woman staring at me. She died looking into my eyes.

On January thirtieth, we landed again on the Bong Son Plains. Gunships and infantry had been engaging a big enemy force that had sort of vanished in an area of hamlets raised on mounds above the surrounding rice paddies. The main action was taking place at a large village that was in the process of being blasted into the air by artillery shells. Palm trees were doing somersaults there as we jumped into rice paddies about fifty meters outside a satellite hamlet and ran forward in a line. We swept up a bank and into a hamlet with palm trees blown down at crazy angles between burning huts.

Vietnamese opened fire at us with AKs and one RPD squad machine gun. In the middle of this racket a baby began crying. Our new medic didn't hesitate for long. He low-crawled in the direction of the crying while enemy bullets chewed-up palm trunks all around him. Doc grabbed a baby swaddled in a blanket and crawled back through that bullet swarm. All of us had heard the baby's cries, but only one of us was brave enough to save it.

The enemy firing abruptly stopped. We searched the hamlet: no livestock, no people, no soldiers. On the far side were cartridge casings and a wide, muddy trail of trampled rice shoots leading from the larger village to the hamlet we now occupied. Gunships patrolling a few feet above the paddies radioed that no one had left the place. We turned around and searched the hamlet again, kicking palm fronds, probing the ground, lifting suspicious items, and found nothing. We wondered out loud how many people were huddling in the tunnels below us. They had prepared for this day for a very long time.

Doc left the baby in the shade of the family bunker where it had been found. His reward was a severe ass-chewing for risking his life over a baby.

January ended with a fruitless overnight ambush high in the mountains. The only enemy contact the previous day was when our point man came face-to-face with a walking skeleton in khaki who couldn't have eaten for days. The poor fellow had either lost his way or was abandoned by his comrades. The point man had seen only an enemy's uniform and an Oriental face. A doll-like heap of brown cloth, tussled black hair, and sinew ended life beside a leaf-strewn trail. The trail overlooked a wide valley framed by purple-green mountain ridges. At the distant end of that valley, a waning sun reflected lime-green and pink rays through mist drifting above a darkening carpet of tree tops.

At the time, I marveled at a day's breathtaking finish and thought very little about a forlorn casualty of war. But I have often remembered him since. If only he could have lived to see that sunset.

I was going on home leave in mid-February. Blue continued making daily landings throughout Binh Dinh Province, doing what it had always done. Once we almost captured a radio transmitter in the mountains, but the commander's decision to approach it after a long patrol gave the station personnel time to escape. We found a smashed bunker, courtesy of Lieutenant Sutliff, and a bloody shirt. Through all these events, my thoughts were on home.

Our friend is dead. The slicks have flown us over this man's isolated hut in the foothills of the Soui Ca many times, and he always ran outside in his red shorts to smile and wave. The pilots say he was counting our choppers and reporting where they were headed. A scout helicopter flew over that place in the half-light of dawn and found him returning from the mountains. The scout gunner took his pack, carbine, and red shorts. Now our friend rests on his belly beside a hedgerow with his naked butt shining in the early sun. The commander has sent us to search the body again and burn his small hut. We had looked forward to seeing him this morning.

We were back several hours later. A gunship had killed a North Vietnamese, and five more were chased into a cave. The slicks orbited to one side as high explosive and phosphorous shells exploded in gray-black puffs and orange flowers streaming dazzling white petals. Fires quickly spread across the churned earth of an open slope. We jumped into a field surrounded by hedgerows not far from where our dead friend rested.

As we rushed to set up a circular defense, a new replacement fired a 40mm grenade into a too-close hedgerow. A fragment dented his helmet and he fell, or was knocked, to his knees. He sheepishly looked around to see if anyone was watching. Several Blues exchanged winks and nods, but let him think that no one had seen his mistake. A North Vietnamese, holding an AK-47 tightly across his chest, ran through a gap in a hedgerow and collided with Arnie Dorsett, a rather large black machine gunner. As the man stumbled backward, his mouth formed an "Oh!" Then he was dead.

We jogged uphill through gaps in hot brushfires. Near the cave at the top we found about twenty abandoned packs and emptied their contents. Blues rifled through a pile of flimsy gas masks, tooth brushes, diaries, extra uniforms, rolled-up hammocks, stick grenades, nit combs, loose bullets and other standard equipment, along with wire-rimmed granny glasses, ornate, curved dope pipes, and one-kilogram, clear plastic bags of marijuana.

Martin looked over at me and opined, "Matt, these guys were heads."

"Yup."

One of the packs had been hit by artillery shrapnel and was coated with drying blood. The owner's diary had taken a shell fragment through its center, which made turning the pages difficult, but Martin pried open the cover sheet and found a neatly penned sentence.

"I wonder what it says, Matt. Let's find Minh and have him translate it."

Minh was munching on a C-ration cracker inside an NVA spider hole. As usual, it had to be the most protected place on the ridge. He took the diary, read the page, and frowned. Minh didn't want to translate the passage for us, so we asked him again. Something in his tone and manner told me that he was sharing part of his culture with barbarians.

"This very beautiful sentence, like something wise old man say. It say, 'Happiness and Sadness I will remember forever.' It good thing to write."

John solemnly nodded his head and said, "He was a sensitive man."

Brown blocks of old dynamite stacked inside the cave were leaking nitroglycerin. There were no enemy soldiers. About eighty meters from the cave was a stench. The NVA were meticulous about sanitation, but here, a miserable forty-by-fifty-meter gulley was covered in watery brown excrement, some of which was flecked with blood. Those people were miserable enough without us. We burned the marijuana and personal items, blew up that dangerous dynamite, and got out of there fast.

The thing of importance that day, besides the death of our friend, was the line from a faceless soldier's diary, a man who also sketched and wrote about butterflies in the mountains. I hope he lived to write and sketch again.

In late afternoon on the last day of Tet, Blue searched a village near Bong Son within sight of an American artillery base called English. Scout helicopters had buzzed a large civilian rally in a nearby field. They couldn't identify the Viet Cong cadres that had to be there, so they chased the whole mob away. Viet Cong flags flew from all the villages and hamlets on the Bong Son Plains, as they did every year at that time. Special cadres even hoisted them in the middle of government-controlled cities. Helicopter gunners had spent the day cutting down flags to decorate those empty walls back home.

The village appeared to be deserted. The women, children and old men were hiding in family bunkers because they were afraid of the scouts and didn't know what our reaction would be to the paper propaganda leaflets glued to the outside walls of each hut - red, blue, and yellow VC flags, pictures of Ho Chi Minh, and many pamphlets written in crude English. They told how the "People's Liberation Forces" were beating "Imperialist" and "Puppet" forces throughout the south. According to one blurb, America had already lost more soldiers and equipment than had been deployed to Vietnam. I made a collection of the better ones to show the folks back home.

A large Viet Cong flag flew in the center of the plowed and furrowed rally field. The platoon formed a sweep line and began walking cautiously toward the flagpole and the village behind it, but I was greedy. That flag was going home with me. I ran to the flagpole, pulled it down, and tumbled as my ankle was caught in a furrow and twisted. I looked back just in time to see most of the Blues scrambling for cover.

After a moment of silence, Haskett jumped up and ran over to me. "You all right, F.O.?"

What the hell was going on? "Yeah. I feel fine."

He started to say something, stopped himself, and then exploded. "Boy, that was the dumbest thing I ever seen anybody do!"

"What do you mean?"

"You're lucky the damned thing wasn't booby-trapped. They expected someone to pull it down, you fucking idiot! The English pamphlets weren't for the benefit of the locals."

Now I felt like a fucking idiot. "Sorry. I didn't think about that. Sorry"

"You could have been a lot sorrier!" He kicked a clod of earth and walked back to his squad.

Now it was Martin's turn. "Still *gung ho*. Huh, Sarge? What are you going to do with a homemade flag?"

"Take it home to Indiana."

Martin pointed to Haskett, who was standing in a little knot of men, gesturing in my direction. "He was looking out for your best interest. You did take a dumb chance."

Martin and I had a visitor later that evening. The lieutenant, who had barely spoken a complete sentence to any of the enlisted men since his arrival, crawled through the doorway of our pup tent home. He asked about my home and family and we talked a bit about the war, then the subject got changed to the propaganda leaflets I had collected in the village.

"Those are nice leaflets," says he. "Wish I'd had time to get some before everyone grabbed them."

"Yes, Sir. I like them all right."

"I sure would like to have some, maybe one of each kind, to take home myself."

So that was why he was here. "Sir, I'd like to help you, but I only have one of each kind. Maybe we'll find some more."

The lieutenant hung his head, so sadly. "I don't know. I have the platoon to keep track of. That's a full-time job. Maybe you could give me a few of yours … if you don't mind." That could be interpreted as a subtle order.

"I'd like to keep them, Sir." He went away mad.

Martin sat silently through the entire conversation with an amused look on his face. We discussed what I should do. The lieutenant had no right to pressure me for my souvenirs. He had run from hut to hut, trying to grab some for himself, but all that were left were pasted on too tightly and couldn't be lifted off the walls without tearing them. We decided that he was in a position to make my life miserable if he had a grudge, so I reluctantly walked to his tent and rustled the flap. He was writing a letter by candlelight and gave me an annoyed look.

I held out my pamphlets to him. "It's Sergeant Brennan, Sir. You might as well have these. I'd probably lose them, anyway." That's the old 'I'm, just a dumb sergeant' routine.

Now he was happy again. He grabbed the leaflets and inspected them to be sure none had damage. "Thanks, Sergeant. I really do appreciate this. Ah, you wouldn't want to part with your flag, would you?" The greedy bastard wanted it all.

"No way, Sir."

The Blues left on a mission the next morning while I hitched a ride on a courier helicopter bound for Camp Radcliff. I was wearing an ace bandage from my brave encounter with a plowed field. When I hobbled into the 9th Cavalry orderly room to pick up my leave papers, a clerk saw the bandage. He pushed his typewriter aside with a guilty look.

"Were you out with Charlie troop this morning?"

My mind made the connection. "No. I'm going home on leave. What happened to them?"

"Charlie Blues got hit in the Soui Ca ….. I was just making out a casualty report."

"Did the artillery radioman get hit?"

"No. They were all grunts."

At least Martin was safe.

Chapter 5

BONG SON

(March-April, 1967)

Snowflakes felt delicate and alien as they melted against my face at the Evansville Airport. I had forgotten about snow.

I proudly showed my family the Viet Cong flag, which meant nothing to them, and when I tried to explain what had happened over the past fourteen months, I couldn't find the right words. The change from a hot world of danger to the lonely cold of an Indiana winter was too abrupt. I tried, but could not remember, the naïve boy who had left the Evansville airport in 1965. I now knew the jungle better than I had ever bothered to know the Indiana woods, and I missed my friends in the Blues.

This Indiana world was dull and different. Things that people of my age held important seemed so trivial, but I knew the truth. It didn't matter who your current girlfriend was, or what model of car you drove, the thing of importance was whether you lived or died. I returned early to Charlie Troop on a cool, blustery March day, telling my family not to worry, and repeating for them our combat credo:

If you don't get hit, there's nothing to worry about. If you get wounded, they'll take care of you. If you get killed, there's nothing to worry about.

The troop had moved north from Hammond to Bong Son, to the site of the graves registration helipad built over the bulldozed graveyard of thirteen months before. Part of the old GR helipad was now a parking lot for scout helicopters. The rest was planted with our tent homes. It never occurred to me that we were sleeping over ancient graves.

Martin had constructed a carbon copy of our "home" at Hammond, so finding the new tent was easy. The Blues were on patrol when I arrived, but a crew chief was cleaning his machine gun in the shade of a lift bird.

"Hi. What's Blue up to these days?"

He recognized me, but faces in the Blues changed too often for him to be sure. "You've been gone a while. Did you get hit or something?"

"No. I went home on leave. Just got back."

"Oh. We're going after the Blues in a few minutes. Want to ride along?" I did.

When the four slicks touched down at a hillside clearing in the An Lao Valley, sweating, tired grunts rushed for seats. I had forgotten how tattered and filthy we looked after a day on patrol. Most of the faces were new. I recognized Hobson, Gould and Patterson. Patterson looked much older than he had before. Hobson had always looked worn around the edges. Gould looked like a fresh-faced choir boy. Martin was on another slick, riding with a new lieutenant, a new platoon sergeant, and Minh. The choppers lifted off from the clearing, nosed over to gain airspeed, and roared across the valley floor at tree top level.

It was twilight, the time when local force Viet Cong returned to their homes after hiding all day in the jungle. As the slicks climbed over the mountains paralleling the plains, gunships spotted armed men running into a hamlet. The slicks made a sudden, tight turn and flew back down the slopes toward a hamlet of well-tended huts and palm groves.

Civilians were hiding in family bunkers, leaving soldiers to fight it out above ground. Two Viet Cong bodies, the last men entering the village, sprawled in a small courtyard beside an enclosed Buddhist shrine. Two Blues slung the dead men's Chinese carbines across their backs and decorated the corpses with Cav patches. A third Blue reached into the memorial shrine and grabbed a stalk of bananas left as an offering for the deceased. He ran ahead, bananas in one hand and rifle in the other.

Clacking bursts and single shots buzzed and ricocheted through the huts from somewhere deeper inside the hamlet. We ran in a sweep line, dodging from tree to tree, until we reached a wide vegetable patch with a hedgerow along its far side. Clack! A bullet from the hedgerow missed by inches. I ran for cover behind a large coconut palm and saw Martin hiding behind the next tree.

"Hey, John. I couldn't get those poetry books for you. I even went to the Indiana University bookstore."

A horrified look in reply. "My God! How can you talk about books at a time like this?"

The new lieutenant was wary of sending us across the vegetable patch. They might catch us in the open and slaughter us. He was still undecided when a man in black jumped up from some bushes in front of me and ran into the patch. He was running as only a man afraid of dying can run. His bush hat and Ho Chi Minh sandals flew off from his efforts. As I leaned against the tree and drew a bead on his back, a replacement ran in front of my rifle, hollering and pointing.

"There goes one! There goes one!" A split second later and I would have been squeezing the trigger. I had that dream for years.

The VC stumbled and dropped his rifle as he entered the hedgerow, turned right, and ran along behind it. His comrades had retreated in that direction. The hedgerow had gaps every twenty feet. As the man flew past the first and second gaps, rifles would bang away, too late to stop him. When he reached the third gap, most of the rifles were already aimed there. He was lifted off the ground and knocked sideways by bullets.

The platoon followed the man's path across the vegetable patch, running in small groups to offer fewer targets. Hobson's men stepped over a discarded Russian bolt-action carbine, someone's future souvenir, and followed the hedgerow. I was with them when they reached the casualty. He was lying on his back in the grass, riddled with bullet holes, but trying to raise his head and say something. All that came out were pathetic gurgling sounds. Hobson turned to me.

"We're going after his buddies. Kill the poor bastard and put him out of his misery."

I held my rifle at arm's length and pointed the muzzle toward the man's head. He smiled and closed his eyes, but I couldn't pull the trigger. I felt ashamed. The man opened his eyes and tried to speak again. I am sure he was asking me to kill him. Gould saw my problem and strolled over.

"Don't worry, man. I can handle it. Give me your Sixteen."

I walked away and stared at the vegetable patch as an eighteen-round burst sent the liberation fighter to his next life. I vaguely heard Gould ripping the Cav patch off his sleeve. He tapped my shoulder and handed back the rifle.

Within five minutes, Gould killed another VC as he rose up from a hidden spider hole to shoot some Blues who had just walked past him. Next, a Vietnamese wounded in the crossfire at the vegetable patch was captured. Door gunners, riding in gunships that sailed a few feet above the palm trees, dueled with clacking AK-47 bursts until only door guns fired. Two more guerrillas were dead.

The slicks landed in trail [in a line] and picked us up from the vegetable patch, from in-between the rows of tomatoes and beans.

An Army of Vietnam unit searched the hamlet the following morning. A Viet Cong from the local force company surrendered to them and told the American advisors a story. His squad of nine men had entered the place the evening before, but U.S. helicopters and infantry had appeared out of nowhere and killed or captured everyone but him.

That first night back, Martin and I drew our two-beer ration and drank cold cans of Pabst Blue Ribbon on top of a bunker. At first John refused to give me details of what had transpired while I was away. All he would say was that the platoon was "doing the same shit."

"Come on, John. I hardly recognize anyone in the platoon. The only thing that's the same is the blue bandanas. Did they all go home?"

He shifted uneasily on the sandbags. "Not all of them. You want to know? I'll tell you."

The battle on March sixth, near a large lake called Dam Tra-O, began like so many others: a helicopter shoot-down. Blue was sent and walked into an NVA battalion. One of Kaneshiro's men was wounded. Kaneshiro ran forward to pull him back and took a single bullet through the head. Our medic ran forward, saw Kaneshiro and the wounded man and charged. He was hit in the ear and knocked down, then played dead as an enemy soldier emerged from his hiding place and stood over him to check his "kill." Doc killed the man with a hand grenade after he returned to his spider hole.

"We lost seven men that day," said Martin. "We spent the night out there, and the only things that saved us were Skyraiders [single engine, propeller-driven close support aircraft] and APCs. You ever smelled what napalm does to people, Matt?" I shook my head. "You should. It's just like smelling roast pork. Let's talk about something else." I had never seen Martin so bitter.

Staff Sergeant Edward Kaneshiro was posthumously awarded the **Distinguished Service Cross** *for extraordinary heroism on December 1, 1966, the day Captain Smith was killed. He had been nominated for the*

Medal of Honor for that action and should have been immediately withdrawn from the field until a decision was reached.

John said that my friend from the forward command post, Sgt. David Blouin, had replaced me and was wounded in the battle. A photograph of David with a bandaged head wound, taken by the famous Vietnam War photographer Dana Stone, made newspapers across the USA.

Sergeants Samuel, Haskett and Jefferson had gone home. Hobson, who had arrived as a replacement in mid-December, was now the platoon's only "old sergeant." Samuel's replacement was Sergeant First Class Kidder, a broad, crew-cut career man who took the Army life seriously. He had told Martin to get a haircut, which put him at the top of John's shit list. Martin referred to him as "a real lifer." Jefferson's replacement was a sergeant from Georgia named Hooten. He was a quiet draftee who had risen quickly through the ranks. The leaders of Kaneshiro's and Haskett's squads were now enlisted men with specialist ratings.

The general opinion in the platoon was that the new ROTC lieutenant, Schultz, treated the men with dignity and respect. They liked him for that, but resented his habit of placing two squads ahead of him on patrol. It was a Blue tradition that the officer walked behind the lead squad. Soldiers said he was a nice, decent person, but not a very brave one. When Lieutenant Schultz moved his patrol position forward, his popularity soared. He became the best platoon leader I was ever honored to serve under. He appeared to be unflappable, always radiating calm to those around him.

A new medic would soon be replaced by a thin, blond man named Brad Smith. Brad had been hit as he carried a wounded man to safety on December first. A bullet had severed one of the nerves in his right arm, so he couldn't completely close his hand. That's how he got his nickname: Doc Claw. The name was used without malice. Doc liked being called Claw.

It is hard to remember the exact sequence of our Charlie Troop medics in 1967. They changed so frequently. Doc Stone, the brave black medic who had rescued Taso on January fourth, left later that same month after a friendly fire incident. He was succeeded by three other medics. The man who was with us the longest was Doc Claw. He made it home more or less intact, although his wounded arm never completely healed.

Doc Smith in his book, ***A Graveyard called Two Bits***, has an interesting take on the ninety-four percent casualty rate among 9th Cavalry medics in 1967:

"The only medic I knew in our outfit who belonged to the elite "6 percent" list (neither KIA nor WIA) looked like the last terrier-mix in a dog pound. He knew he was going to get it. It was just a matter of when, where, and how badly."

The next morning at dawn, Blue was sent to search a bunker where a scout chopper had killed a single Viet Cong. The bunker was located on a hillside that had once been so heavily shelled that the trees were stark and dead and the ground was littered with torn branches. We arrived at the usual red smoke and found a bunker almost hidden by blasted-down tree limbs.

The scout pilot had chased a man there and hovered while his gunner dropped a grenade into the aperture. That was the only bunker on the hillside. We collected the dead man's carbine and walked for hours through a desolate stretch of mountains. It had become a daily routine.

That afternoon, a scout helicopter crew observed a middle-age man standing on the shore of the South China Sea. When the fellow saw the little chopper approaching, he ran to a place on the beach and started scooping away sand with his hands. As the scouts circled back for another look at this strange behavior, the man tried to unwrap oilcloth from around a rifle. He was dead before he could finish. His papers said that he was a reformed VC, released from a South Vietnamese detention center that very morning. He immediately headed for his buried rifle, a piece-of-junk French MAS-36 that couldn't have been fired come hell or high water. The bolt assembly had rusted shut in the damp sand.

On another day, we jumped into deep rice paddies in the Crescent where a gunship had killed a man with a rifle. The pilots were jittery because those paddies were near the place where Blue had lost seven men on March sixth. All we found was the body of an old farmer whose "rifle" was a hoe. A young boy was grinding rice in the shade of a palm tree beside a nearby hut.

"Minh, ask him where his father is."

"He say father there, work in rice paddies." The boy pointed in the direction from which we had come. Schultz told Minh to thank him and moved us out of there in a hurry. We didn't want to be around when he found his father. Sad mistakes happen in war.

Later that day, the platoon was in the Crescent, patrolling paddy fields under a cloudless sky and engaging in an occasional open area pastime. Whenever a helicopter appeared, even if only as a speck on the horizon, it was greeted by random rifle shots from the countryside for miles around. Every farmer with a rifle took potshots at choppers. "Pop!" "Pop-Pop!" It happened so often that when we saw a helicopter, the Blues would sometimes raise their own rifles and machine guns, track it across the sky and make bullets sounds. "Bap-Bap-Bap."

We were doing this out of boredom when our patrol encountered a group of eight women in white pajamas walking toward us along a paddy dike. Something about the self-important way one of them was acting -her clenched jaws, upturned nose and hate-filled eyes- convinced Schultz that she was the one to question.

When two Blues tried to approach her, the rest of the women formed a circle around her and squatted down, wailing and screaming. They were obviously responding to her instructions. When the soldiers broke through the ring and tried to tow the woman away, the others latched onto her legs, waist, torso and shoulders, still wailing and crying, and had to be dragged along with her. Three Blues wrestled her free and plopped her butt down on the floor of a waiting helicopter. As the chopper lifted away, the other women cried and shouted curses at us. But when the helicopter had become a black dot on the horizon, the shouting stopped and seven women calmly walked away down the paddy dike.

In a sweep through a coastal village, the command group arrived at a square courtyard with four tiny huts facing inward. In the western hut sat a woman on a chair over a trapdoor. A soldier told her to move. She didn't. As he tried to pull her off the chair, she bolted, tearing past him to run across the courtyard and disappear into the village. The soldier didn't chase her because he thought she was afraid of our uniforms and weapons.

More quickly than I can tell it, the trapdoor popped open and a stick grenade sailed into the courtyard, followed by a man in khakis. Two things happened. The NVA tripped on the one-inch threshold and stumbled forward at the same time as a Blue fired, removing the very top of his skull. The Vietnamese fell on the grenade, which exploded with such force that the largest piece of him was probably an entire pink brain, quivering on the hot sand about eight feet from the rest. That was a bizarre sight. Grenade fragments had wounded Lieutenant Schultz's two radiomen and the Blue who had fired his rifle.

When I stepped into the courtyard, the wounded rifleman was laughing, "Any man who falls on his own grenade couldn't shoot straight in basic training, either."

Schultz told him to shut up.

Now we were interested in what the trapdoor concealed. The huts were too small for more than one man to freely move around, and no one wanted to lift the lid and get shot, so the lieutenant ordered a safe approach. The hut was torn down and removed. We called for whoever was inside the hole to surrender. No reply. A yellow smoke grenade or two were tossed in and the trapdoor quickly slammed shut. We hoped that the enemy fighters would think the smoke was poison gas and surrender.

Muffled shouts and scuffling sounds traveled through the sand beneath our feet. Another call to surrender received no response. Another yellow smoke grenade - silence below the sand. We lifted the trapdoor and pulled out two bright yellow bodies dressed in bright yellow uniforms. They had been dyed and asphyxiated by the smoke. We were after prisoners that day; no one was supposed to die, but they had been unlucky. As we began to search the village with more care, soldiers filing past the mess in the courtyard muttered coping phrases such as, "Nothing matters," "Sorry about that," and "It don't mean nothing."

Scattered throughout that place were large, long storage bunkers that appeared to be filled from floor to ceiling with coconuts. I searched two of them, up to the coconuts that is, and couldn't get away quickly enough. What made me very afraid was the feeling that those were false walls, and behind them were people who could kill me. Everyone reacted the same way: descending the steps, taking a quick look around, and getting out fast. Those bunkers were a shared secret. They were never discussed.

I found Minh and asked him what was going on. "These people poor," he replied. "Arvin [Army of Vietnam] say no go more than two kilometer or you help VC. Helicopter sink boat. Because no fish, people help VC."

The platoon left that village behind and headed south to the next. The villagers there were hostile and silent. We knew that the local fishermen smuggled enemy replacements and weapons down the coast at night in their fishing sampans. The North Vietnamese would hide in bunkers throughout the day and continue the journey south in darkness. But these people were bothered by more than our search.

Schultz grabbed Minh's sleeve and pointed him toward a crowd of frowning villagers. "Find out what's the matter with these people."

An old, leather-skinned couple finally answered Minh. "They say mortars come two time in three week. They don't know who do it. Last night young girl dies. They say war bad thing."

"Tell them we know nothing about that." Schultz turned to his radio-man. "It was probably the damned Arvins."

We searched huts and bunkers out of boredom until we reached a section of the village where the people were even more sullen than the others. We became more cautious. Hooten grenaded a coconut log bunker and crawled inside with the platoon sergeant's flashlight. He emerged smiling. He had just bagged two communist tax collectors, finding two star belts, two Tokarev automatics, and a thick roll of South Vietnamese banknotes secured by a rubber band. He flashed the money at me and hid it in his shirt as the lieutenant walked up.

"We're almost done here," said Schultz. "Frag all the bunkers from now on. There might be more where those two came from."

Now the game was serious. A soldier approached a bunker with a woman planted squarely in front of it. Schultz watched him trying to pull her away, and told Minh to ask her if anyone was in the bunker. The woman glared at Minh and refused to answer.

"Ask her again, Minh." No response. "All right. Get her out of the way and frag it."

The woman screamed as the charge went off. When the black cord-ite smoke had cleared, Doc Claw climbed into the bunker. A guardian angel was watching over all of us that day. The grenade had exploded beside an infant the mother had hidden in the bunker. The blast had partly collapsed the roof and sprayed the walls with metal, but the child was untouched. Claw returned with the baby in his arms and handed it to the mother. Both mother and child began wailing. When the baby was calmed down, the mother talked to us. The Viet Cong had told the people that we killed children.

———————————

April was another month in the high Soui Ca and the mountains north and west of the An Lao Valley, a wild region almost untouched by the battles raging farther to the east. Our days were spent walking down mountain slopes through sparkling, swift-flowing brooks. I recall those days with the lines from a Simon and Garfunkel song.

"April, come she will,
When streams are bright and filled with rain."

Those words strike a sharp contrast to a line in T.S. Eliot's dark poem, "The Wasteland," where he writes, *April is the cruelest month.* April may be cruel in London or Boston, but seldom is in the Annamite Cordillera of Indochina. The next line, *Breeding lilacs out of dead earth,* could have been written about that other Vietnam, the land of dry, cracked rice fields, dead water buffalo, and burning villages.

Blue often found tiger tracks in the bamboo zone between the elephant grass topknots and the hardwood forests of the high mountains. Sometimes the tracks were so recent that water still seeped back into them, tracks so large that my boot fit inside. On one occasion, the point came face-to-face with a big cat on a narrow game trail. Both of them ran away.

Sometimes Blue followed elephant trails [elephant roads] where small herds had bulldozed a way through the jungle, knocking down trees, stripping branches, and defecating. Once we climbed a mountain and finally broke into elephant grass above the trees. A female elephant and her calf ambled by barely thirty meters away. They ripped out the tough grass that cut our hands and faces with leisurely movements of their trunks. Seeing an elephant in the wild is a stunning experience.

Whole sections of mountains had been burned off by the hill tribes-man, planted in corn, manioc, and melons, and enclosed by huge log fences that looked like the walls of frontier forts. The garden fields made excellent helicopter landing zones. We would land and cross acres of fields to the single entrance of each corral, bypassing the deep elephant pit lined with pointed stakes. Elephants also like corn, manioc, and melons. The trail between the log walls and the elephant pit was so narrow that we moved along it sideways with our backs pressed against the logs. The last obstacle was always a baited tiger trap. Tigers find hill tribesmen tasty. Winding trails led past hastily abandoned wicker baskets full of corn and manioc, and suddenly deserted hamlets of huts on stilts. These might be burned or spared, depending on the whim of the pilots circling far above us.

Once we followed trails under the hardwood canopy for an entire day until we arrived at a single, giant wooden building. Hundreds of pounds of drying tobacco leaves hung in bundles from the rafters. Our fire made the mountain slope smell like a smoker's paradise. When the NVA wanted a smoke, they would think of us.

On another day, rice storehouses were discovered high in the mountains. These were not protected by men, but by booby-traps – a Malayan gate, which was a tree limb bent back and studded with short bamboo spikes, two crossbows linked to vine tripwires; five ancient French bullets embedded in blocks of wood with nails for striking pins, buried upright in the mud of a trail; punji pits covered with twigs and dirt.

The Malayan gate was broken or didn't work. A crossbow arrow narrowly missed the point man, Tom Betts, and almost skewered Doc Smith. We were saved from the bullet traps because recent rains had exposed them. The punji pits could be detected by their slightly different hue from the surrounding earth and vegetation.

We burned the rice and took the crossbows as souvenirs.

While we patrolled the hauntingly beautiful Soui Ca Mountains, Alpha Troop reconnoitered the An Lao Valley. The troop commander's helicopter was shot down there on a sunny mid-April morning. All four aboard were killed.

I flew as a volunteer door gunner on another April morning. A line of elephants was moving down a mountain trail. Each had a double pack of something slung across its spine on wide straps. I was still marveling at how small elephants looked from the air when our two gunships circled back and dived. Rockets and 40mm cannon killed some of the big animals and sent the rest crashing through the trees. I fired my door gun — at nothing.

Many months later, my mother woke me from a troubled sleep. I was shouting, "Oh, no! They're killing the elephants! They're killing the elephants!"

The gunship next flew over a mountain valley with hundreds of huts under the trees. Artillery covered the canopy with bursts, leaving a haze of black and gray smoke drifting through the tree tops. Scout choppers hovered over the trees, dropping white phosphorous grenades on the almost invisible huts.

My pilot looked over his shoulder and said into the intercom, "Know what's going on down below, FO?"

"Looks like they're burning hooches."

"Right!" (*you're a genius; go pick a prize*) "We call it an urban renewal project." He grinned at his wit and gave a thumbs-up signal.

Two men in khaki ran from a hut beside a stream. A scout chopper spat tracers; a phosphorous grenade set the hut afire. My gunship rocketed the streambed while I fired the door gun into the jungle alongside it. As we climbed away from the rocket run, tiny men jumped from toy helicopters far below us. I wanted to be with Martin in the heat, not sitting in the cool seat of a gunship.

Those 1967 forays against vast enemy base camps on the high mountain plateau always confused me. Our choppers would burn huts and shoot a few tracers. Sometimes we would accompany artillery raids where howitzers and pallets of ammunition were slung beneath Chinook helicopters and placed on mountaintops. Surrounding targets would be shelled all day, and then everyone and everything would be gone by nightfall. There never was a determined push to destroy those places. The cavalry division could have done that.

An occasional practice became a habit in those mountains. The rebel yell became so popular among Charlie Troop Blues that I can't picture an insertion without seeing soldiers, black, brown, and white, standing on the landing skids and shouting things like "E-e-e-i-i, ha!" and "Ya-a hoo!" at the top of their lungs. The racket was supposed to scare the enemy, but did far more to boast our courage as the slicks dropped toward landing zones that might be boulder piles, fallen timber, or bomb craters in solid jungle.

We usually jumped from moving slicks, but one landing in five involved hanging from the landing skids and dropping ten or more feet to the ground. Minor injuries were common, but the only man evacuated before the end of a mission broke his leg when he landed on a tree stump. The rebel yells were a blanket over our fears.

Someone tried to shoot down the squadron commander's helicopter from a hamlet in the Crescent, and, as Kidder put it, "That's one man you don't fuck with."

Sturdy homes were burning from artillery shelling as we ran among them, ducking collapsing timbers. Martin stumbled over some cloth beside a shell crater in a brick courtyard, but it wasn't just cloth. We collected three smoke-blackened pieces of an old man, covered him with a blanket from his home, and ran to join the rest of the platoon as they searched caves on a hillside. The caves were old and unused, and the network of trails connecting them was too hard-packed to determine if they had been recently trod. Blue headed back toward the hamlet.

Crack-Crack-Crack! The point man, Gould as usual, shot a North Vietnamese who was walking up the trail from the village. Some of the bullets in the man's AK-47 had been fired, so he probably was the one who had shot at Colonel Nevins' helicopter. Gould slung the AK-47 across his back, stooped and sliced off one of the dead man's ears, leaving a small hole bordered by glistening white cartilage. He muttered, "*Xin Loi*, motherfucker." [*Xin Loi* roughly translates as, "Sorry about that."] Gould held the ear by its lobe and jiggled it over his left shoulder so those following him could see.

In the chow line that night at Bong Son, Gould and the mess sergeant squared off. "Hey, Sarge," said Gould. "Want some meat for your soup?" He dangled the ear over a soup kettle.

The mess sergeant's facial expression was a mixture of fright and fury. "Get that out of here!"

Gould grinned. "Come on, Sarge. This soup never has enough meat in it."

The sergeant pointed his ladle at Gould's nose. "Listen, you monster. If I ever catch you pulling a stunt like this again, I'll see that you're reported for war crimes."

Gould backed away. "Okay, Sarge. I was just having a little fun."

"Take your fun elsewhere."

Gould quickly left his place in line. The ear was never seen again.

Lieutenant Schultz called a platoon meeting that night. We gathered in a filthy mob to hear what he had to say. He began with compliments. "I wanted to tell you that you men have been doing an outstanding job since I've been with you." His statement was greeted by silence. Fuck the lieutenant.

"The main reason for calling this meeting is that Colonel Nevins wants to thank you for getting the gook that shot at his helicopter. He says Charlie Blues have come across again." This caused laughter and a chorus of grunts and coughs. The colonel flew around and played at war while the men under him got killed. Fuck the colonel.

Schultz was embarrassed and tried to laugh. "One more thing. There will be no more mutilation of dead gooks." He was trying to talk our language, but "gooks" sounded uncultured and unnatural coming from him. "The next man who cuts off an ear will be court-martialed. Is that clear?"

Bobbing heads and shuffling feet might have been interpreted as a yes.

"All right. That's all I have. Let's keep up the good work."

More coughs, grunts, and throat-clearing. The lieutenant was probably glad when the meeting ended.

Chapter 6

RICKERSON'S SONG

(May, 1967)

We landed at dawn to patrol a mountain valley on the western side of the An Lao. The gunships had killed three North Vietnamese at twilight the evening before and the first order of business was to open the graves. We found the place after a long walk. Decomposition proceeds rapidly in the tropics. Colonies of red ants already swarmed inside the corpses. There was nothing of value.

The trail led us about seventy meters farther into the trees until we arrived at a field of short, very soft, luminescent grass bordering a large thatched hut. Two perfect rows of seven NVA field packs each sat in that grass. The toe-heavy sandal prints of running men led farther up the hill. Those soldiers had apparently been standing some sort of inspection when they heard the sound of our shovels and fled. Everything was burned.

As the patrol continued, Kidder placed an overweight fellow named Rickerson on point for the first time. Rickerson had been involuntarily transferred from the gunships to the Blues and had a reputation for making mistakes. About an hour later, I sensed something was wrong about a valley we were approaching. I walked down the file to Kidder.

"Sarge, I think there's Charlies in that banana grove down there."

"What makes you think so?"

"I don't know. It's just a strong feeling. Besides, they like campsites like that."

Kidder wore a curious expression. "Well, don't worry. We'll find out soon enough."

"That's what I wanted to talk to you about. There's a new man on point, and he might freeze if there is an ambush or something."

Kidder shook his head. "Let's wait and see, FO. I can't change the point because somebody thinks there might be gooks around. That's what we're here for." And that was a smart statement.

Rickerson almost collided with a man in khakis eating rice on top of a low bunker. The NVA grabbed his rifle and was gone. A whole flock of Oriental fellows disappeared down the trail before Jim remembered to shoot. We passed the unfinished meal and found a large campsite with bananas on carrying poles and baskets of rice drying on top of boulders. Hammocks swung between trees; packs were neatly hung on branches to protect them from insects. I gave Kidder an "I told you so" look and he shot back a "How was I to know?" shrug and expression in reply. Now he took Rickerson off point.

Martin and I talked with Rickerson that evening. The rest of the platoon was avoiding him after the day's screw-up. Left to my own devices, I would have avoided him as well. He had let at least a platoon of North Vietnam soldiers escape unscathed, but Martin had invited him to our tent. The conversation started with the weather and the way we were always soaked with either rain or sweat, then Martin suggested that Rickerson should have stayed with the cool gunships.

He replied, "Gunships! I don't ever want to spend another day with that bunch. You know what they do in the gunships and scouts with the first man you kill? They make you go back to shoot him up until there are only pieces left. Shoot until the pieces are smoking from tracers. That way you're supposed to start liking it."

That rang Martin's bell. "This whole war is sick. Just like the poor farmer with a hoe that the gunships shot. It's all crazy. Somebody said they reported it as a new VC weapon. A rifle made like a hoe. Pretty soon we'll be finding farmers with automatic hoes. All those bastards did was guarantee that the farmer's son will be shooting at us in a few years. How'd you end up in this mess, Jim?"

Rickerson hung his head. "They drafted me, and they put me in the infantry, and they sent me to Nam, but they aren't going to make a killer out of me. All I want to do is go home and forget this nightmare."

Martin jumped up and slapped Rickerson on the back, "I second that emotion!"

It was then that I realized that Rickerson's failure to shoot might have been more than what it appeared to be. His notorious mistakes could be by design.

―――――

Two Blues restrained the prisoner as we flew over the An Lao Mountains. He couldn't take his eyes off the open door of the chopper, clearly preferring a quick death leap to life in a cage.

We found him in a hamlet on the An Lao Valley floor that had been intermittently shelled all night. There wasn't enough left standing to burn. The place was littered with abandoned equipment, but the enemy had fled. A soldier looked inside a bunker and found our prize crouching over a pool of his own blood. He was a tough-looking soldier of about forty, with a crew cut and bulging muscles. Hobson sat him on a table to bandage his bloody legs, and the man tried to kick Doc Claw. Kidder put the muzzle of his rifle against the man's temple and clicked off the safety. He motioned for Minh.

"Ask him how big his unit was."

"He say they two platoon in village."

"How big is his entire unit?"

"He say again they two platoon here."

"Ask him where they are."

"They go back to mountains when artillery comes. He knows American come after artillery. He wounded and tell them go without him."

The prisoner was obviously not a recruit. He was stamped from the same mold that must be used for all professionals in all armies. I was fascinated by how closely he resembled Kidder as they looked at each other with expressions more akin to understanding than dislike.

"What is his job?"

"He say he proud to be aspirant and will soon be officer. He fights French four years, and he in South four years fighting for liberation." We had captured a senior NCO, an officer candidate. He had been a powerful man among his fellow soldiers.

The prisoner began jabbering excitedly. "What's that he's saying?"

"He say he not want to be prisoner." The aspirant tensed his body and glared at Schultz as his words were translated.

Lieutenant Schultz's lips creased into a rare smile. "Tell him, sorry about that."

We laughed.

The platoon left that smoking ruin and returned to Bong Son with our prisoner.

The following day, we patrolled the far northern reaches of the An Lao, near a place where we had seen Korean Marines digging fighting holes a few days before. Crack! Blues crawled through the mud and grass along the trail. Gould had just walked into a patrol of NVA heading south. His rifle had jammed after one shot, but he had managed to hit the point man in the chest. The wounded man's M-14 rifle was passed down the trail to Schultz. It would be easy to follow the blood trail.

When we came to a place where bright gobs of blood had splattered the leaves, Martin stomped his foot in anger. "There's only one thing you can say about Gould."

"What's that, John?"

"The sick bastard doesn't miss a shot."

The serial number of the captured M-14 rifle was run at squadron headquarters. It had been captured from the Marines near a firebase called Montezuma at Duc Pho.

<hr />

Our commander received a report that the Viet Cong had shot a woman the previous night for not giving them rice. If the report was true, the incident would make a good story for anti-communist propaganda. Blue was sent to investigate. Accompanying us were two newspaper reporters and a photographer.

The village was very clean, very prosperous. Put the old headman in a suit and he would have gone unnoticed at a Chamber of Commerce luncheon. Surely the war had not touched these people. Schultz pulled the headman and Minh away from a silent crowd of staring people.

"Minh, ask him if the story is true about the VC killing the woman."

"He say yes, it true. The teacher [cadre] tells people about VC and asks for rice. She say no. They are local squad. They live in those hills." Minh pointed to a line of low hills by the sea. "People never see teacher before."

"Where is the woman now?"

"He say they bury her this morning."

Schultz radioed the information to the gunships, and what he heard didn't please him. "Shit. We've got to dig her up. The press wants pictures of the atrocity."

A pair of Blues dug out the body. The mud wanted to keep their shovels and gave way only with a sigh. The old headman had tears in his eyes. He couldn't understand why we had to disturb her again. A soldier unwrapped her burial shroud and found the body of a woman who would have been a respected elder in any of the dozens of villages and hamlets we had searched. She was about seventy years old with a clinched jaw, executed at close range by a single bullet through the left temple. I am sure that she died defiant. The camera clicked.

As we boarded the slicks, shots rang out from the low hills. It had to be a warning because the range was too far for the shooters to hit us. Gunships swarmed to the attack, rocketing the canopy and making ripping minigun runs. Martin thought he knew why the VC had fired on us.

"I wonder if they felt guilty about our finding the woman."

"I hope so, John. They're murderers!"

He sat in silence for a moment, and then shouted over the roar of the chopper blades, "Yeah, Matt! But so are we!"

Later that same day we landed on the floor of the An Lao Valley and walked from one red smoke to another as gunners marked the locations of North Vietnamese dead. It had been a turkey shoot: the NVA had been scrounging rice, and their bodies were now scattered over a wide area. Each smoke grenade marked the place where a man had been hunted and chased before dying. None of those men, each with a neat haircut and a khaki uniform, had a weapon. Then Hobson found a survivor hiding under a rock ledge on a barren hill. The starving, trembling man told his story to Minh.

"He say his company low on rice and they gamble to get it. His platoon comes to find rice people leaves behind in villages."

"Why weren't they carrying weapons?"

"He say they leaves rifles behind because they add weight if rice found. They think they get back in hills before helicopters come."

We found the last body at dusk. He was a thin man of about twenty-five, lying on his back among saplings beside a peaceful stream. Intestines, resembling small white balloons, protruded from four bullet holes in his stomach. I covered his face with his rain sheet. Eighteen men had died for less than twenty pounds of rice.

We returned at next dawn to empty fields. Their comrades had come for them during the night. We followed a trail into the hills and found a jungle school for the children of the "An Lao Liberated Zone," or the "An Lao War Zone," depending upon your persuasion. A large building held blackboards, homemade desks, elementary textbooks, and notepads with simple mathematics problems illustrated by crude sketches of airplanes, bombs, and stick men. Small huts had been built for the teachers; a well-tended outhouse was located at a discreet distance from the other buildings. All of this we burned and headed merrily back to Bong Son.

Blue is in the southwest An Lao. The banana grove we search is hemmed in by high cliffs. Gunships have killed thirty North Vietnamese in a battle here, and we have come to gather their rifles and papers. Scout choppers hover over jumbled rocks high above us, dropping phosphorous grenades. The NVA shoot like crazy as they run from one pile of rocks to another. Ricochets from gunship door guns shred banana trees and whine around us.

The commander won't let us go higher because there are too many Charlies in the rocks, so we form a line and sweep through the grove. The heavy smell of blood and violent death is so strong that you can almost reach out and touch it, but the bodies are gone. We comb through the grove again and again, mercifully being missed by ricochets from the battle above us, but nothing is left besides battered banana trees. Where have they hidden the bodies so quickly? The stench clings to our noses for hours.

We spent the day walking through an old B-52 strike zone in the An Lao. The topsoil had been blasted away and rain had turned the ground to stone. The North Vietnamese had stayed even here, retreating to caves around the wasteland. My legs ached from the pounding of hard soil; all of us were drenched in sweat.

The lift birds pulled us out in the twilight and were climbing the eastern wall of the An Lao when the scouts saw seven NVA running into part of what had once been An Lao Village. Our slick drivers turned hard left, roared downslope at tree top level, and surfed above palm fronds as we clattered northward up the valley.

Two bodies sprawled over a paddy dike. We ran past them and in among decaying huts, spraying the trees and hedgerows. Hobson's squad gunned down two men who made the mistake of charging the sweep line, and captured a third man who threw away his AK-47 and fell to his knees, begging for mercy with folded hands. The huts were burning as we pulled back to the rice paddies.

Kidder threw a yellow marking smoke and turned around to make sure that his squads were in position. One of the two "dead" NVA on the paddy dike was aiming his rifle at a Blue's back. The banging of Kidder's M-16 sent all of us jumping into the stinking water. Now the man was really dead. Kidder ran over to the other body and emptied his rifle. He slid in another magazine and looked at each of our stunned faces.

"God-dammit! You men better start checking those bodies more carefully! Walker! You were almost a dead man!"

What do you say to someone who has just saved your life? "Thanks, Sarge." Two soldiers slapped Cav patches on the faces of the dead men. We went home.

The following day, slicks took us to a place in Happy Valley where two Phantom jets had just bombed a squad of North Vietnamese as they scrambled up a thinly-wooded slope. This was routine enough, but that wasn't why we were there. The Army was making a training film about the tactics of air cavalry troops, because the Army wanted more of them, and we were the stars.

The platoon landed amid impressive fireworks and burned a new storehouse. Farther up the hill was a khaki-clad figure, sitting with his back against a small tree, facing downhill. He appeared to be sleeping, but he wasn't. A Blue carefully searched the dead man's uniform pockets for papers, all under the watchful eye of a photographer who was filming the scene from a scout helicopter hovering above us. Some of the Blues turned and stage-bowed as our line reached the top of the hill.

———————

Hobson's squad had been scrambled for a mission at dawn. Now they were back at our tents, bitching about lost sleep. Probably surmising that he would be asked anyway, Hobson came over to our tent to tell me where they had gone.

"Scouts shot a gook messenger in VC Valley. We had to go in and police him up. He was fucked up real bad. Don't think he'll make it. Gook had a carbine and a pouch full of documents. Want a souvenir?"

"Depends on what it is."

He handed me the courier's gray canvas pouch, complete with a made-in-North-Vietnam ballpoint pen.

VC Valley was a side valley of the Tiger Mountains on the coast, just across the shallow Bong Son River from our base. Blue was on a ridge above the valley within the hour. From there we had a magnificent view of the town of Bong Son and our base camp with its helicopters and tents. Hard-packed trails ran in all directions on that ridge, but this was the dry season, and there was no way to estimate how recently they had been used.

Rickerson was on point when he heard something rustling through the bushes. The word was passed by hand signals. Kidder knocked down a couple of Blues as he bulled his way up the narrow trail to the head of the file. He was still feeling the effects of Jim's "screw-up" in the An Lao. Our friend was squatting behind a thorn bush.

"What's going on up here?"

Rickerson pointed to a bunker aperture a few feet away. "I've got a Charlie in the bunker, Sarge. What should I do?"

"What have you got between your ears? Frag the damned thing!"

"I don't have any grenades."

Kidder borrowed two grenades from someone else, handed them to Jim, and stood behind him like an umpire to be sure he did everything right. One explosion, and then another to be sure. Jim was ordered to remove the body from the bunker. The man's face looked like hamburger meat; Rickerson turned pale and vomited. Kidder removed the dead man's leather belt, hung with grenades and riddled with fragments, and hurled it into tree branches far down the steep slope. He reached over and patted Jim on the shoulder.

"Nice job, Rickerson. Let's see if we can find what he was guarding." Jim gaped at him and made a few grunting sounds.

The bunker was a lookout post for something on the hill, but we didn't have time to find it. Bravo Troop Blues were in a bad ambush in the An Lao. We trotted in a ragged line down a trail to the valley floor and were taken back to Bong Son to be ready if Bravo Troop needed help.

As we waited in the shade of the slicks, Martin pointed to Rickerson, sitting alone under a stunted tree by the barbed wire. "He's really down in the dumps about what happened this morning."

As two-ship teams of aerial rocket artillery hogs returned from the An Lao and more headed west, *Darling, Be Home Soon* blared from Martin's transistor radio. I heard the words and wondered if our most recent "kill" had people waiting for him in a village somewhere. How many people waited for the men on both sides of Bravo Troop's battle?

Martin was listening as well. "That should be Jim's song," said John. ""He wants to go home even worse than me."

Bravo Troop Blues were rescued without our help. They were withdrawn from the An Lao and given the greatest reward any group of 9th Cavalry infantrymen of that era could receive. Those who had survived the ambush were given the rest of the day off duty.

Blue was landed in VC Valley at dawn the next morning. Here was a narrow valley, bisected by a stream, with rice fields down the center and clusters of huts crowded against the hills on both sides. We soon learned how the place had gotten its name. A soldier slipped and caught himself on the edge of a deep pit lined with bamboo stakes. The trap was concealed by a framework of thin bamboo strips, covered by wide leaves and hidden under a layer of sand. We quickly learned to locate the pits by the slightly darker color of sand over them.

I was walking back-up behind the point man when he stepped through a gap in a hedgerow. Boom! Both of us were knocked down. I ran my hands over my body to find the inevitable holes. There were none. A CBU [Cluster Bomb Unit] rested in the dirt at our feet. We had been lucky.

CBUs are softball-size, yellow bombs filled with explosives and ball bearings. The Air Force dropped them in canisters that broke apart in the air. Not all of them exploded on contact. We sometimes found them scattered through the jungle or precariously balancing on bushes and tree limbs. These were not to be disturbed. The enemy had wrapped the middle of this particular CBU with a band of plastic explosive and linked it to a green nylon tripwire. All we had gotten was the blast from the explosive belt. That booby-trapped CBU was the only time in my experience that an explosive belt failed to detonate a munition.

The point man was stone deaf and was evacuated. My head roared. I walked father back for a few days. My hearing has never been the same.

Punji pits and bundles of new punji stakes were everywhere. We passed a punji stake assembly line with piles of bamboo poles and large bundles of newly made stakes, and climbed the hill behind it to a jungle campsite. Here was a scene that had repeated itself multiple times by now – camouflaged hut, packs and belts on pegs, a corpse in the dirt, all courtesy of the scouts. Everything was burning when we returned to the valley floor to eat C-rations.

The platoon set up a defense in the middle of the valley, around a sturdy brown stucco building with a stream running behind it. The several large rooms and a damaged red tile roof had probably once been the French colonial administrator's home. What remained of the building was burned after our C-ration break.

Schultz formed us into a sweep line and we walked eastward toward a cluster of huts. A gunship roared overhead and AKs opened up from the hilltop in front of us. A door gunner fired back as the chopper banked away. Schultz grabbed his handset for a message as gunships made passes over the target. A real duel began between four door gunners and about ten rifles on the ground.

Schultz shouted, "Gunships taking fire! We're to pull back to the streambed and waited for an air strike!" He listened to his handset again. "It's on the way! On the double! On the double!"

Jets screamed in from the south as we jumped into the streambed. A door gunner dropped a red smoke on the target. An Air Force spotter plane putted over the streambed and fired two white phosphorous rockets where the red smoke floated through the trees. The hot white phosphorous smoke was barely through the tree tops when the first jet released its bomb.

A tremendous brown column of earth from a thousand-pound bomb kicked up from the hilltop. We hugged the bank and ducked while pieces of trees and huge clumps of earth crashed down around us. A slowly tumbling tree trunk snapped off the top of a coconut tree above Martin and me and crashed into the paddies a few meters beyond the streambed. Three more bombs, each making a rain of giant debris, and then the jets were gone.

Echoes from the last bomb still bounced across the valley when two people began scrambling downhill on all fours on that blasted, nearly leafless, hillside. They looked like a couple of animals. One was a woman with breasts swaying from side to side as she scuttled away. Concussion had blown off their clothes.

I grabbed Martin so hard his helmet fell off. "John, I just saw two people up there. I thought they were animals. They were naked."

He didn't believe me. "Aw, come on, Sarge."

Kidder had been listening. "Where did you see those people?"

I pointed. "There, below the crater. They were running on all fours."

"We'll take care of them."

Martin stared daggers at Kidder for a moment, and then glared at me. "You should have kept your mouth shut, Sarge."

The place where the nude people had been was hit by a pair of gunships. As the slope was rocketed time and again, I regretted telling anyone.

When our gunships shifted fire to a trail on the far side of the hill, Lieutenant Schultz led us out of the streambed and formed the platoon into a sweep line. There had been bunkers on the hill until the first bomb scored a direct hit. It left an enormous crater. Beside the crater, a vertical shaft for a deep tunnel had been exposed. A soldier was lowered on a rope to inspect it. He was hoisted back up holding odd items of equipment and two transistor radios stamped with maps of North Vietnam. Everything else, probably including the hill's defenders, had been buried by the bomb.

Pieces of khaki and black clothing were scattered in the dirt; a German Mauser rifle jutted muzzle-down from the lip of the crater, and that was about it. We left VC Valley feeling awed by the destruction one bomb had caused.

Blue was back in the An Lao for another long patrol. Gunship door gunners had killed eight North Vietnamese along a mountain trail leading to a deep gorge and we were there to investigate. Hobson's squad was acting as a separate recon element. I was on point. Hidden in the gorge was a sixty-foot building with long tables, dishes, ladles, and all sizes of pots and pans. The structure was invisible from the air; I located it because something had to be drawing small groups of NVA down that trail. They were hungry, and we had just captured their mess hall.

One of the new replacements found a wide, packed-down trail leading up into the mountains. He was debating whether to follow it when a man in khakis silently walked up and stopped about ten feet away.

The new dude realized he was seeing his first NVA, emptied his entire magazine at him, and missed. The Vietnamese stood there for a moment longer, hungry and confused, and ran back up the trail.

The replacement's ego was shattered. "I let him get away! Didn't even hit him! I don't know how I could have missed at that range."

Hobson was furious. The new man had given away our location for nothing. "I don't know how you could have missed, either. For God's sake, load that rifle. You won't get many more chances to pull a stunt like that."

By the time he managed a weak, "I'm sorry, Sergeant," the rifleman was almost in tears.

The rest of the platoon joined us. We burned the long building and all its food, and pocked bayonet holes in the pots and pans. As the platoon moved off down the gorge, another chowhound died on the trail above us. Sergeant Hooten on point found a large cave behind trees at the far end of the gorge. He yelled for whoever was there to come out, and when nothing happened, he lobbed in a grenade and walked inside.

Hooten returned with a beautiful woman and her small son. She was wounded in her left breast by a sliver of fragmentation, and Claw removed her shirt to treat the wound. The result was spontaneous, electric. Her breasts were well shaped; dark brown nipples stood straight out. The men around her were young – very young and very lonely.

"Look at those tits!"

"Tits nothing! Look at them nipples."

The woman tensed, trying to cover large breasts with small hands. Suddenly, all eyes were on Lieutenant Schultz.

"Sir, no one would ever know if we called her in dead," said Gould.

"Yeah, just say the grenade killed them. How about it, Lieutenant?" said another man.

Schultz defused the situation with a shake of his head. "Forget it. I've already called in the prisoner. Pop smoke! The choppers are on the way in for extraction!"

Gould had the last word. He stood with arms akimbo, facing Schultz. "Shit. What a waste she'll be in a POW cage." Schultz turned away in disgust.

The lift birds took us home.

Soon thereafter, we were landed on the very edge of the South China Sea. A Viet Cong patrol had just disappeared. Our scouts had chased them down the beach into a village, and they had vanished. We jumped from the slicks as a last string of antiaircraft shells from a gray naval ship splintered a coconut grove about fifty meters farther up the beach.

The village was dark and musty-smelling and seemed to be deserted. A haze of light blue smoke from the naval shelling drifted past empty huts. We couldn't find a trace of anything until a Blue leaned against a rotting black coconut log stump and it gave way. Below it was a dark room with exit holes for tunnels or other rooms. Those black stumps were scattered around us, and most of them concealed other entrances. Schultz called the pilots.

"Okay! Listen up! They're going to put delayed artillery on this place to dig them out!" And to his radioman, "Let's let someone else dig out these underground tombs."

We had a rule that you never took the same route twice: too much danger of ambush. But this silent, smelly village was eerie, and we were in a hurry to get away from there. The platoon went the same way back, but it was different. The first hedgerow was booby-trapped with a CBU. The point man had almost tripped the wire. The next hedgerow was booby-trapped with a Chinese hand grenade. Both traps had been placed there after we walked through the first time. A marksman destroyed the booby-traps with rifle shots while the rest of us stayed low. We abandoned the trail and ran straight for the beach, parallel to the hedgerows and past more booby-traps. The artillery shelling began as our slicks lifted off the sand.

———————

I hadn't taken a day off since returning from leave in early March, so May thirty-first seemed like a good day to do just that. No special missions were planned. I had saved six beers from our daily ration and planned to read Michener's book, *Caravans*. All that remained was to check with Martin one last time.

"I'm going to take the day off I've been threatening you with. That means you bring in the artillery if there's any trouble. Think you can handle it?"

"Yeah, Sarge, I'll handle it if I have to. I handled it when you were gone for thirty days. I've got the maps and all the call signs. I hope you have a quiet day." "Sarge" meant that John wasn't happy. He would revert to that little formality when he was uneasy or pissed off.

Making sure that John acknowledged his responsibilities was important, because he wanted to contribute as little as possible to the war. We had gone on artillery raids where I had directed shelling of enemy base camps throughout the day, and John had directed nothing but the barrel of his rifle. On artillery raids, his stubbornness was okay, because we needed just one FO, but this time he would be on his own.

I was reading in the shade of a tree when the platoon saddled up. I stopped John as he ran by the tree. "Where you going?"

"It's no big thing, Sarge. We're going after a chopper that's down with engine trouble. Go back and read your book." He ran ahead to the slicks.

Blue was often taken to secure downed helicopters. On a good day they were down from mechanical troubles; on a bad day they had been shot down. But even choppers that had been hit tried to get away from the place where it happened. The platoon might find dead or injured crew members, or an NVA ambush, but those landings usually resulted in a morning of loafing.

After the slicks returned to camp, a pilot told me, "No sweat. It's down in the secure area east of Bong Son. Nothing out there but smiling farmers." I took my book back to the tree.

I was on my third beer and feeling light-headed in the 110-degree heat when rotor blades began turning. Gunship pilots boiled out of the operations tent and ran for their choppers. One of them shouted to a cluster of door gunners throwing on flak vests and grabbing their machine guns, "Blue's in contact! Receiving fire from a pagoda! One KIA!"

One man was already dead on the "routine" mission. So much for the beer and book. I jumped aboard one of the slicks as it taxied for take-off, and plugged in an extra set of earphones to monitor the action. The ARVN would not let Martin shell the pagoda; the Blues were shooting back with rifles and machine guns. Then the ARVN gave permission. Howitzer shells, called down by John Martin, bracketed the building. Gunships were being shot at along the entire length of the village. An infantry company was landed at the far end away from the pagoda. Enemy soldiers began running back through the village, past the pagoda. The slick I was on would take a squad of Blues to seal off their escape route.

We landed next to a helicopter sitting in deep paddy water. Blues lay face down along a dike, tensing for the fire they knew would come. It didn't. Eight of them ran toward us in a crouch. A replacement gladly let me keep his seat and ran back to the dike for cover. Our slick banked away from the village and circled back to a place where a hovering gunship was firing its 40mm cannon.

Two bodies on a grass embankment were the work of the cannon. One had its left eyeball hanging on its cheek, still connected to the optic nerve; the other's legs were attached only by thin strips of muscle. There wasn't time to think how grotesque they looked. Pop! A carbine round whistled by. Hobson saw the fellow who shot at me and fired a burst down a trench. Pop-Pop! The fellow fired at Hobson. Another burst from Hobson and he was dragging a body from the trench.

I walked down a path between two hay stacks. A Blue, the one who had missed the NVA at the long mess hall a few days before, started shooting behind me. His tracers set fire to both haystacks. Something started popping. Under each haystack was a body. The bullets in their rifles and ammo pouches were cooking off from the intense heat. Fortunately for us, they weren't carrying grenades. The stench of burned meat was suffocating.

The man smiled at me. "I saw one of those haystacks move when the Charlie in the trench fired." He wagged finger. "Better keep your eyes open, Sarge."

Hobson listened to a message from the pilots and shouted, "This is it! This is as far as the gooks got! Platoon's going to sweep toward the grunts! We wait until they bring in the other three squads! Burn the hooches!"

I walked over to the hut behind the grassy slope where the first two NVA had died, pulled a Zippo lighter from my pocket, and lit the thatch. A young woman with a baby in her arms ran through the doorway and beat out the flames with her shirt. She was naked from the waist up, holding a singed shirt in her right hand, and using the baby in her left arm to cover herself. I tried again and she knocked the lighter out of my hand. The third time she slapped me.

"What the hell, lady! If it means that much to you, keep the fuckin' place!" She shouted *"Du ma may!"* which could only be a curse. "Same to you, bitch!"

Three slicks landed with the rest of the platoon. Schultz formed us into a sweep line and we walked deeper into the village, passing a bunker that looked too old to be used.

"Choi hoi! Choi hoi!"

We looked around to see a young NVA soldier standing in the bunker with his hands raised over his head. He was waving a "safe conduct pass," a surrender leaflet that psychological warfare planes dropped by the millions over communist territory.

"*Choi hoi! Choi hoi!*" he shouted in desperation. Minh ran back to the bunker and made the NVA lie on his stomach. They talked rapidly until Lieutenant Schultz and his radiomen arrived.

"What's his unit, Minh?"

"He say he with NVA company that moves here last night. He private and not want to fight helicopters anymore."

"What are they doing here?"

"He say tonight they attack American base at Bong Son."

"Where's his rifle?"

He say he throw rifle in river. We take him prisoner."

A slick took the prisoner away as Schultz got us back into a line. The narrow village was bordered by a small river on the left and rice paddies on the right, so our sweep line could easily cover its width. An old man in black pajamas suddenly stepped in front of us, directly in front of Minh, Martin and me. As we walked forward, he walked backward. Minh shouted, "*Dung lai!*" [stop!]. We knew what would happen if he tried to run, and that's exactly what he did. Rifles banged away. The old man disappeared into the village.

The platoon was out of sight when Martin looked into a hut and found the man lying on the dirt floor. Blood was streaming from a bullet hole through his wrist. He groaned when I placed a field dressing over the gristle.

I started to leave him there, but Martin grabbed my shoulder and swung me around. "You can't do this. He'll bleed to death."

"The platoon left him behind. We've got orders to sweep."

"He's a human being, Matt."

I found Lieutenant Schultz farther along in the village, and his face told me he knew why I was there. "Sir, we have a wounded man back there. He needs a doctor."

Schultz hesitated. "The man shouldn't have run. We've got to link up with the infantry." After another plea, he reverted to his usual, compassionate self. "All right. Get Claw back there and have him look at the wound. I'll contact the gunships and have them pick him up."

Claw gave the man a shot of morphine and led him to a gunship for evacuation. The next day we learned that the old man was the village chief *and* the leader of the local Viet Cong company. It had been his idea for the North Vietnamese to use the village to stage an attack on our base. The plan had failed because a chopper had developed engine trouble and crashed. The Blue landing, covered by gunships, convinced the NVA that they had been discovered.

The village widened as our sweep line advanced beside the river. North Vietnamese squatted like frogs in the tall reeds along its bank. As we approached, they splashed into the water, staying under as long as possible and desperately swimming for the far bank. Heads appeared, gasping for air, and rifles and machine guns fired. Bodies bobbed to the surface of the river and floated downstream until they lodged against an earthen dam.

Beside the dam was a long trench from which the helicopters had received fire. For fifteen minutes, the gunships pumped rockets into the trench while a single defender ran back and forth along it, shooting back - one bullet at a time. A door gunner had finally killed him. We found a young boy in the bottom of the trench, cradling a World War One German Mauser rifle that was longer than he was tall. That boy was a hero in any man's army.

There was something else about that long trench. A home behind it had been burned by the helicopter rockets, and beside the ashes was an animal pen. A mother water buffalo and her calf had been chained in the pen. All that remained were two peacefully kneeling carcasses. The calf had raised its head, mouth open wide, as if calling for help over the charred timbers. The mother's head was turned toward the young animal. If the brutality and sadness of war could be shown in a single photograph, a picture of that scene might do it best.

The battle was over for us. The Blues, the infantry company, the gunships and scout helicopters, had killed ninety-six enemy soldiers.

Our single casualty was Jim Rickerson. Instead of seeking cover behind a paddy dike, he had lain behind a hole in the dike. Carbine rounds, not very accurate, were sprayed from the pagoda, and some hit the water in front of him. Jim was killed by a single bullet, a ricochet.

Martin spoke this of him: "He was a good man. Everyone was always riding him, but he didn't give a damn what they thought. All he wanted to do was go back home. Then he had to lie in front of that hole."

We sat in silence for a long time. Jim was going home.

Chapter 7

GAMES IN THE AN LAO

(June, 1967)

The An Lao Valley was quieter now. Although the valley was the base area for the Yellow Star Division and assorted Viet Cong units, large enemy formations had broken up into groups of between ten and fifty men. Larger units would attract 9th Cavalry helicopters, and with them, the tremendous firepower of the cavalry division. Our mission was to hound the smaller groups until they left the valley entirely.

Blue returned from our first June day in the valley with a dozen pairs of Ho Chi Minh sandals, some packs, and seven bamboo helmets. We had discovered a platoon whose campfire was still glowing hot when they fled. We ran after them as they tossed away most of their non-lethal equipment so they could run faster (and tempt us stop to gather souvenirs). They got away. A show was made of parading the captured items in front of a small cluster of Vietnamese kids by the barbed wire and bragging about the "*beaucoup* VC" we were fighting in the valley. A group of gunship pilots saw the circus and came over.

"Would you guys mind giving us a few of those souvenirs?" asked one.

"Yeah," said another. "We fly cover for you but never get a chance to collect any gook equipment."

Gunship pilots had saved our asses many times in the past, so we gave them everything. There was always more where that came from.

The following day, the platoon was in a deep ravine on the very edge of the valley. Two bodies lay face down in a brook, killed in mid-stride by a gunship door gunner. Hooten on point saw a cave above them and stepped inside. The occupants opened fire. He stepped back, firing his rifle on semi-automatic, and gunned down five NVA. One of them was wounded and still shooting. Hooten's grenade killed him. When he returned from the cave, Hooten was toting an armload of carbines and belts.

"I've got five belts here. They've all got stars. Anybody need one?" A couple of recruits lined up to get their belts.

Hooten's casual bravery would have won him a high medal in 1969 and beyond, but on that day, no one even thanked him.

Hobson's squad killed two more NVA in bushes on the far side of the brook. When he stooped to collect their rifles, he saw they were women. A Blue stripped them of their leather belts and packs. We gathered weapons and a thick stack of papers, jogged back to the stagnant paddy fields beginning about twenty feet from the edge of the jungle, and waited for an airstrike. I sat in front of a trail leading back into the ravine.

Minh shuffled through the documents and made an announcement. "This message center of Third NVA Division. These division dispatches." The discovery would please cavalry division intelligence. Soon they would know the locations, communications, and day-to-day problems of the entire enemy division facing us.

First napalm, and then 250-pound bombs, exploded in the ravine. I turned away after the napalm strike and watched those beautiful, purple-green mountains on the western wall that bombs could never destroy. Then I was lucky. A muddy bootlace was undone and I bent down to tie it. Whoosh! Something hot passed the skin on my neck and a gush of water drenched me.

"What in the hell was that?"

The man beside me stared with wide eyes. "Sarge, you should have seen what just went by your head." He formed a circle with his hands. "A chunk of metal as big as a hub cap."

Even though the fragment's size could have been exaggerated, the skin on the back of my neck was really tingling now.

As the last jet streaked down the valley, we climbed back up the ravine, past sticky black napalm resin hanging from the branches. The bombs had been wasted. There were nine NVA packs, no more, and the trail ended a few feet from where we had been before. The message center had been wiped out.

One of the platoon's side jobs was to detonate unexploded bombs and shells so that the enemy could not turn them into mines and booby-traps. One day we found a real beauty. On a low hill in the middle of a ruined hamlet in the An Lao sat a fat 500-pound bomb. Hooten placed a thick band of plastic explosive around its middle and set a fifteen-minute fuse. We pulled back to a deeply eroded streambed under fallen trees, and waited in the mud for the bomb to go off. Fifteen minutes passed, twenty, then twenty-five. Schultz began casting doubtful looks at Hooten.

"How long did you set that fuse for, Sergeant?"

"Fifteen minutes, Sir. It should have gone off by now."

"We're going to have to check it. Wait five minutes and then take a team to have a look."

"Yes, Sir."

Hooten looked crestfallen. He wasn't happy about the risk of returning to that bomb. When those five minutes were through, he reluctantly left the safety of our streambed. Hobson was resting with his back against the earth bank, a radio handset pressed to his ear. He was interested in what Hooten reported to the lieutenant.

"You ain't gonna believe this. Hooten's squad found Ho Chi Minh prints leading up to the bomb. Some gook stole the C-4."

Hooten set a short fuse this time. His men scrambled down the bank seconds before the bomb exploded with a great roar. After the usual rain of debris was finished, we went back to the hill. No trace was found of the man who had stolen our plastique.

Lieutenant Sutliff is going home in a few days and he wants me to practice directing guns from the air. The Blues need an FO on the ground, so on the next mission, I'm to find a tall mountain and pretend it's a chopper. We have already talked about it a couple of times. That doesn't matter to me right now. I'm stoned out of my mind.

I've smoked grass once before and don't like the way it causes me to lose control. That time I watched moonlight reflecting off the new German razor wire and thought Viet Cong soldiers were staring at me. Martin has been bugging me for weeks to smoke some grass with him, and here I am again. He's my friend, so I'm doing it. The smoke hurt my lungs, but now I only feel the bitter taste in my throat.

A platoon is under attack near a bridge to the west. I never realized how pretty flashing helicopter lights are at night. Explosions are like sparkle-flowers; miniguns make fantastic red streaks through the air that splash back toward heaven. Wow! What a light show!

The lieutenant wants to brief us again about shooting artillery from the air. He would have to pick this night. As Martin and I walk to his tent, I am airborne already, floating about a foot off the ground. The lieutenant is sure to notice that I'm acting strange. Got to be careful.

The light in his tent is too bright. He's saying something, but it's hard to hear because of the light. "Now, Sergeant Brennan, when you have a target, it's either clear or not clear. . ."

"Not Clear!"

He has a curious look on his face. "Ah, Sergeant Brennan, the target has to be either clear or not clear. . ."

"Not Clear!"

I want to say something intelligent, but it doesn't sound that way, even to me. He has a strange look. He's strange-looking. I've never really seen him before. He's too thin, and his crew cut makes him look like a scarecrow. He ought to get some sun. His pale skin is. . .

"Ah. That's all, Sergeant Brennan."

I want to show him that I have been listening. "Not clear!"

Martin laughs all the way back to our pup tent.

And that's the story of the first and the last time I ever smoked Marijuana.

At dawn we jumped into elephant grass on a mountain's topknot beyond the western wall of the An Lao Valley. Thousands of new punji stakes had been concealed there. Walker, the man who was almost killed by the "dead" NVA in the An Lao, punctured his leg. I caught one, too. I pulled up the pant leg and made mud with spit to stop the bleeding. I didn't request a Purple Heart, but was later given one anyway. A grunt platoon from the 12th Cavalry landed after us; two of their men were evacuated with punji wounds. The two platoons separated to search the mountain.

Blue reached a large clearing underneath the hardwood canopy and found the remnants of a feast in months gone by. The bones of dozens of pig lay in a jumble where men had tossed them after gnawing away the meat. Limb bones had been broken open for their marrow. A large unit had dined in this box seat above the valley. Perhaps they had been watching us that day.

I picked one of the few more or less intact parts of An Lao Village in the war zone below, and called down white phosphorous shells on the straw huts. The whole area was soon on fire. Flames spread to coconut groves beyond the village as we added our C-ration cans to the bone pile. Meanwhile, the 12th Cavalry was burning a big hamlet under the canopy; air pockets in the bamboo struts popped like rifle shots. Smoke drifted through the tree tops overhead, and occasional licks of flame flashed through the jungle growth. Fire above and fire below.

When the break was over, Lieutenant Schultz sent Hobson's squad down an overgrown stream. I tagged along. The point cut a path through a maze of 'wait-a-minute" vines, thickets of bushes with inch-long thorns, and giant spider webs. We made our way from boulder to slick boulder, clinging to thick creepers to keep balance. The foliage was so thick and dense that there was almost no light. Then Hobson received a radio message from Schultz.

"Blues are at a small NVA camp. Has a hooch with a guy in a coffin. They're waiting for us up there. Schultz says go down another fifty meters, and if we don't find anything, join up with them."

We climbed further down the streambed. A single shot. Silence for a moment, another shot, then many rifles fired. Bullets smacked into the tree tops high above us. Hobson grabbed his radioman's handset and listened.

'Schultz wants us back there on the double! Platoon from the Twelfth Cav is pinned down. Two men hit!"

I had been the last man in file; now I was the first. On the double became ten minutes of agonizing climbing. We found the rest of the Blues at the bottom of a big clearing. Soldiers from the 12th Cavalry platoon crouched behind boulders farther up, firing at trees higher on the mountain. Random bullets were striking around us as Schultz ran over to Hobson in a crouch.

"They were crossing that clearing. The first shot killed the lieutenant. The second one got a machine gunner through the eye. We're going up to those rocks." He turned to the rest of us and raised his voice. "Everybody keeps his head down and runs 'till we get there!"

We covered the distance in one ragged rush. I rolled behind a boulder and called the artillery lieutenant. "Warbler Three-One. Three-One Mike. Over."

"This is Warbler Three-One. The only thing in range is one-five-five. How does it look down there? Over."

"This is Three-One Mike. Negative on the one-five-five. I say again, negative on the one-five-five. We're in too close for anything but Willy Peterous. Over."

"Warbler Three-One. Roger that. Will adjust from here. Out."

White phosphorous shells exploded in the trees upslope. They might scare the NVA, but the chemical shells wouldn't hurt anyone in those thick woods unless one landed on his head. They did, however, make excellent marking rounds. Jets circled far above the mountain, but we were in too close for bombs. The Phantoms used the phosphorous smoke to mark their target and screamed over the clearing with flames belching from their noses, followed by ragged roars that sounded like the fabric of the sky was being ripped apart. Trees lit up like strings of giant firecrackers. Two jets made two passes each.

After a few inaccurate parting shots from the snipers, the clearing grew silent. Our slicks clattered in to extract the 12th Cavalry platoon. The loss of their lieutenant and a machine gunner had so unnerved the grunts that they shoved and fought each other for seats. The slicks returned for us a short time later, and we watched from above as the first bomb hit the trees. The 12th Cavalry soldiers' fear had infected us as well. The Blue platoon that returned to Bong Son that evening was silent and shaken.

That fight had been the last straw for Walker. He was sure he would be killed if he stayed with the Blues; he wanted to become a door gunner. A gunner with the gunships, Bates, was sure that the Blue platoon was the safest place to be. They went to see our commander the next day, and soon, Walker was a door gunner and Bates was a Blue. The day after the switch, we were scrambled to secure as crashed chopper whose engine had flamed out over the Fish Hook area north of the An Lao Valley. Walker's gunship was down.

Four seriously injured crewmen were pulled out of the wreckage. No one was sure which of the two gunners was Walker. A new sergeant named Paxton rigged the wreckage with demolition charges. The lift pilots took us out of there and pulled into a tight orbit until the gunship disintegrated in a cloud of black smoke. Bates shook his head with relief. He had been right about the Blues after all.

On another day, the sun was brutally hot. Blue had been following a hard trail through barren foothills, past blasted fortifications, bomb craters, and graves in the bottom of bomb craters, when Paxton took two prisoners. They stood together, a young boy and a girl, in the mouth of a cave. Paxton reported to Schultz.

"I was walking up the trail and saw the cave. Next thing I know, the kids are handing me these grenades." He pulled an American and a Chinese grenade from a cargo pocket. "I almost shot them."

Minh questioned the children and turned to Schultz. "They say they brother and sister. Both sixteen year. They medics for NVA, but have not see unit for weeks. All they leave them to fight with grenades. They say killing bad."

Schultz accepted their story. We all felt sorry for them. "Okay. Let's get them back to the valley so a chopper can pick them up."

Hobson's squad guarded the prisoners and brought up the rear as we headed for the valley floor. A short distance down the trail from the cave, Hobson found a wide, bloody leaf attached to a string. He timidly lifted the leaf by its edge and looked at the young girl. She blushed and hung her head.

Hobson dropped the leaf and wiped his fingers on his trousers. "Ha!" says he. "I wondered how they handled that."

The next day we were in high mountains on the western wall of the An Lao Valley when someone emptied an AK-47 magazine downhill at us. Rocket-firing gunships responded almost instantly. Either the rockets or the NVA started a forest fire the roared downhill. As we ran for our lives down mountain trails, fires crackling all around us, I passed a wrecked, decaying bunker. Inside was a delicately painted, chipped China teacup sitting upright in the mud. That treasure seemed as natural in the mud as it would have been on the altar of a Vietnamese family shrine. I am holding that beautiful teacup now, many years after it found me.

Blue had walked since dawn under a burning sun. One last hillside to search and we could go home. Lieutenant Schultz sent Hobson's exhausted squad to make a patrol up a rocky slope. They were back within five minutes, staggering under the weight of a wounded North Vietnamese on a U.S. Army stretcher. Hooten was the last man in the file.

"Where'd he come from Hooten?"

"He was in a cave, Sir, on this stretcher. He's hurt bad. I think he's been hit by artillery."

"Okay," said Schultz. "Have Claw patch him up. Then we can get out of here."

Clack-Clack-Clack! Bullets careened off the rocks in front of us. The platoon was in an open field without cover, but there was a hedgerow behind us. We had been too tired to walk back to the hedgerow before; now we ran back with bullets kicking up grass at our heels. The wounded NVA was abandoned on his stretcher at the base of hill. What followed was like a scene from a grade-B Western. The bad boys were in the rocks; the good guys were down below; everyone was shooting like crazy and no one was getting hurt.

Games can't last forever. It was getting dark and something had to be done before we spent the night in that damned valley. Gunships made a series of minigun runs on the rocks, roaring by a few feet above us. Hot minigun shell casings burned the necks of several Blues. The bad guys tried to shoot down the helicopters, which got their attention away from us.

Schultz shouted to Hobson, "We need a prisoner! Can you get that Charlie up there?"

Hobson stared back through bloodshot eyes. "Why should we risk it? He's the one who got us into this mess!"

Schultz's temper was also short. "Sergeant, I said we need a prisoner! Make an attempt to get him!"

Hobson didn't look at Schultz when he answered. "Okay, Sir. Let's go, Gould!"

We covered them as they ran forward in a crouch, firing long bursts at the hillside. They came running back, jumped the hedgerow, and landed squarely on the backs of two Blues. Groans and curses. Hobson and Gould were panting like dogs in August.

Gould winked at me and carefully avoided eye contact with Schultz as he said, "Gook's dead, Sir. Sorry 'bout that."

The slicks picked us from behind the hedgerow, one load at a time. One of our lift birds had a mechanical problem that day and was grounded at Bong Son, so three slicks were available for pick-up. As a result, the final slick out of there held two pilots, a crew chief, and ten Blues, grossly exceeding its maximum load. Our bird barely made it off the ground, struggling, blades grabbing for air, and flew at tree top level down the valley. All of us held our breath until we landed.

Behind us, an Air Force spotter plane floated down in the twilight, waiting to unleash its phosphorous rockets and bring in its Phantoms. The long day was over.

I cleaned my rifle and reloaded bullets that evening while Martin sketched a scene in chalk by candlelight. I asked him how many magazines he had fired that afternoon.

"One round, Sarge."

"One round? You've got to be joking. Why didn't you shoot more?"

"My foot hurt, Sarge." You can't argue with logic like that. He had fired that one round to be sure his rifle would not jam.

Gould left for his small town in the Midwest the next morning. Other soldiers had become old men almost overnight in Vietnam, but Gould had thrived on war. He looked younger and more innocent the day he left than he did when I first met him.

One of Gould's last acts was the most perverse. Female villagers had been imported from the Bong Son Plains to harvest what was left of the An Lao's rice crop. As the lift birds passed over the harvesters, our door gunners opened up at the LZ. Gould was manning a door gun and firing off-target. That night he boasted that he "bagged" two VC off the books. We were skeptical because he was, after all, a braggart. A day or so after Gould left, Martin found a small article in the *Stars and Stripes* newspaper about two female volunteers who had been machine gunned by the VC in the An Lao Valley as they were harvesting rice. We knew better.

———————

My leave replacement arrived two days later. Now I could go home for sure. Walmsley was a chubby fellow who had volunteered to become an FO sergeant. He looked excited as he walked toward my tent, smiling from ear to ear. He'd lose that fat soon enough.

A big wave. "Hi, Brennan. I can't wait to get started. What's the Blues like? I've heard so much about them."

He was fresh blood. In a month he would be changed forever. "It's hard to explain. We'll be going on a mission later. Why don't you come with us" –you silly bastard- "and see for yourself?"

"That sounds great! I've been trying to get an F.O. slot for months now. Had to extend to get a chance."

So the fools were waiting in line. "The grass is always greener. You might wish you'd gone home."

I would never have followed that advice. The daily rush of adrenaline was becoming an addiction, threatening to overwhelm the historical and patriotic ideals that landed me there in the first place.

Walmsley shook his head and laughed. "Not a chance. Don't be selfish. F.O. experience looks good on promotion boards back in the States." Martin stared long and hard at Walmsley. They were going to love each other.

Blue scrambled for a mission in the mountains a few minutes later. I was on point, trying to impress Walmsley. He had sprained his ankle on the jump and limped badly. "Please, God," I prayed. "Keep him going until tomorrow."

I prowled to the far side of a small NVA camp just in time to see a man's leg disappear through the ceiling of a cave. I motioned for my back-up, a new man nicknamed Tennessee, to get down. I planned for us to remain in a squat because the Blues on an elevated trail behind us had a clearer field of fire. Tennessee was a brave fellow. He ignored my hand gestures and stood up. I played catch-up and stood.

A kid, who looked like he should have been in junior high school, was standing about twenty feet away on top of the cave. He had started firing down at Tennessee when he saw me pop up, and emptied a thirty-round AK-47 magazine in an arc. Both of us fired and hit him, but Tennessee fired last. Tennessee to my right rear was wounded. A bullet had gone dead center through a big rebel flag sketched on the front of his helmet, parting his hair above the forehead. He wiped away a trickle of blood and grinned. A one-inch sapling about two feet to my left rear was bullet-broken.

I attribute our luck to the difficulty of controlling an AK-47 on full automatic.

Martin and I found our enemy among the boulders in a pool of blood. He was armed with a shiny new Russian AK. The fellow had two chest wounds and a broken right arm, but the soldiers only stared down at him. I wanted to know why.

"Why don't you give the kid a hand? He's hurt pretty bad."

"Hell, no! He wounded Tennessee," said one.

"Let the motherfucker die. He wouldn't patch us up if we was hit," said another.

I wanted to change the mood. "Look. Tennessee has probably hurt himself worse shaving." They still wouldn't move.

Now John was beside me. "Come on, Matt. We can handle it."

Doc Claw joined us as we started to bandage the wounds. There had been a lot of men in this camp, but they had left an almost-child as a rear guard. It didn't seem fair to me.

A big pile of captured packs and supplies made a nice bonfire. The wounded boy was fascinated by the leaping flames and raised himself on his good elbow for a better view. The artillery lieutenant wanted to fire some shells above us, where the other NVA had fled, and would check his range with a red smoke marking round. Whoosh! The steel smoke canisters crashed through the tree limbs above us and ricocheted around the boulders. Blues scattered in all directions. I called a ceasefire as the camp filled with red smoke.

The wounded boy laughed, shaking all over with drug-induced happiness. He thought the burning equipment, the red smoke, and the ducking soldiers were hilarious. His glazed-over eyes danced.

The boy needed quick medical help, and the gunships found a clearing where one of them could land and take him away. A squad, every man a new arrival, carried him away on a stretcher. They returned after a few minutes. Schultz was curious.

"Did you evacuate him already, Sergeant?"

"Sorry, Sir. He died on the way to the LZ."

I wanted that boy to live. Back at Bong Son, I began packing a travel kit for the trip home. Martin was beside me when Walmsley limped over to join us. "Hey, Brennan. Know the gook you patched up this morning?"

Of course I knew him. "Yeah."

"Well, those guys in Paxton's squad held his head downhill until he choked on his own blood. They say it's because he wounded Tennessee."

I wanted to scream. Those replacements hadn't been in Vietnam long enough to hate that kid in the hills, and most of them probably didn't know Tennessee. He was just their excuse. It wasn't the experience of war that made them cruel, but rather, something in their training.

"Now you know what you got yourself into, Walmsley."

He didn't know. "Well, that's what we're here for."

Martin exploded. "Aw, shit! Do you have to leave, Matt?"

Walmsley jumped. He didn't even know why John was upset. Tomorrow night those two lovebirds would be crowded together in a six-by-seven-foot tent. That was my last official mission with Brave Fighter Blues.

When this memoir was written in 1974, I edited Tennessee out of the shootout. I thought my reason at the time, anger over the death of that Vietnamese kid, was legitimate. It wasn't.

It's such a good feeling to walk through the gates of Sin City again. So many months have passed. The walled compound is the brothel complex the cavalry division built for its soldiers. It has caused a lot of protest in America, but we are grateful. The girls are clean. Army doctors examine them and give shots every week. The bars have good beer and American music, and the madams treat even smelly infantrymen with respect. Hell, the French took their whores with them in vans.

There is an all-white bar that caters mainly to Southerners and an all-black bar for the other group. The rest of the bars are integrated and have such charming names as the An Khe Star Bar and the Lido. The girls represent all the stocks of Indochina. One woman might be the girl next door. Her father was French, and the Vietnamese of her mother does not show through. Another girl might be from the ghetto. Her father was a Senegalese soldier in the French Army. She wears her hair in an Afro; the black soldiers are very protective of her.

My girl, Mai, is a mixture of Cambodian and Vietnamese. Those people hate each other, but they got together at least once. We spent some days together during my summer in the big bunker, and there was never any talk of money. Mamasan would let Mai "clock out" so we could take naps together. If I had known her under different circumstances, I would be madly in love. She had been my closest friend. When I returned to Camp Radcliff in December for a forward observer course, Mai tried to talk me out of going to the 9th Cavalry. She knew about them and said I would be hurt.

I know that a big shot in An Khe has proposed to Mai, but maybe she has changed her mind. She was having second thoughts the last time we were together. Just to see that beautiful smile one last time. But there is no smile in the doorway. As I turn to leave, Mamasan grabs my arm.

"Sergeant Matt. It's good to see you again."

"Mamasan, where's Mai? The girls won't tell me."

"They don't know you. They're new girls from Qui Nhon. Mai married the major. She lives in a big house in An Khe." A look of compassion crosses her tough face. "Go and see her. She would want to see you, Sergeant Matt."

"No, Mamasan. It's not the same anymore." The soldiers who paid had never mattered, but now she's promised her life to a man, and that's different. I can't sit in the same room with her and just talk; to do anything else would tarnish her vows to her husband.

My lust is gone. I walk down the line of bars and do a stupid thing. Time to have some fun with the big artillery simulator firecracker in my cargo pocket. I toss it through the door of the An Khe Star Bar, and it goes off with an ear-splitting shrick and a loud bang. I didn't know it would make so much noise. A Korean sergeant throws a "Boom-Boom" girl off his lap and tries to hide under a table. Then he sees me standing in the doorway like a big dumb bird and realizes what has just happened. He pulls a big knife from his boot, and I lung for the nearest chair, just as someone tackles me. His buddies are holding both of us down.

I apologize and he accepts, all through the good graces of an English-speaking Korean. He and I sit in that bar for most of the afternoon, drinking and smiling uneasily, trying our best to act like comrades-in-arms. They want me to choose a girl and join in their fun, but all I can think about is Mai. Once the Korean sergeant says something through an evil smile.

"What'd he say?"

"He says you American infantrymen are all crazy."

"Please tell him thanks for the compliment." It's all so stupid. We sit there as friends by a twist of fate while other men are enemies by the same twist.

———◆———

I did walk by Mai's big French colonial home in An Khe later that afternoon, but didn't have the nerve to walk up the steps and knock on her door. I have always wished that I had. She was my first love in every way.

Chapter 8

INDIANA

(June-July, 1967)

That summer's warmth was far better than the chilling days of February. I was home in time for my sister's wedding and wore the uniform. Vietnam veterans were still treated with respect in my hometown in those days. A young man in dress greens stares back from the wedding pictures.

My life in that time felt like I had stepped off a rapidly spinning carousal and couldn't jump back on. I missed the excitement of Vietnam, but did what I could to forget it. I swam, danced, drank beer and little else, and dated five girls. After all, I was a grown man of twenty.

On walks through the fields and woods of Daviess County, I tried to again experience nature without the sweet spice of danger. It was of little use. Everywhere I looked were possible ambush sites or ominous noises. A campsite could be located in that draw. Woodpeckers could be the muffled sounds of machine guns. Those wheat fields on that hillside – how many slicks could land there? There wasn't time to completely forget.

Uncle Art was a scoutmaster. He invited me to a troop meeting and discussion on first aid. I was an Eagle Scout and brought along my first aid handbook. The topics were routine – tourniquets, snake bite, heat exhaustion, drowning, burns, cuts, fractures – until Art asked if I had anything to add. One skill that I felt was vital to any study of injuries, a subject not taught in Boy Scout life-saving and first aid courses, had not been discussed.

"Does anyone know how to treat a sucking chest wound?" Empty faces.

So I walked them through how to treat a friend who has just taken a bullet through the lung, and told those poor kids that the knowledge might be useful someday. I recited what I thought was a funny little joke for them. "A sucking chest wound is nature's way of telling you to slow down."

White, blank-faced stares.

Uncle Art broke the ice by saying, "Well, that's all for this meeting. Let's thank Matt for coming."

The little boys clapped. Years passed before I realized what impact that little speech probably had on them.

Not to be outdone, my Uncle David, a bank president and the family success story, offered to let me make a display of captured equipment in the Peoples' Bank's large front window. I made an easel, covered it with cloth, and used tacks and nails to hang things. I particularly remember two one-dong banknotes of the sort that North Vietnamese soldiers were fond of carrying. They were Viet Minh notes: one from the late 1940s and the other from the early 1950s. Each had a different portrait of Uncle Ho [Ho Chi Minh]. I labeled them "VC Dust," dust being hippie-speak for money in those days.

One day I accompanied an acquaintance, Charlie, on a twenty-mile trip to the recruiting station in Vincennes, Indiana. Charlie was thinking about enlisting in the Army. The recruiting sergeant, an old man of about forty, took one look at the disheveled teenager before him and started telling it straight. There can be danger; you can volunteer for special training, but if the classes are full or your scores aren't high enough, they could put you in the infantry; you might go to Vietnam, etc.

I was more interested in the sergeant's secretary. She was tall and blonde and smiling at me. The last was of great importance. How should I begin?

"Hi."

"Hi." God what a nice smile.

"Ah, do you work here?" She must think that is a dumb question.

"Yeah. I come in on Tuesdays and Thursday to do the typing. Are you thinking of enlisting?"

"No. I'm already in." Maybe I could impress her. "I'm a staff sergeant." [I wasn't]

"Did you ever go over to Vietnam?"

"Yeah. I just got back from eighteen months over there."

"I wondered where you got that deep tan. I figured you might be out working on the railroad." She likes me. I can tell.

"No. It's the tropical sun." That's milking it for all it's worth. "Ah, would you like to do something sometime?"

She was smiling that smile again. "Sure. I'd love to." We went to a drive-in theater that very evening.

I fell head over heels in love. I had a week of leave left, but that passed and then eight more days. I was officially AWOL, but the cavalry division was lenient with people coming back from home leave. I think they were happy that we came back at all. I told Cathy that I was returning to the war and gave her a tiny engagement ring. We had already agreed to save our love for the wedding night, and we promised to be true to each other.

Cathy rode along with my family to the Evansville Airport. It wasn't the same as leaving on a cold morning in March. I was crying by the time the plane left the runway. I had asked for all of it, but I didn't want to go back.

Chapter 9

GROUND RECON

(August-October, 1967)

Delta Troop was the squadron's "rat patrol" unit of three platoons. Each platoon was equipped with a small truck with a mortar team, another small truck with an infantry squad, two jeeps mounting 106mm recoilless rifles, and a commander's jeep and four gun jeeps, all five of which carried a standing gunner manning a machine gun mounted on a steel pedestal. Lots of firepower.

According to Delta Troop veterans I met after the war, the troop's most famous alumnus is Oliver Stone, director of **Platoon** *and* **Born on the Fourth of July**.

As soon as I set down my duffle bag in front of the headquarters clerk's desk at Camp Radcliff, Specialist Abrams informed me that I had a new assignment. The far-from-any-war headquarters battery commander was sending me to Delta Troop. The cover story was that I had survived longer than any other artillery sergeant with the 9th Cavalry, and he wanted me in a safer unit for a rest. I smelled a rat and requested an audience with that joker, but couldn't change his mind. Abrams spilled the beans when I left the commander's office.

'How'd it go?" He asked.

"I still want to return to Charlie Troop," said I.

"The new sergeant likes it there. He wants to stay," replied the smug little prick.

"But I have seniority."

"The captain has made up his mind. Every time you go on leave, your replacement gets wounded. We think you must hang back in fire-fights. Blouin, Walmsley..."

Few times in my life have I been more insulted. I explained that my longevity was the result of not hanging back and often taking the point, and invited Abrams to join us in the field and see for himself. That ended the conversation, but I was still going to Delta Troop.

When I arrived in Bong Son, I left my bag at the Delta Troop pup tent encampment and walked across Charlie Troop's helipad to find Martin. He reluctantly summed up recent events for me.

"Nothing much happened. It always the same shit."

"That's what you said the last time. The clerk at Divarty said Walmsley was hit."

"That was a long time ago. Let's sit in the shade and catch up." Martin limped as we walked toward a tree.

"What's wrong with your foot? Hurt it again?"

"I wish."

Martin was riding with Hobson's squad on July ninth when two lift helicopters, each with a squad of Blues aboard, crashed. He jumped just before his chopper hit the ground and came away with chipped teeth, a busted lip and a back injury. Hobson rode the helicopter down and was seriously hurt. About ten men were injured. Crew Chief Bill Strobel was killed.

The troop had been busy while I was gone. Early, On June twenty-first, there was an engagement near Lake Dam Tra-O, close by where Sergeant Kaneshiro had died. An infantry company from the 5th Cavalry was pinned down by fire from a long, zig-zag trench concealed by hedgerows, and from spider holes dug in front of it. The trench was a transit route from a nearby mountain for NVA troops reinforcing a large force trapped inside a village. A Charlie Troop gunship team was doing recon nearby when the pilots heard distress calls and raced to help.

Gunship pilot Paul Davis, who won a **Silver Star** that day, describes hitting the NVA soldiers moving along that trench "like ducks in a shooting gallery." When Davis could no longer assist, the pilot of the second gunship, Lieutenant Tom Campbell, radioed, "I'm going to make one more pass." Those were his last words. As Campbell's gunship began its minigun run, it was hit by some sort of weapon. The helicopter flipped over, flew upside-down into the ground, and exploded. All four crewmen were killed.

Blue Lift ships were on final landing approach to secure the wreckage of Campbell's gunship when the landing was aborted. The Fifth Cavalry soldiers were already there. Those men suffered heavy casualties while fighting off infantry assaults from three directions. A medic and a rifleman were awarded posthumous **Medals of Honor** for their heroism.

On June twenty-eighth, the cavalry division's 2nd Brigade commander had requested that a Blue platoon investigate reports of enemy activity near Lake Dam Tra-O. A Charlie Troop scout team soon located recent bunker construction in the village of An Hoa. The Blues landed in a nearby rice paddy at 9 a.m., and Lieutenant Schultz organized the platoon into a spearhead formation of three parallel columns. When a machine gun opened fire as the man at the point of the spear prepared to enter the village, the fight was on against a battalion of the 18th NVA Regiment.

Other American units reinforced the Blues in an escalating battle that included an encirclement, air strikes, artillery, tank shelling, and naval gunfire throughout the afternoon and night. American infantry assaults and battlefield sweeps lasted until 4 p.m. the next afternoon. The platoon was under more or less continuous fire (or dodging fragments and debris kicked up by the bombs) throughout most of the affair. Eighty-four North Vietnamese and six American soldiers died.

Schultz described the battle as the largest and most memorable action of his war.

And so it went.

A description of that battle, authored by Staff Historian Steven Schopp and titled, "Battle of Dam Tra-O," *is contained in the document, Unit Historical Report No. 16, from the U.S. Army Military History Institute.*

When I asked my artillery sergeant replacement with Charlie Troop to switch places with me and take the Delta Troop position, he replied, "I like it here. I want to stay." His answer sounded rehearsed.

I returned to Delta Troop in time to watch a convoy of dusty jeeps grind by. A soldier pointed out the artillery lieutenant: a wiry, muscular man, brimming with energy. He was riding in a jeep whose backseat was a jumble of AKs, old American carbines, and Chinese burp guns. I walked over and introduced myself.

"Lieutenant Fortin," he replied. "We made believers out of some dinks in the Tiger Mountains. Haven't seen burp guns since Korea. Why don't we go over to my tent and have a beer?"

Now we could discuss the future over cans of beer. Lieutenant Fortin reached into an aluminum cooler and handed me a cold can of Pabst Blue Ribbon. Everyone in Delta Troop had access to a cooler full of beer on ice.

If Charlie troop had known about it, the squadron would have had a riot on its hands. The Blues were on a strict two beer-or-soda-a-day ration.

Fortin began. "I'm glad to have an experienced recon sergeant again. The other man went home several weeks ago." He beamed proudly. "I was a recon sergeant like you in Korea."

I said, "Glad to be here," and wanted to add, "It's better than Siberia."

"Here's the set-up, Sarge. We have three identical platoons, code-named Red, White, and Blue. There are three artillerymen with the troop – me, you, and the driver. Each of us takes a platoon and acts as the FO."

"Is the driver good at shooting artillery?"

"Yes," he said. "Ted's damned good at it. You'll meet him when he comes in off the road. The way we work it is that you go out on the road for two days and spend the third day on standby in case the air cavalry troops need our help. The standby doesn't go out much, so it's really a free day to write letters, catch up on sleep, or go to town." He winked to emphasize what you could do in town. "You'll be on standby tomorrow so you can get your gear squared away. Any questions?"

I had none.

Ted returned at dusk. He seemed professional and independent. He was a private now, but I had no doubt he would be retiring from the "green machine" in twenty or thirty years. It was written all over him. Ted was a tough city kid who loved danger. He was so different from the John Martin experience that I hoped we could work together without friction. Ted wanted to get some rest so that he would be ready for tomorrow's convoy; Martin would have been finding ways not to go.

I spent as little time as possible with Dusty Delta during the next couple of weeks, riding with the convoys for two days and spending the standby day making landings with Charlie Troop Blues. The troop was operating in a high, nearly treeless river valley called the Song Re. The NVA used it as a highway south into the An Lao Valley and east toward Duc Pho.

On my first day in the Song Re Valley, we sat on a barren plain below a Special Forces camp on a low hill and waited as gunships, aerial rocket artillery, and jets attacked NVA tent camps set up in open areas near foothills farther north. The replacement FO sergeant didn't exactly appreciate my presence, but he kept his distance and limited himself to launching long-range frowns. We spent another day assembling and loading rockets for the gunships.

Things got deadlier as the choppers hunted for enemy camps in the surrounding mountains. Heavy machine guns ringed the foothills around the valley and choppers started going down. One of those killed in a crash was artillery lieutenant Honorio Fidel, Sutliff's replacement. Martin had developed a close friendship with the man, and Fidel's death deeply wounded him.

The fourth day with Charlie Troop was spent in scrub-covered hills that were scorched from a brush fire and pitted with new spider holes. We made no contact. I returned to my tent well after dark to find Ted waiting for me.

"Lieutenant Fortin says no more landings with Charlie Blues."

"Why not?"

"We'll be going out every day now. One of the platoons is going to start guarding convoys to the An Lao. Engineers are going to level some villages with bulldozers."

Martin and I were able to visit together only a few times after that.

*Blue Lift pilot and participant Paul Hart wrote a detailed article about Charlie Troop's Campaign in the Song Re Valley for the December 2011 issue of **Vietnam Magazine,** entitled "Rescue in the Song Re Valley." It is well worth reading.*

During this time a fellow called Chunker Charlie pestered Dusty Delta. This guy would wait until everything settled down for the night and fire between two and four 40mm grenades into the camp at random intervals. I was determined to find out where he was shooting from, so one night after a Blam! I grabbed a flashlight, a compass, and a ruler and headed out to find the crater. The idea was to do a shell-rep: find the hole, stick a ruler in it and use the compass to determine what azimuth [direction] the grenade had come from. I used an empty fifty-five-gallon oil drum for cover as I surveyed the tiny hole with a ruler, a compass, and a flashlight. I jotted some numbers on the palm of my hand and stood up.

Blam! A 40mm grenade exploded about one foot from my left boot. I was knocked to the ground, or dived there, I was never sure which. I clicked on the flashlight just long enough to find the oil drum about three feet beyond the most recent crater knocked over and riddled with holes. I was untouched. Chunker Charlie never did cause any casualties, but he came close at least once.

Late one afternoon, we were heading home, driving in the usual bobbing, weaving manner to avoid possible mines and suspicious places on north-south Highway One. I was riding over the right rear tire of the lead gun jeep when the driver saw a trench that had been dug across the highway after we passed that morning. He assured me that the trench was too narrow to stop a jeep. It wasn't.

The front wheels hit square on and next thing I recall was my helmet flying off. I was catapulted through the air and landed on my head and back. I don't remember much else. The hamburger-size hole in my skin over the right shoulder blade was most painful when the medic first cleaned out the road debris, and whenever he changed bandages that had glued themselves to the wound. The hole shrank each day for weeks and then it was only a scar. I didn't miss a day on the road.

I was an FO once again. A Delta patrol would move down a road behind mine-sweeping teams and set up near areas with enemy base camps. The platoon would blast away with its mortar and two recoilless rifles, and

I would bring in the artillery. On some days I would fire four or five hundred shells, leaving mountains smoking by the time the shelling was over. Eight-inch [203mm[shells were especially welcome. They broke huge holes in the canopy and sent rocks and tree trunks twisting through the air on their shock waves. Those barrages struck the An Lao valley and the Tiger Mountains.

On convoys to the north, we would park the jeeps and trucks on bluffs overlooking the South China Sea and swim naked with laughing Vietnamese children. The Army didn't issue bathing suits, and underwear rotted and caused sores in the tropical heat and humidity. In other words, we didn't wear underwear.

Danger lurked around those beautiful beaches. The engineers would build a sturdy wooden railroad bridge beside the road and complete it every third day. On the fourth morning, the bridge was always burning, sending clouds of dense creosote smoke into the air. The engineers would curse their bad luck and start over. It was almost a game. The engineers did their work and the Viet Cong did theirs.

We never parked our vehicles twice in the same place. A platoon started to do that one day, and a sharp platoon sergeant grabbed a metal detector on a hunch. Yesterday's picnic site was infested with mines and booby-traps. We got out of there fast.

Overlooking one stretch of beach was a three-hundred-foot hill that looked like a hastily dumped collection of giants' rusty brown play blocks. No one wanted to climb it in the shimmering heat, and besides, an American platoon had lived there for some weeks after Delta Troop began guarding convoys north. One evening after we returned to Bong Son, Alpha Troop scouts spotted men running for cover. Their Blues killed four NVA in a twilight battle among outcroppings on the peak. It had been an observation post.

Eighty brave American men died on September sixth, 1967. I knew two of them.

Lieutenant Wheat was a big fellow with red hair, so 'Red" would have been a natural nickname, but he was called Red because he led Delta Troop's Red platoon. We had become close on long road patrols where he enjoyed watching my artillery pyrotechnics. He would sometimes ignore our rotation and request me as his platoon's FO for a day. Red had griped for months about not being able to lead a Blue platoon, and one hot day in early September, his prayers were answered. He was told to pack his bags and leave immediately for Bravo Troop. Red was gone within fifteen minutes. I don't think he ever realized how much he was missed by the soldiers of Delta Troop.

I didn't expect to see him again, but he came visiting a few nights later. "How do you like your new troop?" I asked.

"They're great! Just great! I've never been happier. I've got a tough bunch of boys, and do they ever love to fight." Red was excited by Bravo Troop's latest toy. "Some of the gunships have got police sirens, see. The pilots turn them on when they make rocket runs and it drives the gooks crazy. They run around like chickens with their heads cut off. Then" –he drew his finger across his throat- "Blamo, baby!"

He left after a while, saying he had to get away from the place that had disappointed him so. The next day or the day after, he was riding with Blue platoon headquarters when a heavy hog crashed and caught fire. Wheat was helping extract the injured crewmen when the remaining rockets and aviation fuel exploded. At least three men were killed and others seriously wounded. Pryor Wheat would have been a superb Blue platoon leader. He will always be missed.

The other friend was Walt Phillips, a cheerful, long, and lanky mortar team leader. The sky was never dark when Walt was around, and for that reason, I liked riding with his crew on convoys. During a night attack at Bong Son, a mortar bomb landed in his mortar pit, killing Walt and seriously wounding the other three crew members. I was told at the time that all four of them were dead. When I stood that night in a steady drizzle inside their bloody, damaged pit, all memories of them disappeared from my mind. Erased in an instant and gone for years.

———————

On the morning of September seventh, as we patrolled past destroyed homes in Bong Son Village, Ted remarked, "Poor damn people. This shit didn't even have to happen."

"Yeah. It's a shame," I replied, "but the gooks attacked through the village."

He shook his head. "No. That's not what I mean. The Arvin police caught two NVA scouts selling Cokes to GIs a couple of days ago. They were sitting by the main gate. Guess they didn't make them talk in time."

I remembered seeing those scouts when we returned from a jeep patrol. Muscular men in their late twenties, dressed in tattered khaki and black rags, were crouched beside a wooden crate full of ice and Coca-Cola bottles. I thought it odd that such healthy men of military age should be peddling soft drinks for a living, and blamed the war for their poverty.

There was one casualty during the quiet period that followed. An overweight ROTC lieutenant had joined one of the platoons. We were on foot in the southern An Lao searching an empty village and its crumbling pagoda, and guarding bulldozers as they flattened storehouses and homes, crushed giant clay jars, and uprooted groves of dead, black coconut palms. The village had once been a prosperous settlement of many brick and cement buildings, but it was now overgrown with thick creepers and weeds – abandoned for years. It had been a sweltering morning with heat waves rising from the damp earth. We arrived at an open spot under dead trees and welcomed a break for chow and the chance to cool off.

The new officer had his first C-ration meal brought to him, but there was one extra meal in the ration box. He ran to get it, straight through a field of new, bright white, punji stakes in the inch-high grass. A stake went completely through both sides of his boot above the ankle. So here's this guy with a punji stake protruding from both sides of his right leg, taking horse-straddle steps to avoid hitting the stake against his other boot, moaning and groaning, but still eating. I wonder what he tells people when they ask how he got his Purple Heart.

I finally took a day off-duty. The convoys had been peaceful and I wanted to write Cathy a long letter. An infantry sergeant took my place in the artillery jeep. A blackened, twisted hulk of steel was towed by my tent late that afternoon. I was shocked to realize it was my artillery jeep. The shock was greater when a battered Ted walked toward the tent.

"What happened, Ted?"

"We ran over a mine in that pass south of Duc Pho. The sergeant lost his leg. I think it was command detonated. The gook saw the antennas and thought we were the command jeep for the convoy." (I later learned that the man had suffered a broken femur, but had kept his leg).

Ted's face was cut up and his right arm was starting to turn black. I felt truly guilty for taking time off. "Are you hurt bad?"

"Nothing to lose sleep over. Only a couple of scratches. But you know something? If you had been in that jeep, you'd be missing a leg right now."

Forty-eight years later I learned the man's femur was broken, but doctors saved his leg.

Ted was back on the road in a borrowed jeep the next morning. He didn't want a Purple Heart but he got one.

The convoys to the An Lao ended and standby platoons began going on landings more often. About noon one day, Alpha Troop slicks landed us on a hill within sight of the camp. It just didn't make sense for the enemy to be so far inside a heavily defended zone in broad daylight.

Two bodies sprawled between a rocket crater and the lone bunker on the hill. A machine gunner named Bolton, a small and sad-looking boy whose ragged uniform made him look like a refugee from a poorhouse, lobbed a grenade into the bunker. When the black smoke was gone, he reached inside and tugged out a body. The corpse had a Tokarev pistol on its belt and a small pack strapped to its back.

Pistols were carried by enemy officers or administrators. These were tax collectors. The one with the pistol was an official; the others were enforcers. Bolton found a thick roll of bills in the pack and tried to hide it under his shirt, but the lieutenant grabbed his hand and knocked the roll to the ground. Bolton smoothed his crumbled uniform and glared.

"Come on, Lieutenant. That money can go for a good cause."

"What cause, Bolton?"

"Booze and broads. Have a heart, Sir. It was my kill." The other soldiers looked at the officer and stirred expectantly.

"Sorry, boys. You get paid. The piasters are going to the squadron orphanage." The platoon was picked up, still bitching, minutes later.

Bolton would die a hero's death nineteen months later.

Bong Son base wasn't so safe, after all. On a cloudless day in September, the ARVN police [nicknamed White Mice] and cavalry division MPs made a routine sweep for deserters in the village. Unaware that anything special was happening, an unsuspecting and unarmed Delta Troop soldier walked over to the wire to take a leak. He looked down to see a Vietnamese hiding in the grass underneath the barbed wire. The Delta trooper brought the man in, guarded by the AK-47 he had been lying on. The Viet Cong soldier had been visiting relatives in the village when the sweep began.

That incident reminded me of the day Blue killed, captured, or chased away (I can't recall which) two NVA in the eastern foothills of the An Lao. We captured two French MAT-49 submachine guns. The interesting discovery was a packet of photographs. One photo showed those two posing together on Bong Son's main street with their Mat-49s hanging around their necks.

On another cloudless day in September, the standby platoon I was accompanying was landed by Alpha Troop lift birds beside a small hamlet of about fifteen huts whose roof thatch was gray and brittle with age. A mud dike became a path that passed beneath an arch woven of bamboo, small saplings, and vines, and concealed from the air by overlapping palm fronds.

Vine clotheslines sagged under loads of damp white pajamas; long-handled rice hoes and stubby shovels rested neatly against walls. Displayed somewhere inside each hut was a framed portrait of a kindly-looking Uncle Ho. Several household altars [small memorial tables with sticks of incense and gifts of food for the departed] displayed photographs of smiling young men and one woman posing in French jungle hats: casualties of either the French war or the American war. One family altar featured a recent-model green star canteen. I supposed the photographer hadn't arrived until it was too late. *"Sacrificed for the Revolution"* as the Vietnamese say.

Anything living had disappeared into the nearby jungle or underground. Even the dogs, chickens and pigs were missing. Hidden just below the thatched roof of a large, open-sided building by an earthen courtyard, and stretched between two support poles, was a red banner with yellow lettering. I asked the interpreter to translate.

"Meeting here," he began, meaning the hut was a meeting place. "It say piece of rice is bullet. Piece of rice is blood."

And what did that mean?

"Rice for VC. Grow rice same shoot bullet people enemy." He made a shooting gesture to clarify his point. Grow rice same be soldier. Grow rice same be wounded."

A grain of rice is a bullet. A grain of rice is a drop of blood.

That was a powerful message for a rice farmer and a powerful omen for us. After twelve months of cavalry division campaigning in Binh Dinh Province, and probably thousands of air assaults, openly Viet Cong hamlets were still being found.

The southern An Lao had become so tame that the enemy reverted to a classic guerrilla war of booby-traps and sniping. This didn't help the tank crew killed by a mined 500-pound bomb, but did keep losses at an "acceptable" level. The 9th Cavalry contributed to creating this quiet zone through daylight helicopter patrols and nighttime ambushes. That summer and fall of 1967 was the only time when part of the valley was safe enough to allow small units to operate there and have a reasonable expectation of survival.

Once we were told to search LZ Willy, an abandoned American artillery base at the southern tip of the An lao. Its new cover of shiny, white punji stakes had been discovered by a team of Charlie Troop scout helicopters. We had begun pulling out the stakes when a sergeant, the one who had used a metal detector by the beach, shouted for us to stop until he swept LZ Willy with a metal detector. Fortunately for us, the detector beeped up a booby-trap. A stake had been inserted between the between the striker and primer fuse of a grenade. Follow your instinct; pull the stake out of the ground, and Boom! We swept each stake before pulling (or digging) it out. That slow work put our officer in a foul mood.

I had begun firing big eight-inch shells into a coconut grove below us, walking them south, when six women toting baskets of rice on carrying poles ran from the far end of the grove. The officer shouted for me to drop a shell and "get those bitches." I thought the women might have kept the carrying poles to show that they were noncombatants and refused. He ordered me to give him my radio handset. He would, he said, call the artillery himself. I refused again.

He kicked up a spray of rusty dirt with the toe of his boot and exclaimed, "Well, God Damn! That's a war zone and you know they've been supplying the VC with rice."

"Yes, Sir. I'm still not doing it."

"Well, Hell, F.O.! This war and they're the enemy!"

He sent a patrol to intercept them while giving me the Evil Eye. We captured six incredibly filthy, lice-infested slaves who had been kidnapped from their ARVN husbands near Bong Son and had spent six months digging fortifications and hauling rice. The officer never mentioned the incident again.

I accompanied a Delta Troop ambush on a moonlit night. Our seven-man group was landed near woods and walked west until we found a narrow trail. It was a quiet night. We awoke at dawn and stretched, and then my heart skipped a beat. We had ambushed the mouth of the horseshoe valley where Charlie Blues had been ambushed months before. The raw edges of the B-52 craters had been rounded by rains; grass sprouted from their bottoms and sides. Directly across the valley were gigantic new craters from the 2000-pound shells of the battleship *New Jersey*. A mountainside had collapsed in an avalanche created by the sixteen-inch naval shells: a raw, brown gash surrounded by greenery.

A few nights later, another ambush squad heard splashing sounds coming from a riverbank by a bulldozed village. They directed gunship rockets and artillery shelling at the sounds. Twenty NVA died. The North Vietnamese threw the bodies in the Bong Son River to hide their losses, but they wedged against a dam farther downstream. The ambush squad was never attacked. The tank's crew had been avenged.

We were playing cards in the shade of bunkers when the White Platoon sergeant took off at a run toward four waiting Alpha Troop slicks. "Let's go, White! Alpha Troop's got a downed bird! Everybody to the helipad in five minutes! On the double!"

The slicks took us to a burning village northeast of Bong Son, close to where Rickerson had been killed three months before. Gunships made a series of ripping minigun runs and then we were on the ground, running past blazing huts. A three-man NVA cell ran around the corner of a hut in front of us. Two of them were shot down. The third man dropped his AK and raised his arms in surrender. We began grenading the bunkers that dotted open courtyards.

The platoon sergeant formed us into a sweep line. We began crossing a hedgerow with a square, open pit twenty meters in front of it. A string of machine gun bullets hammered through the bushes. We fired blindly at a hut about forty meters beyond the pit until somebody noticed that the bullets were cutting branches two feet above the ground. The machine gun was firing at an angle.

"It's in the pit! It's in the pit! Fire at the pit!"

Minton took a fragmentation grenade and ran forward. A burst ripped by him and threw off his aim. The grenade exploded behind the pit. With bullets clacking overhead, he unclipped a white phosphorous grenade from his web belt and crawled closer. A muffled Whump! came from the pit, followed by a geyser of hot white smoke. Bullets in the pit cooked off with popcorn sounds. Minton gave a thumbs-up signal and jumped up.

More bullets from the pit, this time fired from a rifle. Minton was trapped in the open. He looked back at us with a face contorted by fear, and knew he couldn't get back to the hedgerow. He sprayed the lip of the pit and heaved another WP grenade with his free hand. Another Whump! and it was over.

Inside the pit were four bodies. They had carried an RPD squad machine gun and two rifles. A fourth man had drums of machine gun bullets in carrying pouches slung over his shoulders. They were horribly burned by the phosphorous. Our soldiers held their noses and fished out the hot weapons with poles torn from the walls of a nearby hut. Through all of this, one smoldering corpse grinned up at us through a charred face.

Minton received a **Silver Star** for his bravery. My reward was some poor verse that haunted me as I stared into the pit.

> *"Death in a pit from phosphorus.*
> *A big grin,*
> *For those who must go on."*

A gunner from the downed Alpha Troop helicopter ran to us from somewhere behind the pit. He still wore a flight helmet and flak jacket and was cradling his machine gun. The White platoon sergeant pulled him to cover behind a hedgerow and questioned him.

"Where's the rest of your crew?"

"A gunship pulled them out as far as I know. Gooks had me pinned and I couldn't make it out."

"Can you tell us what the hell's going on here?"

"All I know is they shot us down with a twelve-seven. This village is supposed to be government controlled, but there's *beaucoup* VC around here. Man! You guys look beautiful!"

It was getting dark as we ran past more burning hooches toward the nearest rice paddy for pickup. We stumbled over a few more NVA bodies on the way out, but I had a complacent feeling about the fight. A bunch of North Vietnamese were already dead; there couldn't be many more around. As the slicks lifted us over the edge of the inferno, a heavy machine gun hammered, sending big tracers arching across the nose of my helicopter. The rounds seemed to come straight at us like red fireballs, then veer off at the last moment and streak away into the black sky.

My complacent feeling disappeared.

I was sitting in the shade of a bunker the next day when Ted walked over with some news. "Hey, Sarge. Know that Alpha Troop chopper you guys went after yesterday?"

"Don't forget that easy."

"I just saw the interrogation report on that prisoner you picked up. There was a battalion of the 2nd VC Regiment in that village. Came down from the Marine area two days ago to attack Bong Son. APCs and infantry are up there now, kicking their asses back north. Their big mistake was shooting at the chopper."

Prisoners and documents were important sources of information. During this time, we received the translation of a document captured in the Crescent. It instructed the NVA to throw away their khaki uniforms and start wearing black pajamas, if the new green uniforms had not arrived.

There began in October a strange series of actions in the Crescent. Alpha and Charlie Troop helicopters caught groups of enemy replacements, all armed with new Russian and Eastern Bloc weapons, making their way to the battered units of the Yellow Star Division. There were turkey shoots as raw troops were surprised in the open or got lost in caves. Hundreds of them died. No one suspected that they were on the way to beef up the Yellow Star for the Tet attacks of early 1968.

Later on, in December, when an entire North Vietnamese regiment assembled for the decisive attack on Bong Son, an Alpha Troop scout helicopter spotted the antennas of its command post. The regiment was surrounded by tracks and infantry, and mostly destroyed.

Binh Dinh ranked forty-ninth out of forty-nine South Vietnamese Provinces in security throughout the war. But the cavalry division's presence made it one of the quietest places during the famous Tet Offensive. While provincial capitals and military bases were buried under rocket and mortar fire, Bong Son was attacked by a couple of long-range recoilless rifle shots from the eastern wall of the An Lao. No one was hurt.

Viet Cong battalions did try to capture the coastal city of Qui Nhon. They jumped the gun and attacked a day before the Tet Offense was scheduled to begin, and apparently failed to take into account the nature of the Korean reaction force. An eyewitness told me that the Viet Cong survivors were lined on the beach and shot.

———————

We passed a cool, spectacular, October day watching white puff-clouds scudding across a cornflower blue sky. The cottony clouds seemed almost close enough to reach down and touch the dark green ridges of the surrounding mountains. It felt like the world was finally at peace, lazily holding its breath as it awaited yet another monsoon season.

After a leisurely training session with Pete, an FO sergeant who was supposed to be Ted's replacement, we returned to camp to find Ted waiting for us. "You're going to Bravo Blues," he said to me. "Sergeant May went home a couple of weeks ago."

I had known David May for eighteen months and trained him in the spring before he went to Bravo Blues. David had become popular with that platoon. His most famous exploit was when the Blues captured an NVA trench and looked deeper into a large village to see something brown moving. A distant assault line of enemy soldiers came into focus. May called in an artillery barrage as they charged, while shouting "Grab your socks and hide your cocks! We got artillery coming in danger close!" That sounds like something David May would do.

I didn't know whether to be happy or afraid about an assignment to Bravo Troop. I wanted to go back to Charlie Blues, and not Bravo Blues. Life in Delta Troop was pretty easy duty, and I had developed a grudging respect for the multiple jobs the troop's soldiers performed.

"Is Bravo Troop still in the An Lao?"

"No. They just went up to Chu Lai to replace the Marines. Lieutenant wants you to pack your gear and catch a chopper back to An Khe first thing tomorrow. Pete's taking your place. I'm here with Delta again."

He waited for a reaction, but I wouldn't give him the pleasure. "All right. Thanks for the news, Ted." Pete looked at me with pity in his eyes. "Hell, Pete, Bravo Troop's not that bad."

By fortunate coincidence, Martin was in An Khe the day I arrived there. He was going home the next morning, so we stayed awake all night, talking about the events of the past year.

"Patterson's on his way to Long Binh Jail," he said. "He was playing cards with a new sergeant, and the sergeant accused him of cheating."

"He always did cheat at cards."

"Yeah. But this was a new dude. It wasn't his place to say. Pat pulled out his forty-five and shot him."

"He's come a long way from the day he tried to play John Wayne in the Soui Ca. This place is like the Old West."

John nodded in silence. "Yeah. Just like the Old West. If somebody crosses you, you shoot him."

"Remember January fourth? I was there a few weeks ago."

"I remember it. I don't ever want to see that valley, not even in my dreams. Remember that big green leech that kept hassling you in the middle of the firefight?"

"That damned leech!" We had a good laugh. "And the Soui Ca. You know? It was such a beautiful place. The mountains were like living poetry."

John had an idea. "Let's propose one last toast to them, Matt." We raised our cans of beer and pretended they were champagne glasses.

"To the Eighteenth NVA Regiment: may they sleep on firm straw pallets tonight, and may their rice rolls be full."

We grew serious toward dawn. We talked about Cathy and the pink panties she had mailed from 11,000 miles away. Martin had found a blond hair trapped in a seam, and the whole Blue platoon had come over to see it. I carried the panties with me on missions for good luck. All of us were obsessed with whether our luck would be good or bad, and almost everyone carried a good luck charm.

John talked about how the last year had affected him. He had wanted a master's degree before, but now factory work would do just as well. Perhaps he would travel the world. He didn't know. He removed from his wrist a copper Montagnard bracelet he had once taken in the An Lao Valley and handed it to me.

"It's the only thing I ever took from a VC. I want you to keep it as a token of friendship."

"Thanks. I'll wear it. I promise that."

When morning came, we climbed a hill to the rocky helipad behind the squadron's buildings. From there a chopper would take John to Pleiku on the first leg of his journey home. I missed him already. He finally broke the silence.

"Matt, you were always the first one on the slicks and the first one off. What's the hurry? Slow down, don't play hero, keep your head down, and all that bullshit. Please come by and eat some of my mother's good cooking when you get back."

"That's a tall order. I'll remember the invitation."

The helicopter's engine emitted its vacuum cleaner whine, and the blades slowly rotated. Martin was smiling as he stepped aboard. I felt empty inside. He shouted something over the noise.

"What?"

"I said, 'I love you, Matt!'"

I couldn't reply, waving instead. As the slick lifted off in a cloud of dust, I felt that my manhood was no longer compromised and said, "I love you, too, my friend."

I still have his bracelet.

PHOTOGRAPH SECTION: 27627574

Alpha Blues, 1966 (U.S. Army)

P/Sgt Wilkerson, Sgt. Lackey, and RTO Cryster on air assault,
Bravo Blues (U.S. Army)

Fryschild under fire with jammed M-16, Bong Son,
Charlie Blues (U.S. Army)

Alpha Blues, 1967 (U.S. Army)

Bravo Blues, 1969 (U.S. Army)

The Author

SSG Kaneshiro, DSC, Charlie Blues, KIA
(Courtesy Gen. S.L.A. Marshall)

Doc Smith (left) recovers gunship crew,
Charlie Blues (Author)

Lt. Eickenberry, Bravo Blues (Catherine Leroy. Time/Life, Inc.)

Sergeant Carter on hawk flight, Bravo Blues
(Catherine Leroy. Time/Life, Inc.)

P/Sgt Samuel, Charlie Blues (Author)

Charlie Blue Landing (U.S. Army)

Lt. Honorio Fidel, FO, Charlie Troop, KIA

Lt. Schultz, Charlie Blues, leads scramble for a downed bird
(U.S. Army)

Minh with captured NVA soldier, Charlie Blues (Author)

Lt. Johnson, Bravo Blues (U.S. Army)

Sgt. David Blouin, FO, Charlie Blues, March sixth, 1967 (Dana Stone, AP)

Mr. Charles Roberts and Author

Lt. Porrazzo, Bravo Blues, KIA (virtualwall.org)

LOH casualty, bamboo jungle (Author)

Lt. Poxon, MOH, Bravo Blues, KIA (Courtesy vvmf.org)

Downed bird, Bravo Troop, Quan Loi
(Photo by Robert Hraban. Courtesy VHPA)

Captured rocket, Quan Loi (Author)

Machine gunner Jim Borsos, Bravo Blues, 1967 (Author)

Chapter 10

FLASHING SABER

Bravo Troop's base at Chu Lai was a far cry from Bong Son with its crude bunkers and razor wire. Blues slept on cots in big squad tents, instead of holes in the ground under pup tent halves. There were jet runways protected by Hawk antiaircraft missile batteries, wooden barracks, asphalt roads, flagpoles, mowed lawns and every form of service the military could provide. Bravo Troop occupied a grassy field with its tents and helicopters. Around that field, rear-echelon soldiers, sailors, airmen, and Marines lived a life scripted in another world.

The troop was identical to Charlie Troop on paper, with a combat strength of ninety-six men (never reached in practice), but the helicopters were arranged differently. Charlie Troop's scout helicopters worked in pairs called white teams; its gunships worked in pairs called red teams. In Bravo Troop, a scout helicopter flew at low level [the low bird] while a gunship covered it from a higher altitude [the high bird]. This was the famous pink team [red + white = pink].

Pink teams were far more effective overall, because, at the time, they had three lethal door gunners [one on the scout ship and two on the gunship flying cover]. But scout pilots and gunners had a high probability of being killed or wounded because of this arrangement. Some did rotate home and most had killed fifty or more enemy soldiers before their tour (or their luck) ran out. The scouts had some genuine heroes, one of whom was Larry Brown. This pilot, with the face of an angel and the balls of an elephant, was shot down seven times, saved many lives among the infantry companies and Blues, and was responsible for the deaths of hundreds of North Vietnamese soldiers over two tours.

A group of gunship door gunners was called the Mag-7. To become a member, a gunner had to kill one hundred enemy soldiers. The group was called the Mag-7 because there were seven founding members. Membership doubled at Chu Lai.

Flashing Saber Blues were used differently from my friends in Charlie Troop. Charlie Blues specialized in long, silent, careful patrols. Capturing prisoners was always a priority. Bravo Troop liked to put its Blues on top of, or beside, the action and let them charge right in. Prisoners were not always a priority.

As a result of their aggressive use, the "old Blues" were tough-as-nails survivors. Scout platoon leader Bert Chole, writing in his memoir, **Flashing Sabers**, describes Bravo Blues this way:

"The Blue platoon was filled with some of the hardest men I had ever encountered in my life. These guys were hard asses who would kill without provocation and without remorse. They had seen too much killing and done too much killing. Death was their constant companion and did not sway them."

A Blue squad leader, Chuck, had been a scout gunner and a gunship door gunner before coming to the Blues, and was nick-named "Red, White and Blue." When Chuck left for discharge, he had been decorated and wounded a number of times, and had killed 173 men over eighteen months.

He would look at me with sad eyes and a hangdog expression and say, "Matt, you know why I extended?"

"Why is that, Chuck?" I always knew what the answer would be.

"Because I like to kill." His obsession really did bother him.

The Blues possessed a few hard core soldiers who had become pro-fessionals at war fighting and survival. Sergeant Bob Lackey, a sinewy

California boy with a large spider tattooed on his right forearm, could usually be found on point, prowling forward like a hard-muscled cat, or at the far end of a sweep line, keeping his distance from everyone else, surviving. There were others like him.

Kenneth Farrell, nicknamed "Hippie Doc," was an ex-member of the Hell's Angels and looked the part. He was a powerfully built man, well over six feet tall. He sported a huge handlebar mustache and a completely shaven head, except for a barbarian topknot. Hippie Doc was a good person and a damned fine medic – that is, if you were fighting on his side. Hut was a huge black machine gunner who wore size thirteen boots and carried an enormous Bowie knife that he kept razor sharp.

Jim Borsos, a tough, wiry, blond California transplant from Canada, carried a machine gun named "The Bad Banana" with its name painted in yellow on the hand guard. He could run with that heavy weapon and its ammo like a leopard chasing an antelope. Two Latino grenadiers called each other Poncho and Cisco after a popular TV series of that era. Poncho was a happy, friendly man of Mexican descent; Cisco was Cuban, fine-featured and more serious. They were deadly accurate with 40mm grenades.

Platoon Sergeant Wilkerson was a hard-driving, muscular man who radiated confidence. Sergeant Willy was idolized by his men, just as Sergeant Samuel had been in Charlie Troop. A blond-haired, blue-eyed lieutenant, Eickenberry, who looked like a junior high school kid, was called Little Boy Blue by the tough survivors in that ungovernable platoon.

Thanh, the interpreter, a skinny, dark-complexioned ex-Viet Cong, was usually in the fight before the Americans could catch up with him. He was the polar opposite of Minh, Charlie Troop's shy, college-educated interpreter. My radioman, Ray, was different from the rest of us. He was a draftee Nebraska Indian, a gentle person, and a frightened one who found solace in drink. He had no friends, perhaps because everyone else was black or brown or white. I could never break through his shell.

My only friend at first was Vic Carter, a draftee squad leader from Louisville. He was tough like the others, but fought mainly to keep his soldiers and himself alive, not because he liked it. I usually rode with Carter's squad on missions, just as I had once ridden with Hobson.

Charlie Troop had its Gould, but this unit had several of them. Four of them had recently been sentenced to twenty years in Leavenworth Prison for the rape-murder of a woman in a village. A night ambush patrol had abducted her from her home. The radioman did not participate and turned them in. He was hustled out of the platoon before the others could kill him. Some of the Blues had obtained his address in the United States and swore that any survivors of the platoon would hunt him down in America. I agreed with what the radioman had done, but I wasn't foolish enough to tell anyone.

A similar incident is described in Daniel Lang's book, **Casualties of War**. *Sadly, that was a similar, but different, war crime in another year.*

Our mission at Chu Lai was to screen for a brigade of the 4th Infantry Division, a First Air Cavalry brigade, and the 196th Light Infantry Brigade. The 4th Infantry Division brigade and Bravo Troop had worked side-by-side since the spring at Turtle Mountain [Duc Pho - formerly Marine base Montezuma] and had fought many battles together.

The terrain in the Hiep Duc and Que Son Valleys where we fought was roughly divided into three parts. A secure zone followed the coast and reached inland past the town of Tam Ky. The soil was poor close to the sea and became richer inland. Next was a contested zone that held fire bases and half-destroyed villages and hamlets. It had been devastated by two years of fighting between our Marines and their enemies. The few people who remained were fiercely hostile toward us. The last area was a "liberated zone," a communist controlled region of rich rice fields and prosperous villages stretching to the mountains.

Marines had operated in the area west of Chu Lai for years. They didn't have our helicopters and had been forced to fight an old-fashioned infantry war with the North Vietnamese too often choosing the ground. Our first recon flights surprised NVA squads and platoons in the open, day after day, in liberated zones that had gone unchallenged for years. They had never fought attacking helicopters like ours and thought that concealment meant lying down and not moving. The toll was high before they started using camouflage again, and the heavy machine guns on the ridges became more practiced. The troop's helicopters began to crash. One of our commanders, Major George Burrow, was shot down thirteen times. Helicopters he piloted were shot-up so many times that we stopped counting. Rescuing the commander became a not-so-funny joke after a while.

Something else was different about Chu Lai. We were fighting 2nd NVA Division troops, and they were not at all like the hunted soldiers of the Yellow Star Division farther south. The 2nd NVA was better armed and had not been bludgeoned by the cavalry division for two years. They were just as ruthless as us. At Chu Lai, we didn't learn to fear the NVA, but they taught us all respect.

The troop flew each morning in a gunship-scout-slick gaggle to an armored base on the edge of the twin valleys. The base was christened LZ Porrazzo after a much-loved Blue platoon leader who had been killed a few weeks before I arrived. Our amazing slick drivers and their assigned Blue squads stood by at LZ Porrazzo while pink teams scoured the ridges and valleys for action.

Artillery support was handled differently in Bravo Troop. There was an airborne artillery lieutenant, but I can't recall any conversations with him. Unlike the close coordination between officer and NCO artillery observers in Charlie and Delta Troops, the ground observer in Bravo Troop was relegated to a purely infantry, extra rifle, role. I still carried maps, radio frequencies, a code book, radio and compass, but was never asked to direct artillery shelling.

Bravo Troop had a reputation to maintain. It had killed nearly five hundred enemy soldiers in the spring while operating out of Turtle Mountain [also called Marine base Montezuma]. In the final analysis, over nine hundred enemy troops would be killed at Chu Lai, and another 305 taken prisoner. You have to think about those numbers to understand why the communists hated the 9th Cavalry so much. In three months, a unit with a combat strength of considerably less than one hundred men eliminated over twelve hundred enemy soldiers from the twin valleys.

In the one-year period from April 1967 to April 1968, Bravo Troop killed over 3000 enemy soldiers.

Chapter 11

ONE KEG OF BEER

(October-January, 1967-1968)

Blue boarded slicks on my second day with the troop and was flown over the flat, rocky countryside west of Chu Lai. I missed the palm trees of the lush Bong Son Plains. Here was an ugly region of stunted trees that resembled dwarf cedars. As the lift birds raced "on the deck" at 110 knots past the southern outskirts of Tam Ky, lines of white dots appeared along the paddy dikes ahead of us. When the slicks reached those dots, the bare, smiling bottoms of hundreds of women, bracing themselves against dikes and squatting in paddy water, greeted us. The slicks flew close and low, hopping over the dikes behind them, wind-whipping shirts, and blowing off straw hats that weren't tied on or held on. Blues on my side of the slick hopped up and down in their seats, waving and shouting. The others leaned over their seats to watch.

"Good morning, morning shitters!" they hollered. "Good morning, morning shitters!"

A few young women waved back. It became a daily routine. I looked forward to seeing those feminine derrieres in the early morning mist.

We didn't remain at LZ Porrazzo for long. Sergeant Willy grabbed his harness and shouted, "Let's go Blue! We got a mission!"

Pilots and infantrymen, all of whom had been lounging in the shade of their assigned slicks, climbed aboard.

The village below us was neat, its rice paddies ready for harvest. Gunships were diving, rocketing a hedgerow and the trees behind it. We jumped into ankle-deep paddies. Three North Vietnamese in green uniforms were dead behind the hedgerow. Three more broke from cover in front of us and charged, hunched over as if running into a headwind. A deafening volley from twenty rifles knocked them down. Random bullets clacked by from deeper inside the village. We belly-crawled among the bodies as a scout helicopter hovered over us. When the gunner fired into the first huts, at least a dozen AKs shot back. Willy listened to a message from the pilots.

"Pull back to the paddies! Pull back! They don't want us in deeper! Pull back!"

The scout gunner was shooting with a continuous chatter, drawing enemy fire as we scooted along the paddy side of the hedgerow. Part of the hedgerow concealed a trench. Carter looked to the side as he rounded a curve near our rice paddy PZ, and saw two NVA below the bushes. He (probably) killed them with a long burst, and lobbed a grenade for effect. We hid behind paddy dikes as the slicks clattered in at rice paddy level to extract us.

That was my introduction to Chu Lai. The NVA garrisoned prosperous villages that were apparently untouched by years of warfare. The vacation with Dusty Delta was really over.

The next day I rode along with Chuck's squad on a one-ship raid. The scouts had cornered a wounded soldier in a stream. The troop commander needed more information about the area and Chuck was under orders to capture the man. As we arrived out of breath at the stream, Hut stepped forward and fired his machine gun in an arc. When the hammering stopped, a man in an unbuttoned black pajama shirt, with a bullet hole below his left collarbone, stood up behind a boulder in the middle of the stream. He raised his hands in surrender. Three rifles and a machine gun fired. The Viet Cong did not seem surprised at what was happening to him. His expression didn't change as he stared straight at us and dropped back into the water with a big splash.

I had never witnessed a summary execution.

When we arrived back at LZ Porrazzo, a scout gunner walked over to the bunker where Chuck's men lounged in the shade. "Why didn't you guys take that gook prisoner?" he said. "We could have greased him"

Hut stood up, stretched to his full height, and laughed harshly. "Man, you know better'n to ask questions like that."

The gunner backed away, afraid of Hut. "What the hell?" he mumbled. "But we do need prisoners once in a while."

———◆———

Thanh brought us a middle-aged Vietnamese woman. She had escaped from a village garrisoned by a North Vietnamese company and our mission was to rescue her family. Pink teams had scouted the area and reported that it looked deserted. Send in Blue.

The troop had a *gung ho* commander, Major Beasley, who loved white phosphorous rockets. This was one of his last missions before going home, and he wanted to do it right. Our objective had been a picture postcard village before gunships made run after run with high explosive and phosphorous rockets, blowing apart huts and setting fire to everything. The attack was brutal, beyond the violence I had known before. Blue landed beside the furnace.

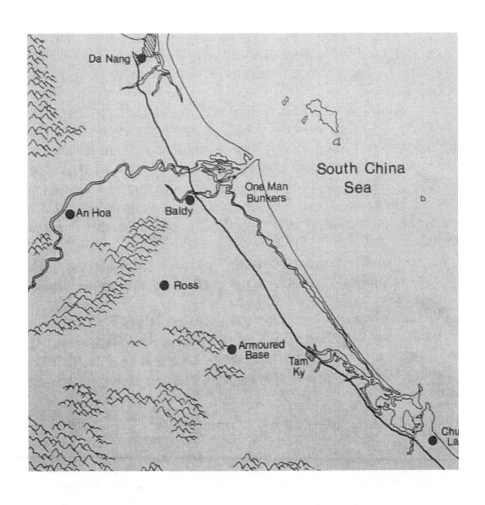

I was walking past a burning haystack when something moved in a bunker in front of me. I hesitated a split-second before firing and an old farmer ran out. The rifleman beside me had seen the whole thing.

"Why didn't you shoot, man?"

"He's a farmer!"

He spat at the farmer and clicked his rifle off safety. "Hell, that's no excuse." This wasn't going to end well.

As if to emphasize the farmer's right to live, the woman ran up to him and grabbed his hands. They embraced, then went together back into the bunker and led out three terrified little boys. Thanh questioned the man about the NVA company we were expecting, and then turned to Willy.

"He says the company is away at another village. They left behind two clerks in this village. They live in a hooch ahead of us."

Willy looked at the pinched faces of the men around him and softly said, "Let's go, Blue. Nobody takes chances."

We left the fires behind us and approached the clerks' home. It looked empty, but a big, rock-walled bunker ran beneath the entire floor. Blues covered the front and back bunker entrances while Hut shouted the usual, brutal words.

"*Lai Day! Lai Day!*"

A green-clad soldier emerged from the front entrance with hands raised in surrender. Hut shoved him out of the way. "Dude's buddy must still be in there. *Lai Day! Lai Day!*"

A soldier emptied his rifle into the rear entrance. The man inside scrambled to a far corner and shot his pistol at nothing. Another long burst through the front entrance, another pistol shot.

"Come out, motherfucker! *Lai Day! Lai Day!*"

A Blue shrugged, ever so coldly, pulled the pin on a grenade, held it for a while, and then underhanded it into the bunker.

After the Boom reverberated off the rock walls, he dragged out a green-clad corpse. He returned a second time and found two pistols (an American .45 and a Chinese Tokarev), a stack of typed papers and carbons, and a portable typewriter in a pea green cardboard carrying case. The typewriter had been sitting on a folding field table similar to ours, except for the lighter shade of green. The farmer wasn't joking when he said they were clerks.

A note: *Bravo's Blues liked to play chicken with hand grenades. The fuse was said to last for six seconds, so standard practice was to hold a grenade for a count of four after the spoon was released. That reaffirmed that the thrower was a tough guy, and gave the target no time to throw back the grenade. Soldiers vied with each other to get as close as possible to that six-second limit. Which fellow had held his grenade the longest was a favorite topic of after-mission bull sessions.*

The prisoner's gaze was shifting from his comrade's body to the open paddy fields, then back to the body. He wanted to run and I hoped that he wasn't stupid enough to try it. Suddenly, a Blue pushed him in the direction of the nearest paddy. The prisoner stumbled and fell. The Blue yanked him to his feet, pointed him at the paddy, and yelled in his ear, "*Di Di!* motherfucker!, *Di Di!*" [*Di Di!* translates as Run! Run!]. He gave the clerk a hard shove and the man ran for his life.

The soldier let him fight his way through water and green rice plants to the middle of the paddy before killing him with a short burst. He turned back to the other impassive faces and laughed, "Got some!"

Behind us, three terrified Vietnamese children clung to their parents' legs while Thanh tried to calm them down.

As the slicks lifted us out of the paddy where the clerk had died, many AKs opened up at a scout helicopter overflying the next village about one hundred meters away. They had been close enough to see the clerk die. Perhaps they were his company.

We were leaving a pleasant region, an Oriental farmer's paradise, that was more prosperous and secure under communist control than the area around Bong Son was under ARVN control. I wondered if the form of government really mattered to those peasant farmers.

———◆———

Tomorrow night we'd make the ABC "Six O'clock News." A red-haired Australian reporter and a Vietnamese cameraman traveled with Lieutenant Eickenberry. The cameraman was dressed like us, while the reporter wore Chino trousers and a neatly pressed safari shirt with lots of pockets. I hoped the enemy wouldn't find that target too tempting to pass up. As the platoon moved out of a rice paddy, a gunship roared overhead, firing rockets at a tree line. I pointed an arm, telling the news team to get down. The photographer snapped a picture.

We ran into a hamlet, making a great show of throwing grenades into wells and empty bunkers. The blast had to just right or they'd turn off the camera and hunt for special effects elsewhere. Some Blues "captured" a couple of scared farmers hiding in a hut. The news people filmed away. Soon the folks back home would see our smiling faces on the boob tube.

I picked up a copy of the *Stars and Stripes* newspaper two days later and saw myself in a blow-up on page one. A mustached soldier with a belt of machine gun ammunition across his chest and Martin's bracelet on his wrist, was shouting and pointing. The caption read, *The Charge of the Third Brigade. A squad leader of the Third Brigade of the First Cavalry Division leads a charge across a rice paddy near Tam Ky.*

That was me telling the newsmen to take cover. My parents sent the picture from our hometown newspaper along with others showing us "fighting in a Viet Cong village" as we lobbed grenades into wells and empty bunkers, and "capturing Viet Cong" as the farmers were led through the doorway of a hut. Other folks received the same pictures from their families.

We also made the evening news. The platoon had been in the hamlet for a reason. Door gunners had shot four North Vietnamese after they left through the rear entrance of an old woman's home. Blue collected weapons and equipment and set fire to her hut. People in America had seen a wailing old woman standing beside her burning home, (the only hut that was torched) but no bodies or weapons. It's possible that the newsmen were unaware of them; it's also possible that someone edited out the footage. The Army was flooded with letters of protest. We were called villains.

About a week after the hamlet incident, Lieutenant Eickenberry called a platoon meeting. He began, "We've got orders from higher up that there will be no more burning of hooches in populated areas. Is that understood?" His answer was a chorus of hoots and laughs. "What this really means is watch what you do when there's newsmen around. Our CO got his ass chewed because we burned that gook's hut."

More cat calls, throat-clearing, and grunts. Someone in the back of the group said softly, "Little Boy Blue, come blow my horn."

That poor, befuddled lieutenant badly wanted to be accepted as part of this platoon, but he was battling with the legacy of the sainted Lieutenant Porrozzo, and the attitudes of men who no longer respected much of anything, particularly higher authority. Eickenberry quickly developed a hearing problem. "What?" A long moment of embarrassed silence, then, "That's all I have. Dismissed."

We swept on-line through a prosperous village in the liberated zone. Several Viet Cong had been killed by a scout gunner, one of whom was shooting from an underwater platform in a well. He would pop up to fire after the helicopter passed overhead, and duck under water as the chopper came around and hovered back over. The scout gunner killed him by dropping a grenade into the well.

As we walked in a sweep line through a grove of coconut trees beside a courtyard, a Vietnamese ran at us, waving a .45 automatic pistol and shouting. He fired a shot and ran into a sturdy home with a brick veranda and a stone-paved courtyard. Hut emptied two entire belts of machine gun ammunition into the home. A wounded man emerged, dragging himself across the courtyard, leaving a glistening trail of blood in his wake. He had been shot through both legs. Thanh knelt beside him and conducted a brief conversation in Vietnamese.

"Are you a Viet Cong?"

"Yes, traitor!"

Thanh drew his pistol and shot the man through the left temple.

Another squad discovered a wounded Viet Cong lying on his back in the grass a few meters from the courtyard. He threw out his hands as if to shield himself from bullets. The bullets sent his body jumping along the grass, tearing him to pieces.

"Daisy," a rifleman with an expensive Japanese camera dangling around his neck, wandered past me. "Has anyone got any color film left?" he repeated time and again. "I just shot my last picture."

Always the same reply. "Sorry, man. I'm all out, too."

As we returned through the village, soldiers set fire to the home by the courtyard where Thanh had executed the Viet Cong. I stayed behind after they had gone, numbly watching an old woman wailing beside the body and the flames. The dead man had to be her son.

Green rice shoots waved in the breeze behind her. That one time, I wanted to stay with her, and not return to LZ Porrozzo with those human scorpions.

I gathered a handful of rice from a drying basket and took it to her, holding it out in the palm of my hand. She stared through me and started crying again. Her arms were raised to heaven, calling down the wrath of something in the clouds. I let the rice fall to the ground and ran to find the platoon. The slicks soon took us back to LZ Porrazzo.

Paul from the cavalry press office had come to visit. He was an old friend of this Blue platoon and spent a lot of time, then and now, flying as a gunship door gunner or making landings. At night Paul would tape-record messages to our families and friends and send them to hometown radio stations, using that as his excuse for staying with the troop. Everyone liked him. He was a quiet, polite, scholarly young man with glasses, whose main ambition in life was to become a professional newsman. He looked like everyone's idea of the nice, clean-cut boy next door, the fellow you wanted your sister to marry. There the resemblance ended.

Paul had won the troop's respect by making the most dangerous landings at Duc Pho. One day there, he was gunning a gunship when they slaughtered an enemy squad in a mountain valley. He volunteered to collect weapons, jumped, and almost got his head taken off by a Vietnamese soldier hiding in the bushes. Paul ran the man down, shot him, and captured a British Webley revolver. Paul was never without his prized pistol. It had a big lanyard ring on the butt and broke open at the top for reloading. He was always eager to demonstrate the loading technique and tell the story of how he had acquired it. Everyone in the Blues marveled that such a nice person could be so brave.

Paul and I talked about the An Lao one evening.

"That's one bad valley, Matt. Bravo Blues were always getting in contact there. In some ways, it was worse than Duc Pho. Duc Pho is what made these guys so vicious. I saw them change. The gooks down there were some bad dudes."

"All they talk about is Duc Pho and the An Lao. Charlie Troop lost a lot of good people in the An Lao, too. I hear the Cav was fighting there, even in 1966."

He nodded. "They've always been fighting there, even the French. No one knows how many men have died for that one place. There ought to be a song about it when the war is over."

"We had one in Charlie Troop. It rhymes with the airborne running cadence."

"Bo-diddy, bo-ddidy, really got to go,
Gonna air assault in the old An Lao.

NVA guerrillas runnin' all around,
Firing thirty cal machine guns a close to the ground.

Four choppers into the old LZ,
One goes down, but not the other three."

"That kind of tells the story. You know? Nobody in America will ever hear about the An Lao. It would just be a place with a funny name."

"They all have funny names."

Paul was with us for a heroic helicopter rescue on November ninth.

Our gunships were reconnoitering two villages beyond a pass while the armored unit from LZ Porrazzo advanced line-abreast toward the western edge of the Hiep Duc Valley. Those villages were the tracks' objective. When a 4th Infantry Division company was landed outside the nearest village, at least a battalion of NVA opened fire at them and the gunships.

Meanwhile, we were on the way to that location. The slick pilots flew us over the green wreckage of Marine Seahorse choppers. Soon the brown wreckage of Army helicopters would litter those same paddies. We passed over a staggered line of knocked-out, boxy green, Marine APCs lost in some forgotten battle. A thousand meters ahead were five burning Army APCs that had been hit by recoilless rifles. Tanks, looking like brown beetles, crawled around hedgerows, firing their main guns into what appeared to be clumps of bushes.

The villages had been bombed by B-52s in the past, but were rebuilt and prosperous-looking. Among the huts were incredibly tall coconut palms, looking like a forest of giant telephone poles. North of the second village was Million Dollar Hill, a grassy hill littered with the wreckage of Marine and Army helicopters, and so named because of the expensive machines that had crashed there. The two brown choppers were ours. The NVA must have thought that they were watching an instant replay of an earlier battle with the Marines.

Our four Blue Lift helicopters arrived and orbited away from the battle. Below us, a gunship crew was sheltering with the 4th Infantry Division soldiers who must have thought that they had just landed in the Seventh Circle of Hell. The grunts we could see were kneeling in deep water behind paddy dikes at the base of Million Dollar Hill.

As memory permits, this is what happened next. Two lift birds were involved in the rescue. The first ship banked away from our orbiting formation, landed in a large rice paddy under heavy fire, briefly deployed its squad of Blues, and quickly lifted off with two of the crew members. A second slick banked away and landed in the paddy. The enemy fire below us increased in tempo until it merged into a continuous crackle that sounded like frying bacon. The Blues on board briefly jumped into the paddy and were driven back by heavy fire. The water around that helicopter boiled with waterspouts, but those gutsy pilots held it in position while the crewmen struggled through the water and were pulled on board.

The Blues on my slick, watching from above, shook their heads and exchanged resigned stares. No one expected that helicopter to make it out of the rice paddy, and none of us wanted to be on the next helicopter to land there and pick up the pieces. Thanks to four very brave lift pilots, the rescue was a success.

During the monster firefight at the twin villages, our new troop commander was seriously wounded and evacuated. Another pilot, Major George Burrow, assumed command. Burrow would become a living legend among the soldiers of Bravo Troop.

As we returned to LZ Porrazzo past the tank-recoilless rifle battle, bullets rattled by from a tiny hamlet of three huts. Our two escorting gunships dived at the target and punched off a few rockets. When they hit, a shockwave and a huge black cloud rose from the hamlet, almost knocking the gunships out of the air and slamming our slicks, flying at about one thousand feet of altitude, sideways. When the smoke was gone, only palm tree stumps and raw earth remained. The huts had disappeared. The NVA had been guarding an ammunition dump. The region was pure death.

Back at LZ Porrazzo, the Blues from a rescue ships were pale and nervous. Paul had been with them and was obviously shaken by the experience. As usual, I was curious.

"What happened down there, Paul?"

He sucked in a breath before answering. "The gunship crew was hiding in some bushes and ran to us as soon as we landed. They had been caught in a crossfire between the grunts and the gooks. God! I've never heard so many AKs in my life. You wouldn't have wanted to be there.

"The crew said the grunts were scared to death. They said the rice paddies in their LZ had deep pits with stakes and steel animal traps in the bottom. They couldn't get their wounded out. They were all digging and shooting at the same time. It was a mistake to put them in. We wouldn't have got out of there at all, if some lift pilots didn't have a lot of balls."

A group of us talked with a rescued door gunner later in the afternoon. He was still trembling from the experience.

"We started making a rocket run on this village, and the whole place opened up on us. The chopper in front took hits and went down. Then we started taking hits. We circled back to draw their fire. Our rocket tubes were so full of holes that they couldn't be used, so we went in with door guns and the last of the minigun ammo.

"The whole ship was shaking from hits. I knew I'd never see the end of that run. I just kept shooting at flashes and hoping I was taking a bunch of gooks with me. Then we auto-rotated [disconnected engine and let spinning blades cushion the fall] into that clearing and saw the grunts waving at us. Poor bastards. They're still out there, and a lot of them ain't coming back."

We heard no more about that battle at the time.

Eyewitness Dick Arnold of the 1/35th Infantry Battalion, 4th Infantry Division recalls three infantry companies with armor support fighting a day-long, stalemated battle with a North Vietnamese regiment. Captain James Taylor of the armored squadron won a **Medal of Honor** that day, probably during the battle we observed from overhead.

That was a more even war than the one being waged in Binh Dinh Province. The 9th Cavalry wasn't fighting squads and platoons anymore. Paul left for greener pastures later that same afternoon.

At some point soon thereafter, I can't recall exactly when, Sergeant Wilkerson went home. On his last mission, we retrieved two bodies from an H-13 helicopter that had been shot down from a bunker on a grassy hillside. The craft had exploded and burned: more evil, disgusting work.

As soon as Blue was on the ground, I gave the bunker's location to an artillery battery and requested a smoke marking round. To my amazement, the red smoke canisters actually hit that bunker – the best shot I ever made. There were a few cheers from scattered Blues, and then the pilots called a ceasefire. Willy was told to get the bodies and get out.

That night Bravo Blues gave me one of *their* blue bandanas.

We were doing hawk flights, one-ship raids, on November thirteenth. Single slicks with Blue squads aboard swooped down to kill enemy soldiers and take prisoners throughout the western Que Son Valley. Finding them was easy because North Vietnamese were harvesting the rice fields alongside the farmers: just look for the green uniform among the black and white pajamas. Those lightening raids were pretty easy duty. I was riding with Carter's squad when our crew chief started shouting.

"Chuck's boys just killed three gooks with carbines. Blue will sweep the area." He paused for a moment and then shouted with more urgency. "Six is down! We'll rendezvous with the other birds and go in to secure him! They have a prisoner!"

Major Burrow had flown into a helicopter trap. They had gone in to capture a man in easily seen khaki, standing in the middle of paddy fields and staring at the sky. It was too easy. The NVA was a decoy, and all decoys were volunteers. Knowing nothing about all of this at the moment, we laughed about the troop commander getting shot down once again. The other helicopters arrived, and our gaggle of gunships and slicks raced northwest. Below us was Major Burrow's gunship, sitting up to its belly in rocky paddies between two long villages.

The slicks dropped toward the downed ship, the door gunners opened up, and the world below exploded. Dozens of flashes from both villages; rapid clacking interspersed with the heavier thumping of a 12.7mm machine gun. A man in green ran along the edge of the village I was facing, fired a volley from his AK at my slick, reloaded and fired again. I shot in his direction until he stumbled, either hit or (most likely) diving for cover.

We were ducks in a shooting gallery. A red tracer came through the open door, zipped by my head and disappeared into the roof padding. Invisible bullets punched holes in the ceiling padding. There was so much noise that it was impossible to distinguish individual sounds.

The slicks came in fast beside the Major's gunship and we jumped ten feet into the paddies from the racing machines. The pilots wanted out of there in a hurry. The fall broke a canteen and a grenade loose from my harness; my helmet was lost somewhere in the muddy water. The slicks crossed part of the long village to the south, pursued by the deep thumping of heavy machine guns and the continuous clacking of lesser weapons.

Carter listened to his radio for a moment and told his squad, "Two lift birds just went down!"

One Blue, a tough, redheaded radioman named Jimmy Cryster, had been hit in the air and taken a bullet through his neck. The rest of us formed a circular defense around Major Burrow's crew and their prisoner. That fellow was drugged out of his mind. He had probably been given something to ease the pain should he be shot.

Two NVA broke from cover in the rocks to our east and ran for the north village. Two Blues killed them. Two more NVA ran from behind rocks about one hundred meters to our west. Poncho stepped forward and carefully aimed. The grenade geysered water behind them. Then he said something to Hut. The next grenade was tear gas that landed in front of the running men and stopped them in their tracks. Before they could recover from their surprise, Hut stepped forward and toppled them with long bursts from his machine gun.

Now bullets came at us from every direction, ploughing into paddy dikes, careening off rocks, kicking up waterspouts. We swam in the stinking water and tried to keep our rifles dry. Unlike AK-47s, M-16s didn't like water.

The major told Lieutenant Eickenberry to attack a ninety-meter-long rocky hump, a low ridge running southwest between rice paddies. Poncho, Cisco, and two other grenadiers fired about thirty 40mm grenades into thick brush along the ridge. They exploded out of sight. Four machine gunners stood up in a line and sprayed the ridge. Bravo Blues were amazing.

Major Burrow turned to our lieutenant and said, "Let's move to the high ground."

Soldiers started backing away from the tiny ridge. We hadn't heard a shot from there, but it had to be well defended. Eickenberry was thinking. "Sir," he said, "I'd like to have a squad check the ridge before committing the entire platoon."

Major Burrow saw how afraid we were. "Okay. Get them moving."

Chuck's squad ran into the bushes and was soon pinned down by a hail of bullets. They came scrambling back. The ridge went silent again.

Chuck reported to Major Burrow. "Sir, there's a trench up there! They were firing at us from along it, but we couldn't see the flashes!"

The major grabbed a radio handset. ""We'll have the gunships hit it."

Two gunships roared in parallel to us, sending rockets crashing down the length of the trench. A scout chopper popped over the ridge and crossed the trench at an angle. Major Burrow listened to the scout's report. A heavy machine gun was in place at each end of the trench. Behind it were rock bunkers about every fifteen or twenty meters. One bunker had been cracked open by a rocket, killing two NVA. Assaulting the low ridge with twenty Blues and four gunship crewmen would probably be suicide.

A scout chopper hovered over a pile of boulders to our north. A single shot, then another. The scouts reported that they had a "gook with a pistol" in the rocks. The scout gunner fired his machine gun as the little chopper made a tight circle and headed back to the rocks, going in for the kill. The helicopter hovered there for a moment before a long burst sent pieces of metal and plastic flying off the airframe.

The scouts weaved about one hundred meters down the rice paddy and crashed. A gunship roared in to pick up the two crewmen. It was chased all the way into and out of the paddies by machine guns from both villages. Later, in the twilight, Carter's squad splashed through seventy meters of water to the rocks. Two NVA raced away through the paddies, leaving behind a World War Two .45 caliber grease gun. Carter jabbed a thumb in the direction of the scout helicopter crash.

"Gook was squeezing off rounds from the grease gun to lure in the scout bird. Then he zapped him. Those boys know what they're doing."

The afternoon was a blur as one chopper after another went down. Other ships flew through the incredible racket to rescue the crews. At one point in the battle, the NVA blew up a shot-down lift ship. A gunship killed a demolition crew as it ran toward another one. Pairs of gunships from another unit (or units) circled over the villages, one drawing fire while the other dived on the weapons. Night came.

A twelve-seven fired from a ruined building to the west. Something had to mark it for the gunships. Two of us stood thirty meters apart and slowly fired tracers at the building. The target was where the tracers crossed. The whole thing took less than a minute, but it was one of the longest minutes of my life. We splashed back into cover before bullets sliced the air where we had been standing. Two gunships rocketed the area around the ruined building. No more fire from there.

Ray had the artillery radio. He had refused to jump with the rest of us and had been fortunate to be on the only slick not shot down. Now he sat at LZ Porrazzo with a bunch of shipless crews. Ray had done this to me twice before, and each time had promised it wouldn't happen again. In truth, I could have volunteered my services to Major Burrow, but his rank and fearless reputation intimidated me. I suppose he might have approached me as well. An artillery officer later arrived and shelled the villages throughout the night.

Shortly after it turned dark, there was a Whoosh! from the ridge. Something erupted in the water beside the gunship. The next shell slammed into its side, breaking it apart like a toy. We pressed ourselves further into the mud and water as the gas tank exploded and thousands of rounds of ammunition began cooking off, as if from a giant popcorn machine. The flames turned the rice paddies around us into daylight as Major Burrow radioed an orbiting chopper.

"Saber relay, this is Saber Six. I just had my bird totaled by a recoilless rifle. Over." A pause. "Roger that. Out." He motioned for our lieutenant. "We've got an infantry company that's going to try to break through to us."

A company of grunts from the 1/35th Infantry of the 4th Infantry Division was landed on the far side of the low ridge. We huddled behind the bushes on our side as the chopper burned and bullets from the 4th Infantry's battle whizzed by close overhead. The little ridge erupted in a drumbeat of grenade explosions and crashes. Our platoon sergeant lowered his handset. His expression said that he had no good news.

"Hell. The infantry didn't make it. They got three killed and five wounded trying to take some bunkers." More crashes. "Now they're being hit with mortars."

A lieutenant, a sergeant, and a rifleman were already dead. The North Vietnamese were using us as bait in a bigger trap.

The flames from the gunship fizzled; the firefight at the ridge was dying, and there was almost complete silence for a few minutes. Major Burrow told us that reinforcements were on the way to our paddy. Six slicks from another unit, guiding on squad leaders' flashlights, brought in a platoon from the 4th Infantry Division. The slicks came in low over the ridge, and we scampered away from spinning tail rotors, thirty jumping soldiers, and one artillery lieutenant. The slicks took off due north over the other village. Someone should have warned them. Strings of big tracers stitched the night sky and something ignited in a ball of flame.

The platoon sergeant was listening to his radio once again. "They lost two choppers to twelve-sevens."

As if to finish the thought, a mortar shell whooshed in and drenched a group of us with stinking rice paddy mud and water. It was mostly quiet after that. The 4th Infantry Division grunts spent the night facing north and east and digging. We had stayed below the low ridge, expecting the NVA to come through the bushes at any moment. They never came.

Dawn on November fourteenth. Two years ago today I sat in a Classroom at USMA Prep School while the 7th Cavalry was landing at LZ X-Ray in the Ia Drang Valley. My eyes were clearer then. I was a patriot who didn't want to miss a war and wanted to do his part to stop world communism. Now I live to survive; I live for the close friendships I never knew in high school; I live for the adrenaline; I live to observe and perhaps someday write about this unforgiving place.

Word was passed that we would be extracted by the troop's one remaining slick, covered by our one remaining scout chopper. That was all that was left of Bravo's twenty-five helicopters.

Larry Brown flew his scout ship along the north village, hopping the helicopter over palm trees and thatched roofs, while his gunner poured down a continuous stream of bullets. Then came the blessed thumping of Blue Lift rotor blades as our surviving slick flew on the deck down the rice paddies separating the two villages. The major and his crew, the prisoner, and a few Blues jumped aboard. It spun around and was gone.

A First Air Cavalry slick carrying four crewmen and four staff officers from the 1/35th Infantry -the battalion commander (Lt. Col. Kimmel), a major, a captain, and a lieutenant- flew toward us from the south at about 1500 feet of altitude. A heavy machine gun hammered a short burst from somewhere and the helicopter began spinning like a top. A door gunner was flung from his seat and fell to his death. The helicopter followed a few seconds later, spinning around in circles before it crashed. Eight more men were dead.

I wanted no more fighting that day. If only Martin was there to talk with. Just to see that reassuring face one last time. I turned to Carter.

"You think they'll have us sweep the villages?"

Our eyes acknowledged each other's fear for a fleeting moment. "Naw," he said. "They'll use the grunts. We only have two choppers left. It's too big for us to handle."

"I don't know if it matters. Tomorrow we'll be in another hassle and might all be dead."

He frowned at me. Those were forbidden thoughts, something not talked about. "That could happen," he said, "but you just don't think about it. Cool it. You've been shot at before."

We were the last slickload out of that paddy. I waited that long because I was with Carter. As or slick flew southward, a light machine gun fired from a village across from where the 1/35th staff officers had just been killed. All of us on my side fired back. The NVA gunners missed.

We were later told that one of the units facing Bravo Troop was an antiaircraft battalion.

My first letter home about November thirteenth states that we lost seventeen helicopters over three days. I'm not sure which units were part of that count, but it included our lost choppers from November ninth and thereafter. At the time, I thought that the fight at Million Dollar Hill had happened on November tenth.

A loss to us (the Blues) meant that a helicopter was battle-damaged out of action or shot down. During the November thirteenth-fourteenth engagement, the First Air Cav's 227ᵗʰ Assault Helicopter Battalion lost four helicopters shot down and three others battle-damaged out.

I once wrote that twenty-seven helicopters were lost that day, but that number was obviously an error.

I found Ray sitting with two pilots on top of a bunker on the perimeter of LZ Porrazzo, staring in the general direction of where we had just been. He saw me coming and tried to avoid my eyes.

"Why didn't you jump?"

He looked away. "The choppers were too high. I was afraid of breaking a leg. I'm sorry. It was too high to jump."

"God-dammit! Everybody else jumped. That's the third time it's happened. I'm not going to make any more excuses for you. Take the next chopper back to An Khe and tell them I said you could come back. I won't make an official report. Get a job driving a jeep or something and lay off the booze. Got it?"

He slid off the bunker. "Yes, sergeant. Thanks."

I had to make sure Ray stayed away from the troop, or the Blues would settle his bravery problems for him. "Ray?"

"Huh?"

"Don't come back around Bravo Troop. Don't ever show your face around here again."

He nodded and quickly walked away. I never saw him again. I don't even know how he left LZ Porrazzo.

The platoon was taken back to Chu Lai one load at a time. The day's troubles weren't over. As Carter's squad got off the slick, a Marine MP wearing a red sleeve guard spotted us. He approached us with thumbs hooked over the top his web belt.

"You guys need a shave." He noticed I didn't have a helmet. "Where's your cover, soldier?"

Carter interrupted the lecture. "Look, our tents are right over there. We'll clean up when we get there."

He put up his hand in a "stop" gesture. "That still doesn't tell me why you look like a bunch of tramps. I'll have to report you to your commanding officer."

I don't think he realized how dangerous those men were, or maybe he did. We laughed. He blushed deep red. "Go ahead," said Carter. "The major looks like a tramp right now, too. Man, we haven't slept in a couple of days, and we spent the night in a fuckin' rice paddy. Get off our case, will you?"

The MP's voice was subdued when he asked, "You guys burps?"

"No. We carry all these guns around because we like how they look."

He shuffled his feet as if he wanted to run away and forget he ever saw us. "Sorry. I was in the burps myself for a while. We just don't see many this far back." I wondered if he was baiting us again.

Carter explained. "We're an air rifle platoon. Sort of a special unit."

"Oh." he sheepishly replied, "I didn't know. Have a nice day."

------◆------

The respite from war lasted overnight. Early the next morning we were back at it. The lone slick was outfitted with four machine guns on bungee cords and became the low bird, looping and twisting over caves and slippery black rock formations along the seacoast. The scout helicopter, crewed by Larry Brown and his gunner, flew cover for us as the (not very) high bird. Blues waited in line to man the machine guns on the low bird; I was able to go on two such missions.

Within a few days, Blue was back at LZ Porrazzo, waiting beside new slicks as the troop's begged, borrowed, or repaired gunships and scout helicopters scoured the countryside. An area of good hunting was the South China Sea coast about halfway between Da Nang and Chu Lai. Just south of a base called LZ Baldy was a place variously called "the one-man bunkers," "the sand spit," "No Name Island," or "Cigar Island."

On a reconnaissance flight along that stretch of coast, a pink team spotted a column of North Vietnamese walking south. The scout gunner killed thirteen of them. Major Burrow wanted the Blues to collect weapons and papers, but first he sent another pink team to investigate. The two teams passed each other in midair, one coming back to our base to refuel and the other heading toward the coast. For about five minutes, the sky above the beach was empty. When the second team arrived, dark blood stains in the sand and drag paths into the hedgerows and palm trees were all that remained. If thirteen bodies could disappear that quickly, trouble was waiting down below. Blue was not sent.

———◆———

The rains were heavier each day. In late November, an infantry company captured a directive instructing the NVA not to shoot at choppers with crossed sabers on their noses. The weather, the directive, our losses, their losses, whatever it was, caused poor hunting. The troop had killed about seven hundred enemy soldiers in less than two months, and had probably captured a couple hundred more. Other units had also inflicted heavy losses.

In early December, we were informed that a helicopter with the squadron surgeon aboard was missing in the mountains west of Duc Pho. Speculation was that it had been raining, visibility was poor, and the chopper was flying too low. Some of the old Blues remarked that another squadron surgeon had been killed with Bravo Troop the previous spring in the An Lao Valley.

From that day forward, a pink team was always searching the region for wreckage. This was a considerable logistical effort for Bravo Troop, because Duc Pho was about seventy miles south of Chu Lai, outside of artillery range, and outside the cavalry division's area of operations. Captain Kushner's chopper had just been passing overhead. Duc Pho had been a liberated zone more or less continuously since 1945. The pink teams were there because we took care of our own.

The wreckage was discovered after a few days. Three bodies were found, but Captain Kushner was missing. Pink teams continued their searches while intelligence began receiving reports that the Viet Cong were parading a captured American doctor through the hamlets. That information allowed us to narrow the search area to the vicinity of the sightings.

One morning, a scout helicopter, hovering across a region of bamboo clumps and thorn bushes, discovered a small, almost invisible, hut. A guard stood to either side of the single entrance. Inside was a Caucasian male on a straw pallet. He was clad only in white boxer undershorts and appeared to be sick. The scout gunner shot the two guards and radioed for back-up. Seventy miles to the north, Blue was scrambled.

As we traveled south over several mountain ranges, the first pink team on site ran low on fuel and headed for home. The air above the hut was empty for the few minutes before we arrived. Our gaggle approached a wild region, far from any villages, almost in the foothills of the mountains, and landed in a huge field of brown grass sown with thousands of old punji stakes. It was surrounded on all sides by thorn hedges and bamboo groves, all of which were the same washed-out shade of brown. The few survivors of the Duc Pho campaign the previous spring were visibly worried as they ran across the punji field toward a scout's red marking smoke.

Hut, lopping along beside me on his long legs, said, "Watch your ass, FO. The gooks down here are bad news."

Chuck shouted to his squad, "Be careful! The whole population's underground! They've got spider holes and tunnels under everything!"

We struggled through the thorn bushes and found the hut. To either side of the threshold was a pool of blood and a khaki NVA field pack. The outside walls were splattered with blood; the hut was empty. We stayed there for more than an hour, probing the ground with sticks, kicking anything that might conceal a tunnel entrance, searching for trails. It was no use. The whole place was covered with several inches of rotting bamboo leaves. Any tunnel entrances were well concealed. We were ordered to withdraw.

It was a sad platoon that boarded slicks for the ride back to Chu Lai. We had been so close. The troop had almost rescued someone, we weren't sure whom, but close doesn't count. Our only souvenir was a small, yellow-star-on-red North Vietnamese flag that someone had discovered in a pack.

Blue never returned to Duc Pho. Our truly heroic squadron surgeon, was released five years later in Hanoi.

December fifth had been a quiet, overcast day. We didn't leave the armored base apart from a few local insertions (not air assaults). The helicopter hop I accompanied put four of us and two nervous artillerymen on a flat plain below and within close sight of LZ Porrazzo. We provided security as the artillerymen hurriedly shot azimuths [recorded directions] with an aiming circle [a surveyor's instrument mounted on a tripod]. Our lift bird, circling overhead like a mother hen, descended, flared, scooped us up, and popped us back over the wire.

Later, the pink teams were making a final circuit over the Hiep Duc and Que Son valleys before we could go home. I was in the middle of a fourth game of chess with a lift pilot when they scrambled us. As the slicks lifted over the barbed wire, the crew chief beside me shouted out the mission. "Somebody shot at the major's gunship in the Que Son Valley! Broke the gunner's arm! Major's mad as hell and wants the gook that did it!"

The slicks dropped toward a ridge north of a base called LZ Ross. Gunships rocketed a grassy knoll while Larry Brown's scout ship hovered over its twin, pumping tracers into a jumble of gray boulders. We jumped onto the grassy knoll as the last gunship climbed away from its rocket run. The platoon sergeant pointed to red smoke floating above short trees and boulders on the other knoll.

"They've got bunkers up there! Chuck's squad move toward the hill! Second squad cover them with your machine gun!"

They ran into a depression between the knolls while the machine gun chipped and scared boulders above them. As the first line reached the boulders, we ran to join them. There were four bodies in American camouflage uniforms beside two boulders. I thought for a moment that we were attacking some sort of ARVN reconnaissance unit until two men in green NVA uniforms raised up from a pit under those boulders about five feet to my right. The opening was very narrow and couldn't be seen unless you stood over it. Lackey and Daisy shot them from a distance of about one foot. Lackey had fired point blank into the other man's head. He wiped brains from his face and helmet and cursed.

One of the two dead men had been wearing eyeglasses. I picked them up off the ground, tried them on, and almost lost my balance: bifocals. He was the first enemy soldier I had seen with eyeglasses. He carried a strange pistol of a type we had never encountered.

A body in khakis was lying face down in a short trench leading uphill from the boulders. I stood at the end of the trench and looked down, searching for bullet holes. The body was suddenly pointing an SKS rifle at my stomach. Lackey and Daisy, one on each side of the trench, shot him as they walked by me and didn't even look back. The last I heard, Daisy was still wearing the man's leather star belt.

Chuck sprayed a bush beside the trench that at least three of us had just walked by. A body rolled away. The man was wearing black pajamas and had wrapped himself so tightly around the base of the bush and under its branches, and lain so still, that he was almost invisible. They were very good at that trick. Chuck stopped long enough to remove a leather officer's belt hung with a Chinese artillery compass, a map case, and a holstered Tokarev pistol, and tossed the rig to me.

"Here, Matt. I got an outfit like this a minute ago. Dude moved when they shot his buddy in the trench. This is great!" He meant the killing.

Larry Brown's helicopter was back overhead, hovering slowly along above the line of Blues. Hot cartridge cases rained down. As usual when we were showered with hot cartridge cases, the danger was immediate and very close. Seven more bodies were strewn along a path running about thirty meters from the end of the trench to the top of the knoll. The scouts had been busy. By now we knew to give each body an extra burst, just to be sure.

Our line crested the knoll and moved downhill through more grass, blasting the jungle beyond another saddle with all weapons. Two NVA ran out of the trees and charged our line, firing short bursts from their AKs. They went down quickly.

More AKs flashed from the trees below us to the left, and in front of us where the two NVA had just died. There were fleeting glimpses of roof thatch in both directions. Two gunships made a rocket run to the left. Another gunship hovered overhead like a noisy guardian angel, firing rockets into the jungle to our front. A long and intact thatched roof was blown into the air about ten feet above the trees. It floated there for a moment, burst into bright flames, and settled back into the jungle, trailed by a lazy, glowing rain of sparks and burning straw. That was a beautiful sight in the twilight, almost like a scene from a Walt Disney fairytale.

All firing abruptly ceased for a moment. We were ordered back to the grassy knoll for extraction, and returned in that direction, walking backwards, firing front and left, but enemy fire had ceased.

Souvenirs were everywhere. The boulder knoll was littered with leather map cases, binoculars, American and Chinese compasses and other debris. Some of the officer casualties wore gold rings inscribed with Vietnamese characters, signifying God knows what. Blues slung their rifles and carried captured weapons, map cases, pistol belts, and documents, etc.

We scooped up a grenade launcher and a laminated map that were taken from one of our crashed helicopters at the battle on November thirteenth. The locations of North Vietnamese and American units throughout the area were carefully noted. I looked down at LZ Ross through a pair of Chinese artillery binoculars and could see every tent, bunker and artillery piece in the base. These had to be forward observers planning a rocket and mortar attack on the base.

We hid trophies under our shirts to conceal them from the officers. Half the platoon looked pregnant by the time we lifted off. The Blues stayed awake until early the next morning, counting booty from the "gook FOs." There was an American .45, six Tokarevs, two Makarov pistols, nine leather officer's belts, a wide canvas belt with a big star on its interlocking aluminum buckle, and five brass star belts. We had never seen Makarovs and thought that they were Berettas.

Major Burrow had heard about the trophies by the next evening and ordered all the pistols collected. These Blues had previous bad experiences with officers taking their souvenirs for 'intelligence purposes" and keeping them. There had been a battle at Duc Pho in the spring where some of the Blues had actually played chicken with heavy machine gun crews to pinpoint their locations for the gunships. That aggressiveness was fueled in part by the discovery that the NVA were wearing new types of hats and belts. Souvenirs had been collected from the Blues and not all were returned. Several of the old-timers thought it might happen again.

To be as fair as possible, we had given all the compasses and binoculars, and some of the belts, to the pilots who were really the heroes of that battle.

I kept my belt, but surrendered a pair of Chinese artillery binoculars, a map case, and a compass. When a group of us went to ask Major Burrow to return our pistols, he told us what we had encountered on December fifth.

"First of all, don't worry about the pistols. We needed them to confirm some things. The pistols will be returned. You men did a good job out there two days ago, but if you had turned the pistols in sooner, we might have known what we bagged and could have inserted an infantry company or something.

"We wiped out what we believe was the command post of the Third Regiment, Second NVA Division. The documents and other evidence show that nine of the seventeen kills were officers. Some of them were division staff, including the division's commissar, and its intelligence officer. There was a full colonel, a regimental commander, three majors and four senior captains. Some of the equipment they had was taken from the troop's helicopters on November thirteenth. You men might be interested to know that the highest ranking NVA officer confirmed killed until now was a captain."

We were interested.

I didn't know it at the time, but that raid marked the high point in morale among the Blues. In many ways it was one of the last triumphs of an era and style of warfare that the Army in Vietnam would rarely again experience. That night we went to a beachside club and celebrated by singing their favorite song for hours.

"Glorious, glorious,
One keg of beer for the four of us.
We're happy as can be,
My comrades and me,
For we are members of the In-fan-try!"

We landed on the knoll a few days later. The trench and the pit beneath the boulders had been used as graves. The back of one body in the pit had been partially exposed by recent rains and was swarming with black beetles. A bloated, purple corpse was left unburied, staring up at the sky from the mud of the trail. He had been punished for something. As I stepped over the body, a large black cockroach crawled from the single bullet hole in its forehead. That would have shocked me once. We pulled the corpse down the trail with a rope tied to its ankle in case it was booby-trapped.

The battle on December fifth resulted in the most high-ranking enemy officers killed in a single air-ground action during the entire Vietnam War. To repeat, among the seventeen dead were the commander of the 3rd Regiment, 2nd NVA Division, three other majors, a full colonel [the 2nd NVA Division's commissar], and four senior captains. The casualties included the 2nd NVA Division's intelligence and operations officers, and most of the 3rd Regiment's staff officers.

Less than a month later, on January second, 1968 the Marines at Khe Sanh Combat Base had a similar success. Five NVA officers were killed outside the wire. Accounts of their ranks and positions have varied, but one of them was most probably a regimental commander and two of the others were regimental staff officers.

On the very day we sang our victory song, another event occurred. Three hundred miles to the south, near a solitary mountain called Nui Ba Ra, was the Montagnard village of Dak Son. Two battalions of North Vietnamese soldiers [about six hundred men] killed 252 civilians there, mostly with flamethrowers, and took the survivors hostage. The victims were, after all, only Montagnards.

Our gunships and scouts completed the destruction of the 3rd NVA Regiment's headquarters staff and infantry security on December ninth. The battle began as a request for assistance from a company of the 4th Infantry Division. It became a daylong battle in which troop helicopters killed ninety-nine North Vietnamese. Major Burrow was in the forefront as always.

Infantry swept through the area as our choppers destroyed each successive NVA position. I listened on my artillery radio as a skeptical 4th Infantry Division battalion commander issued orders to his troops. He told them to "See how many dinks are down there and how many are really dead." A group of Blues crowded around the radio and listened, cursing that colonel for his smart-assed remarks. The company commander's first reply came about thirty minutes later.

"They're all dead. We've got bodies everywhere."

As usual, the 4th Infantry Division took credit for the captured weapons. Their colonel ended the afternoon with praise for our gunners and an apology to Major Burrow. The Blues cursed that battalion commander for days thereafter. We didn't want other soldiers doing our work.

For this action, in which his gunship crew destroyed successive enemy strongpoints and ambushes, and suffered repeated battle damage throughout the day, Major Burrow was awarded the **Distinguished Service Cross** *for extraordinary heroism. He should have been given a dozen more.*

———————

Most of us didn't know Stork's real name. He had once been a Blue and was now a gunship gunner. Each night we held after-action bull sessions to brag, joke, and discuss the day's events, looking for things that might have been done better. Stork was always there, listening, laughing, sharing his own stories, and standing on one leg with the other crossed at the knee. He was long-legged anyway, so Stork was a natural nickname. We liked him because he spent so much time liking us.

Stork didn't show up for our pow-wow one rainy evening in December. Vic Carter asked, "Where's Stork?" and none of us knew. We waited for him each night and kept his place by the tent flap vacant. About a week later, another door gunner reported that Stork had been wounded. Still, we kept his place open until well into January while knowing in our hearts that he probably wasn't coming back.

I always wondered what happened to Stork. Forty-five years later I learned that he died of his wounds. Perhaps he knows how very much we missed him.

———◆———

The twin victories made us media stars for a few weeks. "Where's the action?" someone would ask.

"Go out with the Ninth Cav," would be the reply.

Almost every recon flight or Blue landing was accompanied by news people. There were magazine writers, newspaper correspondents and network camera crews. I once watched a news clip of a small gathering of Blues at LZ Porrazzo, singing *Where have all the Flowers Gone?* for the camera. If memory serves, they look skinny, rumpled, and tired.

The greatest honor was when Cathy LeRoy, the French photographer who had taken pictures of the Marines on Hill 881 and later walked into occupied Hue to photograph NVA soldiers, came to visit in late December. She stayed with us for about two weeks, riding with the gunships and landing with the Blues, time enough for each of us to have a favorite Cathy LeRoy story.

Cathy had dropped out of college in France, sold her possessions, and purchased an expensive camera and a ticket to Vietnam. She told me that she never again wanted to lead a quiet, boring life. Cathy liked to brag about the mortar wounds she had received with the Marines and the five pounds (of fragments) she had instantly gained. She wore fatigues like us, wove her hair in pigtails and carried a flask of brandy on her left hip.

She would serve me spiked coffee at LZ Porrazzo while we waited for the first mission of the day.

Once we were waiting for a mission atop a bunker that gave us a beautiful, panoramic, purple-brown-yellow-green view of paddies, small hamlets, bamboo groves and distant mountains. She poured me a shot of whiskey and asked, "How long have you been here, sergeant?"

"Twenty-four months, but I'm going home for good in three months."

"I've been here nineteen months," she said as she fixed me with unblinking eyes. "I know your type in the Army and Marines. You'll come back, and when you do, I'll have more months in country than you."

She was right, but at the time I only wanted to avoid that stare. "No," I mumbled. 'Not me."

On an early January mission, we secured a shot-down Chinook helicopter that had been transporting a cargo of bodies from a big 196th Light Infantry Brigade battle. A conga line of slicks were loaded with body bags and flew away somewhere. In-between helping us carry and load the bags, Cathy snapped a picture of me, sporting new staff sergeant stripes and doing the same.

Fourteen months later an old safe was opened at Bravo Troop's location far to the south. That photograph was inside along with a combat journal from those days. The officer who handed me the glossy blow-up said he had been reading the journal.

"The Blues were really something back then," he remarked.

"Yes, we were."

Cathy LeRoy once wrote that "The Marines are brave, like the French Foreign Legion, but my favorite unit is the First Air Cavalry. They can do anything." I would like to think that she was writing about Bravo Troop.

Cathy LeRoy published photographs of Bravo Troop in the April thirtieth, 1968 edition of Look Magazine. The following month, a *men's magazine,* For Men Only, *published an article on Bravo Troop entitled, "The Deadliest Chopper Squad in the Air. Here Come Burrow's Bastards."*

Oh, well.

———◆———

A little river, running below and to the north of a hilltop base called Baldy, emptied into the sea. The river formed the northern boundary of the island we called the one-man bunkers. Coastal fishing sampans sailed up the river each night and deposited NVA replacements on the south bank. Men sat in tiny bunkers in the sand all day long, apparently waiting for helicopters to fly overhead. The bunkers were almost impossible to locate and destroy, and most of our pilots dreaded flying recon missions over them. Bravo Troop's scouts and gunships saved many lives by taking out those bunkers when infantry units blundered into the middle of them, but no matter how many enemy shooters were found and killed, more would be waiting the next day.

One rainy day in December, Blue was landed on an island in that little river. Five enemy soldiers had been killed by the scouts before we arrived, and Chuck's squad accounted for three more hiding in tall grass. The affair was like a rabbit hunt with beaters. Blues sank sampans along the beach with grenades and then walked toward a large earth bunker in a sweep line that spanned the island. The platoon sergeant motioned for us to approach the bunker with caution.

"Gunbirds took fire from here. Let's see what we've got."

A Blue looked inside one end of the bunker; a burst missed him by inches. He hopped out of the way while two other soldiers rolled grenades into the front and back entrances. Cordite smoke lingered in the humid air, so Chuck donned a gas mask and crawled inside. He dragged out the inevitable bodies – a man and two women in green uniforms. They had carried medical bags, stick grenades, and two rifles, including a captured Marine Corps M-14. The bunker was a protective storehouse for crates of medical supplies; the island itself was some sort of medical facility. That explained why eleven NVA had put up so little resistance to our attack.

Chuck found a badly wounded little girl under a pile of baskets and rags and carried her out into the fresh air and sunshine. She was dressed in a pint-size green uniform and had waist-length black hair. Chuck gently laid her in the grass and pillowed her head with a medical bag. Daisy raised his rifle and took careful aim. Hippie Doc exploded. He grabbed the front of Daisy's shirt and brushed the rifle to one side. Daisy wrestled away, but was careful not to raise the rifle again.

"Come on, Doc," he said. "She ain't gonna make it. I might as well put her out of her misery."

Doc thrust his finger to within an inch of Daisy's nose and growled, "Back off! You touch that girl and you answer to me, baby."

No one in their right mind would mess with Hippie Doc. Daisy walked away with a hangdog expression, without saying another word.

Doc treated the child's grenade wounds and later carried her to a Medevac helicopter. He asked the medics to do everything they could to save her. The way he treated and protected that little girl is one of my most touching memories of a brutal war. The Medevac chopper that took the child away was painted with big red crosses on its sides, belly, and nose, but that didn't stop AKs from firing as it flew southward toward Chu Lai over the one-man bunkers.

A large town stood on the north shore of the river. It was in the Marine area and we had enough on our hands, but a gunship pilot had reported several Viet Cong flags flying inside the place. As we prepared to leave, a jet flew low over the town, heading toward the mountains about twenty miles away. At least one hundred AK's opened up as the jet flashed by and disappeared to the west.

About five minutes later, Carter listened to a transmission on his handset, turned to me with a resigned look, and spoke five words "They shot it down, Matt."

Carter came over to talk that night at Chu Lai. "The little girl Hippie Doc patched up died. The one-man bunkers got her."

"What a shame. Does Doc know?"

"He knows. I saw him crying out on the flight line. He doesn't want anyone to see him. He's taking it real hard."

Doc was going home soon. He had seen enough.

Another day, another landing. We are south of Baldy in an old B-52 strike zone. The gunships were in contact here. Blues run from crater to crater, hunting the people hiding there. It's a strange group. There's an old man, two women, younger men of various ages. They have an even odder assortment of weapons: American carbines, two French bolt-action rifles, two German Mausers, an assortment of grenades. This is the first bunch of pure Viet Cong the platoon has fought at Chu Lai. From experience we know that the people in this area bitterly hate Americans.

The four Vietnamese killed by the gunships carried large sacks of rice fitted with carrying straps. The sacks are stamped with the "Hands Across the Sea" emblem of USAID. The Blues have shot four more as they rose up from craters to shoot or run. After the northerners we have fought in recent months, these people are like amateurs out for a Sunday picnic. It's too easy. Soldiers are checking a few more craters, slitting the bags, scattering rice and stomping it into the mud. Pissing on it.

A figure in black pajamas jumps over the lip of a nearby crater and runs for a distant hedgerow. Carter knocks it down with a burst, walks across, and rolls the body over with the toe of his boot.

"Oh, my God! It's a little girl!"

Beneath her tiny hand is a hand grenade in the mud.

Another mission to the one-man bunkers. A gunship had been shot down and we were sent to guard it. One squad was still there while the rest of us walked ahead of a company of the 4th Infantry Division. They had been in a battle earlier in the day and weren't anxious for another, especially if we were involved. About a dozen NVA, each of them tall, strong, muscular, and well-fed, were being used as pack mules for two or three heavy infantry packs. They stared impassively ahead, never acknowledging our arrival. I have often wondered what type of unit those big men were from.

We entered a sandy hedgerow area. AKs clacked from small huts to the east, toward the sea, and we charged them spraying bullets. I had an M-79 grenade launcher and fired it like a mortar, trying to put some grenades behind the NVA. We were almost to the huts when we looked around to find that we were alone. The 4th Infantry Division company had changed direction to the south. Now I was sure that they didn't like us. A big Chinook helicopter, with our downed gunship slung beneath it, flew over our heads to the south. At least twenty AKs fired; a Chinook crewman dropped a red smoke grenade to mark the location. Our pilots rocketed the area and told us to watch for more one-man bunkers dug into sandy berms beneath coconut palms.

The entire Blue platoon headed south, firing as we walked. Again we were alone. The infantry company commander had decided to stop and eat lunch. We were openly cursing them, and moods were getting ugly, when Major Burrow called us back for pick-up. No matter where those soldiers walked, they would have to fight again.

When the time came for an R&R to Hong Kong, I boarded a Caribou transport with another Blue for the trip back to Camp Radcliff. The first stop was Baldy. As the plane circled thousands of feet above the one-man bunkers, there was a loud "Pop! The bullet smashed a knob from the instrument panel that knocked the crew chief down. A Red Cross girl saw the fellow go down, fainted and rolled in the aisle. I started laughing. Those damned NVA in the one-man bunkers were at it again. The crew chief had been wearing a flak vest. Only his dignity was hurt.

Bad weather inland that day diverted our flight to the new Air Force Base at Phu Cat in the Crescent, not far from the Korean artillery base where the forward CP had once camped. We walked down the rear ramp of the Caribou and saw an airfield bordered by low wooden buildings, some of which had wide plate glass windows that faced the runway. A shiny jeep, holding two airmen dressed in pressed fatigue uniforms, pulled up beside us. We asked where we could eat.

The driver scowled and replied, "You smell bad. You're not going anywhere until you take a shower and change clothes." They were going to punish us with real showers, not a canvas bag with cold water.

We showered, dressed in clean Air Force fatigues, ate first class food and spent the night in individual rooms with air conditioning and real beds. The next morning, we took luxurious showers, ate a buffet breakfast, used the marvelous flush toilets one last time, changed back into our smelly rags, and were flown to An Khe.

After my short vacation in Hong Kong, while waiting at Camp Radcliff to hitch a chopper ride to Chu Lai, I met a certain Private Page. Page was a tall, good-looking fellow who had been drafted after flunking out of college. He wanted no part of Vietnam and thought I needed a lecture.

"It's not the same in the States now, Sarge," he began. "You've been out of touch. The consciousness of the masses is being stirred. People are turning against our meddling in the affairs of Vietnam. Experience has shown that peoples' wars cannot be defeated."

What's that claptrap he's sprouting? What he's saying sounds a lot like the ideology we're fighting. "What's that got to do with you, Page? You're here now, and you'll fight to live, just like the rest of us. It's not a philosophical question anymore. It's a question of survival."

"Hah! Nobody makes me do what I don't think is right. I'm not going to be a baby-killer. I respect what the NLF [National Liberation Front – Viet Cong] is doing."

Baby-killer? "I respect the NLF, too. You'd be surprised how few babies we have to kill. Listen, what's your job with the troop going to be?"

"A scout gunner, whatever that means."

A scout gunner? Changes were in store for Private Page. "Mark my words, Page. They start killing to live, and then one day they start liking it. It gets like a drug you're hooked on. Tell me how you feel in a month."

He shook his head violently and pointed an accusing finger. "That's not me you're describing. You can't categorize people like that. Our ideals are what make us unique."

Our ideals are paper thin, I cynically thought. "Page, those fancy words you learned in college are mostly just words. Let's wait and see."

We arrived at Chu Lai the next morning.

Carter told me that the past week had been quiet: a couple of helicopter crews rescued and two armed woman killed in foothills north of the Que Son Valley. The women had been wearing American camouflage jungle fatigues. We coveted those fatigues and never were issued with them, but apparently women and high ranking NVA officers had already received theirs. Hippie Doc had gone home to Los Angeles. He may have been a hard character, I don't know, but what I had seen was his compassion for that poor little girl on the island.

———————

Chu Lai had a pleasant side. The defenses of the base were manned by rear-echelon sailors, airmen, and Marines, so our nights were left free to clean weapons and rearm, or sip drinks at a club overlooking a gorgeous white sand beach and blue sea. The club was furnished with wicker tables and lounge chairs under a thatch-roofed veranda. It could have been a Hawaiian scene were it not marred by a rusting Marine LVT [a chunky amphibious vehicle] half-buried in sand some two hundred meters to the north. Chu Lai was occasionally rocketed, but they were after the big planes at the airfield, not our puny helicopters.

The other diversion was pestering rear-echelon soldiers, sailors, and Marines. Blue had never forgiven the Marine MPs for their harassment on several occasions and returned the compliment at every opportunity. The Sea Bees were our enemies only because we vaguely knew that they had something to do with Marines. In all our dealings with the Sea Bees, they treated us with respect. They even let us eat in their excellent mess hall, overlooking the fact that we often smelled like walking garbage dumps and wore Army insignia. We repaid that kindness by stealing two of their big generators.

The Blues made it clear to passing garrison types that our tent street was off-limits to them. The platoon had a legacy, a skull taken in the Ia Drang Valley two years before. No one knew its story, except that it was named Charlie. Old sun-bleached Charlie was placed on a short pole outside the tents. That seemed to frighten them a bit. The Marine MPs complained that Charlie was unsanitary, but he stayed in place.

———————

A historical and reference note on early Battles in the Ia Drang Valley:
Thirteen days before the famous 7ᵗʰ Cavalry landing at LZ X-Ray, Bravo Blues, led by Captain Jack Oliver, engaged in their first firefight in Vietnam. In a brief action, they killed fifteen North Vietnamese and captured forty-three more. Infantry reinforcements arrived. Bitter attacks and counterattacks against the Blues and infantry reinforcements by an NVA battalion continued throughout the day and overnight. Enemy casualties were estimated in the hundreds. Eleven American soldiers were killed.

To read more about the early battles in the Ia Drang Valley, see J.D. Coleman's superb book, **Pleiku: The Dawn of Helicopter Warfare in Vietnam,** *or Joe Galloway and Harold Moore's book,* **We Were Soldiers Once and Young**. *Personal accounts of these battles are also found in* **Hunter-Killer Squadron** *and* **Headhunters**. *Daily reports covering most of the cavalry division's pre-LZ X-Ray operations (excluding late October) are found in the document,* **Long Reach Operation Viewed from G3/I Field Force Vietnam**.

One starry night at the beachside club, four soldiers in tiger-stripe camouflage uniforms abruptly appeared. They stayed close together and avoided eye contact, except with each other. That got my interest. The leader, a man named William Doyle, was sinewy and hawk-faced, with a deep suntan, a tiger-stripe bush hat, and a golden earring. Men wearing earrings were an unusual sight at the time, but what really riveted my attention were Doyle's eyes.

Cold, dead eyes. Prison eyes. Few men carry them. They usually reflect the soul of someone you don't want to know, someone who has given up feeling or caring about his life or anyone else's.

My question about who or what these men were elicited "One-Oh-First Airborne recon" from Doyle. They certainly looked the part.

Those fellows began giggling and whispering among themselves, so I asked a child-sized recon soldier why. His buddies chanted variations of "Go ahead. Tell him."

They had walked a trail along a spine of wooded ridge until a sneeze drove them into cover. Using a backpack for a pillow, an NVA lookout rested on a thick branch high above the trail. He was discovered because he chose the next few seconds to blow his nose between two fingers and flick away the snot. The sudden movement gave him away and started a fatal countdown.

The star-crossed lookout was killed by a stay-behind after the other recon men circled around the tree and engaged his buddies who were eating lunch – the men the lookout was watching out for. The lookout's Swedish-K submachine gun tumbled off the branch along with him and was captured. Swedish-Ks were all the rage as trophies at the time, so the recon men were scheming how to hide this one before some greedy officer grabbed it.

The tiger-stripe boys disappeared a few minutes later, padding away like silent cats, just as they had come. They hadn't even ordered drinks. The memory of Doyle's earring and those disturbing, bottomless eyes remained behind.

In 2013, I picked up a book, titled **Tiger Force,** *about a murderous recon platoon and recognized Doyle in a photograph.*

There is another memory connected with the club. The Blues had a mascot, a fluffy little black dog they truly loved. They trusted that puppy so much that it had gone on night operations with them earlier in the year and barked only once: when it spotted a large tiger watching an ambush team from the very trail they were attempting to ambush. Alerted by the barking, the squad leader used a night vision scope to see the beast. The tiger lingered for a couple of minutes more and then quietly padded off down the trail. The black dog became a friend *and* a good luck charm.

That dog trotted out to the helipad at dawn each day to see off our gaggle of scout helicopters, gunships and slicks. He was waiting beside the empty field when we returned at dusk, or after dark. If we had time to go to the beachside club, he trailed along with tail wagging. He was our family.

My platoon mates had been through a brutal year. Some of them were numbed by the continuous landings, patrols, firefights, and lost friends. Some of them were little more than collections of bone, sinew and nerves that slept little and ate less, but all of them loved that dog.

One evening we were returning from the beachside club and crossed the asphalt road close by our tents. The puppy followed as usual with fluffy tail wagging. He was almost off the road, but he was black and it was nighttime. Quicker than I can tell it, a big Marine truck came racing down the road. The puppy yelped once before it disappeared under the passenger side front tire. We ran back to the dog. An old friend picked it up, hugged the little body to his chest, and howled in pain.

The Marine driver would have been okay if he had kept speeding, instead of slamming on the brakes and running back to apologize. They beat him.

For soldiers who had survived longest, that black puppy had been their only link to a world that was clean, decent, and normal. Most of us cried that night. Some old-timers cried alone in darkness for days. Men who were surrounded by death, and had come to accept it as the natural order of things, had seen a death none of them could accept. The Blues of that era talk about their lost puppy to this day. Their beautiful black friend will never be forgotten as long as one of us who knew him lives, or a single person reads this page.

Christmas was different that year. Most of us had been promised parcels from home, but only about half of us received them. Missing mail became a hot topic of conversation over the holiday season. It's on the way; it must be backlogged; they don't lose mail, etc. Each day we expected the photographs, cookies, fruitcakes, hand mirrors, pocket knives, hot sauce, and other little amenities from home to arrive. But they never did. Later we learned that antiwar protestors had burned Christmas packages on two freighters moored in a California harbor. If one of those losers ever reads this, please be aware that I'm still looking for a case of Vienna sausage and a Swiss army knife.

We celebrated New Year's Eve by quietly sitting on our cots in the big squad tent, reminiscing, telling stories, remembering friends, and getting very drunk. The bunkers around Chu Lai opened up at midnight, creating a distant ring of fireworks with tracers and flares. An AK ripped the air close by our tent. Blues grabbed grenades and rifles, or crawled under their cots. Another clacking burst and we remembered where we were. Hut and Lackey grabbed M-16s and ran in the direction of the firing. They were back within minutes: Hut with a bottle of whiskey and Lackey holding an AK-47. He flung the AK in the dirt and kicked it under a cot.

Our platoon sergeant rushed through the doorway. "Who was firing that thing?

Lackey spat in the dirt. "Some fucking jarhead who bought it from an Army truck driver. Hut hit him a couple of times and took his whiskey."

Hut examined the bottle in the light. "Real Southern Comfort." Then he laughed his chilling laugh and said, "Serves da jarhead right!"

On January third, parts of the 2nd NVA and Yellow Star Divisions attacked bases throughout the Que Son Valley. Our old friends from the Soui Ca and the An Lao had marched one hundred miles north to participate, but the Americans were waiting. Blue had captured plans for the attack when we overran the regimental CP on December fifth. They were defeated everywhere. Now our helicopters hunted down stragglers across the valley.

The slicks circled over the ridge where we had destroyed the regimental CP, then dropped toward LZ Ross, crossing over a staggered line of teenage bodies with close haircuts and green uniforms. Machine guns killed them as they were assembling for the attack, precisely on time. The defenders of LZ Ross didn't know for certain that anyone was there. A two-wheeled cart pulled by a water buffalo was piled high with corpses. The farmer was taking them to LZ Ross for burial. The scene would have been different if a man hadn't gotten nervous that day in December and fired at Major Burrow's gunship.

The last landing at Chu Lai. Blue is on a grassy hilltop west of Baldy that had once been an ARVN artillery base. Below us are railroad tracks running through a pass that are cut in places by big mine craters. There is a white-painted, square concrete post in the thick grass. An inscription reads, "Dan Drachea. 90 days to go. January 1963." What kind of man stood on this barren hilltop five years before and thought of home. Did he live or did he die? The war has been going on for a very long time, even for us Americans.

Chapter 12

TET

(January-March, 1968)

Bravo Troop was preparing to move north of Hue. I was a volunteer door gunner aboard one of a pair of gunships flying north to contact the Marines at our new base. We left the perpetually mist-shrouded pass above Da Nang and arrived over the city of Hue. Below us were pleasant streets and peaceful suburbs. Our pilots flew low level over the Perfume River, a massive citadel, tennis courts, and modern apartment complexes. This was a beautiful city, a side of Vietnam I had never seen. Everything below us was so relaxed, so natural. I wondered whether the people of Hue knew about the war raging in the rice paddies and mountains to the west.

A coastal road guided us north to Camp Evans. The pilots landed outside the barbed wire and we walked through a makeshift gate to a Marine aviation bunker. The Army and Marine pilots eyed each other and exchanged overly polite greetings. One of our captains began the conversation.

"What's the general situation around the camp?"

A marine captain walked over to an acetate overlay wall map. "It's pretty quiet right now. We haven't been mortared in six months. The

major problem our infantry is facing is in this valley to the southwest."
He poked a finger at the map. "They're running into a lot of booby-traps
there."

The map was splotched with red circles. "What do those circles
represent?"

The Marine captain explained. "When we receive antiaircraft fire,
we draw a fifteen hundred meter circle around that point and avoid the
area." He looked guiltily at our captain. "We don't have the helicopters
you have. We can't afford to lose them."

Our pilots grinned at each other.

In future months, after the Tet Offensive was over and things had
quieted down a bit, pink teams made a game of taking out heavy machine
guns. Larry Brown described his method this way:

*"Once we spotted one of them, the gunship would climb up to altitude
and stand off out of range and lob rockets at it. The scout bird would come
on the deck from the direction the rockets were coming and make a run on
the position, just going like hell. The gunship would tell you when the last
pair [of rockets] was on the way. As soon as the last pair hit the ground,
you'd pop up from behind and spin right over the top of them as the gunner
took out the crew. They couldn't elevate the barrels of those things straight
up." Larry Brown's rip-roaring story is featured in the book, **Hunter-Killer
Squadron**.*

Back to the briefing. Our captain pointed to a hotdog shaped village
along the coast northeast of Camp Evans, outlined in red grease pencil.
"How about that long village by the coast?"

"We've had a lot of trouble from there. We consider that stretch of
coast VC territory. They've got twelve-sevens in there so we fly around it."

Major Burrow made his jab. "We don't hide from machine guns. The
Cav will take care of that village." And it did. Five months later, the village of Binh An was flatter than a bulldozed graveyard.

Camp Evans would be a safe place to spend my last thirty days in Vietnam. Bravo Troop came to stay a few days later. The pilots parked the choppers in the same field outside the gate, and we dug foxholes to guard them. That night I sat in a hole in a field and dreamed of Cathy and home. I looked across the flat, open country stretching north toward the DMZ and felt the same emotions that I had experienced twenty-five months before, during that night in the grassy field at Camp Radcliff. I wondered why I had stayed so long and what good I had done by being there.

I was listening to music on Armed Forces Radio that evening when a female voice broke in. The People's Army of Vietnam, she said, welcomed the First Air Cavalry to Camp Evans, "with a special hello to the boys of B Troop of the Ninth Cavalry." She hoped we had written goodbye letters to our families and girlfriends back home. That felt like somebody had grabbed my balls and bungee jumped toward the floor. I hoped the PAVN didn't know just how much damage the boys of B Troop had caused. We later heard a few more Hanoi Hannah broadcasts, but she never again mentioned us by name.

A Marine patrol left through the camp gate at dawn and walked down a narrow dirt road near our foxholes. Each of them carried a heavy M-14 rifle, a flak vest, and not much ammunition. Each of us had at least twenty magazines of rifle ammunition, a smoke grenade, four hand grenades and a belt of machine gun bullets.

A Blue said in a loud voice, "I wouldn't give two cents for the whole bunch."

Someone else quickly hollered, "Cool it, man! They probably think the same thing about us!" The Marines walked quietly past us and never said a word.

Our philosophy didn't help our attitude toward the Marines. They were required to wear protective vests. We believed (wrongly) that wearing a protective vest was a sign of weakness, and considered a machine gun belt and a bandolier of seven rifle magazines protection enough against bullets and fragments. In reality, those protective vests saved countless lives. The only Army

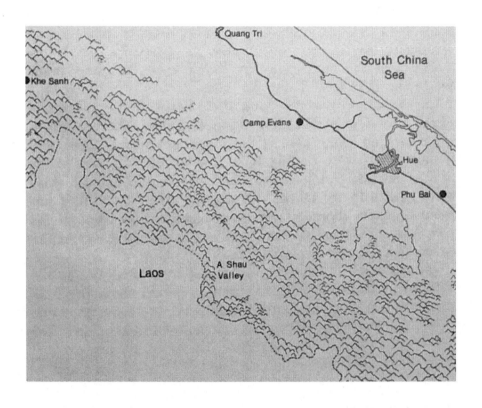

infantryman I ever saw wearing one was saved when he was hit by a machine gun bullet in the chest and walked away with an angry black bruise.

In reality, much of our attitude was probably jealousy over the Marines' famous reputation. They were brave and fought hard with a fraction of the helicopter and artillery support we received. Their individual equipment often looked worn-out. The Marines were highly-trained assault troops, and the military command in Vietnam too often misused them. Their casualty lists are horrendous. To add insult to injury, the Marines' beloved M-14 rifles were taken away and replaced with unreliable M-16s. In some of their earlier engagements with M-16s, the Marines suffered heavy losses.

One of the photographs in this book depicts a Blue trying to clear a jammed M-16 while under fire.

The troop moved inside the wire about two hundred meters from the first night's foxholes. Engineers soon occupied our positions in the field outside the gate. Mortars killed eight of them.

Delta Troop's platoons later arrived and parked in a field behind the engineers. Mortars killed three of them. That same attack wrecked two of our helicopters. The morning after the attack, I found Pete standing beside his wrecked jeep.

"Say, Pete. How are things with Dusty Delta these days."

Pete didn't like the name Dusty Delta. He frowned at my question. "They were better before last night. I'd rather be at Bong Son. They've been mortaring us ever since we started north."

"We'd all rather be at Bong Son. We just came up from Chu Lai. The Charlies up here are different from anything they have down south. Where's Ted?"

Pete laughed. "You won't see him again. We spent the night before last at a Marine base west of Hue. Charlie hit us with about forty rounds of eighty-two mike-mike [82mm]. One landed next to Ted's tent and put holes in all his gear. He was going to come up here for a couple of days, but after that, he caught the first chopper out of there. Didn't even say goodbye."

"So something finally got under his thick skin. I was beginning to think he wasn't human. He hit a mine at Bong Son one day and was back on the road the next. God! How I wish we were back at Bong Son."

He shrugged and looked away. "Maybe, and maybe not. Things are getting hot down there, too. We got into some really deep shit on December sixth." He told me that Alpha Troop Blues were hit and he was with a Delta Troop platoon sent to reinforce them. A platoon leader was killed, and a platoon sergeant and others were wounded.

"What unit was it? The NVA?"

"The Twenty-Second NVA Regiment. They wiped it out before it was over."

"You mean a battalion of the Twenty-Second Regiment."

Pete shook his head. "No, man. I mean the whole damned regiment."

I didn't believe Pete, who could tell a tall tale if he wanted to, until a helicopter I was on flew over the place in early March. Whole villages had been flattened by artillery fire and the paddies plowed by the treads of tanks and APCs. The battle had happened north of the place where Minton won his Silver Star. It looked like a large force had been surrounded by armor and then contracted in upon itself.

A regiment had been destroyed there. The 22nd NVA Regiment, the unit whose base camps we walked through with our prisoner a year before, had been repaid for violating the Christmas Truce and attacking Bird. But the defeat served the communist cause in one sense. By attacking through prosperous government areas, they forced us to destroy that prosperity and the illusion of security, for illusion it surely was.

The departing Marines shook their heads at the swarms of helicopters suddenly filling the sky over Camp Evans. Large gaggles of slicks were landing infantry in the foothills of the mountains west of Hue.

Pink teams were finding targets everywhere. On one of the first days out, pink teams smashed an intended ambush along the road north to Quang Tri, killing about fifty NVA. Shortly after that battle, Private Page strolled past me with an armload of East German and Czech AKs. Last month's ideologue was laughing.

One afternoon, a gunship was shot at by a lone NVA in the middle of a rice field. The man was surprised when the helicopter circled around and dived at him. He stood there gaping, waiting to die. The Mag-7 was welcoming new members. The scouts couldn't believe their "luck" at finding so many NVA so easily. No one questioned why large bodies of enemy troops would be moving around a formerly quiet Marine base. We drew the wrong conclusion. We thought the Marines hadn't been doing their job. The truth was far more ominous.

<hr>

The battle of Hue began for us with a confused report that local Viet Cong had captured a bridge inside Hue. The troop was asked to investigate. I was talking about Indiana with a friendly, fresh-faced pilot named Gary Hanna when his gunship was scrambled for the mission. As the pink teams lifted off, we stood by the slicks, arguing about whether the bridge was really inside Hue. Most Blues were sure that a new radioman had made a mistake.

"Everybody knows there aren't any VC in Hue."

Within two hours, several squadron gunships had been hit and other gunships were receiving heavy automatic weapons fire "at all altitudes" above the city. Major George Burrow described the first hours of the troop's involvement in the Battle of Hue this way:

"Almost immediately we encountered large formations of NVA and VC troops. They were marching in battalion-sized columns (south) toward Hue. We were so low that we could see the enemy soldiers' gold teeth as they gaped in amazement at our choppers. In some cases, we were probably the first gunship or scout helicopter they had ever seen. Needless to say, we were also taken by surprise."

More of George Burrow's story can be found in the book, **Hunter-Killer Squadron.**

One of Bravo Troop's gunships was shot down in Hue and its four crewmen captured. The enemy soldiers were in a crowd in a large open field. When our helicopters roared in to rescue the crew, the Viet Cong split into two groups. Two of our men with one enemy group were rescued. The other enemy group immediately killed their captives: WO Hanna and Crew Chief Delgado.

The two captured crewmen with the first group were rescued by two very brave slick pilots, one of whom was a crazy man: Mr. Maehrlein, also called "Wonder Warthog." Wonder, we said, could fly lower and faster than anyone else, jumping over huts, trees, bushes, and paddy dikes at 110 or 120 knots. Blue squads vied for the opportunity to ride with him. Now he used his piloting skills to save two lives.

Wonder was a gutsy man. He came in low over the outskirts of Hue, saw the burning gunship, buzzed that field, and spotted our two captured crewmen with a group of thirty to forty Viet Cong. Wonder landed his slick almost on top of the soldiers guarding our men. The captives dropped for cover; the Viet Cong ran away, and the slick took them home.

A version of the rescue gives the door gunners credit for killing ten enemy soldiers in that field. That's not what I was told by a door gunner shortly after the rescue. I found him crying in the open bay of Wonder Warthog's slick and asked if I could help. He told me that his machine gun had jammed after a few shots. Wonder had covered for him and killed some, perhaps most, of the Viet Cong by firing a pump shotgun out of his cockpit window. That sounds like something Mr. Maehrlein would do. He received a **Distinguished Service Cross** for the rescue.

On the evening of the rescue, General Westmoreland announced wide-spread attacks throughout Vietnam. Two-hundred-fifty-one American heroes died that day. The bridge had been inside Hue after all.

On February second, a Blue was describing how a big rocket had collapsed a section of concrete aircraft hangar at the Da Nang Air Base and buried a group of screaming Marine replacements who had just arrived from America. The platoon sergeant stopped the usual, brutal talk by asking if anyone had reason to go back to An Khe on a courier helicopter. Minutes later, our slick lifted off and headed south. I watched it lift off over the perimeter wire wished that I was aboard.

The helicopter disappeared. Our pink teams searched for the wreckage for days, but finally gave up until things quieted down around Hue. The crash site was found months later in the perpetually cloudy pass above Da Nang. All five aboard are listed as "Died while Missing. Body not Recovered." Shortly after I left for home, four scout crewmen from the Bravo Troop were captured in two incidents in the A Shau Valley, and are now listed under the same category.

Also on February second, a Bravo Troop gunship was shot down near Hue. The crew was rescued under heavy fire by a big Marine Corps Sea Knight helicopter. Brave men.

On another morning in early February, the slicks took us north to Quang Tri for standby in case a Delta Troop patrol heading north got into trouble. The sky was heavily overcast, so the journey was at low level. Rice fields around the city were cratered by thousands of artillery shells. We passed over a zone of Death - muddy craters, sprawled bodies, water buffalo carcasses, everything swollen and rotting. The land was so silent and still down below us. A neighborhood on the outer edge of the city still smoldered from recent battles. Block after block of ruined houses and deserted streets. The rain made it all seem more pathetic and disgusting. Delta Troop didn't need us.

Then some of us briefly returned to a burning Hue. Our two slicks orbited away from the city as Skyraiders dived again and again into the inferno. Out of concern about negative publicity, the United States was allowing the South Vietnamese destroy their own city. Entire apartment blocks collapsed from the explosions; the air above the city was filled with dust and black smoke. The lift birds touched down in a wide paddy field on the western edge of the city.

We waited as two desperate-looking American advisors splashed across the paddies and boarded the other slick. As our gunships rocketed a suburb from which AKs were clacking, we lifted off, firing our rifles there. My M-16 jammed after one shot. The slicks banked hard north-west and raced away as more bombs exploded along the once-pleasant streets of Hue.

The advisor rescue mission was the Blue platoon's last direct experience with the Battle of Hue. Our services as a recon team weren't needed when pink teams could fly in any direction from Camp Evans and find prey. Most of us didn't like being left out.

Helicopters from Bravo Troop screened ahead of the Army's infantry assault into northern Hue. The scouts also helped beleaguered Marine infantry inside the city. A rain of hot shell casings meant that the scout gunner's target was very close in front of you.

No one in those cold, miserable, rain-soaked days knew the extent of the horror unfolding inside Hue. Throughout the city, cadres were arresting government workers and officials, class enemies, soldiers, families of soldiers, etc. They often worked from lists. The South Vietnam government later provided the names of over four thousand people who were marched away and murdered by the communists. Estimates range as high as six thousand victims.

———————◆———————

The former Marine positions in our sector were little more than foxholes with overhead cover, so we improved them with entrenching shovels, a pallet of empty sandbags, and "anything you can find" for overhead protection and cover. Dark, rolling clouds pelted us with a seemingly endless cold drizzle. My group of nine slept just behind the bunkers under pup tent halves at first, spooning, pressed close together for warmth. Men coming off bunker duty took the warm places of those going on duty. We awoke on two mornings to a crust of ice over the mud puddles around us.

One early afternoon, the platoon watched helplessly as an infantry company got into a brief firefight with North Vietnamese digging bunkers on a facing slope about eighty meters in front of us. The digging had happened suddenly, in broad daylight. We missed it.

Blue soon patrolled past the half-finished holes, raw brown sores in a carpet of green grass, and continued over the hill. The point man heard someone running away and found an NVA pack resting near a fishing pole stuck in the muddy bank of a tiny stream. He wasn't catching anything. On another hill was a neat pile of mortar shell crates. A square pit was already waiting for the tube and crew. That should have been warning enough. Weeks of mortar shelling began that night.

This wasn't how I had planned to spend my last days in Vietnam. Intelligence reported that the NVA tanks that overran a Special Forces Camp on the Laotian border had used poison gas shells, so we were ordered to carry gas masks. I sat each night on a bunker, carrying a gas mask, seven grenades clipped to its waist strap, and the artillery radio. If the NVA attacked, I would do nothing but be an FO and blast the hills and woods to our front. I hoped they would try to use the half-finished bunkers. An artillery concentration was plotted on top of them.

I felt alone. The only time I had spent with the airborne artillery FO in Bravo Troop was what it took to hand over a slip of paper with a new call-sign or radio frequency. A replacement for Ray had never been sent. God knows what he had told them in the rear. My only loyalty was to the Blues. If the artillery targets didn't stop the North Vietnamese and they breached the wire, seven grenades said that they would go no further. Seven is supposed to be a very lucky number.

We were low on ammunition and food when a group of cocky ARVN rangers, wearing red berets and riding atop APCs, shared our perimeter for a night. They had just smashed another North Vietnamese blocking position north of us, on the road to Quang Tri, and offered captured AK-47s in exchange for food. We didn't need AKs and were low on food, so we shared. They had rice; we had some C-rations, and between us, we filled our stomachs. I wish they could have stayed with us longer.

The next morning, we patrolled to an abandoned hamlet to gather baskets of rice. Nearby was an abandoned herd of water buffalo. I had to turn away when Hut shot a water buffalo calf with his machine gun. A slick slung it back to camp in a cargo net. We ate a monotonous diet of rice and water buffalo meat for a week.

Late one night, after a stint on the bunkers, I walked by the mess tent and smelled meat cooking. Inside the tent was a group of pilots and cooks greedily hovering over a griddle of frying steaks. A cook told me to leave – the pilots had flown in the steaks from Camp Radcliff and they belonged to them (and the cooks). I mentioned that the Blues had supplied all of them with the meat and rice they had eaten for the past week. They weren't going to be happy when they found out what the pilots were eating.

Every man in the Blues ate steak that night, with enough left over for the pilots and cooks. That tiny victory was my proudest moment. Air Force cargo planes began low-level parachute resupply drops a day or two later.

We were now sleeping in our big squad tents. Helicopters burned in the field behind us at night, but I was safe. The NVA listened to Armed Forces Radio. When "Holiday" by the Bee Gees played, they mortared us. "Holiday" was my favorite song, so I was usually waiting for it to be played. The North Vietnamese liked it, too. Whenever the song began, I grabbed my transistor radio, ran out of the tent, squeezed into a tiny bunker I had dug into a bank, and waited for the flutter of the first mortar bombs. Then I enjoyed the rest of "Holiday." The Bee Gees sang, "Don't believe that it's all the same."

That happened for about two weeks. The evening I made the connection, there wasn't time to go anywhere but flat. The next time it happened I jumped off my cot and ran while the others looked at me as if I had a screw loose. I explained later. The third time, when I jumped up and ran for shelter, and so did everyone else.

Mortar shells made me feel so helpless. You can fight an enemy rifleman, but a mortar bomb is a blind thing. It seeks you out in your miserable hiding place and crushes you before you know it has come.

Our lives degenerated into a combination of crushing boredom and fear of the sporadic mortar and rocket attacks. A group of comrades who had once thrived on constant action and danger now looked for unfamiliar ways to keep their collective sanity.

One recreation was called the C-4 dance. We used plastic explosive to heat our C-rations and believed that the only time it was chemically unstable was when it was burning. I remember nights in a dirty squad tent, watching soldiers light wads of plastique, then running the length of the tent before leaping through the air and landing full force on the stuff. If a wad had exploded, a Blue would have lost at least a foot.

In 1996, the fellow who ran the C-4 factory during the Vietnam War told me that it *is stable* while burning. If the Blues had known that fact, they would have looked elsewhere for danger.

———◆———

Camp Evans was surrounded by an NVA regiment. Mortar shells exploded day and night, sometimes to the accompaniment of "Holiday." Some nights Camp Evans took a pounding. Our helicopters continued recon flights and did what they could to help cavalry division battalions fighting and dying as they slogged toward Hue, but mortars and bullets were damaging helicopters faster than they could be replaced.

Delta Troop platoons rotated attempts to open the road south to Hue. A patrol would grind past the main gate each day and turn south. They repeatedly fought the NVA at the same place. Muffled crashes, pops and crackles would be followed by gunship runs, and then the jeeps and trucks would come bouncing back through the gate. Bolton was said to be the hero of some of those little battles.

Throughout this period, our pink teams were doing rescue missions north of Camp Evans for small Marine units that were trapped and without support from elsewhere. The Marines were astounded by the gunship runs at tree top level, scout gunners eliminating NVA positions close around them, and our crazy slick pilots, racing in "on the deck" to pick them up. I believe that Bravo Troop made some Marine Corps friends in those hectic days.

One day a scout pilot was wounded so badly that he couldn't hold the controls. The gunner took over and flew the H-13 back to Camp Evans. We constantly monitored our radios to hear what was going on, so we waited. The little chopper wobbled into view and made a rough landing on a grassy slope between our tents and the helicopter parking field. Medics ran to help the pilot. Out of the gunner's seat stepped a dazed Private Page.

"I can't believe it! He told me what to do and I flew the damned thing back! Am I glad that's over!"

"You'll probably get a medal. You saved his life." I had to know something. "Say, Page, what do you think of the scouts now."

"Saved my life, too." His eyes came back into focus. "Know something, Sarge? I got seventy-nine kills. Just up here."

"I thought you were the one who wasn't going to compromise."

He smiled the whole issue away. "People change, Sarge. I like the scouts."

"That's good, Page."

I became a short-timer, living through my last days at Camp Evans. One Friday morning, I had been on the bunkers all night and Carter wouldn't wake me for a trip to the Marine base at Phu Bai. I might get hurt with only four days left in the field. Mortars came when the choppers landed on the airstrip. Two men sitting on my usual side of the slick were wounded before the pilots could lift off.

That Sunday morning, the Catholic chaplain said mass and offered prayers for those who had recently died. He was impressed that every man in the Blues attended his service. The whole platoon must be Catholic. The Blues lined up after the blessing to receive the black plastic rosaries being handed out by a chaplain's assistant. The word was out about those rosaries, and everyone agreed that they would bring good luck. By the next morning, most of us were wearing the rosaries around our necks for ornament. The platoon had finally got religion.

My last memory of those brave men from Chu Lai and Camp Evans is of a group of black, brown, and white soldiers, smiling and waving, with shiny black plastic beads and crosses gleaming around their necks. I will always miss them.

The mortars shells that hit Camp Radcliff landed far away and I wasn't afraid. But there was a personal crisis. Soon I would return to a little Indiana town where people remembered me as a bookworm and an unpromising athlete. But I had been with the 9th Cavalry since nearly everyone there had arrived, and with the cavalry division even longer. Men liked to hear stories about the now-distant days of Pleiku, or the Soui Ca, or Operation Crazy Horse, or about heroes like Sergeants Samuel, Haskett and Kaneshiro.

I never had to buy a beer when a 9th Cavalry Blue was in a club, and here I was, returning to the obscurity of rural Indiana. When Carter returned to Camp Radcliff for R&R, we walked into a grove of young trees behind the 9th Cavalry buildings and I told him that I was afraid to go home.

Carter understood, as he always did. "You'll make new friends, FO. You haven't been out in life much. It happens every time you start something new. There's not a man in the Ninth Cav that wants you to stay another day. You're an example of one who made it. The Blues would lynch you if you stayed any longer."

"But look what's coming. The Cav's getting ready to break through to Khe Sanh and save the Marines. You might need some artillery."

He shook his head. "It's all over for you, FO. If you stayed much longer, we'd all be gone and leave you behind. Just write a letter and tell us about all the pussy you're getting. Go home and start living like a human being again."

Later that day, I walked over to say hello to the Delta Troop commander's jeep driver. He was sitting in the shade of a small tree, the same tree he had been sitting under for the last three days. We talked for a while until I got to my real question. What was he doing there, spending his days sitting under a tree? He told me he was taking a vacation. What kind of a vacation? A vacation. Is it leave or R&R? He finally got tired of being badgered and told his story.

Delta Troop had convoyed to the southern tip of the An Lao for a "fire raid" [bombardment with mortars, recoilless rifles and artillery]. His wasn't the lead vehicle and he had carefully avoided dark patches and suspicious places on the road surface. The grassy road shoulder where the troop commander told him to pull over and park appeared to be undisturbed. A mine explosion killed the other occupants of the jeep: the troop commander (a captain), Delta Troop's first sergeant, and a major from squadron headquarters who was riding along as an observer. When the driver regained his senses, he was "crazy," as he put it. But the mine detonation was now five months in the past.

He whispered for at least the third time, "They think I'm crazy."

I wished him luck and wondered just how sane he really was as he resumed a silent, blank-faced vigil under that little tree.

I spent the last night at an NCO club. Paul the newsman was there, along with Jerry, his replacement. Jerry was still chubby from American food and beer, 'Stateside fat" we called it, and Paul was going home.

He jerked his thumb in my direction. "Matt here has just completed twenty-seven months with the Cav and something like three hundred air assaults (more like 350). That must be some kind of record." He asked in a low voice, as if afraid of what the answer would be, "What did the Blues do during Tet?"

"Nothing. We sat inside the wire at Evans and got mortared. I dug a little bunker and marked the days off on a calendar. How about you?"

"Nothing much."

Jerry was restless. He wanted to say something and fluttered his hand to get my attention. "Nothing much? This guy's too modest. He shot fourteen gooks in Hue. They gave him a Silver Star the next day. Come on, Paul, tell him about it."

Paul blushed. He seemed like such a gentle fellow. "Did you really do that, Paul?"

He blushed again. "Yeah. You know how they build things up after they happen. I was hiding in a shop in the center of Hue. The odds were about even. They came by in pairs. All I was trying to do was save my neck. The best part is that the newsmen I was supposed to be baby-sitting heard about it and offered me a job when I get back. It's what I've always wanted to do. I can't tell you how excited I am about it."

Three days later, I was a civilian, boarding a jet in Seattle for the long flight home.

Chapter 13

A LONG SUMMER

(March-October, 1968)

Returning home was more complicated than I would ever have imagined. My sister, Ann, had offered to "keep an eye" on Cathy while I was gone, and she reported that Cathy had been dating other men. That scenario had been reenacted a million times in Vietnam; I wanted no part of it at home. Cathy admitted that she had been dating and wanted to stay engaged, but I was unable to communicate with anyone and said goodbye. My belief was that adjustment is something best done alone. I began doing manual work or exercising to exhaustion, hoping that sleep would follow. If all else failed, I drank myself to sleep.

A month passed. I was desperately in need of someone to talk with. One chilly April morning, I threw a sleeping bag in the back seat of my new Plymouth Valiant and headed for Texas to visit Chuck, formerly of Bravo Blues. The morning mists, drifting through tree tops in the Ozark Mountains, reminded me of daybreak in the Soui Ca. The poverty of people living along the back roads –the trash, unpainted, falling-down homes, and junked cars – was something completely outside my experience.

While driving along a superhighway between Dallas and Fort Worth, I passed a large billboard poster of me leading the "Charge of the Third Brigade," as advertisement for a local television station. There I was, frozen in action beside a Texas highway, thousands of miles from that rice paddy in the Que Son Valley.

The understanding and support I expected at Chuck's home didn't happen. I told him about the billboard, and he replied that he wouldn't drive near it because it reminded him of the Blues. He kept his medals in a tiny cardboard box on his dresser. He would line them up at the foot of his bed at night and drink himself to sleep. He was trying to forget 173 dead men.

Chuck's parents gave me a detached welcome. They probably didn't want anyone around to revive his memories of the war. We talked of our common experience and then we were silent. The visit had been superficial and damaging for both of us. I returned home to Indiana and never heard from him again.

Next I enrolled in a junior college and lasted one week. The boredom of a classroom was insufferable. I became infatuated with a local girl, but her father didn't want her dating an ex-soldier. I thought it was poetic justice when they drafted her brother. Then I hooked up with two fellow veterans, Ed and Bob, and we began a summer of drinking and generally raising hell. The low point was the night we spent in the county jail.

Five veterans, two of us wounded as recently as the Tet Offensive, celebrated the Fourth of July at a dance in a neighboring town and left for home about 2 a.m. When we got back, Ed suggested that we stop at an all-night diner. We were hungry and Ed liked to tease the waitress, a teenage girl whose father owned the place. Ed would ask her out, and she would reply, "I like my Daddy better," which, of course, led to endless speculation.

We pulled onto the edge of the gravel parking lot and exited the car. I stepped out into the grassy border and promptly lost my pipe: a short thing with a large bowl and a square stem. I was on my knees, running my fingers through the grass, when a cop car pulled up. The officer asked me what I was doing and I replied that I was looking for my pipe. When he heard the word, "pipe," you could almost see the wheels spinning in his head. He thought it was that other kind of pipe.

The officer asked to see our IDs. My friends complied. I didn't. He asked for my driver's license. When I didn't move, my friend, Ed, a former air policeman, said the fatal words, "Officer, he doesn't have to show you his ID."

Driver's licenses were printed on thick paper and not laminated at that time. I took mine out of my wallet, popped it in my mouth, chewed it a bit and swallowed it. All five of us, two of whom had recently been wounded in the Tet Offensive, went to jail for a night. Sorry, guys.

I dated Leila, Ed's cousin, that summer, but ours was a star-crossed romance. Leila's father didn't want her dating a military veteran, ironic because he held a well-paying position at a nearby military base. One example: we had a secret date planned for a Saturday night. I wanted to surprise her with flowers, a bottle of champagne and two expensive wine glasses. Father caught wind of it and said she had to stay home to serve drinks to his guests at a dinner party. When she failed to rendezvous, I drove to her home and left a wine glass on her front steps. Daddy found the glass the next morning on his way to church and she got the trouble.

We became engaged in early August. I bought a six-hundred-dollar engagement ring, a lot of money in those days, and proposed. She accepted for a week and then returned the ring. Leila said that she would like to pick her own ring, but not just yet. I suspected daddy had squelched our "infatuation." I was only able to see Leila a few more times. Even so, when I returned to Vietnam, I dreamed for a year of coming home and marrying her.

When I had returned home, I didn't draw the automatic six months of unemployment insurance to which I was entitled. That would have helped. My savings ran low, so I hired on to drive spikes on a railroad track gang. Railroad work was a welcome change. Work hard for eight hot hours a day, and there wasn't time to be bored, and no need to drink to sleep. I would work on railroad track gangs three more times during my life for the same reasons.

Boredom was always a problem. Every day was the same as the one before. If a person was lucky, he could look forward to living like that for fifty more, painfully long years. I had become addicted to constant danger and its adrenaline reward, and the constant security of life in Indiana was unbelievably melancholy.

I enrolled in Indiana State University for the fall semester with the usual menu of freshman classes: Intro this and Intro that. ISU was an alien place with a student life that seemed trite and incredibly petty. Students dressed to impress and attended classes to find dates for the weekend. The pursuit of knowledge was far down the list of reasons for being there. Greeks controlled most of the campus social activities.

A fraternity on campus, claiming to have a majority of veterans, urged me to join, but they had been clerks, truck drivers, supply and support personnel: worker ants with air-conditioning. We had nothing in common. I wasn't aware at the time that only ten-to-fifteen percent of Vietnam servicemen served in combat positions. Some of those fellows told elaborate, false war stories to sorority girls who couldn't distinguish a combat veteran from a lump of modeling clay. Similar losers would later add phony atrocity stories to the mix.

Veterans were a curiosity in Indiana in 1968. We weren't yet ignored, not called dope fiends and psychopaths, but no one seemed to care about our experiences, except other veterans. The questions I received came from young men who might be drafted. They wanted to know what to expect. I advised people to avoid the infantry. Those kids would be disenfranchised veterans themselves in a few years.

ISU students carried umbrellas even in the lightest rains. Having spent months in heavy rains, sometimes with no dry clothing at all, I found those umbrellas the most ridiculous part of student life. With all my heart, I hated those umbrellas as a symbol of just how superficial my new life had become. When other students told me, "You ought to buy an umbrella at the campus bookstore," I silently cursed umbrellas yet again. My escape from these strange customs was to study extremely hard. In four weeks' time, I had read most of the semester's assignments and all of its simple textbooks, and read them a second time.

There was too much time to contemplate the country to which I had returned. America had changed in the three years I had been away. Not only were fashions and hairstyles different, but also the prevailing morality. "Free love" was a threatening concept. The days when a girl could get a bad reputation for taking a sip of beer after the prom were fading into history, but that was the culture I grew up in. Now, young men and women were playing together at an amazing clip, but I sensed that the real losers in that game were the women.

The racial tension at ISU struck me as ludicrous. Blacks and whites were not on speaking terms. That was confusing after experiencing the integration and sharing I had so recently known. Julian Bond, who struck me as a rabble-rouser with a cute face, arrived on campus and gave a fiery speech that ended with, "God told Noah, here's a sign. No more water, fire next time." That speech did nothing to bring people closer together; it only made the racial divisions deeper.

The great men, Robert Kennedy and Martin Luther King, had died that summer. It should have been a time of healing. I felt that I had returned to a nation of burning ghettos, political assassinations, morality gone haywire, and petty competition for money, power, and status symbols. I missed the action, the sharing, the comradeship, and the simple life-and-death choices of Vietnam. I began repeating to myself a motto I had read somewhere, *"A soldier's place is in war."* There was also my unfinished book that needed its last chapter written when we won the war.

The Vietnam War was being debated and I couldn't understand why. I had never questioned the reasons for the war. I thought we were winning and felt guilty about leaving before the fight was finished. I believed that Vietnam required our sacrifices because it was a just cause. There had been so much Chinese equipment that it was easy to believe that America was stopping Chinese expansion into a region that had been a tributary state prior to the arrival of the French. Yes, I have always been easily deceived.

In early October, I was part of a line of students snaking out of a building between classes when I walked past Daisy, formerly Daisy of Bravo Troop Blues, and did a double take. He had stayed longer than me, and had become a Loach gunner during the Khe Sanh relief and the A Shau Valley campaign. He was still mourning the loss of a good friend, Richard Martin, another Loach gunner. Martin's three-man crew had apparently had been captured and marched away after a shoot-down in the southern A Shau. They were never seen again.

Daisy had admired a large American eagle tattoo on Richard Martin's back and had planned to visit his friend's home in Hawaii and get the same tattoo. Now Daisy was an ISU freshman. We hugged each other, skipped classes, went for a beer, and drunkenly decided that life in Indiana was too boring. We would go back to Bravo Blues. One of us did.

On a rainy day, also in early October, I withdrew from all classes. It went well until I reached the history professor's office. He asked me why I was leaving, and when I told him, he gave me a lecture on the immorality of the Vietnam War. I didn't know what in the hell he was talking about, and certainly didn't want to hear it.

As I was leaving his office he asked, "Did you even bother to take the exam?" Yes. He rummaged through a stack of marked-up papers and looked up. "Wait! You got the highest score in the class. Son, the war is immoral."

He didn't convince me.

The Army recruiting station was in a second story office two blocks away from campus. I made a deal with the recruiting sergeant. I would reenlist if I could go straight back to the cavalry division. He made arrangements over the phone while confiding that he was in the recruiting business to avoid going back to Vietnam. He could stay in America as long as he met his monthly quota of volunteers. He wanted to stay and I wanted to go. Whatever half-baked ideas I used to justify my return to Vietnam, going back was the greatest mistake of my life.

My dorm was one of two towers. An all-male building faced an all-female building. A resident of the other tower was a pretty, petite, dark-haired freshman girl who was already known as "Jean-Jean the Machine." I had seen her around and wondered why such a pretty girl had to be so promiscuous. On my last evening in the all-male dorm, at 8 p.m. sharp, the residents on my floor gathered in rooms facing the all-female tower.

The lights went on in a room across from us. Jean-Jean the Machine walked to that room's big window, lowered her blue jean pants to around her ankles, turned around and bent over, mooning God knows how many testosterone-addled undergraduates. Cheers echoed through the hallways.

And that's how I remember ISU.

Chapter 14

AN LOC

(October-November, 1968)

One week later, I arrived at the Oakland, California replacement center. Tiers of bunks were filled with silent draftees, waiting as if for their own funerals. The boasting paratroopers of three years before were distant memories. There was a Special Forces sergeant in the barracks, a quiet man who set himself apart from the herd of long-faced draftees. He had fought for two years in Laos and North Vietnam, had gone home for eight months, and was returning for the same reasons as me. He was lonely, bored, and disillusioned.

To know someone who had wrestled with the same problems, and made the same decisions, made me feel less alone. We waited together for the flight across the Pacific. The SF man and I spent our last night in Oakland with the unpleasant duty of roster NCOs. We carried clipboards and were required to take roll every hour, and then every half hour, to make sure that none of the draftees had deserted. Now, no one was bribing replacement center personnel for an early departure.

The Special Forces sergeant and I bade goodbye at the Tan Son Nhut Air Base outside of Saigon. The base was larger, cleaner than in 1965, and was now the busiest airport in the world. The paper trash and garbage that had littered the surrounding fields three years before were long gone. Instead of climbing aboard big transport trucks, we were driven to Camp Alpha in air-conditioned buses.

The road to Alpha was lined with tanks and APCs. The crews flashed two-fingered "V for victory" signs as our buses drove by. Nine months before, the usual greeting had been a "thumbs-up" gesture. The new sign meant "stay high," not victory. I knew something was different about those soldiers. I didn't understand what that difference was, but some of the discipline and confidence that I had grown accustomed to seeing in Vietnam seemed to have slipped away.

I returned to Camp Radcliff over the same jungle ridges that had so impressed me three years before. At least the war hadn't changed the mountains. The airstrip at An Khe was now heavily protected by barbed wire and infantry bunkers. Knots of soldiers, many of whom wore Marine Corps fatigue hats and carried K-bar knives, imitation being the most sincere form of flattery, rested in the shade of the concrete-floored, wooden terminal building. As a dusty infantry patrol returned through the barbed wire at the far end of the airstrip, I mentioned the added security to a soldier standing beside me. He explained.

"The VC set up a machine gun on the edge of the airstrip last summer. Killed some guys going back to the World. Gooks got away Scott-free."

Brown Army buses, windows covered with chicken wire to deflect terrorist grenades, took us to Camp Radcliff. The drivers wore starched uniforms and neat baseball caps. The sandbagged dump trucks and their ragged drivers had disappeared long before. Sleepy An Khe had become a prosperous town, teeming with children and crowded with Chinese restaurants, Korean tailor shops, Indian clothing and brassware stores, and Vietnamese laundries, souvenir shops, barbershops, and massage parlors.

The replacement center had morphed into a complex of wooden buildings equipped with concrete floors, electric fans, lights, and office machines. Once the complex had consisted of three small tents and a grassy field. Instead of sleeping on damp grass, we slept on steel bunks with firm mattresses, coarse mattress covers, blankets, and pillows.

The following morning I was assigned to an artillery battalion. A clerk explained that pilots were receiving artillery training in flight school, so the 9th Cavalry wasn't using artillery FOs anymore. A slick took me and two other men on the 230-mile trip north to Camp Evans. The door gunner told us that we were aboard a new model of Huey lift helicopter [UH-1H] that was fitted with a more powerful engine than before.

We passed west of Hue and followed Highway One to a sprawling military base. Camp Evans was several times larger than it had been in February. Most of the inhabitants lived in big sandbagged bunkers, reinforced with thick wooden crossbeams and steel plate. The place bristled with howitzers and helicopters and seemed much safer than the surrounded camp that I remembered from the days of the Tet Offensive.

The clerk at the 21st Field Artillery Battalion was sympathetic. He offered to send me to a grunt company as a forward observer sergeant. I asked him if a transfer to the 9th Cavalry as a Blue infantry sergeant might be approved. A young major overheard the conversation from the next room, stuck his head through the doorway, and nodded a greeting.

"The transfer will be approved. You're too highly trained to be an infantryman, but requests for the infantry have the highest priority. Why don't you go over and ask them for a transfer? Bravo Troop is where it's always been."

I found the Blues living in the squad tents we had erected in January. I tried all four tents before I found someone I recognized: Hippie Doc's replacement, Dwayne Melugin, the only man left from the platoon I had known in March. Doc Melugin led me to his cot, and caught me up on what had happened while I was away.

The Blues made landings around Khe Sanh in March, but most of the NVA had fled or been killed by pink teams, artillery, and air strikes. Doc described Khe Sanh after the siege as a huge garbage dump, filled with trash and demoralized Marines. He said that you could spot the newly arrived cavalrymen at Khe Sanh by the way they behaved when rockets were fired. The cavalrymen would wait for the black explosions and snap pictures. The shell-shocked Marines would dive for the nearest foxhole or ditch.

Bravo Troop had been the first American unit to return to the overrun Special Forces Camp at Lang Vei. Later in April, pink teams had reconnoitered the A Shau Valley and destroyed many targets before a massive cavalry assault was launched. Antiaircraft fire in the valley was heavy and often radar controlled. The Blues were kept busy rescuing or recovering shot-down helicopter crews.

The most frightening time was the three days the Blue platoon spent guarding an airstrip near an abandoned Special Forces camp on the western edge of the A Shau. It was being used to evacuate heavy equipment and supplies. The troop was one of the last units in the valley. Melugin said that the airstrip was under sporadic fire from 130mm artillery in Laos. The guns would fire, and then growling, heavy tracked vehicles, easily heard at the airstrip, would move them to new locations.

A Blue had been killed by a pressure-detonated artillery shell mine in a coastal village in the spring. Some of the old Blues had gone home and others had been hit in an ambush in May. Reconnaissance operations had become rarer after the ambush. The Blues were now being used mainly to secure downed helicopters and their crewmen. We talked a bit longer before Doc pointed to a tall man walking along the barbed wire.

"First sergeant's back if you still want to talk to him about coming back to the Blues. It's a lot safer where you are."

"Thanks, Doc. I'll be seeing you."

The first sergeant saw me walking toward him from the Blue tents and gave me a suspicious look. "What can I do for you?"

"Top? My name is Brennan. I was an F.O. with the Blues for fifteen months."

He nodded. "I've heard about you, Brennan. The old first sergeant said you had a hell of a lot of air assaults under your belt. You probably know that we don't use FOs anymore. The pilots bring in their own artillery if it's needed."

"Since you don't need an FO, can you use an infantry sergeant? I spent most of my time playing infantry, anyway."

His eyes lit up. "We can use all the experienced sergeants we can beg, borrow, or steal." The first sergeant lowered his voice. "Right now we have a bunch of Shake and Bakes. Most of them can't lead a horse to water. What unit are you with?"

"The Twenty-First Artillery. I'm putting in for a transfer here as a grunt."

"Okay, Sergeant. When it gets here, it'll be approved."

I had to ask one final question. "Top? Before they left, did the old Blues say anything about me to you?"

He nodded. "They said you were funny." (as in platoon comedian) The answer was not what I had hoped for or expected, but at least they had remembered something of me.

I returned for a last look at the Blues. The platoon sergeant and three of the squad leaders were products of the Army's new ninety-day NCO school, commonly referred to as "Shake and Bakes" or "Instant NCOs." It was now possible to enter the Army and be a staff sergeant seven months later. There were two volunteers in the entire platoon. The rest were draftees. The toughness and aggressiveness of previous years, the lone wolf stares and the quick reflexes, seemed to be lacking. What would Carter, or Hut, or Hippie Doc have thought of those soldiers?

I began to realize what was different about the Vietnam Army of late 1968. Something had happened to the Army's spirit after the Tet Offensive. The confident, disciplined soldiers of 1965 through early 1968 had largely been replaced by draftee officers, sergeants, and enlisted men. The old NCOs and volunteers had either served their time in Vietnam, retired early, or were dead.

I returned to the 21st Artillery and began completing transfer forms. The young major wished me good luck and assigned me as a liaison NCO with the Army of Vietnam until the paperwork had gone through channels.

Two days later, the cavalry division moved almost six hundred miles south to positons northwest of Saigon. We were going to the aid of the 1st Infantry Division, the Big Red One, whose artillery bases were being attacked along the Cambodian border. The artillery battalion headquarters loaded its equipment on trucks and drove down the road toward Hue. A short distance south of Camp Evans, the convoy passed the dead and twisted trees where Delta Troop had fought its daily battles during Tet.

The road was safe; security was lax. We passed marching companies of ARVN troops, armed with M-16s and AKs, and everyone smiled and waved. We drove on through Hue, past the modern apartment buildings that the bombs of February had gutted. All that remained were blast-blackened concrete shells and sagging floors. The convoy arrived in the Port of Hue where Korean stevedores hoisted our vehicles aboard a fleet of LSTs.

The LSTs were at sea by evening, heading south along the coast. I spent the next few days on a deck covered by an array of dirty brown vehicles, each flying a rebel flag, a pirate flag, a sports team pennant, or what-have-you from its antenna. Between the vehicles were shelters made from ponchos and canvas pup tent halves. It looked like a seagoing gypsy camp. Below deck was a nightmare of seasick men and slippery vomit, so I stayed on the bow, enjoying the warm sea breeze and sometimes seeing the lights of a port city gliding by off starboard. "The Tavern" by Mary

Hopkin was the hot new song on Armed Forces Radio. I listened to it over and again.

The LSTs approached Saigon down a winding river through the Rung Sat Special Zone. Rung Sat means "killer swamp," and it certainly looked the part. It was a flat sea of red-brown mud, covered with scattered bushes and short, twisted trees. Ninth Cavalry helicopters with yellow crossed sabers painted on their noses patrolled the banks. They made me feel proud. I waved at a couple of the gunships, as if the crews could possibly recognize or remember me.

Hoists unloaded our trucks at New Port outside of Saigon, and we prepared to spend the night in squad tents a short distance from the docks. I had never seen Saigon. A night at New Port would give me that opportunity. I was strolling through the New Port gate when a spotlessly dressed MP grabbed my arm.

"Where do you think you're going, Sarge?"

"For a walk. I want to see Saigon."

He shook his head. "Nobody from the Cav's permitted off base."

Fucking MP. "I'm a big boy. I'll be back in a few hours."

The MP wasn't very good at being hardnosed. "I can't let you through here, but there's a hole in the wire about fifty meters from here. If I wasn't looking . . ."

I headed in the direction he pointed, but he wanted to talk. "I always wanted to go to the Cav MPs. The Cav's a tough unit."

"Yeah, but MPs have the same job all over. You'd just be directing traffic and kicking people out of bars." His hurt expression made me quickly regret my nasty comment. "Maybe not. The Cav MPs do make combat assaults."

I didn't tell him that Cav MPs worked with some evil critters called the Vietnamese National Police, or more commonly, White Mice. They usually did cordon and search landings in safe areas to search for black market goods and South Vietnamese deserters.

"What's duty like around here?" I asked.

He was smiling again. "It's pretty good since the attacks in May. Saigon hasn't been rocketed in months." A jeep with an MP sergeant and his driver pulled up to the gate. My new friend pointed to the rear seat. "Still want to see Saigon?"

"Sure."

"Why don't you go on patrol with my buddies? They're going right through the city."

The jeep crossed the New Port Bridge and headed down a modern highway toward Saigon. I bounced along in the back seat with a grenade launcher across my lap. The MP sergeant who handed it to me turned around in his seat.

"You know how to use that thing, Sarge?"

"I shot one once or twice." I slid a 40mm grenade into the chamber.

The sergeant jumped, twisted completely around, and snatched away my elephant gun. "Hey! We'd better unload this thing. It might go off if we hit a bump." I dreamed of new names for rear echelon MPs.

The sergeant told me that we were going to cruise down Tu Do Street, the famous Rue Catinet of the French War. What wonderful news! Every serviceman in Vietnam had heard about Saigon's legendary red light district. I had wanted to see it for years. My only regret was that the tour would be from the back seat of an MP jeep. We had reached the business district when a building in front of us lit up for an instant, followed by a thunderclap shock wave, my first experience with 122mm rockets.

The jeep raced down Tu Do Street, passing flashing neon signs and a milling crowd of made-up girls in miniskirts, drunken GIs and Vietnamese pimps. The driver turned the corner and inched around a bucket brigade throwing water on a burning building. More thunder rolled by as a building in the next block caught fire. The MP sergeant hunched down in his seat and pulled his helmet over his ears with both hands. The driver hit the accelerator and raced the jeep all the way back to New Port through dark, suddenly deserted streets. My tour of Saigon was over.

The artillery headquarters convoyed to the northwest at dawn. The first few miles were on a modern four-lane highway. Army bulldozers and road-graders were out in force, working at making more interchanges. Then we turned onto a poorer road, a narrow highway that had once been paved and still was in some places. Several hours into the journey, my truck passed a 20mm Vulcan minigun mounted on an APC. The thing was firing at something, belching an ear-splitting roar. As the sound of that monster receded, we heard President Johnson announce a total bombing halt over North Vietnam. He said the halt was in the interest of peace, but peace means different things in different places. The soldiers around me were angry.

Late in the afternoon, the convoy arrived at the Quan Loi base in rubber plantation country near the Cambodian border. The scenery there was breathtaking - rolling red earth hills covered with straight, well-tended rows of rubber trees. The plantations were cut by straight roads. Rubber workers' hamlets were laid out in carefully planned squares. This symmetrical world had nothing in common with the mountain forests and populated coastal plains of Binh Dinh Province. The plantation country was far more beautiful than the Bong Son Plains at ground level, but couldn't equal their splendor from the air. The long, straight rows of rubber trees seemed too regular, too artificial.

As we entered the front gates of Quan Loi, an infantry unit from the Big Red One returned from patrol. They wore custom made black base-ball caps, black scarves, and too-neat jungle uniforms. A bulletin would soon remind us that cavalry division regulations required soldiers to wear helmets and carry their weapons at all times. Frequent fistfights between members of the two divisions, over hats and helmets, were sometimes accompanied by taunts of "Bloody Red One" on one side, and "The Horse they Rode and the Line they Crossed" on the other.

The cavalry division would soon remove (fire) about two thousand civilian trash haulers, laundry washers, floor sweepers, hooch maids, and others from the base. We did most of these things for ourselves. In spite of being security risks and doing jobs that had more to do with comfort than war, suddenly unemployed civilians had relatives fighting with the Viet Cong. They might have resented the sudden loss of income and no longer had to worry about hitting Uncle Nguyen at his day job. Round-the-clock shelling of Quan Loi intensified.

The headquarters slept that first night in tattered, long-unused GP tents whose canvas sides were punctured, ripped and torn. They provided us with a stunning view of the rolling plantation hills. I was awakened at dawn by the crash I had been subconsciously hearing for nine months now. An 82mm mortar had fired a single shell. The headquarters moved to the other side of the Quan Loi base that same day. That evening, a leisurely mortar barrage tore up our tent camp of the night before. Forward observers were being used here. The NVA had fired a ranging [marking] shell, made their adjustments, and waited for darkness to kill us in our sleep. Unfortunately for them, the tents were empty when the mortars landed.

———◆———

I became a liaison NCO in An Loc, about three miles down the road from Quan Loi. An Loc was a sleepy provincial town, very neat, clean, pleasant and charming. It had schools with children in uniforms, kids on bikes, pretty girls in traditional *Ao Dai* flowing dresses, and an excellent Chinese restaurant. Reminders of the colonial past were everywhere. The brown stucco architecture was French Colonial, and the signs above shops were printed in both Vietnamese and French. The entire local economy was based on the French-owned rubber plantations.

The French were supposed to be neutral, but they were on good terms with the local Viet Cong. The NVA used plantations as sites for their mortars and rocket launchers, but permission was seldom given to shoot back at them. The French were reimbursed for every damaged or destroyed rubber tree. The French in Vietnam had fought their own war with the communists. They knew who was going to win this one. They took what our side offered while remaining on good terms with their future masters.

I worked in the ARVN advisor's compound in An Loc, reviewing intelligence reports and sending the best targets to the gun crews. The reports gave quick notice of what had changed since March. Entire NVA divisions waited across the border in Cambodia, some with tanks, multi-barreled rocket launchers, and heavy mortars. We were facing the equivalent of five NVA and Viet Cong divisions. The enemy was surely preparing for another Tet.

The story of the cavalry division's nineteen-month fight against those large enemy units is superbly told in J.D. Coleman's book, **Incursion**.

On my off-duty nights, I sat in the bar at the An Loc advisors compound and talked with an ex-sergeant of my age. He was an "officer" in a guerrilla force called the Green Lizards. They assassinated village chiefs and made hit-and- run raids to capture prisoners. The Green Lizards were a strange crew of Vietnamese, French, Americans, Cambodians, and probably, a German or two. They kept a low profile. I never saw more than two of them at a time, and they never spoke to regular troops, so my nationality assessment may be a tad off-center. At the time I had never heard of the Phoenix Program, and perhaps it hadn't been named, but that is exactly what the Green Lizards were doing. They may have been CIA mercenaries.

One evening at the bar, the "officer" told me how they had killed a communist hamlet chief that morning. They had been chased down a road by the hamlet's Viet Cong unit, and had destroyed the place with artillery shells. I asked him what good it did to kill the chief and then destroy the hamlet. He couldn't answer that. Our conversation ended when 82mm mortars exploded nearby and we crawled under a heavy oak table for protection.

Mortars were the bitter side of An Loc. They had become a daily menace since the arrival of the cavalry division. Mortar shells crashed across the compound every day. Some days they landed on the lawn of the province chief's mansion, and other times they sprayed an ugly statue of a South Vietnamese infantryman with fragments. The NVA were after that statue. Once a schoolgirl at recess was killed. The schoolyard was in a direct path from the statue, and I'm sure the child's death was an accident. The statue and the compound would be mortared again most nights.

Two nights before I left An Loc, the Viet Cong blew off the town gate with an RPG and held a propaganda rally in the town square. The government garrison locked themselves in their homes until the commies left at dawn. The next evening I listened to Quan Loi being shelled by rockets, mortars and recoilless rifles. The barrage was bigger than anything I had ever heard. On my last day at An Loc, I sat breathlessly in a bunker as mortars marched across the ARVN advisors' compound. Then a jeep took me to Bravo Troop.

The enemy no longer had a shortage of equipment and was confident enough to fire barrages or single shells around the clock. I laughed to recall the familiar dawn crowds of 1966 and 1967. The morning after each rapid mortar attack, people rushed to pry out tail fins as souvenirs. An officer and a private racing for the same crater to get a souvenir 82mm paperweight was a common sight. No one bothered to collect mortar tail fins after the Tet Offensive. They were too common.

Chapter 15

THE MOUNTAIN OF THE OLD MAN

(December-February, 1968-1969)

I became a fire team leader in the Blues and was soon learning firsthand how things had changed. The old Huey gunships were being replaced with Cobra gunships [snakes]. Cobras were faster and carried more weapons, but they didn't have those lethal door gunners, and didn't always fly at low level. Cobras carried 76 rockets as opposed 48 on the older Huey gunships, but I would take a Huey down low with two door gunners over a snake with a minigun any day. Cobras became flying gun platforms supporting the scout helicopters.

The old H-13 scout choppers, the bubbles, had been replaced by the more maneuverable Hughes LOHs [Light Observation Helicopters], nicknamed Loaches. Loaches resembled brown eggs with four stubby rotor blades on top. They too often burned when they crashed. Air crewmen now wore Nomex flight suits which were fire resistant; the suits didn't burn, but they sometimes melted with awful results.

A newer model M-16 was replacing the rifles that had caused so many Army and Marine casualties. The new rifles incorporated the changes to powder, cartridge cases, chamber, and buffer that were made to the older M-16 rifles to (unsuccessfully) stop jamming problems. The Singer Sewing Machine Company now manufactured the receivers. Singer M-16s did not jam.

The new concern for casualties changed the role of the Blues. Slicks no longer routinely flew on the deck. The Blue Lift pilots approached landing zones from higher altitudes and then descended. Missions usually involved air crew rescue or recovery, rather than shoot-'em-up heroics. Helicopter rescues had been considered easy duty on the open plains of the central coast, but here, in heavy jungle, they were never easy. Serious crash injuries were common. As in other years, our immediate medevac capability usually kept alive those who were not killed outright.

Once men wearing blue bandanas were considered "max crazy" and deferred to within the 9th Cavalry and throughout the cavalry division. Because of the present dangers of scout flying, Loach pilots and gunners had moved ahead in the pecking order. Other members of the troop repeated scout exploits just as they had formerly done with the Blues. It is said that you never step into the same river twice.

The enemy was the same soldier as before, but now, in most units, he was imbued with superhuman characteristics. He was described as tough, hard core, and battle-hardened. That attitude had more to do with sagging morale than with reality. North Vietnamese soldiers did have more munitions and more automatic weapons, were harder to see in their green uniforms and green pith helmets, and did carry an improved version of the RPG, but other than that, they remained the same: mostly farm boys who were as much out of their element in the jungle as we were.

My squad had nine soldiers. The squad leader was a draftee, like six of the others. The exception was Private Krueger, a German citizen who had volunteered for Vietnam duty. He had come a long way to fight and was disappointed that we didn't make more landings.

Krueger would have loved the Blues of 1967. He followed orders without question or comment, unlike most of his American comrades.

My main headache was Granite, a draftee from the mountains of Tennessee who recognized no authority from anyone born north of the Mason-Dixon Line, or, for that matter, anyone from outside his valley. His favorite profanities were "nigger" and "Yankee." Orders had to be repeated and explained; if he couldn't or didn't properly obey an order, he got angry or argued about it. Riding herd on him was like trying to herd a mosquito, but Granite did love a good fight. He was in the squad because there weren't any niggers. There was at least one Yankee.

On the first mission after my arrival, the slicks carried us over the B-52 crater fields marking the Cambodian border. We jumped into that moonscape. The North Vietnamese had remained even there by digging spider holes in the sides of bomb craters. We patrolled through the leafless white trees of a defoliated forest and found new bunkers, but the enemy had retreated across the border.

That first landing disturbed me. The platoon sergeant walked point while two squad leaders conducted all reconnaissance activities. I would be doing the same thing by the end of this tour of duty. The rest of the platoon had followed the sergeants, bunched together without proper spacing. After that one landing, I realized that this platoon was a shadow of the former Blues.

In truth, if it had been otherwise, if I had returned to the same intensity of purpose and steady combat that I had left six short months earlier, I would have stayed in Vietnam until my luck ran out or the war ended.

The Blues sat by the choppers for two days until Dusty Delta moved into squad tents down the road from us. I wondered what the jeep soldiers would be like now, so one evening I walked over to their tent camp. I found Pete leaning against a scarred, often-repaired artillery jeep.

"Peterson! You're still around!"

"Brennan, what in the hell are you doing back?"

"I was bored. How are things with Dusty Delta?"

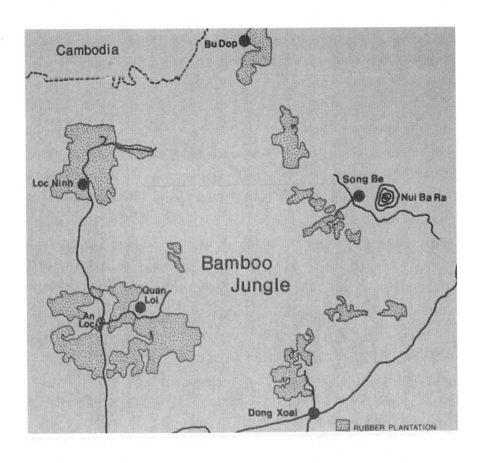

He frowned. He still didn't like that name. "Good. The troop's a lot tougher than it used to be."

"Pete?" I asked. "I thought there weren't any FOs with the Ninth Cav."

"There aren't. I'm the last one. They let me stay until I get tired of it, and I've about had it. I'm going home in two weeks. Been here twenty-nine months now."

Pete told me that Dusty Delta had left its vehicles and operated as an infantry company of three platoons in the mountains around Khe Sanh. The countryside was among the most beautiful he had ever seen. Later, the Delta Troop company walked into the northern A Shau Valley with the 101st Airborne.

Delta Troop's biggest day came in June, when it initiated and participated in a battle with a battalion of the 812th NVA Regiment in Binh An, that village northeast of Camp Evans that Marine pilots had avoided. Enemy losses were 244 killed and 33 made prisoner. Pete said that the survivors were sealed in their bunkers by APCs.

Pete invited me to join Delta Troop's road patrols through the rubber plantations, so I spent six days on patrols around Quan Loi. Meanwhile, the Blue platoon was still waiting for a mission. I rode with whichever platoon Pete was covering that day. The platoon would drive down straight, red earth roads, park their vehicles along road shoulders and patrol through the rubber trees. We ate C-rations in those neat little workers' hamlets. The villagers always gave us armfuls of bananas and breadfruit. Breadfruit tastes like a cross between bananas and oranges, and it is delicious.

One day a sniper shot at us from deeper inside the plantation. The platoon charged past rubber trees bleeding sticky white sap from our bullets, only to find a few cartridge cases and a French bush hat in the mud of a shallow trench. The sniper had escaped down a fire lane through the trees. Those men were acting like a Blue platoon.

On the sixth day, we patrolled north through a hot scrub country of brush and dead trees until we arrived at the rubber town of Loc Ninh.

About a mile outside of town was the wreckage of a column of APCs. Several of them had "splash holes" in their armor [aluminum armor melts and splashes when hit by an RPG]. The lead vehicle had been reduced to massive chunks of metal by a powerful land mine. Those armored vehicles had been part of an ambushed rescue force.

The town was battered and half-ruined by the pre-Tet battles of a year before. Some of the buildings had been demolished by RPGs, and many of the stucco walls had disintegrated under machine gun fire. We turned the jeeps around on the manicured lawn of a beautiful French villa on a gentle rise that appeared to be undamaged by the fierce battles that had raged just down the road.

Pete said his goodbyes that night at Quan Loi. "I'm leaving because my mother's afraid I'll get shot. I promised her I wouldn't extend again."

I told him not to give up like I had done. Then Pete was gone.

I returned to a Blue platoon that was still waiting by the slicks. I didn't understand the reason at the time, but the hiatus was caused by a landing that almost happened the day before I rejoined the troop. Two scout Loaches spotted men with military haircuts hiding in a hamlet; Blue was launched to investigate. Meanwhile, a force of APCs and tanks from the 11th Armored Cavalry Regiment began moving through a rubber plantation toward the hamlet. They quickly became engaged with an NVA battalion inside the plantation. Slicks carrying the Blues were descending, on final approach to the landing zone, when the mission was aborted.

Once, Bravo Blues would have been inserted so they could get a piece of the action, but this was a different, more cautious, time. Fifty-eight North Vietnamese were killed in the battle.

In early December, our Loaches found an area of heavy enemy activity east of Quan Loi. A scout crew discovered a long NVA column walking out of the jungle, down a streambed, and back into the jungle in the direction of a bunker complex. They shot up the group, which was said to include a North Vietnamese general, and hovered down to capture a 57mm recoilless rifle, a .30 caliber machine gun on wheels, an RPD squad machine gun, and several AK-47s. Fifty-seven millimeter recoilless rifles were carried by command groups.

The weapons were put on display at Quan Loi. I was looking at the strange, wheeled machine gun when Bolton walked up. I was seeing him at close range for the first time in fourteen months and he looked ten years older. Pete had told me that Bolton was now a scout gunner, but he had apparently been keeping a low profile.

Bolton looked fondly at the trophies and asked, "Aren't they something, Sarge?"

"Yeah. Did you have something to do with getting them?"

"Of course," he replied. "The gooks never knew what hit them."

Bolton told me that he wasn't leaving Vietnam. His main problem was finding a new war when that one was over. "Maybe they'll need mercenaries in Africa again." After that conversation I knew he was there only to die. He later died a hero's death, firing a machine gun to hold off the enemy soldiers who had shot down his Loach.

In the area where the command group was attacked, Loach crews found evidence of fresh trails, bunkers, cooking fires, and many people. Scout pilots Rick Chesson and George Hamilton recommended a B-52 strike. Instead, an infantry company, call sign 'Heavy Bones," was landed. The NVA were waiting in bunkers around the clearing and opened up with mortars, RPGs, heavy machine guns and other weapons. Tracers and their little pea green flamethrowers set the dry grass on fire. The grunts took heavy casualties, including twenty-seven killed. Division barely got them out of there.

A B-52 strike hit the area that same night. The following day, one of our Loaches rescued the last cavalryman in the clearing from inside a bomb crater. He had survived bullets, fire, a B-52 strike, and a rare and lucky miss by premier scout gunner Doug Glover.

———————

The day before the Christmas Truce began, we landed in a plantation of mature rubber trees and patrolled down the last row beside a boundary of woods. Black telephone wire was strung high in the trees of that woods; next came pieces of Plexiglas, torn sheets of helicopter skin, and then most of a tail boom balanced on the upper tree limbs. We arrived at a great bowl blasted out of the tree tops. The limbs and branches had begun to mend themselves and sprout twigs, so the blast had occurred about a year before, probably during the 1968 Tet Offensive. The enemy had rigged a mine in the trees, perhaps with some kind of pressure trigger, and waited to bag a slick. No one could have survived that blast.

On Christmas day, a few Blue volunteers were offered the opportunity to fly as scout observers. My crew was reputed to be one of the best: pilot Rick Chesson and gunner Doug Glover. I sat in the right front seat with a red smoke grenade in my right hand and a rifle across my knees. The idea was to mark a target for the high bird with a red smoke. A truce was in effect, so we hoped that the most lethal weapon used that day would be bundles of glossy First Air Cavalry Division Christmas cards tied up with twine.

The North Vietnamese were easy to find that morning. The weather was chilly and their camp fires were blazing to high heaven. I would see similar fires extinguished almost instantly, but these continued to burn. Below us were thatched roofs and cleared spaces with picnic tables, just like those found at state parks in America. At any other time, we would have tried to start a battle and they would have tried to shoot us out of the sky, but instead, we bombarded them with Christmas cards.

Later we were flying in circles or figure eights down a red dirt road that ran straight through a rubber plantation. I was dizzy from watching whirling while Chesson and Glover looked earthward for trouble. Doug Glover excitedly shouted something over the intercom that I couldn't understand. By the time I would have dropped the marking smoke on the pilot's command, we were past them, and Rick Chesson was calmly explaining that Glover had spotted a file of NVA on the road. Chesson recalls their eyes being wide with fear. Glover wanted to open fire with his machine gun, but a truce was in effect and the order was not given.

We leveled off for a moment and saw a young Vietnamese, probably the "tail-end Charlie" of the file, gaping at us. His green pith helmet was tipped back on his head like a straw hat. He looked exactly like what he probably was – a farm boy seeing his first helicopter. We were gone by the time our Christmas cards hit the ground.

Mr. Chesson stated that he might have allowed Glover to fire had he known that another Loach was being shot up a few kilometers away.

Shortly after the Christmas Truce ended, a Loach flew over tall jungle trees, dropped into a clearing, and discovered a classroom. Cobra gunship pilot Bob Stamm repeats the scout pilot's description of the scene this way: a man on a podium, using a pointer to highlight a drawing of a helicopter on his blackboard, was lecturing a group of North Vietnamese soldiers seated in bleachers. The scout gunner opened fire and killed several of them.

"What a surprise," wrote Stamm, "when he had a pink team fly right into his midst and begin cutting down his class where they sat."

Stamm directed the Loach out of the clearing and rolled in with rockets and miniguns. Then his copilot discovered that they were actually over the border in Cambodia. Stamm called "Stormy Weather," code for an inadvertent border violation, and the pink team beat a hasty retreat back to Vietnam. He estimates that fifty or more enemy soldiers died. Because of the action's location, the troop commander at Quan Loi told the pilots to consider that it had never occurred.

Once a scout chopper left Quan Loi at dawn and flew toward Cambodia over a field of B-52 bomb craters. The gunner saw a man walk out of a wood, yawn and stretch, and stroll over to a crater. He was pissing into the muddy bottom when the Loach got back to him. He died before he could finish.

Another Loach surprised a column of NVA resting beside a bulldozer near an abandoned Special Forces Camp. The gunner killed eighteen men on the first pass. Snakes and bombers finished the work. The war was fast becoming a remote control affair, fought with machines and steel rather than flesh and blood.

On December twenty-ninth, the slicks took us near the Cambodian border, to a place where oily black smoke rose from a dead wood. A Charlie Troop Loach had been shot down and was burning. It was a damp, drizzling, overcast day when we jumped into a forty-meter-wide clearing of wet grass surrounded by shabby hedgerows. Charlie Blues came in right behind us. Everyone I had known was gone. Charlie Blues left to recover the scout crew's bodies, but our platoon made no real effort to protect the clearing. The platoon sergeant and all the squad leaders gathered in front of a hedgerow and posed for photographs.

Charlie Blues returned carrying three body bags and were extracted by their lift birds. Our slicks followed. As we were lifted out of the clearing, the slicks flew over the hedgerow where the sergeants had been mugging for the camera. Behind it was a bunker in the grass; crumpled in front of it were two bodies in green uniforms. Their AKs were lying beside them.

As we gained altitude, the air rattled with the sound of a heavy machine gun. Two barrels were flashing in the shade of some trees below us. Shadows made the muzzle flashes easy to see. I emptied three magazines at the flashes and shook the man next to me until he started shooting. Our tracers disappeared into the trees around the barrels; the twin machine gun stopped firing. We probably didn't hit anything.

A familiar face appeared in the doorway of our tent that evening. Private Page hadn't changed much, except now he was a specialist who sported a big handlebar mustache.

"Page? I don't believe it. Did you extend?"

"Yeah, Sarge," he said. "I heard you're back. Brought you some news."

"What news?"

"I work over at troop operations. Anyway, Charlie Troop called a couple of hours ago and said you guys killed an NVA this morning. I checked and found out that you were the one who did the shooting."

"You mean the twin twelve-seven?" (or whatever it was)

That's it. They said to tell you it was good shooting." Page remained standing in the doorway. He needed something else. "Sarge, would you do me a big favor?"

"Sure."

"Come here a second." He led me to a tent occupied by a small group of enlisted men from the operations section. He pointed to the upturned faces. "They don't believe me. Tell them I got a Distinguished Flying Cross and killed ninety-eight NVA in those first days at Evans."

I looked at the man who had called us baby-killers a year before and nodded. "It's true. He did it." They looked at Page with new respect.

We were after the crew of a downed artillery observation Loach. It had been hit by a heavy machine gun in a place we called the "bamboo jungle." Agent Orange had destroyed the leaves of most trees, and the sudden flood of sunlight had caused normally small clumps of bamboo to grow into a tangle of giant yellow, green and purple stalks.

The slicks hovered down between tall white trees, one ship at a time. We hung from the skids and dropped into a clearing created by an old bomb crater, crossed a trail and stepped around a bunker where someone had been eating C-rations minutes before. Juice was still dripping from a can of Ham and Lima Beans. If the NVA wanted that meal, they could have it. A man ran to us from behind a clump of bamboo; the squad leader on point almost shot him. He was the artillery forward observer from the downed Loach, and he was crying.

"God damn! Am I glad you guys are here! The pilot's hurt real bad!"

The injured pilot was lying on a bed of red jungle flowers, a few feet from where the Loach burned on its side between clumps of bamboo. Doc Melugin dragged him farther away from the flames and spread ointment over his burned chest, face, and arms while I got rid of the munitions. We strapped the pilot to a jungle penetrator stretcher and he was hoisted up through the trees by a medevac helicopter. It was time for us to get out, but the nearest bomb crater clearings were too small for the slicks to use as "hover holes."

The circling pilots sounded hysterical. "Blue Mike, this is Saber Red. Move to the yellow smoke and prepare for extraction! Move to the yellow smoke! Move quickly! I say again, move quickly!"

We reached one of the bomb craters as a Loach arrived with chainsaws and axes. Two squads worked like demons to cut down small trees and bamboo stalks while my squad searched the jungle immediately around the crater. The bomb blast and wild growth had created an almost solid wall of vines and bamboo. We found nothing. When the slicks came in to get us, one ship at a time, their blades chopped bamboo all the way in and out.

We had just arrived back at Quan Loi and were walking to our tents when the jungle, about five miles away, erupted with a string of black explosions, followed by the rumbling thunder of a B-52 strike. The bamboo jungle had been declared a no-fly zone the night before, but the artillery Loach pilot had flown over anyway. We had been extracted just in time.

Page came visiting again that evening. We had been best friends since I confirmed his war story and I could tell he had some interesting news by the way he was grinning.

"You boys had a close call this morning."

"That's putting it mildly."

"Hey, Sarge. Guess what the scouts found after the strike."

"Let's see. Craters?"

A sadistic grin. "Oh, better than that. They found five smashed twelve-sevens in the area where the Loach went down. They were all around you in the bamboo. Oh, Yeah. I almost forgot. There was a dead gook ten meters from your hover hole."

Page, the bearer of ill tidings. "Thanks, Page."

The next afternoon, we landed for a rare recon patrol in an abandoned plantation of old rubber trees. Our point squad leader came face-to-face with an NVA on a narrow trail. Both of them fired until their rifles were empty, missed completely, turned and ran. As the squad leader ran past me, the fear on his face reminded me of Patterson's expression the day his rifle jammed in the Soui Ca. The difference was that Patterson had been in Vietnam for two weeks at the time. The squad leader had been with the Blues for about nine months.

On another day, we were taken to one of the few unbombed regions along the Cambodian border. The Air Force had dropped electronic movement sensors there, and they had detected something. Our target was an open field of saw grass sandwiched between jungle to the north and south. I wondered why the camouflage-crazy NVA would infiltrate through grass instead of jungle.

We carefully approached a trail identified by the scouts, a trail made by wild water buffalo: not a single human footprint among hundreds of hoof prints. And we found a movement sensor. It was camouflaged to resemble a green metal tree, but was out of place in the light brown grass.

The story of the infiltrating water buffalo bounced around the troop for months thereafter.

Then the scouts found a "mortar." The Blues walked for hours through an old plantation of tangled, decaying trees that had been heavily shelled in the past. Red smoke marked the mortar as a scout gunner poured tracers into the plantation. Among the rotten branches was the upturned tail section of a 500-pound bomb, rusty with age and looking for all the world like a mortar tube. Krueger was watching me. He was curious.

"You don't look surprised like the others, Sergeant."

"It's happened twice before."

"Where?"

"In nineteen-sixty-six and nineteen-sixty-seven, when the Blues were at Bong Son"

"Oh. Where's Bong Son?"

What was the use of trying to explain? Those events had happened a million years ago. "We'll talk about it sometime. Okay?"

"Yes, Sergeant." Krueger made a fine soldier. He only asked the proper questions.

The next day about noon, we returned from a plantation patrol just in time to be scrambled for a mission in the bomb crater strip along the Cambodian border. I arrived at my tent, heard the siren, and turned to leave just in time to see a familiar face go by. Bob was a blond-haired young man whom I had known when he was a platoon leader's radioman with Bravo Blues. He was a quiet, soft-spoken fellow who was liked by everyone.

Bob told me that he had been bored and missed the Blues, so he reenlisted to come back, by a now familiar story. I welcomed him back, excited to have an old comrade from the hard days in the platoon, and hopefully, in my squad. He nodded without speaking and stared away at something far off in our past.

After the border patrol was through, I went looking for Bob. No one knew who, or where, he was. Finally, a squad leader told me that Bob was gone. "He went to see the major." That was code talk for someone who needed out for whatever reason, the philosophy being that damaged men could make mistakes or hurt morale. To my knowledge, those folks were never refused, and were usually sent away on a chopper the very same day. I never saw Bob again.

Somewhere in this time-frame we received a boyish-looking young platoon leader. Lieutenant Poxon was a shy but friendly person who was all business. He usually stayed with the pilots and came around us only for missions. I am sure that this was his way of maintaining the separation he thought was required of his position.

The nights in late January and February were spent guarding a mountaintop in War Zone D. Its Vietnamese name was Nui Ba Ra, but we also called it by our translation, "The Mountain of the Old Man." The slicks would come in over white limestone cliffs and clinging jungle to deposit us on the summit. The mountain was the highest point in the province; you could see for many miles in all directions.

A small ARVN infantry platoon and a three-man American radio relay team were already there, so the defenses were prepared: bunkers, several rows of barbed wire, and a ring of deep trenches. The sleeping quarters were sandbagged steel conex shipping containers.

The entire position was at most fifty meters across. We could easily defeat a large force from behind those close-knit defenses, but the South Vietnamese soldiers didn't want us to prove it. Some of them glared at us and others cursed when we test-fired our weapons into the tree tops below us. When Blues lobbed grenades down the steep sides of the mountain, Arvn soldiers would shake their heads "no," wave their arms in a Vietnamese stop gesture, and put index fingers to their lips. Their expressions said, "Be quiet. Don't piss off the men who really own this mountain. They might think it's us making the noise."

The place was very rocky, and mortar blasts could turn rock splinters into deadly shrapnel. I was leading the squad, so I called my men together. "I want everyone to sleep in the conex containers, not on top of them. If mortars ever hit this place, they'll get everyone who's not under cover."

Granite objected as usual. "Aw, Sarge. The conexes are hot. The other squad leaders aren't making their men sleep inside. The guys on the relay station say they haven't been mortared since September."

"Granite, if only you knew how many times I've heard that. Now we're here. The gooks hate the Cav, and I promise you, we will be mortared. You have to sleep in the conex containers or you'll be hit by flying pieces of rock."

Krueger backed my judgment. "I think the sergeant is right. It would be safer."

Other men nodded in agreement. After all, it was their lives I was talking about, and I was going to sleep in a conex container even if no one else in the platoon did. Granite wandered off, muttering under his breath about "that brown-nosing Kraut." Krueger looked away in hurt silence.

Nui Ba Ra was a place with a reputation. War legend had it that a 101st Airborne platoon had been overrun there some time in the past. The Viet Cong were said to have left their heads on stakes along the barbed wire. There had been attacks since, but the Blues got off lightly. The outpost was mortared a couple of times during the Tet attacks of 1969, and NVA infantry tried to capture the place one night in late February. The Blues stopped them in the wire, but there was a more frightening thing. Dawn revealed a Viet Cong flag flying from a pole outside the wire. The flagpole was booby-trapped with a round Chinese claymore mine. That claymore is what the Blues remembered about Nui Ba Ra. Let me tell you why.

A claymore mine blasts out hundreds of tiny missiles in an arc or a cone. The American claymore is a marvel of engineering. It is an outwardly curved rectangle of high impact plastic backed by a steel plate. On the front of this little gem are the words FRONT TOWARD ENEMY. This evil thing is placed against a tree or boulder to protect the firer from back-blast. The explosion follows the line of least resistance, hurling out a lethal shower of ball bearings.

The Chinese varieties came in several sizes, for revolutionaries of all ages, but all were brown and bowl-shaped. And no ball bearings for the Chinese! The few I handled had a hinged door in the front to allow the mine to be filled with whatever was at hand. I once visited one of my soldiers who had been hit by a Chinese claymore. His souvenir was a steel nut removed from within an inch of his spine. Claymores were usually detonated by a man in hiding who was waiting for someone to walk in front of his mine. In my opinion, they were the most brutal weapons used by both sides during the war, partly because of their effectiveness, and partly because of the way they were fired.

In May, 1966 a Delta Troop claymore ambush wiped out an entire group of fifteen NVA on a mountain trail as they tried to escape Operation Crazy Horse in Happy Valley. Also in May, 1966 while I was on a flight from Pleiku to Cam Ranh Bay, a soldier from the 173rd Airborne Brigade told me that every other man in his squad had been killed in a claymore ambush. He was taking a tied-up bundle of five M-16s somewhere.

*The full story of Delta Troop's claymore ambush is told in General S.L.A. Marshall's book, **Battles in the Monsoon**. It is worth reading.*

The first night on Nui Ba Ra, we watched artillery and flares over the war zone below. Many miles to the east was a sea of light. Perhaps it was Saigon. At about 4:00 a.m., a B-52 strike tore apart dark jungle to the south. Those strikes had once been called "heavy artillery" and were now called "arc lights." For the first time I realized how appropriate the most recent name was. For a long instant, the strike zone looked as if an intensely hot electric light was burning above the jungle. Toward dawn, a firefight erupted to the southwest. Strings of tracers crisscrossed, bounced skyward and flickered out. That was a typical night on the mountain.

February twelfth was our turn. Two Loaches were down on the edge of the rubber trees. The first one, George Hamilton's chopper, had been shot down by a heavy machine gun over big rubber log bunkers; the second had attempted to rescue the crew. Red smoke marked our landing zone beside French plantation buildings in a large, rectangular clearing. The main building looked like a brown tropical imitation of a Southern mansion. The outlying buildings appeared neat and well-tended.

Our four slicks approached the LZ in trail [each slick following the one ahead of it]. My squad was on the first one. The rubber trees began winking like Christmas tree lights. Cobra pilot Rick Chesson describes an aerial view of the scene to this point:

"The plan was to insert the Blues, but as the slicks flared on final, hundreds of NVA opened fire on them. The trees were full of NVA who were lying along the shallow fire breaks between rows of trees. They were also in trenches inside the rubber trees. On the other side of the landing zone, the NVA occupied the plantation buildings."

Much more of the captivating and understated story of Chesson's Vietnam tour, entitled "Flying Tigers," can be found in the book, **Hunter-Killer Squadron**.

A machine gun fired tracers from an upstairs window of the mansion as our lift bird came in fast and hovered down a dirt road beside a grassy swale. The men on my side jumped. The clacking roar of AKs continued until the slick was out of sight above the rubber trees. Four of us squatted in the dirt and looked around. We were alone in the clearing. The last three slicks had been driven off by the intense fire. The four Blues on the other side of our slick had not jumped. One of them and the ship's crew chief had been wounded. Our team included Doc Melugin, a new rifleman, a new fire team leader, Sergeant Ruby, with the squad radio, and me. That radio and some courageous pilots saved our lives.

The clearing was suddenly silent and eerily peaceful, like siesta time in the antebellum South. It was a picture perfect day. Small white clouds floated through a blue sky, nudged along by gentle breezes above the tree tops. Around us were the cool, green leaves of a mature plantation whose trees marched away in silent rows in all directions. Then someone spoiled it. A single rifle fired a lonely bullet into the morning calm. As in most firefights, it was that first, solitary shot, and it boomed like a cannon.

We dove into the swale and belly-crawled along it as a brushfire slowly ate its way toward us. Dozens of AKs opened up as a Cobra dived for a rocket run. The rockets exploded against the front of the mansion, raising clouds of brown and gray dust. The machine gun continued firing from an upstairs window with open shutters.

I shouted to the others, "Hit that window. They've got a thirty caliber up there!" and then emptied a magazine to show them where to shoot.

Plaster and paint flew around the window as the barrel swung in our direction. They couldn't aim well because of our bullets, and seemed to be having trouble depressing the barrel enough to hit us. I told Ruby to call the gunships about our problem. He got a quick response.

As Rick Chesson recalls, Cobra pilot Bob Stamm heard our plea for help and shouted over the intercom, "They're getting their shit blown away! We've got to help!" and down they went.

Ruby pulled a smoke grenade from his harness and shouted, "Pop smoke! The gunships are making a run on that building!"

Stamm's Cobra roared at low level across the plantation, dropped into the clearing, and came to a hover level with that second story window. He fired rockets at the mansion while Chesson raked the rubber trees on the other side with the gunship's minigun. Chesson states that enemy bullets missed the Cobra because the NVA were doing what they had been trained to do – lead [fire in front of] a helicopter. But this one was at a hover. Perhaps their instructor had been a man with a blackboard on a podium in Cambodia.

The wall around the window disintegrated and the snake lifted away. The machine gun had gone silent. A dazed soldier in a green uniform stumbled through the front door and ran in our direction. He didn't see us. Doc Melugin shot him.

Doc sucked in a deep breath and shook his head. "He was heading right at us! Man, I got him!"

The brushfire was getting closer. We lay in the swale with our feet almost touching and faced in four directions. I was facing the rubber plantation that began about forty meters away. Something brown was moving there. I focused on a man in a khaki uniform and jungle hat, pack and AK, motioning on a sweep line of soldiers behind him. Troops fresh from Cambodia, still wearing khaki uniforms!

The soldiers in the sweep line dodged from tree to tree while the leader ran straight at us in crouch, triggering short bursts from his AK. I took careful aim and squeezed off a three-round burst. The leader flopped on his back beside a rubber tree, legs kicking and jerking. The soldiers behind him quickly disappeared into cover, so I emptied the rest of the magazine into the plantation at ground level. The NVA had taught me a hard lesson: always shoot the leader.

Ruby told the gunships that the rubber trees were full of NVA, a fact that the pilots already knew. We popped more smoke and two Cobras made a low-level run parallel to us, filling the air with the buzzing crack and red tracking smoke of flechette rockets. They thundered by just above the tree tops like prehistoric birds of prey.

Clack-Clack-Clack! Bullets dug into the lips of the swale. The swale was on fire, the mansion side was quiet, and the NVA in the rubber trees were dodging flechette rockets. The bullets must be coming from neat piles of rubber branches about halfway between us and the trees.

I raised my head to look at the nearest pile. Clack-Clack-Clack! The burst kicked dirt in my face and eyes. I pulled a pin on a TNT grenade and waited. They would keep their heads down when the gunship pilots made their next run. When two slicks dived, I tossed the grenade. A black explosion scattered the branches. Somewhere among them was (probably) a dead man. The other Blues cringed from the unexpected blast.

"Hey! Everyone take one of these concussion grenades. We can use them on the branch piles if they try to use them for cover." I passed out three of my five remaining TNT grenades.

Ruby took a concussion grenade and listened to a transmission on his radio handset. "Pop smoke! Gunships are making a minigun run on the edge of the rubber!"

The Cobra dived, and then the whole world was roaring. We were lost in a cloud of dust and flying dirt. Doc Melugin rolled over on his back and groaned. Ruby gaped at him. The Cobra was coming back around for another minigun run. I grabbed Ruby by both shoulders and shook him like a rag doll. He was that limp.

"Tell them they were shooting at us! Quick, man, before that snake makes another run!" Ruby tried to say something. "Don't fuck around! Do it!"

He fumbled with the handset and found his voice again. "Red! Red! That smoke marked out location! I repeat, that smoke marked our location! Call off the snake! The medic got hit by that run! I repeat! The medic got hit by that run!" The Cobra climbed away.

Doc used his teeth to tighten a field dressing around his arm, looked around at our concerned faces, and said in a calm voice, "It's okay. I know how bad a wound is. It's just a flesh wound." He managed a weak smile to show us that the wound didn't hurt.

Ruby finally received the merciful message. "They're going to try and get us out. They want us to throw all our smoke grenades at the woods for a smoke screen."

The new rifleman guffawed. "Yeah. Let's throw all two of them."

The brushfire was a few meters away now, but to run would be suicidal, so we low-crawled farther down the swale. Ruby and the rifleman threw two red smoke grenades at the rubber trees and I lobbed my last two TNT grenades into more branch piles.

A beautiful lift bird flanked by two rocket-firing Cobras dropped into the clearing, flared and touched down just behind us on the road. We ran to board it. Doc and Ruby ran backwards, spraying the rubber trees. The rifleman and I ran around the nose of the helicopter, firing at the mansion and the outbuildings. As I hopped up on the floor of the chopper and grabbed a seat strut, a line of bullets kicked up dirt in front of the lift bird's nose. "Wow!" I thought. "Just like a World War Two movie!"

Our rescue ship lifted off over the brushfire. The rubber trees started winking again. My left foot went numb as we banked away from the outbuildings. When I stepped off the slick at Quan Loi, I had trouble walking. I knew I had a foot wound because of the numbness, the ripped leather on top of my new boot and blood on the grass, but I refused to acknowledge it. Thanks to far too many war novels in my youth, I thought that people with foot wounds were cowards who shot themselves to get out of combat. Russians had executed their soldiers with similar wounds during the Second World War.

I sat down on the grass, pulled off the boot, and stared at what looked like a large red dot on my precious big toe. It was a lucky hit. The bullet had gone through the toe joint. The injury still didn't hurt, so I put the boot back on. At the aid station, the first painful event was when a doctor cut off my new boot. I saw the scissors aimed at the top of the boot and shouted for him to stop. He ignored me. I had waited a long time for those boots. Then he stuck a piece of wire completely through my toe and twirled it around. That hurt like hell.

I was tagged for evacuation and waiting for medications, but sneaked out of the tent with one bandaged foot and hitched a jeep ride back to Bravo Troop. I wanted another crack at those North Vietnamese in the rubber trees. Pink teams, artillery, and jet bombers were engaged until nightfall, but Blue was never sent back.

The entire leg was swollen and throbbing by the next morning. I limped to the headquarters tent and begged for a lift to the aid station. Two days later, I arrived at Camp Zama Hospital in Japan. Memories of the trip north to Japan are hazy. My companions were at least Doc Melugin and a scout gunner.

The scout gunner had earned the nickname "Crazy Man" a few days before. His Loach had been shot at from a maze of bunkers. It had been shot at mainly because the pilot had hovered there while Crazy Man stood on a landing skid and pissed on the bunkers. Now he had a bowl full of Darvon tablets begged from sympathetic nurses and was intent on staying high until he was healed and could piss on more NVA. Crazy Man had been shot through the foot.

Bravo Troop had three Loaches shot down during that battle. Several snakes and lift birds also suffered battle damage. Pilot George Hamilton and two crew chiefs were killed. Five other troop personnel were wounded. Sixty-six North Vietnamese dead were counted. Our brave scouts had intercepted an NVA battalion on the march toward Saigon for the 1969 Tet Offensive.

Rick Chesson states that an infantry battalion was inserted the next morning. Soon thereafter, a unit dressed in NVA khaki uniforms and carrying AKs, emerged from the rubber plantation and linked up with the infantry. They said that Bravo Troop had engaged an NVA unit that they had followed from Cambodia. The phony NVA unit was, of course, the Green Lizards I had seen at An Loc.

Three days after our battle, Alpha Troop lost five men when a slick with an infantry squad aboard was shot down. On February twenty-third, Delta Troop fought its way through an NVA ambush in a rubber plantation near Quan Loi and suffered eight men killed. This was in the same area with the friendly villagers that I had patrolled with Pete in November. He had gone home just in time.

Two-hundred-and-one other American heroes died on February twenty-third, the first day of the 1969 Tet Offensive.

Chapter 16

HOSPITAL

(February-March, 1969)

The hospital in Japan was a turning point in my life, but in the first hours, I was angry that they had sent me so far for such a little wound.

The man in the next bed was a Special Forces staff sergeant with a broken femur. His team had ambushed a trail in Laos and caught the NVA in a claymore and machine gun crossfire. Instead of waiting to die, the North Vietnamese had charged the machine guns. One of the Vietnamese had shot the SF sergeant as he himself was being killed. The sergeant was tired.

"I've been in the Nam for thirty-five months, and I've never seen men like that. Each year they get harder and better armed. Those dudes wouldn't die out there. We kept hitting them and they just kept coming. I'm glad this happened to me. They're getting too much heart. Just too much heart."

He left for home leaning on a cane and smiling like the cat that ate the canary. He said he hoped some "good guys" would need a mercenary in a few years. He preferred Asia to Africa, but would take what he could get.

On the other side of me was a Marine Corps platoon sergeant. He had been wounded by mortars in the northern part of the A Shau Valley and was afraid that his missing eye would force him out of his beloved Corps. Beside him was a paratrooper riddled by a claymore mine.

I rolled my wheelchair to the mess hall one day and heard the grating voice of my nemesis, Specialist Granite. I thought I was mistaken, but there he was, wrapped in bandages and trying to bully another soldier out of beer money. I couldn't escape that hillbilly, not even in Japan. If I wanted to eat lunch, I had to pilot my wheelchair right past him. Of course, his eyes lit up when he saw me.

"Granite, how did you get here? Did you get hit on February twelfth, too?"

"Naw, Sarge. They mortared Nui Ba Ra."

"Were you inside the bunkers like I told you?"

"Nope," he said with a guilty look. "We was sleeping on top of them." As if to justify his own actions, he added, "They got the Kraut, too. Through the eyes."

"I warned you guys. That should leave about one man in second squad. Maybe we should have a squad reunion while we're here."

Granite became the motor for my wheelchair. We had a few good days of wheelchair races and wheelchair snowball fights, and then one day, I could hobble. One of my first walks took me by the camp library, and I was hungry for books. I asked the clerk if he could recommend anything, and he led me to a well-stocked section on Southeast Asia. I stayed there from morning to late afternoon. After scarcely two weeks, I had read every book on the shelves on Vietnamese history and politics, the French war, and the American war. Then I reached some conclusions.

The Army was falling apart. The evidence was all around me. Nothing that one man could do was going to change that. It was going to be a long war. I couldn't possibly stay around to see the end of it. If I wrote a book someday, it would be a story that began with no beginning and ended without an ending.

I reread **Street without Joy** and **Hell in a Very Small Place** by Bernard Fall, and Lucien Bodard's **The Quicksand War: Prelude to Vietnam**, and realized only too well that our war was an extension of a war against foreigners that Vietnam had been waging for a very long time. I thought about all of the wasted bravery and suffering. In the chaos of 1969, draftees were killing other draftees. Better that they all return to their farms and rice paddies. I had wasted most of three years fighting nationalism, rather than communism or Chinese expansion, always steadfastly convinced of the justice of our cause. Now I was confused.

A Marine staff sergeant of about my age joined me on a bench outside a beer hall one cold March day. After we exchanged war stories for a while, he pointed to a group of young soldiers and Marines who were horsing around (called "grab-assing" in the Army) waiting for a theater to open.

"Did you notice how much alike they are?" he asked. "The only way you can tell which ones are Marines is by their khaki belts. My first tour was in nineteen-sixty-five in Da Nang. Every one of us was a Marine volunteer. Now there's more draftees in the line units than anything else. They fight well when they haven't got a choice, but it's not the same. You know?"

I knew.

A few images of that hospital have remained with me. A terrifying (to me) head wounds ward: shaven heads, railroad track stitches across skulls, grown men struggling to learn or pronounce simple words, large clocks over double doorways at both ends of a long ward, some of the patients who can speak incessantly asking, "What time is it?" I remember to hate snipers once again.

In the next bay is a tiny, frail 101st Airborne child-paratrooper wounded by a mortar shell in the A Shau Valley: wounds and tubes everywhere, both legs and one arm in suspension, a cheerful greeting for anyone passing by, the overwhelming stench of rot. We visit each day. I praise his recovery in person and pray for him in private.

An Americal Division surfer dude gut shot in the Que Son Valley: long blonde hair, a deep tan and pearly white smile, broad shoulders and a seashell necklace, entrails displayed outside his body cavity in clear plastic.

A cheerful, upbeat 173rd Airborne lieutenant calls himself lucky to have lost "only a foot" to a land mine, and be alive and away from the Crescent.

And on it went.

Chapter 17

SKY PILOT

(March-May, 1969)

When I returned from the hospital, Bravo Troop was temporarily stationed in a part of the sprawling command and supply center near Saigon affectionately called Disneyland East. We lived in modern two-story wooden barracks and slept on steel bunks with springs and mattresses. The accommodations were luxurious. Many of the buildings had air conditioning and the rest had big ceiling fans. Paved roads were lined with hotdog stands, ice cream parlors, clubs, restaurants, and swimming pools. The Saigon Army knew how to fight a war.

The lost Blues of February twelfth and Nui Ba Ra had been replaced. The platoon sergeant and three other Instant NCOs had gone home. When I asked someone if they had left any instructions for me, he replied, "Well, not really, except the platoon sergeant said, 'That *gung ho* son-of-a-bitch [me] told those men to jump.'" I didn't have to.

Lieutenant Poxon was still leading the platoon, and we had a new platoon sergeant, "Bigelow." He was a nervous black man in his forties who had spent the previous four years in Germany doing everything in his power to avoid Vietnam service. Doc Melugin's replacement was Doc

Ring. He was plump and pink-cheeked and looked more like a cherub than a medic. The only "old" NCO was Ruby, now a squad leader.

To my great joy and excitement, Granite remained in my squad. He had been promoted to specialist, so I made him a fire team leader over his bitching and objections. I figured he had learned enough by rote to be able to lead a team. The other fire team leader was Sergeant Randy Spear, a lanky fellow who had been with the Lurps [Long Range Reconnaissance Patrol teams] before coming to the Blues. A new policy allowed Lurps to request a different assignment for the last half of their tour. He had chosen the Blues because he thought we were safer. Randy was a mature man with an easy way about him. We enjoyed talking about his wife and two children back home, and my heart's desire, lovely Leila.

The platoon had made a few landings to collect weapons and papers from Loach contacts and had killed five NVA on the first landing launched from Disneyland East. Those North Vietnamese had been inside one of the least militarized areas in Vietnam, and had apparently been returning from R&R along the coast of the South China Sea. The platoon's longest day was spent in the blasted wilderness of the Ho Bo Woods. The Ho Bo Woods had been a dagger aimed at Saigon during the French war and the early part of the American war. B-52s and artillery had reduced it to an emptiness of collapsed tunnels and rotting corpses.

The troop discovered Binoctal at Disneyland East. The drug could be bought over the counter at Vietnamese pharmacies; it gave men a sense of general well-being, and a false feeling of strength and courage. An ex-Lurp named Parquet was stopped by two MPs after they watched him walk into a deep ditch. He beat them senseless. On another night, a group of Blues tore up an NCO club and put some rear echelon types in the hospital. Another Blue attacked the mess hall with a white phosphorous grenade because he thought the cook was harassing him.

Most of those events stemmed from Binoctal use. The MPs could never prove that we were responsible for any of these incidents, but they knew. Late night lineups in front of the Blue barracks became a familiar ritual. Binoctal was addicting. I later spent weeks watching the occasional soldier shaking and sweating as his comrades helped him through a painful withdrawal.

Our stay at Disneyland East was mercifully short. We secured a few downed helicopters and made several landings in a desert region of red sand dunes and jagged boulders. The desert people lived in hardscrabble clusters of little stilt houses set about twelve feet off the ground. Whenever the natives stepped out on their small front porch platforms and saw us, they hustled back inside, snapping shut the rags that passed for doors.

One sunny morning in April, we loaded the troop's equipment on slicks and returned to Quan Loi. It was good to be leaving. There were no Vietnamese pharmacies at Quan Loi.

The rubber plantation country was different when we returned. The NVA had begun using Chinese 107mm multiple rocket launchers, and these hit the base around the clock. The rockets were usually fired singly or in pairs, but sometimes a salvo of twelve would roar in and smash something. We learned to eat Quan Loi's red dust and like it on our first day back. By the second day, we could detect the Boom! when the rockets were fired and use the five-to-seven seconds before they hit to find cover. Soon we had soldiers walking around with two-tone uniforms: rust red in front and green in back.

The cavalry division fought back when it could. Once, aerial rocket artillery Cobras rocketed the bamboo jungle for an entire afternoon. That stopped the rockets for two glorious days. Another time, Blue landed at a rocket launching site. All that remained were long detonating wires and blackened patches where the rockets had been leaned against termite mounds and fired.

The twelve-barreled launchers were heavy and couldn't be moved around easily, so they were commonly fired from the edge of the untouchable rubber plantations and then wheeled back underneath the trees. But all a man needed to fire a single rocket was a lightweight, single-tube launcher or a rise in the ground and a fair idea of how far it would travel.

Quan Loi was a big target; even inaccurate rockets would hit something. The Boom-Roar-Crash! of rockets became a fact of life, like sleep or rain.

———◆———

It was nearly dusk on April twenty-fifth and lightly raining when the slicks carried us on a thirty-minute ride to the northwest. We passed an abandoned Special Forces camp and circled over a wild region of massive rounded hills and valleys untouched by bombs and defoliants. Below us was primary growth triple canopy forest. Those interesting hills were excellent sites for heavy machine guns. Another slick hovered into a valley far below us, and I silently prayed, "Thank you, God. They're sending in someone else."

Then the crew chief beside me cupped his hands and shouted in my ear, "Rappel! Medevac ship shot down by twelve-seven extracting Special Forces Team! Other bird's ropes are too short! We're going in!"

Our pilots dropped straight down beside those ominous hills, and crossed over a road with branches forming a canopy above it. We hovered over 120-foot tall trees. Directly below us was the smashed helicopter, lying on its side among clumps of bamboo. The white background of the red cross was clearly visible in failing light. When the crew chief threw down the rope, the specialist in front of it looked at me with pleading eyes.

"I can't do it, Sarge! You go first!"

I was numb with fear. "I'm scared, too! Go! God-dammit! Go!"

He hooked his D-ring on the rope, leaned back on the skid and disappeared. My turn. I hooked up, took a deep breath, and jumped backward, riding the rope in fifteen-to-twenty-foot drops. When I was about thirty feet from the ground, the slick dropped a few feet and popped back up, tangling the rope in the bamboo. I was flipped upside down.

Every movement of the slick slammed my back against a large tree. It hurt. As I hit the tree again, I saw huge burlap sacks beside a wide trail, somewhere beyond the wreck.

The specialist finally untangled the rope, and I lowered myself to the ground. Next came a new rifleman and Sergeant Bigelow with a radio. The slick left us in that terrifying place. The specialist climbed over the belly of the medevac chopper and smashed the lock on a medicine chest with a short fire ax. He stuffed Methadrine bottles in his leg pockets while the rifleman gaped at him. Bigelow was hiding under the tail boom, shaking and talking to himself. I ran over to him.

"Is the radio on the right frequency?"

He looked up with a dazed expression. "I can't remember." He picked up the radio and handed it to me. "Here. You take it."

Bigelow had his radio set to ground communications channel. We needed to talk to the aircraft. I tried various frequencies until I found or remembered the ground-to-air channel. I don't know how to this day because, call it what you will, I had not been given those numbers. I heard the pilots talking and wondered what I was supposed to say.

"Birds. This is Blue Three-Two. We're on the ground." (Obviously, you idiot).

"Roger that, Blue."

Now that we've got that out of the way, "Ah, Birds. Do you have any instructions? Over."

"Roger, Blue. Check the downed bird for wounded. We have a medevac on the way to your location. Over."

"Blue Three-Two, roger that."

Three men, Cambodian trail watchers in tiger-stripe uniforms, were in the wreckage. One was crushed beneath the side of the chopper and already dead. Another was pinned in the wreckage and couldn't be freed without a cutting torch. The third man was lying free inside the ship. He was the only one we could hope to save, but save is the wrong word. The two living men had been shot in the head after the chopper crashed. I knew in that instant that we had a hidden audience.

A medevac chopper hovered over us and dropped a jungle penetrator stretcher. It almost crowned Bigelow. He scurried away to hide under an umbrella of bamboo stalks. I gave the trail watcher first aid, trying to keep the brains inside his skull with a field dressing. We strapped him to the stretcher, attached the winch cable, and watched him disappear up through the trees. The medevac nosed over and raced away. It was dark and raining when I radioed a Loach hovering above us.

"Birds, this is Blue Three-Two. Over."

"White One-One, go."

"Blue Three-Two. How we gonna get out of here?" Fuck protocol.

The scout pilot replied in calm, soothing voice, "Roger that Blue. Medevac will hoist you out. Destroy what you can't salvage from the downed bird and prepare for extraction.

I passed on the news. The pinned trail watcher was moving, but not responsive. I told the specialist to kill him. It was an act of mercy. We riddled the instrument panel and radios with volleys of rifle fire. The NVA had already taken the trail watchers' weapons. A jungle penetrator snaked down through the trees. The rifleman hooked his rappelling harness to the device. Up he went.

Screw this! I handed the radio to Bigelow and followed on the second hoist. The trip up through the trees seemed to last an eternity. It was raining hard. The racket from miniguns, heavy machine guns, rockets, and helicopter blades was deafening. A Cobra slowly hovered over the medevac helicopter, firing rockets into a hilltop hundreds of feet above us. I was watching the white flashes of exploding rockets when four hands grabbed my harness and pulled me aboard.

The specialist was thirty feet in the air when the winch cable flashed and broke. The specialist landed in a seated position on the tail boom of the wrecked helicopter with enough force to break it away from the rest of the aircraft. That cushion saved his life. I wondered if he had broken any of his Methedrine bottles. Our Medevac nosed over and raced away into the night sky.

I returned to Quan Loi with the worst backache of my life. I tried to help carry the wounded trail watcher to a tent operating room, but the sudden weight doubled me over. Instead, I walked behind the stretcher and explained what had happened to a waiting team of three medical people. I walked to another GP tent and sat down in the red dust.

When my eyes focused, I saw five more Cambodians in tiger-stripe uniforms. At first I thought they were a hallucination. Coming to my senses, I mimicked rappelling and bandaging, and pointed to the operating room. They thanked me with bows and the folded hand gesture of homage, and left to see their friend. A medevac crewman walked into the tent.

"Hi, Sarge. We got your buddies out. They were dropped over at Bravo Troop. I'll take you home in a jeep."

"Thanks. I'll walk over. I need the air right now."

He sat down in the red dust beside me. "That took a lot of balls what you guys did. I've seen a bunch of people leave Fifteenth Med alive because you guys got to them before the NVA did. We think a lot of the Blue platoons."

"Thanks. I was scared. All that kept going through my mind was, 'This is a green hell. This is a green hell,' I hope I'm not going crazy."

He shook his head. "Don't worry about it. That was a bad place. You can tell the folks back home that you got to see one of the meanest parts of Cambodia close up."

"Thanks."

A Headquarters, 9th Cavalry summary of the action states that a lift ship (piloted by Blue Lift leader, Captain Bob Marshall) hovered over the downed helicopter while the riflemen rappelled into the wreckage *with complete disregard for their personal safety*. I'm sure the author of that report was blinded by bullshit.

That green hell was in my dreams for weeks. Another dream began troubling me as well. Dressed in a jungle uniform, I was helplessly spinning, falling face down and spread-eagled through the air inside an endless dark tunnel, never reaching bottom. I would wake up scared and soaked with sweat.

Then I became a young-old man for about a month. My black hair turned light gray.

One afternoon, the MPs came around to search for communist weapons and confiscated several, including an AK-47 that one of our point men favored. He had fitted an NVA rifle grenade launcher attachment to the barrel which gave the weapon a slightly different sound. The MPs failed to discover a false wall in my squad tent room that concealed a mounted RPG-7 launcher and four AK-47s. The MPs' excuse was that a man carrying a communist weapon might be accidentally shot. No one had seemed to care much about that in the past. We couldn't know that Special Forces teams were salting enemy ammo caches with exploding bullets.

A day or so after that, we were scrambled to secure a Loach that had crashed and burned in Tay Ninh Province a few hundred meters from Cambodia. As Randy Spear and I jumped off our slick and ran side-by-side deeper into the clearing, bullets whistled around us. I thought a slick crew chief was firing off target. Sergeant Spear dropped as if hit by a sledgehammer. One moment he was beside me; suddenly

I was alone and he was face down in the short grass. We were trapped inside a large clearing surrounded by defoliated jungle. Air strikes did not faze the North Vietnamese around us

Ruby's squad was pinned down by a machine gun in the trees, probably the one that had stitched Spear across the back. They jumped up and rushed it, shouting at the top of their lungs. One last burst from the RPD, then silence. The NVA gun crew had run away, leaving behind a green pith helmet. That display of bravery from normally listless draftees stunned me. A Loach hovered over the white trees where the NVA machine gunners had disappeared. Da-Da-Da-Da-Da! A twelve-seven fired skyward from the bamboo jungle a few meters in front of us. Perhaps the machine gun crew had run away to draw us in deeper. We pulled back to the edge of the clearing.

Camouflage-painted Australian Canberra bombers streaked in over the tree tops, dropped below the trees as they raced across the clearing, and popped up to drop cluster bombs on the twelve- seven positions. We could have used those hotshot pilots back in the day.

As the CBUs exploded with a continuous crackle, Granite rose to his knees and shook a fist at the dead trees. "Love they neighbor," he hollered, "but bomb the fuckin' Cong!" He looked so ridiculous – a skinny hillbilly shouting at a dead jungle.

We jogged north beside the burning bamboo, heading toward the greasy black smoke column from our downed Loach. Another Loach flew over the crash site, and AKs opened fire at it. Then they turned their assault rifles on us. I dived for cover when bullets began kicking up clods of grass and dirt in front of us. Would Blue ever get off this clearing?

Bigelow shouted that the pilots would direct 155mm artillery shells along the northern edge of the clearing. We crawled into old artillery craters for cover. The ground was soft, the craters wide and deep. The first two shells were close, sending fragments smacking into the ground around us. Granite and I squeezed together and hugged each other as the next four shells whistled in. Hot concussion sucked the air out of the crater and bounced us off the bottom. Two men in the next crater started screaming.

Granite whispered across the inches separating our faces, "It doesn't look like our day, Sarge."

I wanted to reply, "It never looks like my day when I'm sharing a crater with you."

A Loach flew near the crash site until a burst from an AK tore up the floor beside the gunner's feet. The chopper veered off to one side and raced back over the craters. Another RPD clattered from the north, showering us with dirt clods and bits of rock, but hurting no one. A Cobra hovered over us and sprayed the area with its minigun. Four thousand rounds per minute chopped down the giant stalks of bamboo. Granite and I took turns slapping red-hot cartridge casings off each other's uniforms and necks.

Major Stewart radioed Lieutenant Poxon to wait in the craters for reinforcements. A slick landed behind us. Four Blues heaved the wounded men aboard like two sacks of grain and ran back to their craters. The pilots swung the tail boom around and flew away over the southern edge of the clearing, over more AKs. I changed frequency on my squad radio and listened on the air-ground channel as an infantry battalion commander talked with Major Stewart.

"Saber Six. Golden Lion Six. Over."

"Saber Six, go."

"Golden Lion Six. We have an element on one-one bravos on the way to your location in two lifts. Have your element mark their positions with smoke. Over."

"Roger that, Golden Lion. White will mark Lima Zulu with red smoke. Over."

"Ah, roger. How big is your element? Over."

"About one eight, over."

"One eight?" He asked. "Those boys down there have a lot of balls." Maybe a lot of balls rolling around in our heads.

The North Vietnamese stopped their target practice when twelve slicks came in from the south, followed by twelve more. I had never seen more than four slicks in a landing. A hundred or more grunts ran north and threw themselves down around us. By God, it felt good to see them. Those fellows packed real muscle.

Four aerial rocket artillery Cobras roared overhead to blast the northern tree line. The grunts charged north and led us into the bamboo jungle. The NVA were gone. A filthy, grim-faced infantry sergeant walked back down the line to Lieutenant Poxon.

"The wreckage is up front, Sir. We found the bunker that probably got them. They left these behind." He held out a pair of Chinese binoculars, an officer's star belt with a holstered Tokarev, and an AK. "They killed some gooks before they bought it. Looks like a lot of gooks were watching this landing zone."

We gathered the burned pieces of the pilot and gunners and left the infantry company in that loathsome place. Later, Doc Ring and I were sitting inside a bunker and talking about the day's events.

"Do you think Spear made it, Doc?"

"I don't think so," he said. "He looked pretty white when I put him on the slick."

"Just once I'd like to see a decent man live through this. He went through enough shit with the Lurps."

Just then, Granite stuck his head through the entrance and shouted in his grating voice, "Hey, Sarge! Spear's dead!"

I felt like he had hit me with a baseball bat. "Get out of here!"

"Don't come down on me, you fuckin' Yankee!"

"Get out of here, asshole!"

He left and then Doc left, and I sat in that bunker for hours, crying. It wasn't only for Randy Spear, but for the wife and two little girls he loved so much. Tomorrow a man in uniform would knock on their door.

One of the soldiers had kept the NVA machine gunner's pith helmet. A slogan was penned on its side, and I asked Con, our new interpreter, to translate. Con read the words and spat.

"What's it say, Con?"

Con, an ex-Viet Cong himself, spat again into the red dust. "It says he has come south to kill Americans. He prays that he has the chance."

I passed a Blue squad tent that night. The men were singing the favorite song of the last few months.

"Sky pilot!
How high can you fly?
You'll al-ways, al-ways, al-ways
Crash and die!"

They had never heard of "One Keg of Beer."

<hr />

One of my team leaders and I were on duty at the Quan Loi gate bunker. An APC unit was parked in the rubber trees behind us and a track crewman ran over to warn us to stay under cover. Mortars had killed three of his buddies the night before. They had been sleeping in pup tents between the tracks, but they were staying inside those hot metal coffins tonight.

The night started off quietly enough until Quan Loi shook with the rapid thunderclaps of Russian and Chinese rockets, and the sharper crashes of mortar bombs and recoilless rifle shells. The barbed wire, not more than one hundred meters away, echoed with the sound of exploding RPG warheads and massed rifles. I could hear the attacking soldiers shouting to each other. I am not sure what they were hollering, but it was probably *Xung Phong!* [Forward! Charge!]. The team leader laid grenades along the sandbags while I rechecked the bunker's machine gun.

The shelling lifted away from the perimeter bunkers and hit deeper inside the camp. It continued sporadically for hours. Two NVA companies had cut through the barbed wire and tangled with two rescue columns. The first column had consisted of Big Red One infantrymen riding in cargo trucks. That column was hard hit. The second involved tracks from the 11th Armored Cavalry Regiment.

The 11th ACR tracks had been stationed farther down the road near An Loc. A line of flares, oscillating under their parachutes and making their hollow, haunting "Tump-Tump-Tump" sounds, slowly moved our way over the plantation. When the first APC roared down the road in our direction, we swung open the gate. A clanking, grinding convoy thundered past us and turned right (our left) toward the battle. RPGs, rifles, and the heavy machine guns mounted on the tracks engaged in one hell of a battle.

Stray bullets smacked into the sandbags of our bunker all night long. The enemy retreated just before dawn, sending a parting gift of seven RPG rockets fired at about their maximum range from a ridge across from the base. They exploded in a line, in fountains of red sparks, on the road just behind our gate. Those spark-flowers were absolutely beautiful. Then there was finally silence.

The Blue platoon was sent to patrol the attack area in the early morning half-light. Evidence of the battle was everywhere. We passed a burning truck and a smoking APC. The truck had been the first vehicle to arrive with reinforcements; the APC had been the lead vehicle of the armored column. Both had been stopped with RPGs. Two bunkers had been completely destroyed by RPGs. Other bunkers were blackened and collapsing.

Twenty Americans had been killed. One NVA body remained. He was a teenage boy, lying next to an equally young, blond GI. There was no blood or obvious wounds. In an accident of death, their hands were touching. Both corpses wore green uniforms and similar jungle boots. One of our new men kicked the American corpse, thinking he was a dead NVA. He recoiled in horror when I pointed to the blond hair.

A grassy slope leading down from the wire and up from a depression toward the rubber plantation was littered with bloody bandages, packs, magazine holders, AKs, RPG warheads, demolition charges, long-handled green wire cutters, and dozens of green NVA concussion grenades. If just the men who had left their packs and weapons behind had been hit, at least thirty of them would be out of action for a while. A last 107mm rocket roared directly overhead as we tossed armloads of equipment into a jeep trailer. It blew apart an empty squad tent about sixty meters behind us. Rocket Man's aim was a bit high.

Smoke rose above the rubber trees throughout the day. APCs and Sheridan tanks from the 11th ACR had trapped some of the retreating NVA. Jets dropped bomb after bomb, and Cobras dived into the smoke on long minigun and rocket runs. The thunder rolling across the tree tops was deafening at times.

Because of that attack, the Blues spent most of the next two weeks filling sandbags, laying more barbed wire and erecting RPG screens of cyclone fence around the bunkers. The NVA contented themselves with using us, the flight line, and our tent area for rocket-shooting and mortar practice.

The attack described above was a small part of a nationwide communist offensive that killed 284 Americans on May twelfth and thirteenth, 1969.

Mr. Murray was a slightly built man with a thin mustache and the kind of swagger I have since seen among the tough Irish street kids of Boston. He and his gunner had over one hundred kills, so he was damned good and he knew it.

Mr. Murray was the only scout pilot from that era the Blues got close to. Scouts had their culture; we had ours. We were too often sent to bring back the burned bodies of helicopter crewmen and didn't particularly want to know them first. But Mr. Murray was different. He survived. He was the pilot every gunner wanted to fly with, because he was lucky and could bring them home safely. Murray was said to be an acrobat over the jungle, giving his bird a grace it didn't naturally have. He sometimes chased enemy soldiers with the Loach, shooting at them with a .45 automatic. It was hard to imagine that side of him.

As time went by, other scout crewmen would come and go, but Mr. Murray kept right on flying. The Blues began to regard him as a good luck charm and, rarest of things, began talking with him. He was different – a philosopher who would tell you why things had to be the way they were. We could talk to him about any subject, and he would listen and give an answer. The officer-enlisted man gap ceased to exist for us. Murray's favorite song was *Scarborough Fair*. He compared us, the soldiers in Vietnam, to the scarlet battalions of Britain, fighting for a cause long ago forgotten. He was probably right.

Murray had a flair all his own. The gunner decorated Mr. Murray's Loach with half-moon gravestones topped by crosses after each successful mission. Above them was his motto, "Death is My Business, and Business has been good." That seemed so out of place next to *Scarborough Fair*.

Mr. Murray made it through an entire tour with the scouts. Then one evening he told a group of us that he was signing up for six more months to save some money for his future marriage. We couldn't believe what he was doing and tried to talk him out of it. That didn't succeed.

Mr. Murray disappeared out of our lives –home on leave for thirty days- got married and returned to us. He was back one day in late April or early May, 1969 but he was changed. The old cockiness was gone. He told me that asking for more time was a mistake. He wanted to go home to his wife.

Things were the same for a week or two. A few more half-moon grave-stones appeared on his Loach. He was a charmed man once again until we scrambled for a scout chopper, down and burning on the edge of a rubber plantation. As we orbited over the fire, the word spread. "It's Mr. Murray! It's Mr. Murray!" A Sioux machine gunner, Raymond Bad Yellowhair, rappelled alone into the scrub jungle in an attempt to save Mr. Murray. Raymond was too late. He deserved the **Silver Star** he was awarded,

You could almost reach out and feel the cloud of depression that hung over us that night. We missed Mr. Murray. I will always miss him. He was our friend.

Morale was nonexistent by the second half of May. The Blues were being used mostly for guard duty or construction. Sometimes a few of us could fly on Nighthawk missions. A Nighthawk team consisted of a lift ship outfitted with a powerful searchlight and four machine guns, followed from higher altitude by a Cobra gunship. The slick was blacked out, while the Cobra had all lights on and flashing. The idea was to get the enemy to fire at the gunship and attack them with the four machine guns. Blues waited in line to fly on Nighthawk missions. They weren't much, but they allowed a few infantrymen the chance to escape boredom and random rockets and fight back.

Nighthawk flights worked well for a few weeks. Convoys of sup-ply sampans were shot up and sunk, and jungle way stations, with campfires blazing to high heaven, were attacked. My two flights were really uneventful. On the first flight, we discovered campfires along the Cambodian border which winked out almost instantly as the Cobra approached. We fired blindly in the jungle where the fires had been and surely hit nothing. The Cobra fired a few rockets. My second flight was even more unproductive. An occasional tracer round streaked out of the black jungle toward the snake. We couldn't find a target to return fire.

For about a month, I set up a real bomb-making factory for the scouts, assisted by a couple of Blues and scout pilot Rick Chesson. The bombs were used for tasks like cracking open bunkers and destroying ammunition caches along trails. We started with one-quart cans and steel ammo boxes that were packed with plastic explosive around a hand grenade and secured with duct tape. The hand grenade set the charge off. We graduated into big cans with ten or more pounds of plastique and TNT grenades as fuses. It was always a compliment to our bomb factory boys to watch those little Loaches fly away with an assortment of different-sized bombs cluttering up the floor in back. So we made bigger bombs. We had to quit after one of them almost blew a Loach out of the sky.

When the Nighthawk missions stopped because a slick got riddled with antiaircraft fire, nothing was left for us to do.

Major Stewart, our troop commander of this era, was, without a doubt, the most caring commander I served under. Late one afternoon, Blue was almost landed at the site of a newly established command post in the bamboo jungle. It was located in the center of a wagon wheel of trails, each protected by a round Chinese claymore mine. The insertion was cancelled toward dusk in favor of aerial attacks. The next day I wrote a few paragraphs and handed the sheet of paper to Major Stewart - Blue is ground recon; we are supposed to take prisoners, and so forth. He replied the following day.

"I read it, but if Blue makes contact and one of our ships goes down (somewhere else), there'd be no one to get out the crew. Your mission right now is standby for downed aircraft. We have to be careful how we use you."

When I think back now, especially with regard to those commanders who would not have hesitated to insert a platoon near nightfall in the middle of an enemy force of unknown size, I appreciate his sound judgement and gentle handling of my intrusion upon his responsibilities.

———————

Meanwhile, the quality of some replacements was deteriorating. For instance, when I was in Germany in 1965, missing two 9 p.m. bed checks was an automatic court martial. Requests for Vietnam duty were being denied. By 1969, disciplinary problems, drug offenders, and petty criminals from Germany were being dumped on the Vietnam Army. These folks were automatically a problem. If they were corrected, they would say things like, "What're you going to do? Send me to Vietnam and put me in the infantry?"

Radicalized black soldiers thought they were gaining power, and crackerjack Southern white soldiers thought they were losing it. A couple of folks had obvious nervous disorders. Some had trouble understanding and following simple orders. But most were solid, working class folks who had been swept up by the "Green Machine."

In 1967, an excellent recruiting source was the pool of young offenders to whom judges gave the choice of jail or military service. Most of them had done tiny crimes, like taking the neighbor's car for a joy ride, but they were bolder than the rest of the population. That made them good infantry material. I didn't encounter any of them in 1969.

Some unruly soldiers from Vietnam were being sent to the 9th Cavalry for punishment. Other soldiers with long service in Vietnam had requested the Blues because we still had a reputation. We had two of those. One was just disappointed. The other had a longstanding drug problem. The second time he offended, I made him gone.

Most of them were just putting in their time, doing the best they could and counting the days until they could go home. But bad apples stand out. By 1969, these types of problems were occurring throughout Vietnam.

Morale remained highest among the helicopter crews.

Lieutenant Poxon and Sergeant Bigelow never visited or walked among our tents. That might have become the pattern if Bigelow hadn't spilled a pail of boiling water on himself. A lot of people thought the accident wasn't really an accident. Bigelow's departure made both him and the Blues very happy. Now something had to change. Our new platoon sergeant reported to Lieutenant Poxon that same night. He was Reb Herron, a scout mechanic and gunner, smiling a boyish smile that hid a fierce reputation.

Reb, looking every inch the professional soldier, was a tall, athletic man in his late twenties. I had first heard of him at Disneyland East where the rumor mill had him spending a lot of time bitching about the lack of Viet Cong. But such impressions aren't much to go on. He was probably a new dude who wanted to see some action. But Reb wasn't new.

He had already served tours in Vietnam as a Special Forces man, an ARVN advisor, and a Bravo Blue squad leader. He was in Vietnam for several reasons, the most important of which, besides his obvious patriotism, was that Reb was a natural soldier. He was cool and fearless in combat and seemed to think of war as an exciting game that he couldn't possibly lose. And he was right.

In October 1966, Reb's squad was crossing a vine rope bridge in the Soui Ca when an AK stitched him. The doctors told him that he would never return to combat because of his injuries, so he went home to Georgia to be discharged. He reenlisted for noncombat training, spent a year in America learning how to repair helicopters, and talked a clerk into fixing his records so he could return to Vietnam.

Now Reb was back in a Bravo Troop where no one knew him. He started as a mechanic and begged his way into not only repairing Loaches, but gunning them. Other gunners said he was fearless. When a man tried to bully him out of beer money during our sojourn near Saigon, Reb pulled out his .45 automatic from its shoulder holster, held it to the man's temple, and asked him to reconsider. He did. All Reb's scheming and planning had been aimed at rejoining a platoon he remembered as an elite fighting machine. He was finally back with the Blues.

Reb called a meeting of the squad leaders his first morning as platoon sergeant. He was smiling as we filed into his cramped room. A smile for each of us. "Okay. This will only take a minute. Major Stewart wants the Blues to start going out more, so tell your men to get their gear squared away. We're going to be bopping down trails, so emphasize silent movement and security."

He paused for a moment, probably thinking about events that had happened long before. "The Blues aren't what they used to be, but that's going to change. This platoon, that you are honored to be serving with, used to kill more gooks than the infantry battalions. We were called the Headhunters. It was different then."

The other squad leaders had no idea what Reb was talking about. They stared at him with blank faces. The changes were swift. Blue squads were reintegrated, white and black troublemakers were sent away, and the platoon began practicing nighttime alerts, ambush techniques, and silent patrolling beside our flight line. I can't know Reb's mind, but suspect that, with so much experience, leading Blue platoons in 1969 and 1970 was child's play for him.

The first landing of the "new Blues" near the vast Michelin Rubber Plantation was not a smashing success. The slicks came in over a field of bomb craters baked cement-hard under the tropical sun. The slicks hadn't been going out much, either. Mine had a new pilot. He was flying too fast, unsteadily, and dumped some of us into the deep craters. I fractured my ankle on the rock-hard lip of a crater and fell in.

The wobbling helicopter caused the crew chief to lose control of his machine gun. His bullets sent the rest of my squad jumping for cover in the craters and destroyed a rifle and a grenade launcher that had been left behind. Another slick returned for a man with a dislocated knee, then we were finally ready to begin the patrol. I laced my left boot tightly to stabilize the ankle. That and natural endorphins took care of the rest.

My squad led the way down a wide trail toward out target. We stopped when we reached a four-foot-high grassy bank, the outer wall of a large depot, and spread out along it. That wall was nearly invisible from the air. Inside it grew more bamboo jungle with firing slits peeking out from under clumps of bamboo. A Loach flew over the wall. Clack-Clack-Clack-Clack! AK fire from a clump of bamboo at the base of a large dead tree. The gunner poured down a stream of tracers on pass after pass until the chopper suddenly banked away. The gunner had been shot through the leg.

Lieutenant Poxon told our grenadiers to hit the firing slits with their grenades. I was listening to the steady Blam! Blam! Blam! reports of the elephant guns when Reb ran over in a crouch. He sat with his back against the earth wall and smiled.

"It's not like the old Cav is it?"

"Hell no. We would have gone in under the scout's fire and grenaded that bunker. The gunner wouldn't have been hit that way."

Reb nodded in agreement. "And that's not the half of it. Those chunkers will tell the gooks we're here and give them plenty of time to *Di Di* out of here."

"Yup."

He was right. We found a few items of personal equipment and the trademark bloody shirt. It seemed as if the NVA always left behind bloody shirts as consolation prizes.

The fighting bunkers under the bamboo were connected by covered trenches with vegetation growing on top of them. The bamboo, bushes, and grass usually hid one bunker from the other at ground level. I instructed my squad not to enter a covered trench until the connected bunkers were cleared. "Cleared" meant a shout of *Lai Day!* [Come Out!] and a wait, then a burst of rifle fire followed by a grenade. Every man but one obeyed.

I approached a bunker, shouted, waited, fired, and threw a grenade. In the few seconds before the grenade detonated, I heard high-pitched squealing. Then a Boom! followed by a whining sound.

"Who is that?"

From the companion bunker, hidden behind a clump of bamboo, I heard the grating voice of none other than Granite.

"That Yankee son-of-a-bitch tried to kill me!"

Granite had ignored my orders and gone down into a bunker without clearing it. He crawled down the trench with his trusty .45 automatic until he saw sunlight, then bullets, then a grenade. He turned around and went squealing back toward the original bunker. The blast knocked him flat and gave him a nice whole body bruise, but he got no fragments. He was very fortunate that I hadn't thrown a powerful TNT grenade.

We continued carefully searching tunnels while Loaches shot NVA rabbiting over the far wall of the depot. I grenaded a large living bunker and walked down the wooden staircase to have a look. It was a big room, complete with bunk beds, pinups of Vietnamese swimsuit beauties, a Big Ben style alarm clock and the latest edition of the NLF newspaper. The newspaper had a feature article on how to shoot down cavalry division helicopters. The front page had a half-page drawing of two men in NVA jungle hats firing a machine gun at a slick with the crossed sabers of the 9th Cavalry on its nose. The helicopter was diving directly at them.

The drawing sent shivers down my spine. They had precisely identified us as the enemy, and that reminded me of the night Hanoi Hannah had welcomed "the boys of B Troop" to Camp Evans. Ironically, a soldier from a slick with crossed sabers on its nose had just stolen their newspaper article about shooting down slicks with crossed sab... Oh, whatever.

A photo section showed NVA infantry overrunning a Marine position, and a row of dead GIs. They were typical soldiers with mustaches and sideburns and longish hair, lying in the grass along a trail. One of them had what looked like a peace [ban the bomb] symbol, partly hidden by his shirt, worn around his neck.

The depot was a comfortable place to live. In a large open pit were a table, chairs, a little potbellied stove, and a sea chest full of china and chopsticks. The pit was cool and shaded under a canopy of French camouflage parachute silk. Everywhere were crates of canned fish, sacks of rice, and baskets of fresh greens. Boxes and crates were stacked all over the depot. I hope someone collected all of them, because we didn't have time to do it. The occupants could easily have stayed and fought, but these were supply personnel, the equivalent of our truck drivers and typists. We took what we could carry and set demolition charges to some of boxes left behind.

On the way back to the crater field, Ruby's squad on the left flank found a park of robust, green-painted bicycles, most loaded with more supplies. Blues had found and destroyed cargo bikes at Bong Son and Chu Lai, but didn't understand their importance to the enemy's war effort. Cargo bikes were the pack mules of the North Vietnamese supply chain. They could be loaded with five hundred pounds of supplies and pushed all the way from Hanoi to Ca Mau. We took two or three bikes back to Quan Loi as souvenirs. Ruby's squad blew up the rest. Scout pilots and gunners were soon using the green bicycles for trips between the tents and their Loaches.

The doctors put a plaster cast on my ankle. I spent the days digging a deep coffin hole beside my cot. The wall of sandbags around the tent wasn't as much protection as a hole in the ground; I put an air mattress in the bottom for a soft landing during rocket attacks.

Then I contracted a less severe case of what I suspect was Break-Bone Fever, the condition that afflicted me in Happy Valley three years before. After a couple of days of light headaches came that familiar, painful, "bone-broken-with-a-baseball-bat" feeling in the right humerus. A smart person would have gone to see a doctor, but now I knew the pain would pass. I had a useless right arm for two or three days and then began feeling better.

The Blue platoon was making daily patrols around Quan Loi. At night I would listen to their war stories. One afternoon they landed near Nui Ba Ra and found a supply depot with hundreds of cases of mortar shells and rifles. They brought back two "souvenir," yellow-painted, 120mm mortars rounds and set them up as sentries by the doorway to my squad tent. Granite swaggered into the tent that afternoon wearing an NVA star belt and holding another, now rare souvenirs. He refused to believe me when I told him that the entire platoon could once have worn those belts.

Con prowled by with two AKs strapped across his back. Two NVA guards had shot at him. He crept up behind their bunker and dropped in a grenade. That's where Granite got his belts.

Con was a dangerous man. He had been a loyal Viet Cong until a North Vietnamese squad had killed his wife and children. He called it a mistake and wouldn't say more, except that he hated the NVA. His eyes would become harder than any I had ever seen when he silently ran through the jungle like a hard-muscled cat. I hoped his former comrades were not as brutal and efficient as him. He called the communist gooks, just as we did, and one night I asked him why.

"Con, do you think it's right to call the VC gooks and dinks?"

He shrugged, "It makes no difference to me. Everything has a name. Do you think the Americans are the only ones who do that?"

"I don't know. I suppose not. I never really thought about it."

Con's eyes glassed over for a moment and he smiled his hard smile. "My company in the jungle" –he swept the countryside around Quan Loi with an arm- "called you big hairy monkeys. We kill monkeys, and" –he hesitated for an instant before continuing- "we eat them."

Chapter 18

THE HIGHLY DECORATED RAT

(June-July, 1969)

Lieutenant Poxon died on June second. A helicopter night patrol had engaged or detected two large trucks in Tay Ninh Province near the Cambodian border. An abandoned artillery base nearby looked like a good place to land the Blues for a patrol to a possible truck park. The artillery base appeared to be unoccupied. Scouts overflew the base for hours, dropping tear gas and white phosphorous grenades to flush any NVA. The enemy remained hidden. A decision was made to insert Blue.

The platoon was ambushed as soon as they jumped from the slicks. The North Vietnamese had dug spider holes in the corners of the big inward-facing artillery bunkers and waited for the helicopters to arrive. That was their latest favorite trick. Lieutenant Poxon tried to rescue a mortally wounded machine gunner and was himself wounded. He then attacked and destroyed a machine gun crew with a hand grenade before being killed. It happened quickly and accounts varied, but everyone agreed that Poxon went down shooting. His was an astonishing and unexpected display of bravery from a normally quiet man.

About twenty NVA were killed by the Blues and a reinforcing infantry platoon from a nearby firebase. All agreed that Reb had saved the day, but I never heard that from him. After the artillery base was cleared, the Blues were pinned down by AK fire from the surrounding jungle. The pilots said it came from more enemy soldiers waiting to spring a trap. The quick victory at the bunkers confused the NVA and caused them to fire too soon. Artillery, scouts and gunships broke the ambush

Reb had borrowed my web gear [also called load-bearing equipment or harness] before the scramble and returned it as soon as the slicks landed at Quan Loi. "Best set up I've ever used," he said through his perpetual smile. Then he told me his story.

He used grenades to clear the NVA positions and gave a detailed description of how each of them had died. He especially liked the man who squealed like a pig until a white phosphorous grenade turned his spider hole into a crematory oven. Reb's story included the squeal. He said the Blues acted like they were running through another drill at Quan Loi. If Bigelow had been there, the platoon would have been lost.

*Lieutenant Robert Poxon received a posthumous **Medal of Honor** for gallantry in action and conspicuous heroism. Machine gunner Joseph Scott had only been with the Blues for about a week and, sadly, few of us knew him. He died a brave death.*

Lift Platoon Leader and former gunship pilot, Captain Robert Marshall, was quickly appointed as the new Blue Platoon Leader.

Four days after Poxon's death, Bravo Troop lost a slick to ground fire. A well-liked crew of two pilots and a crew chief were killed. NVA sappers attacked Quan Loi that same night.

Clashes with NVA scouts and patrols had become a nightly occurrence, so no one was surprised when the enemy attacked in force. The battle in our sector was aimed at Bravo Troop's tents, and our flight line beside the perimeter obstacles. Mortars and rockets crashed around the helicopters in a steady drumbeat while Bravo Blues and a platoon from Delta Troop defended the flight line. At least five sappers died there. The NVA may have mistaken a field hospital to the north for our tent area. Medical personnel were using their sandbagged tents as fortresses. The sappers used demolition charges and RPGs. Flashes and red spark showers.

Cobra gunships rocketed the little valley between our flight line and the rubber plantation. Aerial rockets detonated in the bamboo and grass, and AKs fired tracers at crazy angles. Sappers were being hit and were pulling rifle triggers by reflex. Two twelve-sevens damaged blacked-out Cobras by firing tracers along the red streaks from their miniguns. A Cobra limped back to squadron headquarters at Phouc Vinh with a wounded pilot.

"Spooky," a big Air Force C-130 transport plane equipped with flares and miniguns, attacked the twelve-sevens. Tracers from Spooky's miniguns were like flowing pencils of red light: meandering lava flows from the heavens. One of the red pencils found a twelve-seven. Fat tracers from the heavy machine gun stitched an arc across the night sky. The machine gunner had apparently continued squeezing the trigger after he was shot. The dueling continued until just before dawn.

I was still in a plaster cast, and had spent the night in an open pit with a good field of fire and a front row seat for the clashes north and south. My companion was a Blue, an Italian kid from New York City, who was going home the next day and was sure he wouldn't make it through the night. Our whispered conversations reminded me of my nighttime talks with Corda so long before. He eventually calmed down.

Twenty dead sappers had been counted by the time I hobbled out to the flight line to help search for survivors. Those sweeps were deadly serious. After the last attack, two NVA hid for two days in a drainage culvert located just across a dirt road from our tents. They surrendered to a passing First Infantry Division truck driver. If two regular NVA grunts could hide for that long, sappers could pull off an even better disappearing act.

The flight line was pitted with rocket and mortar craters; several choppers were smoking wrecks. The bodies of three sappers sprawled beside a slick; more lay face down below the wire obstacles. These were older men with powerful builds, not teenagers with crew cuts. Each of them wore American-issue green boxer underwear with the fly sewn shut and Ho Chi Minh sandals. They wore wide belts, hung all around with green concussion grenades that looked like soda pop cans with stubby handles, and fist-size lumps of plastique with grenade primers that were wrapped in clear plastic. Three-AK magazine holders were strapped across their chests and backs. Their assault rifles had commando-style folding metal stocks. One sapper had worn a belt taken from a French Foreign Legionnaire. The wide brass buckle was engraved with *Legio Patria Nostra* [The Legion is Our Fatherland].

A sapper had died cross-eyed from a painful groin wound. He was on his back with clenched hands stretched above his head. One Blue pried the hands open and placed a Pabst Blue Ribbon can in each of them. Another man stomped on the forehead, leaving a dirty boot print above the crossed eyes. A chaplain walked onto the flight line, seeking to comfort the wounded and whatever else chaplains do. A 107mm rocket roared in and destroyed a Loach inside the revetment beside which my group and the chaplain were standing. The revetment's walls contained the explosion. If they had not, I wouldn't be writing this.

The Loach mechanic was furious. He jumped up from the oil-stained dirt and cursed. "Those fucking bastards! I spent three days getting that chopper up and they got to fire a fucking one-oh-seven! Fucking gooks!"

The chaplain tried to calm him. "It's alright, son. The important thing is that no one was killed."

The mechanic grinned maliciously at the chaplain and pointed at the three dead sappers. "They were killed, Sir."

The chaplain gaped at the scene for a moment, and uttered three words – "Oh, my God." He sat down in the dirt beside a blackened revetment and began crying. A group of us stood around for a moment, trying to think of something comforting to say. We left him there. I hope I never again see a man of God sobbing. It makes you wonder where your tears have gone.

Smoke columns rose above the rubber trees until darkness. Tracks had cornered some of the retreating sappers. It had been an attack by a sapper battalion from Tay Ninh Province. They had force-marched through the jungles of War Zone C to launch the assault. A wounded sapper said that his battalion wasn't given enough time to study Quan Loi's defenses, and had suffered as a result. He didn't apologize for the attack, just for the lack of proper preparations.

I'd had enough of being handicapped by that hot, itchy, damned cast, so I chipped it off with the open bayonet of an SKS rifle. Bizarrely, I got into a fist fight with Charlie, another squad leader, who said I was going to get myself killed and then punched me. That's tough love. We ended up hugging each other.

The Blues were conducting foot patrols around the base. The platoon was permitted to patrol around Quan Loi, so long as we were reasonably close to a road for helicopter pick-up in case of a downed chopper. We soon found the blood-stained twelve-seven donut emplacement from the sapper attack.

Donut emplacements were circular, shoulder-high trenches around an earth pedestal. They looked from the air like big donuts. A heavy machine gun would be mounted on the pedestal, giving the gunners an all-around field of fire. This particular donut had been hit by a minigun stream from Spooky. One side was bathed in black blood, as if the gunner had suddenly exploded. Below the blood spray was a Chinese stick grenade in the mud. I wiped it off and slipped into my left cargo pocket, and there it stayed for the last three months of my war. That grenade became my good luck charm.

One evening we were placed on standby for a helicopter that had crashed in the rubber trees less than a mile from Quan Loi. At dawn we patrolled through a tiny rubber village whose friendly inhabitants I remembered from those jeep patrols with Delta Troop. Reb soon located the village elder and led him over to Con for questioning.

"Con, ask him if there are any VC around here."

The two Vietnamese talked for a moment before Con looked back at Reb. "He says they are many. They come each night in small groups to watch Quan Loi."

"Does he know the VC shot down a helicopter last night?"

"Yes. He saw them do it." Reb's mouth popped open. "He says they set up a big machine gun in the rubber trees each night and wait for the helicopters to fly over. The VC put it near the village because they know the people are afraid and the Americans won't fire artillery in the rubber trees."

The elder looked at Reb with a frightened expression. He didn't know how his news would be received. Reb smiled at the old man and said, "Thank him, Con. Thank him for being honest with us."

We walked a short distance to the anti-aircraft site and then returned to Quan Loi.

We had begun going to eat in small groups to avoid needless casualties from rockets and mortars, getting food at a new wooden mess hall and dispersing to eat in sandbagged culvert bunkers or open pits. Three days after the sapper attack, a rocket killed our mess officer as he watched to ensure that the line of soldiers waiting for food was widely spaced.

Four of us had been eating in an open pit when we heard the rocket fired and dived for cover. It roared directly overhead and crashed on a slight rise about forty meters behind us, where sat the mess hall. I think we were the target, because our pit was in clear view of the firing site on the edge of the rubber plantation, and because the mess hall area was partially hidden by trees on that side. Gunners tended to aim high when firing 107mm rockets at line-of-sight targets.

Sad to say, the four of us heard shouts, but were too numb to care about what damage the rocket had done. We continued eating lunch.

The random shelling seemed to intensify each day. Much of it was directed at our helicopters; the flight line began to look from the air as if a miniature B-52 strike had hit there. Several times in broad daylight, choppers exploded from rocket or mortar hits. Once a string of mortar bombs marched past our tents, filling them with holes above the sand-bags. We rolled over and went back to sleep. Rows of ruptured 107mm rocket motors lined the tops of the sandbag walls. Everyone who wanted one had a 60mm or 82mm mortar tail fin paperweight.

One night a big 120mm mortar leisurely shelled the troop's tent area. The result was mostly thunderous tree bursts. The men in my squad ran into a nearby culvert bunker. A wounded man was screaming for help when a recruit tried to run out of the door to help him. I grabbed his shirt and pulled him back inside.

"You're afraid!" he hollered.

"No. Just careful. Wait until the next round hits."

After the blast, another tree burst, we dragged the fellow to safety.

I found a crater, got a direction and distance to the mortar pit, and ran to the troop's operations bunker. The duty officer greeted my data with skepticism. Where would a Blue learn to plot a mortar location? I explained that I had once been an artilleryman. He told me to take my information to the brigade operations bunker. I walked to that big bunker over a carpet of blasted down branches and tree limbs. There, a smart-assed captain told me to leave the mortar plotting to them. My plot, if accurate, was in the rubber trees, said he, and they couldn't fire there, anyway. I went away mad.

The next morning, I scrapped together five equally pissed-off Blues who had mortar training. We drove a truck to the rear area of an infantry battalion. The cavalry division wasn't carrying mortars in the field anymore, so the battalion's weapons were stored at Quan Loi. I talked a reluctant supply lieutenant into lending us an 81mm mortar, "off the books" for three days. We picked up some unauthorized crates of mortar bombs and fuses at the base ammo dump.

We set up the mortar behind the flight line, practiced dry-firing it, and waited. If the NVA mortared us again, we would shell the rubber trees; permission to fire be damned! We took turns babysitting that mortar for three unusually quiet nights. The rocketing continued, but no more mortar attacks occurred in our sector. Late in the third afternoon, we repacked the tube, legs and baseplate in gun grease and return them to the supply officer. We were mortared again that night.

Blue landed a short hop from Quan Loi to investigate a trail used the night before. Trails speak, and this one scared the bejesus out of me. Many men had been carrying heavy objects in the direction we were traveling. Their sandal prints had sunk deeply into the mud. We set up an ambush in a glade of soft, iridescent green grass beside the trail, and received word that a hill just across a tiny brook was heavily bunkered and peppered with stacks of ammunition crates. Cool-as-a-cucumber Reb wanted to go after the hill. I didn't have a good feeling about that. Major Stewart soon ordered us to pull back.

We climbed a slope and reached a clearing large enough for our four lift ships to land. While we waited, one of my men found an 82mm mortar crater and dug out the tail fins. Soon more of us, including Reb and I, had 82mm tail fin paperweights. There was no opposition on extraction and no report on the mortar craters.

Reb had been inviting me to Major Stewart's nightly briefing. At the next night's briefing, Major Stewart mentioned that Lurps had landed at dawn in the clearing and were immediately hit by mortars. Reb and I exchanged shocked looks as it dawned on us what those mortar craters the day before had meant. The NVA had been expecting someone to use the clearing as a helicopter landing zone and had registered mortars there. They held their fire when we left, assuming other Americans would return. We kept mum. The hill had been hit by an air strike after the Lurps were pulled out. No sense revealing our stupidity now.

Another day's patrol through the rubber trees around Quan Loi had exhausted me. It had been more of the same – disarming booby-traps, collecting the odd piece of abandoned equipment from the sapper attack, chasing another NVA watcher through the woods. All I wanted to do was sleep, but first I had to find out why Reb was visiting, smiling his disarming smile as usual.

"Well, Matt. I hope you like being platoon sergeant."

"Platoon sergeant? What are you talking about?"

"I'm going on thirty days leave to Europe, starting tomorrow. You won't have all the responsibility. The captain from the lift ships is going to be platoon leader." Another smile.

"Reb, you're dropping this in my lap and giving me a slick pilot as platoon leader?"

"Right on. Just pretend he's not there. Nobody's got any doubt that you can handle it. The major recommended you for the job."

"Do I have a choice?"

"No."

I didn't want the responsibility, but nothing much changed. Blue continued patrols and landings, and the captain left most of the decisions to me. At night, the captain and I attended troop briefings. In one briefing, Major Stewart told us that Bravo Troop was killing more NVA than any other cavalry division unit, including the battalions. He said that 126 had died during the previous month. I thought back to the months when two-or-three hundred enemy casualties were about average. Much of the fighting in those days had been on open coastal plains, and the 9th Cavalry was still using those lethal gunship door gunners. Our operations now were over dense bamboo and thick jungle.

Blue continued daily patrols around Quan Loi.

We had a scout gunner, "Prince," who had a certain presence, almost like a dark-haired angel of death: an angel with a machine gun riding on his shoulder. Prince was trim, handsome, courageous and self-assured, and I envied him his good looks and his poise.

A pink team and the Blue platoon were reconnoitering adjacent parts of the bamboo jungle when the pink team's Loach was hit hard from a bunker complex about a kilometer away from us. The Loach crew tried to escape. The aircraft flew about three hundred meters before it ignited in mid-air and crashed. The NVA who shot it down were pinned in their bunkers by the Cobra. A single lift bird pulled four of us out of a bomb crater PZ and took us to the crash site. We hung from the skids and dropped in amongst bamboo, stumps and logs. Two men were left at the LZ to wait for fire extinguishers and body bags while I chopped a path through a jumble of vines to the wreckage. Captain Marshall was right behind me.

The Loach had burst into flame and dropped like a rock, burning a hole straight down through tree limbs, bamboo and thick jungle vines, and landing on its skids. A new warrant officer had been aboard for an orientation flight, along with the pilot and his gunner. Three black, smoldering bodies sat upright in their seats, staring straight ahead through hollow sockets. The pilot's jaw was frozen open in a final prayer or a cry for help. The corpse looked like it was screaming. I wanted to run far away from there.

The captain stumbled into the burn zone, saw that awful scene, and mumbled, "I'm sorry. I can't take this." He headed back to the others. The scout pilot had been his friend

I unloaded my rifle and used the barrel as a stick to knock glowing-red grenades and belts of machine gun ammo out of the flames. I had done this once before, but if I had known the risk, I would have stayed a safe distance from that Loach. It was now time to recover our comrades. An electric shock hit me when I recognized Prince in the right gunner's seat in back, but only by a golden charm he always wore around his neck. Now it was a dazzle in a sea of black. Prince was no longer beautiful.

The captain and the other two soldiers arrived carrying fire extinguishers and body bags. The next hour or so was a horror. Extinguishing sizzling bodies with fire extinguishers and choking on the thick smoke, donning heavy rappelling gloves and trying to drag bodies out of their seats. Having arms rip away instead. I did most of it alone. I knew this work. The others had never handled burned corpses. We carried the body bags back to the LZ.

I attached the top carrying handle of the last bag to a rappelling rope. A slick crew chief hoisted it skyward. Then I daydreamed. Someone was shouting. I looked toward the place where Captain Marshall was speaking to a rifleman. It wasn't coming from them. More shouts. I looked up to see a black horror.

Prince's hot skull was slowly burning through the rubberized canvas of his bag about twenty feet above my head. The skull emerged into the light of day, trailing an attached spine with rib cage and pelvis. It resembled a hideous black spearhead. I was momentarily transfixed by this, the most gruesome and terrifying sight I ever encountered, and then jumped away as the thing suddenly broke free and crashed at my feet. The crewmen's shouts had saved me from being killed by a corpse. It would certainly have broken my neck. We waited until our friend cooled down.

That event cured me of envy for a lifetime.

———◼———

We supported, extracted, and rearmed Lurp teams throughout the summer. If they had a problem, the troop could help solve it. On a late July afternoon we returned from a Lurp affair on the Cambodian border soaked to the skin from a hard rain. The big news that day was that America had landed a man on the moon. I don't recall anyone being much interested or impressed. The big news for us was that a rocket had destroyed our supply room.

Also in July, there was an extraction mission for a Lurp team in contact. We set up a perimeter without knowing where they were until a bush flopped sideways and six camouflage-suited soldiers climbed out of the same hole. That was fancy hiding.

We soon received another lieutenant. He was Murphy, a West Point officer who didn't act like one, a cavalryman, and a compassionate and friendly person. The soldiers liked him instinctively. I liked Lieutenant Murphy as well, but would miss working with Captain Marshall who had successfully led both a helicopter platoon and an infantry platoon for weeks by then. Murphy would be my eighth and last Blue platoon leader.

The first landing with Murphy was not a textbook affair. I was supposed to be training him and tried too hard. Blue was landed beside a muddy stream in the bamboo jungle, and a scout pilot told us to follow the trail northeast to a bunker complex. I took a compass reading and moved the platoon down the trail – to the southwest. It was my mistake, but no one stopped us.

We followed a silent trail for hours, picking up discarded concussion grenades, and a few heavy belts of twelve-seven ammo. This was the trail that the sappers used to retreat from Quan Loi. They must have been demoralized and running to have tossed away so many munitions. We eventually arrived at a clearing, found a small pack with demolition charges (and a nest of scorpions) in the bushes, and were extracted.

Major Stewart was impressed by the ammunition we brought back. He commented at the briefing, "That's the way we should use the Blues, as a separate recon force. If they find something interesting on the ground, they should go after it and not always follow the directions of the scouts."

He didn't reckon with the fact that his Blue platoon sergeant was an idiot. I wondered what the major was talking about for a moment and then realized what had happened in the clearing. I avoided Major Stewart's eyes as he continued the briefing.

Murphy jabbed me with his elbow and said, "I thought we went the wrong way."

I replied in my lowest whisper. "You should have said something, Sir." That had to be a great first impression, as in, Sergeant Brennan can't even read a compass.

In late July, we were assailed from other quarters. One of the big squad tents had been claimed as its own territory by a large rat. The rat would help itself to packages from home, nibble through packs of cigarettes, and hurl itself through the air at night, landing on blankets or hanging from mosquito nets, scaring people half to death. The rat was getting bolder each night, so the tent's occupants decided that enough was enough.

For three nights in a row, they stayed awake after the lights were turned off, hoping to ambush the rat as he went about his mischief. On the fourth night, a Blue looked under his cot and saw the animal chewing on a pack of Winston cigarettes. I was startled by his shouts. I arrived at the tent to find an enormous rat, with a well-developed set of balls, backed into a corner on its hind feet, clutching a pack of cigarettes and baring its teeth. Granite was aiming his .45 automatic at it. I grabbed the pistol. The rat darted between Granite's legs.

We chased the marauder from cot to cot for the next fifteen minutes. The chase ended when I threw a bayonet and pinned the gutsy little fellow to the plank floor. Nicotine kills; quit now. It was sad that the rat had died, but the tent's occupants wanted to make an example for all other rats to heed. Someone hung the rat by the neck in the doorway of the tent using twine from a package it had gnawed through.

Granite had an idea. "We can't leave him like that. He was a brave rat. Why don't we give him a medal?"

"Got any suggestions?"

Doc Ring had joined us. "I've got one," he said. "Hold on a minute." He ran back to his tent for a moment, returned with a National Defense Medal, and pinned it on the rat's chest. Although this was a Vietnamese rat, we hoped that he wouldn't have been offended by an American decoration. Eventually, I went to bed.

My good friend Granite shook me awake the next morning. "Sarge! Sarge! Wake up! The new rear area captain wants to see you!"

I looked at the bedraggled hillbilly. Granite was worried, and that was a bad sign. "What's it about?"

"He's over at Third Squad's tent! He said to get your ass over there!"

The captain's shaven head glistened in the early morning sunlight. He was staring at the rat. A Bronze Star and an Air Medal had been added to the creature's noble chest. I tried to sound as cheerful as possible.

"Good morning, Sir. What can I do for you?"

He looked at me as though I had come for his garbage. "Are you the platoon sergeant?"

"Yes, Sir. That's me."

He pointed a stubby finger at the highly decorated rat. "Do you think this is funny, Sergeant?"

"No, Sir!" But I think it's hilarious.

"It's unsanitary; rats spread disease, in case you didn't know. Have one of your comedians cut it down." Now the threat. "I'll hold you personally responsible if something like this happens again."

"Yes, Sir." Fuck you, Sir. "Okay Granite, cut this thing down and bury it with full military honors." The captain winced.

That damned ridge-runner clicked his heels and snapped a mock British salute. "Right, Sarge." We were marked men.

———◆———

There had been articles in the *Stars and Stripes* newspaper for several days about a newly opened road east of Nui Ba Ra. The road was supposed to be rebuilt and secure for the first time in years. "The pacification of Blank-Blank Province continues on schedule," et cetera. After three years of reading such propaganda, I was not surprised to learn that a Lurp team had made contact almost as soon as they landed beside the road. We were sent to reinforce them. I wished some howitzers were in range of the "safe" road.

The slicks landed in trail [in a line] along the road. The place didn't look at all dangerous. The silent green mass of Nui Ba Ra towered above us, and that felt like seeing an old friend. The road surface was graded and well banked, and Rome plows had leveled the jungle for at about two hundred meters on either side.

Blue walked in a sweep line toward a wall of small trees and thin, thickly growing bamboo on the west, stumbling along over rotting trees and branches. Clack-Clack-Clack-Clark! I fell backward, flipped over and wiggled under a big tree limb. The enemy fire was light and not very accurate. One string of bullets snapped through a branch and stung may face with a few tiny wood splinters. We fired back until a Cobra made a long rocket run across our front. Silence.

We reached the bamboo and followed Lieutenant Murphy with the point squad as they headed north in a file. Somebody observed movement in the bamboo beside us and we began firing bursts at small groups or individual NVA who walked parallel to us, about thirty meters inside the jungle. Their game was safer than it looked; the flood of sunlight along the edge of the plowed area had created a densely packed wall of tough bamboo that deflected our little high-velocity bullets. Our watchers were behind that growth, in amongst larger bamboo stalks. They would drop out of sight when we fired, then pop up again a few meters ahead.

Red smoke blossomed by a trail leading into the bamboo, and a man in camouflaged jungle fatigues stood up right beside me. He had hidden himself well. The Lurp sergeant jerked his thumb in the direction of the smoke.

"Red marks the team's location. Where's your platoon sergeant?"

"That's me. What have you got here?"

"I'm not sure. We were inserted on the road and set up an ambush about fifty meters inside the bamboo. About twenty minutes later, I saw what I thought was another Lurp team ahead of us. They had camouflage fatigues and flop hats, and their faces were painted with battle grease, just like us. Then I noticed that they were carrying AKs and I shot the point man. I'll show you where it happened." The sergeant led me down the trail until we arrived at a pool of bright red blood at the base of a tree. I asked him to have his team walk in a file beside us, between the bamboo and the road.

The scouts told Lieutenant Murphy to check a ridge farther north. The strange walk continued for about 150 meters, until we climbed a gentle slope toward the place where red smoke marked bunkers. Wham! Wham! Wham! The NVA stopped our point with Chinese grenades, just like the one I was carrying in a cargo pocket. They sprayed us with their AKs, firing high. Wham! Wham! A man close by had the leg of his trousers blown open. I caught a fragment above the elbow when I braced my hands to push up and see what the hell was going on. I knew better. Stay flat when grenades explode and you're usually safe. Wham! Wham! A Loach flew over our heads with the gunner firing like crazy. It reached the bunkers, spun around, and raced back over us. The gunner had taken a bullet in the ass.

Four Cobras rocketed the bunkers with big seventeen-pound warheads. The detonations shook the ground beneath us. Over the years, rocket warheads had changed from six-pounders in 1966 to ten-pounders thereafter, but those new seventeen-pounders really packed a punch. We had already seen them snap mature rubber trees like matchsticks. As the last Cobra climbed away, Murphy ordered the point squad to rush the bunkers. Nothing was left but a few bloodstains. More bunkers stretched into the jungle as far as we could see.

The pilots told us to return south to another ridge, past the place where the Lurp team had made contact. A Loach hovered there, dropping white phosphorous grenades on something. We headed in that direction, firing at more NVA beside us in the bamboo. They continued their game of disappearing and reappearing.

I was with the point squad when we arrived on the south ridge. Overlooking the road were new machine gun and recoilless rifle pits, skillfully concealed with dead branches. Marks in the hard earth showed where weapons had been emplaced and sighted along the road. Fields of fire for the coming ambush were marked by branches stuck innocently among the other scrap wood.

A big NVA unit had carefully prepared its killing field and was waiting for the first convoy to pass. That unit was large enough to occupy the jungle along at least three hundred meters of roadway and send out a specialized recon force on short notice to attack our Lurps. It also had soldiers who liked to play chicken with M-16s.

There was none of the thick bamboo along this ridge and no watchers. The scouts radioed that the bunkers behind the weapons pits were empty. I sent Henry, a very professional black squad leader (Granite's new boss) to find out for certain. As Henry's squad entered the bamboo, Granite followed me on a recon into the bamboo about forty meters to the south of their location. Three firing slits peered out about twenty meters inside the bamboo. The bunkers were so well hidden that they looked like random piles of bamboo leaves. We dropped on our stomachs.

A roar of rifles and machine guns swept over Henry's squad, and we sprayed the firing slits we could see. About five AKs shot back at us. Bullets snapped through young bamboo stalks inches over our heads. We pivoted around and executed what may have been the fastest ground-hugging belly-crawl in military history. I tumbled into one of the recoilless rifle pits with Granite hard on my heels.

He huddled in a corner, gasping for air. "I thought they had us dead to rights, Sarge."

"Me, too. I ain't never moved that fast."

I told the machine gunner in our pit to fire short bursts at the place we had just left. As his bullets snapped through the big bamboo stalks, Henry ran out of the jungle, leaped a series of branch piles, and dropped into the pit beside me. He was bleeding from a deep bullet wound through the Trapezius muscle above his shoulder blade.

"They've got bunkers everywhere up there. Two of my men got hit by a gook machine gun."

"Where's your machine gun?"

"Gunner's shot. They won't let us get close to him. I'll need another machine gun to lay down a covering fire and get him out." He turned to the machine gunner in our pit. "Want to play hero?"

I waited for his answer and hoped I wouldn't have to make him go. This fellow called himself Panther. He called Sergeant Henry an Oreo [black on the outside; white on the inside] for being an NCO in a white man's war. Panther spat.

"What are we waiting for? The pinned man's a brother."

I had to grab hold of Henry's shirt to give me time to bandage his wound. Seconds later, Henry, Panther, and Granite where running back into the exploding bamboo. Perhaps once, light-years before, I had been stronger or braver, more foolish or more patriotic, but now I was afraid to go with them. I made excuses to myself.

A long, hammering volley from Panther's machine gun, and the squad backed out of the bamboo, dragging the two wounded men and firing. Bullets snapped through the brush piles around them. No one else was hit. More bullets snapped over my pit and a similar pit occupied by Murphy's command group. The only respite was when Cobras rocketed the bamboo and the NVA turned their weapons skyward.

Granite returned carrying the wounded gunner's machine gun. When a slick landed for the casualties, he jumped from my pit and ran back along the bamboo, firing the machine gun at the bunkers. Other men ran behind him with spare ammunition belts. He was the last man to board a slick, still firing. Granite, in his insane rage, had covered our withdrawal without even knowing it. All our weapons were firing as the slicks lifted off, banked away from the bunkers, and flew us away down the "safe road."

That night I wrote Bronze Star recommendations for Panther, Henry, and Granite.

Lieutenant Robert Jella, the Lurp team leader, wrote a letter in 1970 stating that I saved the lives of his team that day. I don't agree, and neither would Lieutenant Murphy, but it was a nice and much appreciated thought.

Less than two months after our experience, a Delta Troop road recon patrol encountered two NVA battalions in bunkers beside that road. The patrol fired its jeep-mounted machine guns into the bamboo without knowing for sure that the enemy was there [called a recon by fire]. The NVA thought they had been discovered and initiated an ambush meant for a much larger American unit. Sergeant Donald Skidgel won a posthumous **Medal of Honor** for his heroic actions that day.

———◆———

A couple days after the "safe road" experience, I was in Bien Hoa, ostensibly to check on pay records, but really to get away from the rockets for a few hours. There I learned that SSG Brennan was now 2LT Brennan. I returned to Quan Loi that afternoon and was commissioned the next morning in a ceremony on our flight line. All I could think about was how wonderful a target our formation made for those watchers in the rubber trees.

My new assignment was an infantry battalion near Saigon. I spent my last night with the division at an officers' club in Bien Hoa. There I met a shaven-headed headquarters company commander who had been a police lieutenant in New York. We were scheduled to fly home on the same day. The fellow looked like the Telly Savalas TV character, Kojak.

"What made you give up a reserve major's commission to come here, Sir?

"It's simple, Lieutenant. I got tired of those young punks on the street telling me what Vietnam was like and justifying their actions by it. He changed his voice to a higher pitch and mimicked them. "It's the war, man. I get flashbacks." He paused and lowered his voice. "When I go back, they won't be able to feed me any more of that crap."

We were joined at our table by a young, tow-headed lieutenant from the 7th Cavalry, Custer's old outfit. He said I reminded him of his little brother back in Virginia. The lieutenant talked about nothing but his recent experiences in the jungle.

"Man, we're hurting Charlie out in those boonies. Finding big caches and blowing bushes on him every time he bops down the trails. But, man, I'll tell you something. Charlie's been here a long time and this is mostly jungle. Not many places to land." The lieutenant continued, "We've been hit by one-twenty mortars in our last three Lima Zulus [landing zones]. I think they've got every clearing in War Zone C watched and zeroed in." He made a scream like a big mortar shell.

I remembered the "Heavy Bones" ambush, the LZ watchers who killed Sergeant Randy Spear, and the 82mm tail fin paperweight fiasco.

The next day I traveled to a transit unit in Long Binh and was told that my paperwork would come through in about three days. My cot was in a hot GP tent, crowded together with about twenty other junior officers and senior NCOs. The wait got boring very quickly. Then I discovered that next door was the famous 93rd Evac Hospital. I was soon sampling the food at the hospital's excellent canteen, and hanging around, trying to meet people.

I quickly developed a circle of acquaintances because they considered me an oddity: an unwounded soldier with long service in Vietnam, three Purple Hearts, and no good reason to be at the hospital. The first day and evening, I was taken on tours of the various wards and living quarters. The accommodations were luxurious. The doctors, nurses, and orderlies worked hard and spent their off-duty hours in air conditioned rooms with nice stereo outfits, refrigerators and most of the amenities of home.

I was introduced to a couple of doctors and their Vietnam wives and shared their liquor. Those couples already had spouses back home and were making do while they were overseas. I spent about an hour watching an Oriental neurosurgeon, seated on the floor in the middle of his elaborate living quarters, doing some sort of craft as his admirers came and went. He had an almost godlike status among the hospital staff.

The following evening, I followed a pretty nurse to her quarters and marked time in the canteen until about midnight. The nurses' quarters were posted with "Do Not Enter" and "Off-Limits" signs, but the door wasn't cinched shut. I entered a long corridor with a row of doors to the right, and large, banded, five-foot-square, cardboard boxes against the empty left wall. The first priority was to meet a nurse. I knocked on every door; no one answered. I climbed on top of a big box and fell asleep. There may have been copious amounts of alcohol involved.

The next morning I was awakened by a tiny scream. Someone with a terrycloth bathrobe and a round bottom was hurrying away toward the exit door. A residential door opened a crack and snapped shut. Time to go.

I returned to the canteen in late afternoon and was joined at a table by a Medical Corps major who I had been hanging around with. He had some news.

"The MPs are looking for a young lieutenant who broke into the nurses' quarters last night. Know anything about that?"

"Could be."

The major smiled. "If I were that young lieutenant, I would leave here as soon as possible."

I never went back.

Chapter 19

XUAN LOC

(August-September, 1969)

I wanted a First Cavalry Division platoon, but was instead assigned to an infantry battalion. A staff officer there briefed me with a pointer and a wall map. Here is a summary of what he said.

"The brigade is operating in the jungle for the first time in years. That's the reason you were sent here from the Cav. We need your knowledge of the jungle. The battalion is experiencing light contact around Xuan Loc" –he rapped the map with his stick –"but Delta Company had a heavy contact last week," -he pointed to an area of low ridges and thick jungle- "and lost a lieutenant and nine men."

"What unit are we fighting, sir?"

"Most of the contact has been with the Thirty-Third NVA Regiment. You've surely heard of them. They're supported by local VC battalions."

I had heard of them. The 33rd NVA Regiment had started the battle in the Ia Drang almost four years before. In one of the great ironies of the war, it would be the first and the last unit the First Air Cavalry Division would fight in Vietnam, across seven bloody years.

I nodded to the major, "The Cav fought them in the Ia Drang."

"Well, they still around." He smiled proudly. "It's a good feeling to be fighting NVA, instead of local guerrillas and booby-traps. The battalion commander is excited by the change. This has opened up a whole new set of options." Then he made an offer I should not have refused.

"Would you like to join the S-3 [Operations] staff?"

I have made quite a few dumb choices in my life, but the stone-stupid, wrong-headed decision I made ranks right up there with my refusal of a direct commission over three years before. I had spent about twelve months in various operations positions and wasn't eager for work that didn't feed my addiction to danger. I was living the last days of my last tour of duty in Vietnam, and hadn't seen the grunt war firsthand. Forty days with an infantry company, in what I thought was a relatively safe area, didn't seem like such a big deal. Perhaps there would be new experiences to write about one day.

"I'd prefer a line company, Sir."

"Are you sure? You've been in the field for a long time."

"Yes, Sir. I'm sure."

"Do you have any preference of assignment, Lieutenant?"

"No. It makes no difference to me."

"All right. We'll send you to a company that needs a lieutenant."

———◆———

Five days later, my new company returned to our Xuan Loc base from three days in the hills. I was concerned. The company commander moved with a "Tiger Team" of five bodyguards dressed in Vietnamese Tiger stripe uniforms whose only duty seemed to be to protect him. They often behaved toward the other soldiers in a condescending manner and this bred resentment.

The platoon leaders had not received situation briefings and never would receive them. Soldiers in my platoon were careless with weapons and very noisy on the march. There was work to be done.

Platoon Sergeant Buser told me that the company had been in serious action once during the previous year. The rest of the time had been spent in a swampy, overgrown area called the Pineapple Forest, a place infested with occasional snipers and booby-trap-setting will-o-wisps. Two weeks before my arrival, the platoon had killed five Viet Cong by charging up a jungle hill. He was justifiably proud of their feat.

"Gooks opened up from a bunker and second squad was pinned. Then we got on line and charged the bunker."

"Did they have a machine gun?"

"No, Sir. Just rifles."

"That charging on line is dangerous business, especially if the enemy has automatic weapons. The safest thing is to work up from tree to tree with covering fire. That's how we'll do it from now on."

"Okay, Sir." His body language told me that he didn't like that order.

The company was next sent on a series of patrols in the rugged foot-hills around Xuan Loc. I soon discovered that no amount of badger-ing could make the soldiers walk quietly. They refused to walk down trails, no matter how old, unless I took the point. They would cross trails quickly while making brief inspections to the left and right, so I began doing area reconnaissance and telling them to watch what I was doing.

On several occasions, we almost surprised groups of Viet Cong eat-ing rice or bamboo shoots, but our noisy approach scared them away. One day the platoon crossed a trail where many people had been walking a short time before. Nobody noticed, or chose to notice, the signs, so I showed them.

I wondered how the platoon was doing on night ambushes and LPs [Listening Posts], so one evening I accompanied a squad on a night ambush. The squad leader led us about one hundred meters away from the company position and settled into a deep gulley. It actually was a good location.

"This is it, Sir."

"No. It isn't." Our assigned position was one hundred meters deeper into the woods.

The riflemen told me that they did ambushes that way – find a protected place and hunker down until morning. According to them, every squad in the company did the same thing. That night I was weak and let them get away with that little deception. It was too dark and dangerous to move. After that, Sergeant Buser and I accompanied ambush patrols and LPs on alternate nights. That fixed the problem. When we returned to Xuan Loc, I called a platoon meeting in a grassy field.

"Look. I've seen things that might get you in trouble if we make real contact. The most important thing is that everyone is too noisy. I'll say it over and over again. The jungle is silent. You guys have to be silent or the NVA will hear you coming from a long way off. The little groups run away, but the heavies will stay and fight. If you are trying to scare them off by making a racket, forget it. Tie down your canteen; carry your rifles so they don't clank against grenades. Things like that can save your life."

The leader of the Second Squad, the heroes of the fight on the hill, interrupted. "But, Sir. We did okay against those five VC. They even had a claymore."

"Let's talk about that hill. They had a claymore, but they didn't use it. You did fine, but you were fighting local yokels. That charging stuff doesn't work against automatic weapons. Another thing. The claymores you saw in the Pineapple Forest were booby-traps. Up here, chances are that a claymore's going to have a man behind it, waiting to blow you away. If a lot of people expose themselves, Charlie's going to take you out. You guys are here for one year. Those same Charlies have been fighting Americans for a hell of a lot longer."

I wanted to add, "and fighting a lot tougher Americans," but that phrase could have been used in a talk with almost any group of infantrymen in the Vietnam of that era. It wasn't their fault at all. Selective enemy targeting had gutted the Army's leadership – the experienced leaders who could have helped them learn how to survive were usually dead, disabled, or retired.

I ended the talk with a demonstration of the quiet heel-toe walk used by the Blues. They began practicing that walk.

The lecture was greeted with no enthusiasm. Most of them probably thought I was another officer trying to make their lives harder than they already were. We sat together and cleaned weapons, and I prayed they wouldn't have to use them until I had more time.

I met a new lieutenant at the officers' club that evening. A crisp young man with shining eyes, wearing parachute wings and a ranger slash, pulled up a chair at my table. He had seen my Cav patch. He told me that he had graduated from West Point and immediately volunteered for Vietnam. He didn't want to miss the war. The lieutenant had requested service with the First Air Cavalry Division, but had been sent here instead.

I saw much of my former self in him: unquestioning loyalty, no good sense of danger, a craving for excitement. He wanted to know what medals I had gotten and I told him. He wanted to know about the cavalry division, so I told him what he wanted to hear. I knew what he would be like in the jungle, so I cautioned him to be careful at first and rely on the experience of his NCOs – if he was lucky enough to have experienced NCOs.

"Most of all, don't take chances with your life. You can only lead if you're alive after the shooting starts."

"Don't worry," he said. "I'll be okay."

The lieutenant was dead three weeks later. He took one man with him to search bunkers along a trail. A machine gun killed them. I had known what his fate would be that night in the officers' club. I mean that literally. I knew.

The company was in trouble five minutes after landing beside a jungle road. A man in khakis walked into the middle of the next platoon up the road, saw his error, dropped to his knees in the three-foot-tall grass and began crawling away on all fours. The platoon leader arranged his men in a circle and hollered "*Choi Hoi*!" [Surrender!] Soon all of them were shouting. As the NVA scampered back and forth, the circle moved with him.

"There he goes!" "He's getting away!" "God-dammit!" He had crawled between two soldiers and escaped.

The company set up squad-size, outward-facing ambushes in the woods for 150 meters along both sides of the road. It rained heavily throughout the night, and every time the downpour stopped, ground mist drifted and rolled through the trees. NVA moved noisily around us all night without ever presenting a clear target. They were playing with us. I had the misfortunate of positioning my ambush squad over an ant colony. At dawn, we were not only sleepless and soaked from the rain, but covered with hundreds of tiny red welts.

One of my squads had the wires to its claymore mines cut and hadn't seen a thing. A squad from another platoon watched a man walk up a mine and piss on it. They thought he was an American. Another squad in that platoon had a mine turned around.

I walked to the captain's position at dawn, passing a stream below the road. Ho Chi Minh sandal prints muddied its banks, and the impression of an RPG-7 rocket launcher was etched in the mud. On a rise on the other side of the road, with a clear view of the captain's command post and his "Tiger Team" bodyguards, at least two enemy soldiers had lain behind a big tree stump. No one seemed aware of, or had bothered to investigate, that obvious ambush site. I told the captain what I found. I don't know what was reported back to battalion headquarters, but the slicks had landed us at the precise location of a large enemy unit.

The company again broke up into squads and sent out morning claymore ambushes to either side of the road. I remained with a squad at the anchor position beside our landing zone of the day before. About noon came a crash, a delay, and a short burst of machine gun fire. One of my ambushes had made enemy contact without causing or taking casualties. That was the signal for the withdrawal of all ambushes back to the road. The soldiers who had fired the mine stumbled past me a few minutes later. One of them was holding an NVA bush hat. I was curious.

I grabbed his arm. "What happened up there?"

He blushed. "Sir, a patrol of about nine NVA walked down the trail where we had the 'bush."

"Why didn't you get any of them? Have the claymores turned the wrong way?"

"Sir, the point man had a grenade launcher and they looked like Arvins. I thought we should warn them."

"They all look alike. What were they wearing?"

"Brown uniforms and cloth hats."

It would have been funny if the game wasn't so damned deadly. He was lucky he didn't try to shake hands with them. "Next time, remember the Arvins wear green uniforms and steel helmets like we do."

Another blush. "I will, Sir."

I quickly briefed the squad leaders about the khaki, black, and pea green color of enemy uniforms, information that I had taken for granted that they knew, and told them to spread the word.

The company was resupplied by helicopter a short time later and C-rations distributed. We prepared to follow the road deeper into the jungle. When one of my men went into the woods to take a final leak on the side of the road opposite the failed claymore ambush, he left his rifle behind. He looked up to see a man in khakis leaning against a tree, smiling as he watched him pee-pee. When I heard his story, we organized a sweep line and moved about seventy meters into the woods. The NVA was long gone. That soldier may remember the ass-chewing that followed.

The men we were facing wore khaki uniforms and cloth jungle hats. Regular NVA troops in the south wore green uniforms and green pith helmets. Our adversaries had gained a lot of skills and experience fighting somewhere, but probably not in South Vietnam. They were a playful bunch who caused no damage, except to our pride, when they certainly could have. A 1967 Blue platoon would have eaten them for breakfast.

My platoon led the way until the company took a break. Platoon Sergeant Buser, my brave radioman, and I went ahead about 150 meters while the company rested. That sounds foolhardy, but I trusted my instincts to keep us safe. We found a side road with fresh tire tracks leading up a hillside. The road junction was marked by a wooden sign nailed to a tree. It had a phrase in Vietnamese beneath a five-pointed star and crudely drawn skull and crossbones. The hill had to be booby-trapped and mined at a minimum. Sergeant Buser's whisper sounded like a cannon shot.

"What do you think, Sir?"

"The hill is off-limits for some reason. It's late afternoon. If we go up the hill, we're asking for a fight. I'm not risking it..."

He nodded. "That's the way I feel. Besides, artillery might be hard to get."

I didn't need to make excuses. "Let's find a route around this hill."

And we did. The entire company followed us as we continued along the main road, filing by that uphill road and its sign with nary a comment. Again, I don't know what the captain reported.

The company camped that night on a hill covered with rotting branches and leaves. I was trying to sleep when a North Vietnamese mortar thunked several times from the next ridge hump, about eighty meters away, shelling a target somewhere in the valleys below. We took no action. I was lucky to be awake. A thick black scorpion, about five inches long, was crawling across my chest. I threw the ugly thing off with a quick jerk and killed it with a loose canteen. Scorpion nests were everywhere on the hill: another sleepless night.

We left the hill at dawn and passed tiger traps and bees nests on the border of a populated valley. Ancient logging trucks rumbled by our column. We waved to the drivers, but they acted like we didn't exist. Someone was watching them. These were vegetable farmers and loggers, at least during daylight hours. The company rested among the huts of their shabby, tumbledown hamlet. Again, no one was speaking. A convoy of trucks arrived for us. I didn't feel tired or breathe easily until we were driven away.

A few days later, we climbed a hill and entered an open area populated by thousands of tough saplings that grew so densely that they formed a wall. We couldn't walk through or past them without chopping a path with machetes. It was brutally hot and machete men were rotated frequently. After hours of this, with no end in sight, our point man came upon a small, dead tree towering a bit above the saplings. He didn't see the hornets' nest until it was too late.

Hornets ranged along the column, stinging people, spreading the joy. Some of us became light-headed and dizzy from stings. The point man was stung many times and went into shock. The captain was furious, not because the man was hurt, but because the medevac helicopter that hoisted him out gave away our location to everyone within earshot. We eventually cut our way out of that damned place.

We had been on patrol in light jungle for two days. Around us were squad-size camps where the NVA had been eating mackerel from cans with Saigon labels. Coca-Cola bottles littered the camps. Once my platoon crossed a trail where men had passed so recently that the stiff grass was still snapping back from the direction they had taken. I showed my squad leaders a resting place hidden under a canopy of bent reeds interwoven with vines and long grass. We returned to the trail.

"What does this grass tell you?"

Blank stares and an awkward silence.

"It's wet, so gooks can walk by and bend it without the stems breaking. It'll bend in the direction they're going and then snap back for about fifteen minutes. What about those Ho Chi Minh sandal prints in the mud?"

The Second Squad Leader stepped forward. "Looks like maybe a squad came by." He looked again to be sure of his estimate.

"Three or four at most. The water is still seeping back, so they passed here quit recently. Most of our boot prints haven't started filling up yet. You learn a lot from trails: what the Charlies are eating, what they're wearing, what kind of weapons they're carrying, how many there are, and where they're headed. You've got to know the signs and keep on your toes."

I had become almost desperate, worried that my instructions hadn't made a dent in their thinking. Real danger could be just a day or a week away. And then, as if a switch had suddenly been thrown, my soldiers began moving more quietly, asking questions, reading the trails. I felt my nagging was finally reaching them. They made me proud.

The battalion's recon platoon was at Xuan Loc when we returned. They were volunteers and a different breed of cat. Several days before, they had ambushed a group of important North Vietnamese in the hills. A personal letter of commendation from Uncle Ho [Ho Chi Minh] was found on one of the bodies. Another NVA had been wearing a little star with a green background awarded by the Viet Minh to veterans of Dien Bien Phu. It looked like a carbon copy of an award I had once worn in Cub Scouts. The star was pinned on a recon soldier's shirt.

I walked to the mess hall and loaded a tray with hot food and fresh bread. We lived for that delicious Army bread. The battalion commander, a major whom our company commander called "the colonel" because, he said, the fellow was "on the (promotion) list," was seated by a window. Hereafter I call him "The Major."

The Major was a lean, muscular man with close-cropped hair and a deep tan, arrow straight, looking every inch the professional soldier-athlete. He gave me no smile or other greeting, just "Come over here, Lieutenant."

"Yes, Sir." I sat down my food tray and walked over to his table

"I don't believe we've met." He introduced himself.

After we shook hands, he indicated that I should have a seat at his table. "What university did you attend, Lieutenant?"

He had hit a sore spot. I had spent most of my time since high school graduation in the Army, and my lack of education embarrassed me. "None, Sir. I only have a high school education. I got a direct commission."

A condescending look. "Oh."

"Sir, I intend to go to college when I get back to the States."

He wasn't interested. He stared out of the window with the back of his head turned toward me. I would see the back of that head on another occasion. "See that you do," he said as he continued staring through the window. "It's very important."

"Yes, Sir. Thank you, Sir."

I didn't think that he noticed me leave the mess hall with the tray of food but a few days later, the captain informed me that The Major wanted me as the next recon platoon leader.

"No, thanks," I told him. I was leaving the field in about three weeks, my men were improving, and soldiers from other platoons were trying to volunteer for mine.

There was a rubber plantation on the north side of our patrol base. A one-armed Frenchman and his Vietnamese cook lived there in a one-story, brown stucco house. The middle-age Frenchman was an ex-soldier with a crew cut and a barrel chest. He told us that he had fought the Japanese in 1945, and the Viet Minh for years thereafter. He had lost his arm to a sniper. He pulled a tattered map from a teakwood desk drawer and showed me where he had fought – places in North Vietnam I knew nothing about, and An Khe, Pleiku, Kontum, and Binh Dinh Province that I knew all too well. He didn't speak English, but one of the other lieutenants remembered a few words of college French. What was left unsaid was replaced by gestures.

We were talking one evening over glasses of his excellent wine when a report came over the radio. Another company was under machine gun fire inside a rubber plantation. The Frenchman excitedly grabbed a map and gestured for me to show him where the battle was taking place. I almost did. I looked past his smile to his Vietnamese cook, standing about ten feet behind him so she couldn't be seen. She was violently shaking her head and crisscrossing her hands, palms outward, in a "stop" gesture. I understood and picked a cassava plantation surrounded by rubber plantations miles away. The Frenchman was skeptical of my plot. We assured him that, yes, that was the place.

We told the captain what had happened and never returned. I later heard that several Viet Cong visitors had died in ambushes near the Frenchman's house.

Soon thereafter, the company returned to Xuan Loc for a two-day stand-down. My platoon was more self-assured, more comfortable with their new skills, and was gelling into a fine outfit. The afternoon we arrived, two Red Cross girls organized a baseball game. Do you want to play lieutenant? No. The game began.

The ladies walked over to where I was watching the game and made small talk. They were having a party that evening. Would I like to come? As an officer, I was finally able to say what I thought, although what I thought might not have been accurate.

"For years I've watched donut dollies play games with the enlisted men and sleep with the officers. Why would I want to attend your party?" The Red Cross girls ignored me and walked away.

I tried to relax that night at the officers' club. Judy Collins' song, "Both Sides Now," was playing when a chubby military history buff plopped down on the bar stool next to me. He wanted to talk about Verdun, and Stalingrad, and Dien Bien Phu. I wanted to listen to Judy Collins. He tugged on my shirtsleeve to get my attention, so I decided to tell him how I felt.

"It all comes down to the depressing business of scared men trying to kill other scared men."

He wasn't listening. "If the French only had more one-five-fives at Dien Bien Phu and hadn't left all those one-oh-fives back at Hanoi…"

"What bullshit! My friend, it doesn't matter how many one-oh-fives the French had at Dien Bien Phu. The only thing that matters is that thousands of men died like slaughterhouse pigs."

That reached him. "That's a pretty speech, but we have to face reality. War will always be with us, at least in our lifetimes."

He had a good point and I knew it. The most effective politics are backed by steel. But I deeply, fervently hoped to see the end of wars in my lifetime. "But can't you see how insane this all is? We hunt each other from tree to tree, like game."

The chubby lieutenant shook his head. "No. It will always be that way." He left to find someone else to talk with about Cannae and Tannenberg.

<hr>

We were in a rubber plantation, crossing parts of a bunker system that probably stretched for miles. This had been a regimental camp during the 1968 Tet Offensive and had been used on and off since then. North Vietnamese still lived in parts of it, even as we blew up some of the hundreds of deep log bunkers. It was a strange region. There were artillery-smashed bunkers and rows of graves in places (some of which were opened to verify what was buried there) and NVA living in other places.

We were always followed. All the company had to do was pass a quiet rubber workers' hamlet. The smiling workers might be part of the local Viet Cong cell. I don't recall us ever questioning them. I had spent years tracking men; now we were the ones being tracked and watched. One dark night, one of my squads ambushed the day's trail and blew a claymore that probably killed a tracker. We found his pack hidden under a pile of rubber branches. Blood and drag marks.

On another day, there was a skirmish in the rubber trees between one of my squad patrols and about a squad of green-clad NVA. A grenadier started the fight by targeting a man carrying a large burlap sack on his back. The grenadier's shooting was so good that the 40mm grenade buried itself in the sack of bananas the Vietnamese was carrying without exploding. We later ate the bananas and buried the grenade. The patrol may have wounded others. It chased the NVA up a trail until a stay behind whirled out from behind a tree, sprayed a burst, and disappeared downhill. The lead man was hit. We used machetes and small chainsaws to clear a one-ship PZ for medevac.

On our last night in the plantation, another of my ambush squads, accompanied by Sergeant Buser, blew claymores at rustling noises in the darkness. They found two dead wild boars at dawn. The Americans left the carcasses alone, but our Vietnamese scouts shoved each other and cursed, fighting over cuts of meat. Each of them walked away carrying a haunch over his shoulder.

Those Vietnamese scouts hated each other. Both had been NVA soldiers, but one had been a private, and the quiet, muscular fellow had been a lieutenant. They had a major point of disagreement that sometimes ended in fistfights, or more correctly, open-handed smacking sessions that resembled fistfights. The private had walked down the Ho Chi Minh trail through Laos and Cambodia. The story went that the lieutenant was flown almost to the border of South Vietnam by a Soviet made helicopter. The private couldn't forgive the officer for his easy trip south.

We left the plantation and cut a path across a series of deep, bamboo-covered ravines. People shadowed us throughout the day. They were playing the game I had first seen along the "safe" road. A man would walk parallel to the company column until somebody fired. He would disappear for a moment and then reappear. The unnerved soldiers in the platoons following mine began shooting at shadows. The little squad camps we found had been hastily abandoned.

The company finally reached a plantation of young trees and set up a night position about three hundred meters inside the rubber. I sent a squad under Specialist Gomez to ambush the trail we had made. Almost at dark, Gomez radioed to tell me that five Viet Cong, dressed in black pajamas and carrying old American carbines, had just climbed out of the last ravine. The captain broke into the transmission and told Gomez to shoot them. Gomez refused. He said that his compass didn't work and he wasn't certain where he was. I looked around to see a pissed-off captain beckoning for me.

"Lieutenant Brennan, get the hell over here!"

"Yes, Sir!"

I ran to the rubber tree where he had set up his command post. "Brennan, did you check your squad's leader's compass before they went on ambush?"

"No, Sir. I didn't."

"That's your job isn't it? Making sure your men are properly prepared for missions?"

"Yes, Sir."

"From now on you will check all equipment before the ambush goes out. You will then make a report to me. Is that clear, Lieutenant?"

"Yes, Sir. It won't happen again."

"You'd better be damned sure that it doesn't."

Leaders were required to personally check each man's equipment, but I had never seen it done for a compass. The chewing out was a farce, staged for the enlisted men who had heard Gomez's radio messages. The captain and I both knew that the leader of nine Americans, lavishly armed with a machine gun, claymore mines and seven M-16s (two with attached grenade launchers), had refused to engage a tiny VC patrol armed with World War II carbines. If we admitted the fact, we would have to report a mutiny.

The Viet Cong spotted Gomez's squad a short time later and cautiously withdrew back into the bamboo. The squad came dragging back to camp shortly after dark. Gomez walked quickly by me and headed for the shelter of a rubber tree out of my line of sight.

"Gomez?"

"He turned around slowly, not wanting to hear. "Yes, Sir?"

"Let's see that compass." It worked perfectly. The florescent needle spun around and pointed in the right direction. "Why is it working now and didn't before?"

He shrugged his shoulders and held out his hands, palms up, in a helpless gesture. "I can't explain it, Sir. Maybe it was magnetism or something."

"Yeah. Or something." Gomez cringed at the words. "You're relieved as squad leader. Turn all your duties over to Flores. Don't go around the captain. He wants to bust you back to private." I believed in second chances.

"Yes, Sir," he said. "I'm sorry."

The following days in the young plantation were a time of pleasant patrols between rows of rubber trees and long rest breaks in the shade. The grass was soft; the weather was cool and clear. There were gentle breezes, no rain, and naps on banks of freshly mowed grass. Everything had a picnic atmosphere about it. We listened one day to Cobra gunships and Phantom jets attacking a Viet Cong company two miles away. The young trees muffled sounds and made the fighting seem a world away. Danger was that close, but my war was over. I dreamed of Leila and home.

Staff Sergeant Buser left for home during this time. I immediately missed his counsel and the respect he was given by our fellow soldiers. His replacement, a staff sergeant and veteran of a previous tour with the infantry brigade, soon arrived.

The company returned to another part of the extensive bunker system in the plantation. After a long walk through the earthworks, we spent the night inside a rubber log fortress. The irregular walls had been carefully constructed from interlocking logs to look like accidents of nature. In reality, this was a well-sited defensive position on high ground.

Shortly after dawn, we were awakened by a high, momentary whine of jet engines, soon followed by the distant rumble of a B-52 strike smashing something. Hearing B-52 engines was a rare event because the jets flew so high, but I heard them for few seconds that morning.

When the company moved to a grassy clearing on the edge of the plantation, I lost my squad leaders. I arrived to find them standing with the company first sergeant beside a headquarters helicopter. The captain called me over and informed me, without any prior warning as usual, that they would be flown to Xuan Loc for leadership training.

Seeing the puzzled look on my face, he added "It's only for three days, Matt."

My platoon now had a new platoon sergeant, a specialist or two, and lots of privates. We boarded a gaggle of slicks. Forty-five minutes later, we were cutting a path with machetes toward the B-52 strike zone. The rest of the day was lost in a churned-up expanse of former jungle. We left the wasteland at dusk and spent the night in untouched jungle. The captain had told the platoon leaders nothing about our mission, but the bombers had obviously missed their target.

We awoke to a cloudless sky and a beautiful, golden sunrise. It was September fifth, my mother's birthday. I had spent over one thousand days in Vietnam and had only six left that mattered. My platoon led the company column over steep, wooded hills. Once there was a loud rustling in the tree tops as we moved downslope. A large troop of noisy, chattering langur monkeys passed by overhead, running from something in the direction we were heading. At two places we encountered lightly-used trails. In early afternoon, we climbed a rocky ridge above a swamp and sat among the jagged boulders to eat our rations. I sent two fire team-size patrols [four men each] to recon our flanks along the ridge. They returned to report more colonies of black scorpions.

Two resupply slicks hovered at the edge of the swamp below us while the crew chiefs pushed out rations, ammunition and explosives. The company would be in the jungle for at least three more days. Normal platoon rotation after the lunch break did not happen. We remained in the lead, so I put my best squad, Second Squad, on point. I could trust them to be careful.

Second Squad that day consisted of five PFCs [Privates First Class]. The leader was PFC Moore, a man who had quickly picked up jungle patrolling and reconnaissance techniques. I considered him a rising star in the platoon. All five of them worked carefully and well together.

Moore's squad led us off the rocky ridge, continued about one hundred meters along the edge of the swamp, and then back into the jungle. About fifty meters in, they encountered a wide trail running perpendicular to them at the base of a hill. It looked dangerous. My halts to conduct reconnaissance were not always appreciated; I had been warned to report the reasons for delays and continue reconnaissance only with the company commander's approval. I radioed the captain.

"We have a trail with fresh Ho Chi Minh prints and animal snares. Request permission to recon the area before continuing. Over."

From his usual position, two platoons back in the line of march, he radioed, "This is Six. Permission denied. We have one thousand more meters to go before dark. Keep moving. Over."

"Three-Six, roger that."

The leader of another platoon, Sergeant Tom Marcotte, monitored our transmissions and chimed in with his favorite phrase, "Grandma was slow, but she was old."

The point advanced about thirty meters up the hill with the fifth man in column separated from me only by a large, black log. I was straddling that log like the back of a mechanical bull when my radioman handed me the handset.

"They've got something, Sir."

"This is Three-Six, go."

"Three-Two. We have a claymore hanging in a tree up here. We are investigating."

If the men by the mine made any sudden move, we would have many casualties. They had to keep acting in a normal way. The squad leader asked for instructions; I told him to wait, knowing full well that his five-man squad might be sacrificed to save those behind them. It is numbing, gut-twisting, to know that men's fates are in your hands, that you are talking to a dead man. I slid back behind the log and used hand signals to quickly get the rest of the company spread out and into cover. When they were eating dirt behind me, I told the point to get down.

Boom! The continuous chatter of a machine gun was drowned out by four more Booms! The Vietnamese had been waiting from more of us to enter their killing zone.

The captain radioed, "Three-Six, this is Six. What have you got up there?"

"Six!" I angrily screamed at him through the handset. "We're pinned down by motherfucking claymores!"

I scrambled on all fours away from the log as two machine guns and about forty AKs turned the slope into a shooting gallery. I had never experienced such heavy fire on the ground. I dropped my pack and rolled onto my back in a shallow depression. Earth kicked up all around; bullets clipped grass and vines. White tracers streaked by two inches above my face. I was terrified, trapped, waiting to feel the bullets hit me, sure that I was about to die.

I silently prayed, "My God! My dear God! We're in the middle of a kill zone! Please, please let me live!"

The enemy abruptly stopped firing. I rolled on my side to find that every sapling along the trail had been chopped down by claymores and bullets. Moans and groans filled the jungle. I positioned what was left of the platoon behind the trail and evacuated the wounded to the swamp. At one point, I braced a man with a bullet gash across his shin and started to help him toward the swamp. I wanted an excuse to go back to the swamp and hide. My radioman saw me leading the wounded fellow away and knew I wasn't coming back.

"Sir! Where are you going? You can't leave us here!"

I was ashamed and handed the wounded man to another soldier. If I ever left that trail, I wouldn't have to guts to return.

With the wounded evacuated, I arranged the survivors in a line and moved them about twenty meters forward, up against the bamboo and trees above the trail. I rolled and crawled back to the black log where I had been when the nightmare started. A machine gun raked the top of the log, tearing off a few chunks of bark and traversing left. They were probably keeping our heads down for the next act.

My radioman and I crouched on our knees behind the black log, popping up, quickly firing, and dropping down to reload. We emptied six magazines at the place above us where the machine gun's muzzle blast was pushing aside leaves. The machine gun stopped firing; shouts echoed through the suddenly quiet jungle.

Whoosh! Whoosh! A rocket-grenade skimmed the top of the log, ricocheted off a tree limb and went hopping along the ground toward the swamp. Another hissed by to the left, hit the ground, and fish-tailed into a clump of bushes. There was such a racket that I couldn't hear them being fired. I never knew how many RPGs were fired or why they failed to detonate. It may have been that the warheads were striking dense bamboo at a short range and failing to arm.

I thought the RPGs were preparation for an infantry assault, so I pulled my line of soldiers back about ten meters to below the trail, giving them better fields of fire and some protection behind the few trees.

Two snakes circled far above the swamp. I could hear them, but couldn't see them. As our marking smoke drifted up through the tree tops, I directed their rockets. Each run was met by dozens of AKs from our hill and at least three others.

"Three-Six, this is Tiger Tree-One. How was that last run?"

"Three-Six. Bring it in closer."

"Roger that, Three-Six. Rolling in hot." More rockets.

"Three-Six, Tiger Three-One, over."

"Tiger! We need it closer!"

"Roger that three-Six. Understand closer." More rockets.

"Three-Six. Tiger Three-One, over."

"This is Three-Six. Rockets are suppressing November Victor fire. Bring it in closer, right in front of the smoke. Over."

"Tiger Three-One. Are you sure you want it there?"

"This is Three-Six, roger that. We're behind trees. That smoke is right in front of the bunkers."

"Roger that you want it closer. Keep your heads down."

Fragments smacked into the trees. The second Cobra fired a salvo of flechette rockets that sent nail-darts cracking overhead. The pilots had not informed me that they were going to fire flechette rockets, which required a safety radius, but they did the trick. Small branches and leaves rained down, but the NVA fire abruptly stopped.

"Three-Six, this is Tiger Three-One. That was the last of our rockets. We took hits on that last run. Can no longer assist. Pop smoke and my teammate will expend forty mike-mike and minigun."

"Roger that. Smoke popped. Out."

They left after the second Cobra made two more gun runs. The jungle was silent for a few minutes until random bursts of AK fire started up again. I placed a machine gun by a small tree in front of the trail and told the team to fire random bursts across our front to keep enemy soldiers under cover. The rest of us collected belts of ammo to feed the gun.

At that point, I rose to my knees on the trail and twice shouted "Fuck Ho Chi Minh!" at the bunkers on the hillside above us. All firing abruptly stopped for about forty-five seconds.

I sent a three-man machine gun team about thirty meters to the right front. They crossed the trail, disappeared behind a clump of bamboo, and were chased back across the trail by long machine gun bursts. They tore past the bamboo clump at a dead run, heading for the swamp. So, I placed another machine gun team beside the trail, covering that right flank. Three men in green uniforms ran past the bamboo clump where my machine gun crew had retreated. They were headed for the swamp and the wounded. Our machine gun by the trail killed them.

Flashes of green cloth moved up a small tree a few meters above us on the slope. The tree wasn't a good choice of perch: branches shook and leaves rustled.

"Shoot that tree! Spray it! Spray it!" He fell heavily through the branches, bounced once and was still. The tread pattern on the soles of his boots, a reverse image of our own, could be seen below the bamboo stalks.

I was behind the black log when Sergeant Marcotte's platoon spread into a line behind us, flattened themselves, and belly-crawled up the slope, firing as they moved. Bullets were hitting both sides on my log. The friendly fire was more dangerous than the machine gun on the other side of the log. I shouted for them to cease fire. Sergeant Marcotte crawled up to my log.

"We're going after the wounded."

"Don't do it. They're dead for sure."

"Captain's orders. Hang in there."

A brave black rifleman organized and led the charge into a clacking roar of rifle and machine gun fire. They stumbled back down the slope dragging a dead man and four wounded by their legs. One of the wounded was from my point squad. His blood-drained face was covered with dirt and he had a mouthful of leaves. Suddenly, his eyelids fluttered and he looked up from his dirt bed with eyes full of pure faith and trust. He spat out the leaves and started to say something to me. His eyes glassed over. You never forget something like that.

Sergeant Marcotte beside me said, "They've got a lot of AKs up there! The rest of your men are fucked!" Dead.

I radioed the captain. "We just shot a sniper out of a tree. Have four confirmed NVA KIA. If we're going to stay here longer, we need the FO. Over."

"Three-Six can you handle it from there?"

Yes.

He soon sent another message. "FO has first round on the way. You direct from there."

The artillery lieutenant gave the guns a first target out of earshot. I didn't have a map, so the initial targeting was his responsibility. I began dropping the shells two hundred meters at a time. I would radio the direction and corrections to him; he would send the information to the gun crews on his radio frequency, and call back on my frequency when the shells were on the way. The process would then repeat. Although he was an unnecessary middleman, he probably had to convince his superiors that he was doing his job.

My plan was to pull back about forty meters to the edge of the swamp and bring in "danger close" delayed fuse artillery to plow up the bunkers that had to be there. The one-half second delay would allow the shells to crash through tree limbs and drill into the ground before detonating. The fifty-to-sixty-meter distance from the closest targets was necessary because some of the shells might hit tree trunks or rocks and ricochet.

As an artillery shell exploded with a muffled crump about four hundred meters away, the captain called a ceasefire. I was told to direct an attack by an Air Force spotter plane. The Air Force was transitioning at that time to twin-engine spotter planes that carried more rockets. Bravo Troop had experienced problems with the new planes' accuracy as the pilots learned the ropes, so I was wary. We were in too close for bombs, and when the pilot had trouble pinpointing our location, I directed his rockets at a hill from which we had heard firing, but not the one above us. The pilot could contribute to the battle while we remained safe and sound.

As the last set of rockets hit, a man ran up our trail from the swamp. I thought the FO was finally coming forward. But it wasn't the FO. The Major flopped down beside me.

"You call those rockets close, Lieutenant?"

"No, Sir. That's a FAC and I wa . . ."

"Why haven't you got a position by that log in front of you?"

"Sir, there's a machine gun on the other side of it. I think they're in bunkers, and I'm planning to pull back about forty meters and get some artillery in there. We're to close in to crack the bunkers."

Our machine gun was still spitting out random bursts as The Major continued. "We don't know that they're in bunkers! You're not pulling out! Get your men up past that machine gun."

Then, for some ridiculous reason, I remembered something in my leg pocket. When I had first encountered that trail, I had found several one-inch-square contraptions on little stilts, constructed from bamboo and vines, and had kept one of them. It looked like a tiny cage. The Major had been in Vietnam for a while. Maybe he would know what it was.

"Sir, can I ask you one question?"

"Sure."

"What's this?" I pulled the cage thing out of a cargo pocket and handed it to him.

He gave me a venomous look, crushed it between two fingers and flicked it away over his shoulder. Then I was again staring at the back of his head. His arrogance was suffocating and humiliating. The Major thought that he was talking to a coward.

He crawled up to the black log (where he remained throughout the remainder of the afternoon) followed by Sergeant Marcotte. I crawled forward with ten nervous men until we were against the bamboo where the RPGs had been striking. The Major looked my way.

"Have all your men got grenades, Lieutenant?"

"I'll check."

"See that you do. Each man should have a grenade to throw when the NVA try to close with us."

Try to close with us? The enemy soldiers weren't about to leave their bunkers and trenches when they were doing so much damage without exposing their asses. Any grenades we threw would hit the bamboo and bounce back on us. I whispered to each man not to use a grenade unless we pulled back from the bamboo.

The Major, all balls and a few cards less than a full deck of jungle skills, led the battle after that. He wouldn't let us pull back to hit the hill with artillery. No more artillery; no more close rocket runs; no more spotter planes; no more confirmed enemy casualties. We took about ten more casualties from bullet swarms and snipers when we should have been cracking open bunkers.

The man beside me lost part of an ear to a bullet fired from somewhere behind and above us. He was disoriented. As I led him back to the edge of the swamp, we almost tripped over our seriously wounded platoon sergeant. The platoon medic later told me that the platoon sergeant had lost his nerve when the shooting started and ran away to hide with the wounded. A ricochet ripped open his back. Close by was Gomez, recently of "non-working compass" fame, squatting in the water and trying to look invisible. I was concerned and asked him where he was hit and how bad it was.

After a silence, he finally said, "I'm not hit, Sir."

I didn't understand. "Then why are you back here?"

"I don't know." He looked away for a moment. "I'm scared."

"Let's go back up there. We need all the rifles we can get."

Gomez shook his head. "No, Sir. I can't do it."

For the first time, it dawned on me that Gomez wasn't hurt. "Let's go!"

With eyes full of terror and shame, Gomez said, "No!"

"Gomez, it's your ass. If we both get out of here . . ." I took his ammunition pouches and ran back to the trail.

At some point, Sergeant Marcotte was wounded by a machine gun bullet when he rose up from behind the black log. Two men grabbed his arms and dragged him kicking and cursing back toward the swamp. The flak jacket he routinely wore saved his life and gifted him with a large chest bruise.

Later in the afternoon, The Major told me that he had spotted a bunker on the hillside. The battle was prolonged for another hour (and at least two sniper casualties) until a Loach crew delivered four LAWs [Light Antitank Weapons – small 66mm rockets in disposable tubes]. The soldier who brought them forward fired where The Major pointed. The first two rockets thudded into the ground without exploding - a common fault with those weapons. The next two exploded with deep crashes. Two direct hits on a fallen tree. That was the major's bunker.

We withdrew to the swamp. There was one last exchange of fire with the enemy and then The Major covered our pullback with rockets that detonated along the crest of the hill far above us. This was followed by two closer 40mm passes. The little grenades made a lot of noise in the first of three canopies of branches overhead, but did no damage.

The Major gave me a triumphant look and said, "Now, that scared them, Lieutenant."

And that's all it did. He was settling for scaring them.

The company lost twenty-nine men killed and wounded that day. My platoon suffered five dead and thirteen wounded; the reinforcing platoon lost two dead and nine wounded. I eventually led the survivors - a combined platoon of about twenty-one men.

I spent the night squatting in the water with a machine gun across my lap and several belts of bullets hanging on branches above the swamp water. The next morning, the captain sent the combined platoon away from the swamp on patrol. About forty meters from our positions and the command post in the swamp, all of which was visible through the trees and bamboo, we found a new, wide, muddy trail. A lot of men had silently walked past us, headed in the direction of the wasted B-52 strike. My combined platoon had secured the *other side* of the swamp.

We returned to find four twisted body bags and a pile of useless weapons. Off to one side were my four returned squad leaders, looking white-faced and thoroughly shocked. Soldiers from another company were resting on their packs and smoking. I found one of their lieutenants seated on a mud mound in the swamp, and pointed to the four body bags.

"Did they die quickly?"

He nodded. "A claymore messed them up real bad. The gooks didn't take their rifles or radio, so you must have scared them. There were some unexploded RPG rounds up there."

"Yeah. I bet we scared them. They didn't take the damned rifles because they don't need them. They don't have to capture stuff anymore."

I walked back into the jungle to the tree where I had lain while directing the gunship runs. From about four feet on up, embedded nail darts made the trunk looked like a pin cushion. One wrong correction, or an inexperienced pilot shooting a hair off-target, and those darts would have nailed us. No pun intended.

To the left of the tree stood a low three-legged wooden stool of the type Vietnamese use for meals. That particular stool had taken its share of scrapes and dings and had aged to the weathered gray of an old fence post. The stool belonged to a soldier we called Kitchen. Kitchen, being a massive fellow, loaded his pack with ration cans that other men wouldn't (or couldn't) carry, until it bulged and the straps sank deeply into his broad shoulders. When Kitchen tied that stool to his pack as a final touch and stood up, he looked more like a lumbering tinker than an infantryman.

To be honest, I had never paid much attention to Kitchen, except to wonder why he carried so much extra weight. Now I missed him terribly. I never learned how badly he was wounded, but his three-legged stool will sit, lonely and deserted, in a clearing beside the nail tree, throughout my eternity.

I never climbed that hill. I was told that there was a bunker upslope from the black log with shell casings and dried blood. The hill had three trenches with bunkers and a larger bunker with bloody bandages that had probably been used as an aid station. We had faced a Viet Cong "hard hat" force, probably a battalion of elite VC infantry.

Michael Lee Lanning writes in his book, **The Only War We Had***, that 135 bunkers were counted. That's more bunkers than we had soldiers when the fight began. Artillery could not have missed.*

On the two-day walk out of there, we found small, squad-size camps scattered through the jungle. These were now frightening places. A very brave chaplain accompanied us on the walk; his comforting presence helped all of us. Elephant trails of bulldozed trees, flattened vegetation, and large balls of manure led to banana and cassava plantations which, in turn, led to a road. Our trucks arrived about an hour later. I climbed into the cab of a truck piloted by a smiling driver. He had no right to be grinning. He recoiled against the door when I glared at him.

"You guys had a hard time of it from what I hear."

"Yes. Why are you so damned happy?"

Now the big secret. "Sir, I got good news! Have you heard the latest?"

"We've been out of touch for a few days."

"Sir, Ho Chi Minh is dead! The war might be over in a few days."

I thought back across four years to the soldier who had hitched a ride with our dump truck in An Khe Village. We had believed that the war was almost finished. There is always that hope among soldiers. I looked at the teenage driver straining to hear my response.

"Don't count on it, partner." My answer disappointed him. He was crestfallen.

Gomez was waiting for me when the trucks left us at an ARVN camp. "What are you going to do with me, Sir?"

"Nothing."

His eyes widened in disbelief. "Nothing?"

I told Gomez that he was a coward who had abandoned his platoon when they needed him most. But any investigation would have to include the other men who had not come forward, or who ran away. I was thinking about my platoon sergeant, the captain, the FO, and others. I told him to get a job driving a jeep or whatever in the rear, and asked him to someday think a kind thought about me.

His expression was a mixture of gratitude and relief. He saluted like a recruit. "Yes, Sir."

I was through with cowards and heroes. I just wanted both of us to go home. There was a book locked somewhere in my mind. Someday I might have the strength to write it.

I spent the last night in the field on ambush in a safe area near the ARVN camp. The next morning after we returned to the camp, the FO lieutenant asked if I had a few minutes to talk.

"Sure do."

"The captain and I discussed it," he began. "We both have families to take care of, and you are all alone. We thought that if one of us (came forward and) was killed, more people would suffer. I'm sorry, but I thought you deserved an explanation."

That's the old "You can be killed, but not me," philosophy.

Our platoon medic said a similar thing. The captain told the medic to stay with him (and his bodyguards) in the swamp, treat the wounded there, and not go forward. Seeing him would have been a comfort.

Gomez and I left for Xuan Loc the next morning. Gomez quickly disappeared, I know not where. His name was never again mentioned.

From Xuan Loc, I traveled to the company rear area at Disneyland East. I arrived in time to hear Armed Forces Radio describe our battle: moderate American casualties, twenty to forty NVA dead. That body count was tripe. Later, President Nixon said that American forces had been engaged only in defensive operations for the past month. If that were true, my draftees would be alive. I wanted to live to vote for anyone but him.

I learned twenty years later that enlisted men from the two platoons I tried to lead on September fifth nominated me for the Silver Star. I am forever humbled and honored.

Chapter 20

TWILIGHT

(September-October, 1969)

I had to make a last trip north, had to see the Blues one last time. At the Quan Loi base that first evening, Lieutenant Murphy, a few Blues I had known before, Reb and I, caught up on events. The big news items were a large sapper attack on Quan Loi in August, and the troop's recent defeat of an NVA recon company on the Cambodian border. Reb proudly told me that he had been written up for a **Silver Star** for that action.

Granite had come unglued during a fire attack and had driven a truck up and down the flight line while 122mm rockets exploded there. He was currently under observation at squadron headquarters in Phouc Vinh. Because Phouc Vinh was the first stop on the journey back to Disneyland East, I made a mental note to check on him.

Murphy invited me on a last mission the following day. The scouts had killed three NVA on an infiltration trail on the border. The lift ships carried us past Nui Ba Ra, over one of the new "instant LZs" blasted out of the jungle by a 10,000-pound butane bomb. We landed in a grassy swamp and followed a trail into the jungle. I was impressed at how silently everyone moved. I had forgotten about that.

The trail was a well-engineered affair, floored with woven bamboo mats and concealed by branches and bamboo trained together with vines. Along both sides were pieces of uniforms, torn NVA jungle boots, bits of thin plastic ponchos, rotting packs and scraps of packaging for Vietnamese and American rations. The trail had been used for years. We followed it into Cambodia. As a snake thundered down the trail a few feet above the trees, I dreamed of how that kind of firepower and close support might have changed the outcome of my recent battle. The Blues were more fortunate than they knew.

The rest was the same – bullets, Loaches, a camp burned. Some of the last bullets I fired in anger were at woods on the edge of the swamp where two green-uniformed North Vietnamese soldiers had disappeared as the slicks lifted us out. The brand-new Blue beside me stared wide-eyed until I shouted for him to open fire.

Later that afternoon, I sadly headed to the flight line where I had been commissioned an eternity before. I knew that I probably would never see any of the Blues again, and never again ride the skids into a landing zone. That had once been my life, but it was really over this time. I had known, at least in passing, seventy-three men who died during my service in Bravo, Charlie and Delta Troops, and God knows how many more wounded, whisked away and never seen again. I remembered the dead and gravely wounded soldiers from the battle on September fifth - men I loved and will always be proud of. I didn't want to forget a single one of them. Someone had to remember.

My overnight stay at Phouc Vinh was humbling. I was invited to the squadron officers' mess for dinner. During that dinner, Major Stewart stood up, introduced me to a hall full of officers, and led them in a standing ovation. I never forgot that kindness.

The following morning, while I waited for a helicopter ride back to my infantry battalion headquarters, I spotted the squadron surgeon who was monitoring Granite. We ended up in a squad tent, facing each across four feet, seated on two stacks of C-ration boxes. I was asking the surgeon, a paratrooper major, about Granite's mental state when, from the tent's entrance, came that familiar, grating voice.

"Well, look at this! The damned Yankee is a great big lieutenant!" etc.

Granite walked over, stood next to me, and began telling the surgeon how I tried to kill him with a hand grenade. Next thing I knew, he pulled his .45 automatic out of its holster and fired a bullet that missed two pairs of knees and hit between the surgeon and me. I am sure that was an accident. But then he held the muzzle of the cocked .45 a few inches from my left temple and began growling over and over again, "I'll kill you!"

Each time he said "I'll kill you," I ordered him to "give me the god-damned gun!" While this insanity was going on, the squadron surgeon and I made eye contact. I flicked my gaze to a crate of something beside the tent entrance. The surgeon blinked a response.

As Granite continued to threaten and growl, I jerked my head toward the crate and exclaimed, "What's that?" Granite looked there for an instant. The surgeon, with lightning fast reflexes, sprang forward and snatched the automatic with both hands before Granite could react.

Granite was shouted at the surgeon, "Give me back my gun!"

The surgeon calmly told Granite to leave the tent, and said that he was going to keep the pistol for a while. Granite hung his head and meekly left the way he had come. I never saw him again.

I returned to the infantry battalion in time to deliver pay in a jeep to our company at the ARVN camp. Per regulations, a pay officer was armed only with a .45 automatic, a rule every bit as stupid as the one requiring platoon leaders to carry binoculars in the jungle. I held the pistol in my lap and felt completely naked without an M-16. We passed a tiny position, really only a ring of razor wire enclosing a sandbagged wooden tower beside the road. There was something there that tied my stomach into a knot and made me afraid. I still don't completely understand why.

The outpost had repulsed an NVA probe the night before, and within it stood a young Popular Forces [local militia] soldier with an M-16 slung across his shoulder as he waved a green pith helmet and an AK-47. He was hopping up and down, grinning and shouting something to us. In that instant I remembered the untouched Viet Cong hamlet we had found after so many landings at Bong Son two years before and knew that we would never win.

The land grew less open beyond the tower. A few hundred meters farther, we received a burst of AK fire from a rubber plantation on the passenger side. A bullet skidded off the hood, and the driver floored the accelerator. I emptied my popgun at the trees, slid in another magazine and fired again. Then we were at the ARVN camp.

And just like that, my shooting war ended.

The final days at the infantry battalion headquarters lasted an eternity. I visited with my wounded soldiers in the hospital, and spent the rest of my days on minor duties. At night I drank cheap champagne and relived the last battle, trying to win it and save my soldiers. I still do.

I began to find fault and see humor where there was none. I was drunk when a captain in a jeep wanted to tell me about the body of his Red Cross girlfriend. "You've probably seen her around. She's a natural blond" –a wink- "and she has one of the nicest . . ."

"Your rear echelon son of a bitch! You sit back here and plug your damned donut dolly while men are dying out in those hills! God-damned coward!"

He reached for the notebook and pen that all correct officers carry in their left breast pockets. "What's your unit, Lieutenant?"

Some friends made excuses and pulled me away before he could get my unit and name, and report me.

On another night, I climbed on a tabletop in a Senior NCO Club and challenged anyone in the place to a fight. A group of master sergeants, first sergeants, and sergeant-majors laughed me through the door.

One night I was pissing in a buried fifty-five gallon oil drum, half-filled with sand and painted with the words CLEAR ALL WEAPONS, and thinking how funny that was, when the company first sergeant walked up behind me.

"Clearing your weapon, Lieutenant?"

"You got it, Top."

He waited for me to finish and put his hand on my shoulder. "Look. If you keep drinking like this, you're not going to have a liver left when you get home."

His concern irritated me. He should go away and leave me alone. "I got things to forget."

He coughed and spat. "Stop feeling sorry for yourself, Sir. Nobody's blaming you for what happened out there. The F.O. broke down one night and told me you carried the show. He said that everyone else was afraid to go forward. Hell, they put you in for a Silver Star."

"Fuck that piece of tin! They're only trying to cover their asses. Nobody came forward but the colonel [formerly The Major] and he got a lot of people hurt. I was with a Blue platoon. They were a team. Then they sent me to this sorry unit. Why can't the training camps send us men who can take orders and stay alive?"

The first sergeant raised his voice after patiently listening to my babbling. "I know about the Cav. I was with them in Korea. I saw your Blues beat up a dozen MPs here one night in March. But you don't mean what you said about Bravo Company. It's people who make anything good or bad, not numbers. You know how the platoon was shaping up. Every enlisted man wanted to be in your platoon, because if anyone could keep them alive, you could."

FLASHING SABER

He was right. I had loved those men. "Yeah. But now they're all dead or wounded. I'm leaving the green machine."

Top was tired of my self-pity. His eyes hardened and his voice had an irritated tone when he spoke again. "Six men are dead. It could have been a lot more. Look, Lieutenant. You've got a good career ahead of you, but what you do after you leave here is your business. You'll be going home in a few days. Try to cut down on the booze and pull yourself together."

I thanked him in a sullen voice, and he was gone. Time to clear my weapon again.

I wanted to stay drunk until I boarded the plane for home. Drinking seemed to be the only way to get through those last days. I was drinking champagne in the officers' club when two muffled explosions came from the direction of a USO show. Officers, bartenders, and waitresses ran through the exit door and scurried into a bomb shelter outside. I was left alone in a big room with a bottle, seriously eyeing the drinks everyone else had left behind.

I shouted at the empty tables. "Those idiots! Anyone can tell those are grenades and not mortars! What they need is a one-twenty-two to really scare them!"

As I sipped my champagne in that big, empty room, I didn't question why someone would lob grenades in the middle of a sprawling American base. Two black soldiers had tossed grenades into a crowd of whites. Two GIs had killed two other GIs and wounded many more. I was witnessing the beginning of the disintegration of an army, once a truly formidable army.

Once the problems of other men helped me forget my own. I read in the *Stars and Stripes* newspaper that a battalion of the 18th NVA Regiment, our old friends from the beautiful Soui Ca, had tried to ambush a convoy in the Deo Mang Pass. I remembered the tough Koreans along the pass, doing martial art training in their white underwear. The article said that the Koreans had driven the NVA back into the mountains with heavy losses. Martin was long since home, so I raised a silent glass and toasted those brave men of the Soui Ca one last time.

"To the Eighteenth NVA Regiment: may they sleep on firm straw pallets tonight and may their rice rolls be full."

On my last night in Vietnam, I met two infantry lieutenants who were replacements for my unit. We quickly established that all three of us were from the same area of southwestern Indiana. I asked if, by any chance, they knew lovely Leila. They did.

One of them replied, "We flew her down to the Playboy Club in Louisville last weekend."

The other said, "We got her away without her daddy finding out. You know what he's like."

I knew.

The First Cav sniper found me at the Tan Son Nhut terminal. I had known him at Quan Loi, and he wanted to recite his latest deeds. On his last mission in Vietnam, he had wanted to do everything right. He had broken the legs of a young NVA with his bullets and waited patiently all afternoon while the boy screamed for help. At dusk, two other Vietnamese crawled out of the jungle. He killed all three of them.

"Only cost Uncle Sam thirty-five cents, Matt." He laughed.

I walked away reminding myself how much I hate snipers. When a man lines up distant humanity in the crosshairs and squeezes the trigger, he loses his soul. It certainly never makes him a hero.

———◆———

Enlisted men's baggage was routinely searched when they boarded "freedom birds" for the twenty-two hour flight to America. That search provided an opportunity for some unethical military policemen to steal souvenirs from combat veterans. As a former enlisted man who had returned from Vietnam on three previous occasions, I knew the arguments, shouting and cajoling necessary to retain a star belt, a French bush hat, a genuine NVA trench shovel, or a green star canteen. The MP predators claimed that such items had intelligence value, but all of us knew that the only value our souvenirs held for anyone else was for bragging rights and manufactured war stories. I was now an officer and wasn't searched. I should have been. In the cargo pocket of my jungle pants rode my lucky Chinese grenade.

I boarded a one-quarter-empty plane for America with many of the people I had traveled to war with one year before. Their faces were more serious, thinner, tanned. There were fewer infantrymen and pilots. The shaven-headed police lieutenant from New York was there, heading home to tell the street punks what the war was really like.

Our landing a year before had been delayed by a mortar attack. The return flight was delayed by more mortars. As the jet left the runway, I tensed for the twelve-seven fire that would surely come. They would never let me leave after what I had done to their country. Only the roar of the jet's engines.

As we crossed the coast of Vietnam, so high above white sand and blue ocean, my mind screamed, "They're letting me leave alive!" While the jet crossed the Pacific, I swore over and again that I would never bitch about leading a quiet life. I should have died many times and hadn't. I wanted to use that gift of life to help better a world that I had once helped to destroy. "Dear God in heaven. It's finally over!"

The loudspeakers at San Francisco Air Terminal blared the same song that had played continuously for two years by then: "If you come to San Francisco" (*be sure to wear some flowers in your hair*). It was Moratorium Day, 1969. The terminal swarmed with antiwar demonstrators. Hippie-type people dressed in paisley shirts, embroidered peasant blouses, tall buckskin boots, moccasins, outrageously wide belts, bell-bottom trousers, and fringed leather clothing were everywhere. Some of them wore colored glasses, rose and light blue being favorites, and most of them sported long hair. The hippies passed out antiwar literature, sang songs of protest, and recited names from lists of war dead. Were my dead draftees yet among them?

While heading across the terminal for a flight home, I passed a particularly large group of flower children gathered around a man speaking from a small platform. Part of me wanted to be a love-and-peace crusader like them, like some of my comrades in 1967 wanted to become. The other part missed the excitement and adrenaline rushes of war and blamed the antiwar movement for spoiling everything.

I stroked the lucky grenade through the rip-stop fabric of my left cargo pocket and wondered how those hippies would react to the sight of a real weapon from a real war. *"Just hold it out and watch them scatter."* The urge to keep the grenade almost overwhelmed me. What would my future be like with no good luck charm and no defensive weapon?

Twice I headed for the military arrivals gate, hesitated, and turned back toward my departure gate. The third time I strolled across the terminal and found the stainless steel receptacle labeled "Contraband." Pasted below it was a drawing of a red bullet inside a white circle with a diagonal line across it. That container was the Army's way of anonymously collecting what people shouldn't have had in the first place. The grenade clunked down among the lucky bullets and explosive trinkets already there.

I missed my grenade for a long time.

I caught a jet for home. Beside me was a Marine recruit, just out of boot camp, muttering about the damned hippies. I wasn't sure exactly what they were. Many of them probably used that phony culture as an easy avenue to acceptance, drugs, and sex, but much of what they were saying was true. The war had been lost for a long time.

I watched my beloved country glide beneath the jet until the snow-capped mountains of Colorado disappeared behind us. Then I opened Heinlein's new book, *Stranger in a Strange Land*, and began to read.

It was a fitting title.

———————◆———————

In the spring of 1970, a Bravo Troop Loach drew first blood in the Cambodian Invasion when a scout gunner dropped a hand grenade into the bed of a truck carrying North Vietnamese soldiers.